CLASSICS *Illustrated*

CLASSICS *Illustrated*

A Cultural History, with Illustrations

by William B. Jones, Jr.

McFarland & Company, Inc., Publishers
Jefferson, North Carolina, and London

Frontispiece: Unidentified artist, No. 64, *Treasure Island* (1969 reissue of March 1956 painted-cover reissue).

Library of Congress Cataloguing-in-Publication Data

Jones, William B., 1950–
Classics Illustrated : a cultural history, with illustrations / by William B. Jones, Jr.
p.   cm.
Includes bibliographical references and index.
ISBN 0-7864-1077-9 (illustrated case binding : 50# and 70# alkaline papers) ∞
1. Classics illustrated (New York, N.Y.) 2. Kanter, Albert Lewis, 1897–1973. I. Title.
PN6725.J67   2002   741.5'0973—dc21   2001044514

British Library cataloguing data are available

Manufactured in the United States of America

On the front cover: Classics Illustrated *covers. Clockwise, from left*: No. 133, *The Time Machine* (1956 original); No. 68, *Julius Caesar* (1960 painted-cover reissue); No. 149, *Off on a Comet* (1959 original); No. 29, *The Prince and the Pauper* (1955 painted-cover reissue); No. 4, *The Last of the Mohicans* (1956 painted-cover reissue); No. 1, *The Three Musketeers* (1956 painted-cover reissue).

On the back cover: No. 11, *Don Quixote* (1953 painted-cover reissue).

McFarland & Company, Inc., Publishers
Box 611, Jefferson, North Carolina 28640
www.mcfarlandpub.com

For my father, William B. Jones, Sr., who gave me the map;
for my mother, Marie W. Jones, who taught me to read it;
for my wife, Susan, who kept watch on the voyage;
and for my sons, Will and Stephen, who brought
the treasure and poor Ben Gunn home at last

Acknowledgments

Classics Illustrated may be the most misunderstood comic books in the history of sequential art. Assorted cultural arbiters dismissed the adaptations as vulgar corruptions of the literary masterpieces upon which they were based. Certain comics champions, judging them by the standards of what they knew, which is to say superhero comics, condemned them, in essence, because they were not superhero comics. Collectors often ignored the series because of its complexity—with 169 U.S. titles (not to mention the *Juniors*, *Special Issues*, and *World Around Us*), entailing multiple reprints, variant covers, and new interior art, making sense of *Classics Illustrated* seemed akin to the task of mastering *Finnegans Wake.*

Yet, from the early 1970s onward, a dedicated group of experts in the evolving field of popular culture—including Hames Ware, Jerry Bails, Raymond True, Jim Sands, Bill Briggs, Mike Sawyer, and Dan Malan—made strides in tracing the convoluted history of what was promoted as "the World's Finest Juvenile Publication" and building a solid foundation for research. Their various labors of love resulted in such reference sources as *The Who's Who of American Comic Books*, *The Classics Reader*, *The Classics Collector*, and *The Complete Guide to Classics Illustrated.*

I have been fortunate in having the generous assistance of most of the authors and editors of these works while writing this book. I owe an immense debt of gratitude not only to them but also to many others who shared their memories and expertise. I am deeply grateful, as well, to those whose encouragement sustained my efforts during seven years of copyright negotiations, artist interviews, and manuscript drafts.

At the inception of this project, the unqualified enthusiasm of Michael Frawley of Frawley Enterprises proved instrumental in setting the copyright machinery in motion. His kind attention to my early inquiries and requests certainly made the crooked straight and the rough places plain. Richard S. Berger of First Classics, Inc., followed through with a permissions grant of liberal scope that has allowed the generous use of illustrations for this book.

Without the generous assistance of the Central Arkansas Library System and its director, Dr. Bobby Roberts, who authorized a grant for artwork reproduction, this work would quite literally have been impossible. My thanks extend beyond the reach of words.

Hames Ware of Little Rock, co-editor with Jerry Bails of the original *Who's Who of American Comic Books* and internationally renowned comics and animated art authority, was my Virgil, guiding me through the *inferno* and *purgatorio* of comics lore—the maze of artists and styles—with unfailing courtesy and patience. He sharpened my critical sight and more than once saved me from what the Earl of Rochester termed "error's Fenny-*Boggs* and Thorny *Brakes*."

So, too, did Jim Vadeboncouer, Jr., of Bud Plant Illustrated Books, Palo Alto, California. In a marathon session, he ploughed through the manuscript and called to my attention various matters of nuance and fact that only his trained eye could catch. I am grateful to be the beneficiary of his expertise. Naturally, however, I am solely responsible for any errors of fact, failures of judgment, or lapses in taste.

The author of the *Complete Guide to Classics Illustrated* and a specialist in the history of illustrated books, Dan Malan of St. Louis supplied countless insights and numerous contacts. The importance of his two-volume *Complete Guide* for any serious collector or student of the U.S. and foreign *Classics* cannot be overstated. All of us stand on his broad shoulders.

Raymond S. True of Libertyville, Illinois, the founding father of the hobby, whose efforts in systematizing the publication sequence in the early 1970s made intelligent collecting possible, has been an invaluable reference source and an untiring champion of my efforts. When I began collecting *Classics* the second time around, as a law student looking for something to take my mind off *Prosser on Torts* or *Corbin on Contracts*, Ray guided me to original editions of *The Moonstone* and *Lorna Doone* that I cherish as emblems of more than twenty years of friendship.

No words of appreciation can express my heartfelt thanks to John Haufe of Kettering, Ohio, who supplied me with photographs of Albert Kanter, illuminating comments and an article on his friend L.B. Cole, critical essays, filler details, news about recent developments concerning *Classics Illustrated*, and years of cheering support and helpful advice. His boyhood experiences in Ohio and mine in Arkansas have struck us both as amazingly similar, though he had sense enough to order *The Bottle Imp* from the publisher before it was too late.

Rudy Tambone of El Segundo, California, is an amazing resource for anyone interested in *Classics Illustrated*. His "Classics Central" website is a research tool of the first order, and it has been strengthened with the copyright acquisition of Dan Malan's *Complete Guide*. With deadlines looming, Rudy provided well-documented filler information for early issues missing from my collection, enabling me to complete the Appendices for this volume.

A longtime friend and respected *Classics* dealer, Philip J. Gaudino of Port Washington, New York, has come expeditiously to my rescue too many times on this and other projects over the years. I have enjoyed our phone conversations about the psychology of collecting and the impact of the generational shift on *Classics Illustrated*.

I am much beholden to Bill Briggs of Toronto for his extraordinary gift of the entire run of *The Classics Reader*, a 1970s and early 1980s fanzine. I am grateful as well to Ron Prager and Jim McLoughlin of New York for lending their time and offering their recollections. These three gentlemen are among the world's leading experts on the subject of *Classics Illustrated*, and I have been moved by their kindness and breadth of spirit.

For his witty words of encouragement and approval, I am deeply obliged to Hal Kanter, the respected screenwriter and director whose father, Albert Kanter, launched *Classic Comics* and watched over its growth for thirty years. Mr. Kanter generously supplied an unpublished photograph of the founder of our feast.

Among the artists who have taken the time to respond so graciously to my impossibly lengthy queries, I wish to thank Lou Cameron, George Evans, Gray Morrow, Norman Nodel, and Rudi Palais. Herb Feuerlicht was most gracious in sharing memories of his late wife, Roberta Strauss Feuerlicht, under difficult circumstances. Harley Griffiths, Jr., provided invaluable details of his father's life and career. I must single out Mrs. Louis Zansky for her kindness not only in loaning me photographs and articles about her late husband but also for allowing me to examine her file copy of the 1942 Saks-34th *Robin Hood* Christmas giveaway—one of only a handful of copies known to exist.

Special thanks are due to Wade Roberts and Rick Obadiah, whose 1990 conversations with me about First Publishing's *Classics* venture were the immediate inspiration for the present enterprise. Madeleine Robins, editor of *Classics Illustrated Study Guides*, always proved willing to take time from her busy schedule to share our common enthusiasm.

I can't adequately express my gratitude to the many friends, colleagues, comics dealers, or fellow-collectors who have helped me, such as *Overstreet* advisor Michael Tierney; Philip Martin, Karen Martin, and Ed Gray of the *Arkansas Democrat-Gazette;* Steve Duin of the *Portland Oregonian*; Mike Nicastre; Clint Miller; Jan Emberton, Cary Cox, and the staff of the Central Arkansas Library System; and Ava Hicks (a tireless champion of the civilized institution known as interlibrary loan), Timothy Holthoff, Jacqueline Wright, and Carol Hampton of the Arkansas Supreme Court Library.

The generosity of Bonnie Slawson of Hot Springs, Arkansas, who gave me her *Classics Illustrated* collection when she read about my project, touched me deeply. A substantial portion of the artwork reproduced in this book was taken from the issues she provided. Vida Bolding of Little Rock contributed several *Classics Illustrated Junior* issues to the cause.

For his professionalism and patient endurance, I am grateful to Larry Pennington of Peerless Photography, a division of the Peerless Group, Little Rock. Having spent 11 hours on the artwork shoot for this book, he uncomplainingly allowed me to return two days later to "capture" five overlooked images.

Sandy Scoggins of Annapolis, my cousin and perpetual booster, and Julie McKenzie of Baton Rouge, who assembled my proposal and suggested layout options, kept the faith even when I had lost it. The persistence of Gary N. Speed, my intellectual-property attorney, helped in a very real sense to make this project possible. My agent, the late Charlotte Gordon of New York, made unstinting efforts on behalf of a book in which she believed while fighting a gallant battle against cancer.

Dee Brown—chronicler of the American West, mentor, and friend—was a constant source of encouraging words and good counsel. Stevensonian scholar Barry Menikoff of the University of Hawaii offered invaluable advice and immeasurable moral support, not to mention a well-timed and much appreciated nudge. Novelist and fellow attorney Grif Stockley started me on my way, and I'm grateful to him for the travel tips. It's been a rewarding journey.

Finally, I wish most of all to thank my parents, who have encouraged my writing from the days of the "Isle of Gems" stories to the present; my wife, Susan, for her support and understanding through a project that is older than our second child; and my sons, Will and Stephen, who have their dad free for fireflies again.

William B. Jones, Jr.
Little Rock, Arkansas
Summer 2001

Table of Contents

Introduction: "Good Stories"

This is a book about memory and a moment in cultural history. It is also about stories and storytellers, both those who use words and those who draw pictures. It begins, as you might expect, with a story.

In the 1950s, Hall Drug Store stood at the corner of Kavanaugh Boulevard and Hayes Street in a Little Rock neighborhood known as the Heights. The 19th president's name would soon be sacrificed in a fit of civic boosterism, and plain Hayes Street would become the grander University Avenue. In time, the Heights, an enclave of quaint bungalows, would succumb to the invasion of overstated affronts to the principles of architecture. The old Hall Drug Store building still stands on its corner, though now it houses an upscale café.

Until the pharmacy closed with his retirement in 1997, Bill Dutton, J.V. Hall's son-in-law and successor, filled prescriptions in bottles adorned with the same blue-and-white labels that he and the original proprietor had used for more than 40 years. Apart from out-of-state sojourns for college and graduate school, I remained a loyal, lifelong customer.

On an evening close to Christmas 1955, when I was five years old, I went with my father to Hall's to pick up a prescription for my mother. While Dad was chatting with Mr. Hall, I spotted a spinner rack of comics, each of which bore a bright yellow rectangle in the upper-left-hand corner of the cover. One issue near the top leapt out at me—*Davy Crockett*—a name I had no difficulty reading, even if the buckskin-clad figure on the cover looked nothing like Fess Parker. (The coonskin-cap craze may have died down several months earlier, but I clung to the faith well into 1956.)

Up to that moment, I had shown absolutely no interest in comic books; I suppose I was vaguely aware that they were bad for you. Still, I asked Dad to confirm that Davy Crockett was indeed the subject (you never could be too sure at five) and begged him to get it for me. As an only child, I needed to do very little begging.

There was something about that yellow rectangle that made an impression. Even where Davy Crockett was concerned, it seemed to confer more authority than the Disney imprimatur. I asked Dad what the large black letters in the yellow rectangle spelled, and he said, "Classics Illustrated."

"What does that mean?"

"Good stories," he replied.

For 30 years, from 1941 to 1971, *Classics Illustrated* (originally known as *Classic Comics*) introduced GIs, bobby-soxers, and their baby-boom children to "Stories by the World's Greatest Authors"—a category that encompassed Homer's *Odyssey* and Frank Buck's *Bring 'Em Back Alive*, Shakespeare's *Hamlet* and Talbot Mundy's *King—of the Khyber Rifles*, Goethe's *Faust* and Owen Wister's *Virginian*. Although the comic-book series of literary adaptations and biographies was disparaged by educator May Hill Arbuthnot and attacked by crusader Fredric Wertham, it gradually won the applause of skeptics and the affection of at least two generations.

By the mid–1950s, with more than 100 titles published, a *Junior* fairy-tale and mythology series under way, and sales in the millions, the Gilberton Company's *Classics Illustrated* had become as much a part of growing up in postwar America as baseball cards, hula hoops, Barbie dolls, or rock 'n' roll. The ubiquitous yellow banner attracted a variety of young readers, whether they were students who wanted to take short-cuts through *A Tale of Two Cities* and *Jane Eyre* or kids who simply enjoyed the exploits of d'Artagnan and Natty Bumppo.

I belonged to the latter category. The yellow rectangle was reassuring, and I failed to comprehend that the names "Shakespeare" or "Conrad" or "Dostoevsky" were supposed to be imposing. All I knew was that they— or their adapters and illustrators—told good stories.

In the months after my discovery of *Davy Crockett* at Hall's, I found *Moby Dick* and *Robin Hood* at Corder's Model Market at the other end of the block, *Treasure Island* and *The Call of the Wild* back at the drug store, and *Benjamin Franklin* and *The Oregon Trail* at the downtown Woolworth. My barber, Loy Scoggins, humored my mania and secured a longtime client, giving me well-worn copies of *The Deerslayer* and *The Adventures of Tom Sawyer* from his magazine pile. By age six, I had become a collector. I began circling the numbered titles I had acquired on the back-cover reorder list of *Waterloo.*

The pictures and whatever words I understood carried me through extraordinary adventures. I remember losing myself in a new copy of *The Three Musketeers* at my parents' New Year's Eve party as 1957 dawned. While the Little Rock school crisis unfolded on the other side of town later that year, I was absorbed in the *Classics Illustrated* retellings of *The Last of the Mohicans, The Scottish Chiefs,* and *Mutiny on the Bounty.*

By the time I was

Davy Crockett (November 1955). The author's introduction to *Classics Illustrated.*

eight, the series had become the fulcrum of my imaginative life. Photographs from 1958 show me holding copies of *Kidnapped* outside the White House, *20,000 Leagues Under the Sea* next to Old Ironsides, and *In the Reign of Terror* beneath our very model of a modern metallic Christmas tree. Wishing to preserve my *Classics,* I began having them bound at the Little Rock Library Bindery, not realizing—or subsequently caring—that I was seriously compromising their future collectible status.

When I should have been learning the rudiments of multiplication and division, I was committing to memory the numbers and titles on the Gilberton reorder list.

Robin Hood **(painted-cover edition, November 1955). An early favorite.**

covered that some issues were harder to find than others, so I traded *Classics* with schoolmates, obtaining out-of-print editions of *Julius Caesar*, *David Balfour* and *Rob Roy*. During recess at Jefferson Elementary School, a couple of friends and I founded our own short-lived *Classics* club and staged playground reenactments of *Caesar's Conquests*, *The Iliad*, and *The Three Musketeers*. Convinced I was d'Artagnan, I challenged a bully who had taken a neighborhood girl's bicycle and quickly discovered that comic-book swords were no substitute for a pair of experienced fists.

For my ninth birthday, my mother took me to the Siebert News Agency warehouse in Little Rock, where I was allowed to select as many *Classics* as I wanted from a room that seemed stuffed with piles of them. Occasionally, when inspecting the spinner rack at Safeway or another store, I would come across a discontinued rarity such as a 1951 original issue of *Crime and Punishment* and would carry it triumphantly, like the recovered Grail, to the check-out counter.

Nothing else I read as a child had as significant an impact on my developing imagination, which

My mother brought me a get-well issue every bedridden day during bouts of measles or mumps. Returning from business trips to New York, my father would produce from his briefcase crisp copies of the most recent editions, which I always believed came straight from the publisher's offices at 101 Fifth Avenue.

The obsession strengthened its grip in 1959. I dis-

was peopled with such historical and fictional good and bad guys as Vercingetorix, Lady Macbeth, Ivanhoe, William Wallace, Joan of Arc, Quasimodo, Don Quixote, Cardinal Richelieu, Lorna Doone, Alan Breck Stewart, Uncas, Ishmael, Hiawatha, Huckleberry Finn, Flashman, Rima the Bird Girl, and Raskolnikov (all pronounced with varying degrees of accuracy). With their childish,

The author, age 8, lost in revolutionary France. (Courtesy of Marie W. Jones.)

and other works have appeared in comic-book adaptations, told an interviewer that, as a child, she "adored" *Classics Illustrated.* Among the titles she remembered with affection were *Jane Eyre, Lorna Doone,* and *Moby Dick.* "Not only did these comics give us an early appreciation for novels we would later read," she said, "they were a thrilling art form in themselves. I can still remember some of the drawings quite vividly."[2]

Writing about collecting the series during the 1940s in his memoir, *A Drinking Life,* journalist Pete Hamill fondly recalled the original *Classic Comics* as "a kind of road map to the real books."[3] Demonstrating the hold that the colorful adaptations had for more than half a century, he recited the first ten titles in publication order and threw in another five early editions for good measure.

Hamill also notes, in passing, that the series was renamed *Classics Illustrated* "for some reason."[4] That reason, as this book will endeavor to show, had everything to do with the purpose of the series, as envisioned by its creator, Albert L. Kanter—and with the cultural forces against which the comics industry was contending in the late 1940s and early 1950s. The series not only survived the vicissitudes of the postwar anti-comics campaign but also emerged as a juvenile-publication powerhouse in an international market.

Along with its companion lines—*Classics Illustrated Junior, Picture Progress, Classics Illustrated Special Issues,* and *The World Around Us*—*Classics Illustrated* embodied the Horatian ideal of mixing usefulness and pleasure, delighting generations of young readers while instructing them. Other comics reserved space for advertisements for Charles Atlas bodybuilding programs or mail-order monkeys that fit in tea cups. Inside cover space and back pages in the Gilberton series were devoted to "Who Am I?" literary quizzes; synopses of great operas; biographies of the particular book's author, "Pioneers of Science," historical figures, and sports heroes; articles related to the subject of the book adapted; practical science experiments; and even capsule histories of Great Britain and the American Civil War.

A student of popular culture can learn much from *Classics Illustrated* about postwar America's assumptions about the interests and capacities of its children. Shakespeare's language may have been abridged, but it was

improbable plotlines, the tight-underwear guys in other comic books—Superman, Batman, Green Lantern, and the rest—seemed pitiably weak heroic substitutes for Athos, Porthos, and Aramis. When it came to villains, I knew that Magua and Madame Defarge could wipe the floor with the Joker and the Riddler.

Through the fusion of pictures and text that comics artist Will Eisner has termed "sequential art," I was transformed by the power of the stories told by Robert Louis Stevenson, Mark Twain, Charles Dickens, Jules Verne, Sir Walter Scott, and Alexandre Dumas—as interpreted by artists Louis Zansky, Henry C. Kiefer, Alex A. Blum, Lou Cameron, George Evans, Norman Nodel, and others.

Of course, I wasn't alone. Romantic poetry scholar Donna Richardson, in an article for *American Heritage,* recalled her first encounter with *Classics Illustrated—The Iliad,* with its cover painting of "chariots and men wearing skirted armor"—purchased at age seven at her local drugstore. "The stories had the imaginative energy of fairy tales," she noted, "but seemed more satisfyingly real and serious than the Disney and DC comics available on the same rack. Every week I'd obey the exhortation at the end of each issue: 'Now that you have read the *Classics Illustrated* edition, don't miss the [added] enjoyment of the original, obtainable at your school or public library.'"[1]

Novelist Anne Rice, whose *Tale of the Body Thief*

never rewritten. Sydney Carton may have been painted to look like Tab Hunter on the cover of the 1956 revision of *A Tale of Two Cities*, but he still went to the guillotine. Though trimmed to 64 or 48 pages, Javert's obsessive pursuit of Jean Valjean and Edmond Dantes's implacable quest for vengeance were faithfully represented. The ugliness of racial hatred was not disguised in either *Uncle Tom's Cabin* or *Pitcairn's Island*.

Goethe and Dostoevsky were not considered too great a risk for the series; Jane Austen and Louisa May Alcott were. Boys and girls alike enjoyed *Classics Illustrated*, but the bottom-line perception at Gilberton, reflecting the prevailing view among other publishers, was that the vast majority of comic-book readers were male. Yet ample evidence to the contrary was available: in 1949, romance comics became the fastest-growing category in the industry; a 1950 Dayton, Ohio, study revealed that comic-book readers were nearly evenly divided by sex, with males accounting for 52 percent and females for 48 percent.[5]

Even so, the occasional appearance of a *Wuthering Heights* or a *Black Beauty* notwithstanding, the *Classics* re-order list was dominated by such action tales as *Men of Iron*, *Men Against the Sea*, and *The First Men in the Moon*. Practical experience indicated that, while girls would buy "boys' books," boys wouldn't be caught dead with "girls' books." (I can remember vividly the unrelenting ribbing I took in the fall of 1960 from a fifth-grade friend who was with me when I found the long-out-of-print, recently reissued *Alice in Wonderland* on a grocery-store rack and, innocent completist collector that I was, searched my pocket for enough change to buy it.) As late as the early 1960s, whenever editor-in-chief Roberta Strauss Feuerlicht needed a sure seller, she would order another Jules Verne or G.A. Henty script from editor Alfred Sundel.

Classics Illustrated was the most significant, successful, and influential publication of its kind. "They were the only comic books my parents would let me buy" is a familiar baby-boomer refrain. Growing up in Pittsburgh under such an injunction, a future attorney who enjoyed the series but wanted to savor the pleasures of the forbidden learned to detach *Classics* covers so she could hide copies of *Batman* and other proscribed comics. "If only I had known that I was destroying their value," she remarked somewhat ruefully.[6]

Albert Kanter, founder of *Classics Illustrated* and its subsidiary series, deserves recognition as one of the great teachers of the 20th century. This book tells the story of his educational enterprises and explores the subsequent incarnations of the original series under the banners of the Frawley Corporation, First Publishing, and Acclaim Comics. Dan Malan, in his indispensable two-volume *Complete Guide to Classics Illustrated*, and Mike Sawyer, in a scrupulously documented article for the *Journal of Popular Culture*, have already detailed the fortunes of the Gilberton Company and the Frawley Corporation, and I am indebted to their scholarship and good examples. Their writings were principally directed to collectors and specialists; it is my intention to address not only fellow travelers but also both an academic and general audience interested in the treatment of serious literature in popular culture and in the comic book as a distinctive American art form.

Enthusiasts have been exceptionally well served by Malan's thorough studies of the American and international series and definitive survey of *Classics*-related collectibles. Given the emphasis of this book on art, artists, and adaptations, I have not attempted a detailed discussion of such items as boxes, binders, notebooks, slides, or giveaways—nor have I delved into the minutiae of cover and color variations or the arcana of *Long Island Independent* or *Nassau Bulletin* print runs. These topics appeal primarily to hobbyists and are largely outside the scope or the purpose of this work.

This volume will explore the nature and quality of *Classics Illustrated* adaptations and will survey the work of the individual artists who gave them life. No other study has yet attempted a comprehensive review of the art of the series, which has been largely neglected and consistently underrated, or a chronicle of the careers of the artists in connection with their work for Gilberton. Ancillary series, including *Classics Illustrated Junior*, *Picture Progress*, *Classics Illustrated Special Issues*, and *The World Around Us*, will also be examined. The more recent series issued by First Publishing and Acclaim Comics, which featured illustrations by outstanding contemporary artists or recolored reductions of the original *Classics*, have had a less significant cultural impact and thus will receive less attention.

A chronological review of *Classics Illustrated* art and adaptations reveals the evolving seriousness of purpose that animated the efforts of publisher Albert L. Kanter, editors Meyer A. Kaplan and Roberta Strauss Feuerlicht, scriptwriters Ruth A. Roche, Kenneth Fitch, and Alfred Sundel, art directors Alex A. Blum and Leonard B. Cole, and artists George Evans and Norman Nodel. When he launched *Classic Comics* in the fall of 1941, at the peak of the so-called Golden Age of comic books, Kanter was attempting to wean young readers from *Action Comics*, *Detective Comics*, and *Marvel Comics*, employing the same medium to win new adherents to the works of Dumas, Scott, Cooper, Melville, and Dickens. As the series progressed, the emphasis on its character shifted from comics to illustrated books and led to the new name, *Classics Illustrated*, in March 1947.

The change of focus, however, led to something of an identity crisis for *Classics Illustrated.* Many educators looked at the issues and saw comic books, pure and simple. To the extent that the series in the early years (1941–44) bastardized the originals—and one need only look at the 1943 edition of *Dr. Jekyll and Mr. Hyde* to see how corrupted a text could become—the critics reviled *Classics* as worse than regular comic books because they polluted great literature and subverted high culture. The fact that only a handful of adaptations took the liberties attributed to all was strategically ignored.

This point of view persists to the present, and it is not uncommon to hear the assertion that it is impossible to turn, say, *Faust* into a comic book without trivializing it or—the most withering contemporary indictment—rendering it middlebrow. One cannot counter so absolute a prejudice with reasoned argument; one can only hold up the *Classics Illustrated* version of Goethe's masterpiece and trust that the adaptation by Alfred Sundel and the illustrations by Norman Nodel will persuade.

In any event, the series was never intended to replace the original works (as the Walt Disney versions of *Winnie-the-Pooh* and *The Little Mermaid* threaten to do). It is unlikely that anyone who read the sequential-art abridgments of *The House of the Seven Gables* or *Silas Marner* as a means of avoiding Nathaniel Hawthorne or George Eliot would have read those authors in the first place. What *Classics Illustrated* and its offspring did with increasing skill between 1941 and 1962, when original-title production ceased, was to make the realms of the literary and historical imagination accessible and immediate.

While the complaint from one side of the cultural chasm was that the *Classics* were too much like comic books and were therefore meritless, the cry from the comics camp was that, with their lack of original stories and innovative art, they bore too little resemblance to comic books and were therefore meritless. Indeed, many comics authorities tend to judge *Classics Illustrated* on the basis of the often badly drawn first 22 issues, published between 1941 and 1944, and to be unaware that some of their culture heroes—Jack Kirby, Reed Crandall, George Evans, Joe Orlando, Al Williamson—worked for Gilberton and helped raise the quality of the artwork in the late 1950s and early 1960s to a level unsurpassed in the industry.

Although New York was the center of the comics universe, many of the key figures in the *Classics* story were out-of-towners—from Russia, Kansas, Hungary, California, Italy. Some, including the founder of the series, were Jewish immigrants who found themselves engaged, somewhat ironically, in a reverse method of assimilation, interpreting and popularizing what had been essentially the cultural canon of the Anglo-Saxon Protestant establishment of the Northeastern United States.

At least one of the *Classics* artists and one of the scriptwriters were African-American, an exception at the time. Two of the artists and two of the scriptwriters were women, another anomaly in the 1940s and '50s. A collection of steady professionals, a few eccentrics, and a genius or two left their individual imprints. The most forceful personality of all, the editor who reshaped the publication in the 1950s and '60s, was a young woman with an unswerving devotion to what amounted to a calling. The history of *Classics Illustrated* is their story, and, whenever possible, I have allowed them, or their surviving family members, to speak for themselves through interviews and correspondence.

I have never forgotten the moment when, at the age of ten, I turned from Alex A. Blum's *Classics Illustrated* rendering of *Hamlet* to my mother's old high-school Riverside edition, and the words danced to life on the page. If this book serves no other purpose, I hope that it will set in perspective the efforts of the artists, editorial staff, and publisher who filled millions of children around the world with an early and enduring passion for what my father called, quite simply "good stories."

I

Albert Kanter's Dream

It was a quintessentially American dream—an immigrant child, a self-made man, a visionary concept, and an unqualified triumph. Before *Classics Illustrated* and its companion series were displaced by televison and an exploding consumer culture, they could be found in the largest cities and smallest towns of the United States. In time, the books would also appear in 26 languages in 36 countries, including Canada, Australia, Brazil, the Netherlands, Italy, Greece, Japan, the United Kingdom, Argentina, Mexico, Turkey, Hong Kong, Germany, Norway, New Zealand, Sweden, Denmark, Iceland, Finland, Ireland, France, Belgium, the Phillipines, India, Singapore, and Malaysia.[1]

The dreamer in this case was Albert Lewis Kanter (1897–1973), the eldest son of a Russian Jewish family that had fled the Czar's pogroms and in 1904 had immigrated to Nashua, New Hampshire. An eager learner, he read voraciously, even after he was obliged to quit high school in 1913 because of his father's poor health. Kanter, bouyed by his lifelong sense of humor, began working as a door-to-door salesman. The New Englander's peregrinations in time took him to Savannah, Georgia, where he met and married Rose Ehrenrich. There, the couple had three children, Henry (Hal), William, and Saralea.[2] (The two brothers eventually would play vital roles in the *Classics Illustrated* story.) Albert passed along his love of history and literature to his children.[3]

Seeking to improve his situation, Kanter moved his family to Miami, Florida. A real estate venture soured with the arrival of the Great Depression. With the assistance of his brothers Maurice and Michael, Kanter relocated to New York and landed a job as a publisher's representative for Colonial Press, selling, among other items, sets of works by Mark Twain, Jack London, and Rafael Sabatini.[4] Eventually, he found himself working for Elliott Publishing Company, selling surplus books and designing a widely used appointment diary for doctors and dentists. With his customary inventiveness and energy, he also created and produced a battery-operated toy telegraph set and a crystal radio set.[5]

In 1940, Elliott Publishing Company began repackaging pairs of remaindered comic books in a 128-page format called *Double Comics*. Pairs of coverless comics from different publishers were bound together with new covers and sold for the price of one. It was the new industry's Golden Age, when fresh series and entire genres were born every few months. Looking at the issues recycled by Elliott and at developments in the market, Albert Kanter had an idea.

From a tradition extending back to 17th-century broadsheets and the 18th-century satirical series of William Hogarth, James Gillray, and Thomas Rowlandson, Victorian England produced the forerunners of comic books in *Punch* (1841) and other humorous magazines that combined illustrations and text. Gilbert Dalziel, whose *Judy* (1867) had imitated the *Punch* format, created what comics art historian Roger Sabin regards as the first comics publication, *Ally Sloper's Half Holiday* (1884), a tabloid blend of strips, cartoons, and narrative.[6]

Recent research has shown that the first American comics-style book was an import. Swiss artist Rudolphe Topffer's *Adventures of Obadiah Oldbuck*, a 40-page, panel-filled supplement to the periodical *Brother Jonathan*, was published in New York in 1842. Topffer's work had been translated into several languages and was popular in Europe and the United States. American editions of *Obadiah Oldbuck* and other comic-strip books by Topffer remained in print until 1877.[7]

The first American newspaper comic appeared in Joseph Pulitzer's *New York World* in 1895. Drawn by

Albert Lewis Kanter, circa 1945. (Courtesy of Hal Kanter.)

Richard Outcault, *The Yellow Kid* was a single panel rather than a strip and featured a streetwise urchin with an attitude as brash as his yellow nightshirt that soon gave its name to a brand of journalism. Outcault went on to create, perhaps as a moral counterweight, the insufferably sanctimonious Buster Brown for the *New York Herald Tribune*. Les Daniels views Outcault's odd couple as a microcosm of comics history, a recurring cycle in which subversive impulses are periodically diluted by the power of conformity.[8]

By the turn of the century, comic strips such as *The Katzenjammer Kids* by Rudolph Dirks had become popular fixtures in American newspapers. During the next 25 years, the national mythology would be enriched by Winsor McCay's *Little Nemo in Slumberland*, Bud Fisher's *Mutt and Jeff*, George Herriman's *Krazy Kat*, George McManus's *Bringing Up Father*, and Harold Gray's *Little*

Orphan Annie. With the appearance of Hal Foster's *Tarzan* and Philip Nowlan and Dick Calkins's *Buck Rogers* in 1929, the stage was set for the arrival of the next decade's superheroes.[9]

Book reprints of popular newspaper strips began in 1897 with *The Yellow Kid in McFadden's Flats*, which featured Outcault's outlandish hero.[10] *Funny Folks* (1899), a compilation of color and black-and-white comic strips by F.M. Howarth that originally appeared in *Puck* magazine, was the first book to emphasize sequential narratives.[11] The name by which the format would thereafter be known was introduced in Saalfield Publishing Company's *Comic Book* (1917).[12]

In 1922, *Comic Monthly*, which was closer to the standard comic-book format, began a 12-issue run. At the end of the decade, George Delacorte, who would later gain renown as founder of Dell Publishing Company, produced a 13-issue tabloid series titled *The Funnies* that included some original features.[13] But the publication that sparked the comics revolution was Eastern Color Printing Company's *Famous Funnies*, which offered "100 Comics and Games-Puzzles-Magic" for a dime and lasted from 1934 to 1955. Major Malcolm Wheeler-Nicholson's *New Fun* followed in 1935 and Dell's *Popular Comics* in 1936. With the appearance of Wheeler-Nicholson's and Harry Donenfeld's *Detective Comics* (later the home of Batman) in 1937 and *Action Comics* (introducing Superman) in 1938, the Golden Age was under way. Captain Marvel, the Blue Beetle, and other caped or masked competitors soon followed.[14]

In the meantime, a distinctive aesthetic, supported by its own vocabulary and grammar, had evolved along with the medium, and art schools were filled with aspiring comics illustrators. As the demand for original artwork and stories accelerated, New York studios known in the trade as "shops" grew rapidly, beginning with one founded in 1936 by the colorful Harry "A" Chesler (d. 1981). Certain shops established exclusive relationships with different comic-book publishers and developed distinctive house styles. By the end of the decade, four major comics art shops had emerged, headed by Chesler, partners Will Eisner and S.M. "Jerry" Iger, Lloyd Jacquet, and Jack Binder.[15] Two of these—Iger's and Jacquet's—would figure prominently in Albert Kanter's enterprise.

Comic books have generated controversy from the beginning. As early as May 1940, children's author Sterling North blasted the phenomenon in a *Chicago Daily News* editorial, terming it a "national disgrace" and urging parents to introduce their children to such adventure classics as Charles Kingsley's *Westward Ho!* and Robert Louis Stevenson's *Treasure Island.* Magazines exhorted teachers and librarians to fight the good fight.[16]

It was clear to many, however, that for most children the comic book was simply too compelling a medium. *Parents' Magazine* sought to address the problem by producing a series of wholesome, fact-filled comics designed to wean preadolescents from the rapidly proliferating superhero fare. The result was *True Comics*, which inaugurated its nine-year run in April 1941 with features on Winston Churchill, malaria, the Marathon run, and Simon Bolivar.[17]

At this point, Albert Kanter's idea began to take shape. With an autodidact's fervor, he dreamed of a means of introducing young readers to the classic literature that had sustained him over the years. The hundreds of thousands of copies of *Double Comics* that poured out of Elliott Publishing Company—and perhaps the recent example of *True Comics*—supplied the immediate inspiration. Kanter would create a comic-book line that would devote each issue to the adaptation of a single literary work. The concept was brilliant in its simplicity and had the merit (and the attendant risk) of never having been tried.

Not that there had never been comics-style versions of the classics. In 1921–1922, newspapers carried George Storm's 22-week comic-strip serialization of Johann Wyss's *Swiss Family Robinson* for the McClure Syndicate.[18] Major Wheeler-Nicholson had produced a daily newspaper adaptation of Robert Louis Stevenson's *Treasure Island* in 1925 before revisiting the pirate yarn and introducing a subsequently aborted *Ivanhoe* ten years later in *New Fun*. In 1936, Wheeler-Nicholson's *New Comics* (National Periodical Publications) serialized Jonathan Swift's *Gulliver's Travels*, Charles Dickens's *A Tale of Two Cities*, and H. Rider Haggard's *She*.[19] *Treasure Island*, drawn by Harold deLay, began a four-issue run in *Doc Savage* in 1940, and the popular tale appeared in ten issues of *Target Comics* in 1941–1942. Still, no one had thought of self-contained abridgments of individual titles in the comic-book format until, in 1941, Albert Lewis Kanter dreamed his American dream—*Classic Comics.*

Most American dreams, of course, require capital. Kanter's friend and future copublisher, Raymond Haas, brought along his business partner, Meyer Levy, to finance the new enterprise, which remained nominally an Elliott operation until the spring of 1942.[20] Kanter made arrangements with Lloyd Jacquet's Funnies, Inc., shop for production of the artwork, and Malcolm Kildale assumed primary responsibility for the first issue, a 62-page adaptation of Alexandre Dumas's *The Three Musketeers* that appeared in October 1941. (See color section.) Two pages at the end of the comic book were devoted to a biography of the author.[21] Production costs were approximately $8,000 for an initial run of about 250,000 copies.[22] By the 1950s, between 250,000 and 500,000 copies of first editions were printed, and reprints numbered between 100,000 and 250,000 copies.[23]

Despite limited distribution, for which Kanter relied primarily upon his considerable sales skills as he canvassed various outlets in the New York area, No. 1 did well enough to encourage the publication of a second number, an adaptation of Sir Walter Scott's *Ivanhoe*, in December 1941. By the time *Classic Comics* No. 3, *The Count of Monte Cristo*, was issued in March 1942, the new enterprise was outgrowing the limited space it shared with Elliott Publishing Comany. Kanter's partner Raymond Haas was able to offer not only a building but also an unused corporate name and corporate papers. Some time earlier, Haas had bought out a failing chemical firm that had been named the Gilberton Company by its founder, Hamilton Gilbert, who had supplied chemistry sets with illustrated instruction booklets to thousands of young Americans. Although it was impossible, because of America's sudden involvement in World War II, to secure the dissolution of the original certificate of incorporation, the charter was amended on March 13, 1942, to permit publishing.[24]

Thus, as the Gilberton Company, Albert Kanter moved to Haas's building at 510 Sixth Avenue, suspending publication of *Classic Comics* until August 1942 to accommodate the changes. Three years later, with the war winding down, the publisher obtained dissolution of the original certificate of incorporation but retained the company's name.[25] Gilberton it was, and Gilberton it remained for more than twenty years. In the meantime, during the war years, Kanter purchased paper allotments from New York-area publishers, whose company names—Elliot Publishing Co., *Long Island Independent*, Island Publishing Co., *Nassau Bulletin*, *Queens Home News*, *Sunrise Times*, *The Courier*, and *Queens County Times*, along with Raymond Haas's Conray Products—appeared in various reprinted editions.[26]

From the beginning, *Classic Comics* were unique in the industry. Apart from in-house promotions such as "Coming Next" notices or reorder lists, the series carried no advertising. It was a deliberate break with comic-book convention on the part of Kanter, who hoped thereby to retain editorial independence and to strengthen the publication's appeal to educators. In addition, the back-of-the-book section in each issue was reserved for educational or patriotic filler material, including author biographies, poems, and reports on the war.[27] By the 1950s, these articles displayed an increasing level of sophistication and were tailored to complement the work they accompanied—for instance, a biography of Bonnie Prince Charlie was appended to Robert Louis Stevenson's *David Balfour*, No. 94 (April 1952), and a description of Elizabethan playhouses served as an epilogue to Shakespeare's *Romeo and Juliet*, No. 134 (September 1956).

Producing 64-page comic books with a war in progress and paper rations in effect called for some strategic maneuvering, and, while Kanter was able to purchase surplus paper, the amount available was not sufficient for the standard *Classic Comics* length. In August 1943, with issue No. 13, *Dr. Jekyll and Mr. Hyde*, the page count dropped to 56, where it remained (with the exception of No. 26, *Frankenstein*, a 48-page issue) until January 1948, when rising paper costs forced a final reduction to 48

pages with issue No. 45, *Tom Brown's School Days*.[28] Even with the shrinkage, *Classics Illustrated* (as they were called by that time) were longer than most comic books, which generally ran to 32 pages.

Gilberton's first competitor appeared in 1942. *Famous Stories*, a series published by Dell, issued only two titles, *Treasure Island* and *Tom Sawyer*, before folding. The artwork in the two Dell books, however, surpassed anything *Classic Comics* had produced at that point. Meanwhile, the Jacquet shop ended its affiliation with Gilberton after issue No. 4, *The Last of the Mohicans* (August 1942), and a gifted freelancer, Louis Zansky, who adapted and illustrated issue No. 5, *Moby Dick* (September 1942), assumed the duties of de facto art director, bringing some improvement to the series as a whole and visual charm to the titles he drew.

In 1943, Gilberton received an extraordinary financial boost. Kanter negotiated the sale of *Classic Comics* editions to the American Red Cross and the army post exchange for distribution to service personnel. He also introduced gift boxes containing five different titles for shipment abroad.[29] *Classics* authority Dan Malan has estimated that between five and ten million copies were sent to soldiers.[30] Other comic-book publishers benefited from the reading habits of GIs, who, more than any other demographic group, were responsible for the growth of the comics industry in the early 1940s.[31]

Another significant development for *Classic Comics* occurred in 1943. Gilberton began reprinting earlier editions, further setting the publication apart from other comic books, which were typically one-shot productions with relatively short shelf lives. Only *Classic Comics* built a catalogue, keeping its earlier titles in print while regularly issuing new ones. Eventually, more than 1,200 reprint editions would appear in the American series alone, with estimated peak monthly sales of between two and four million.[32] The venerable founder would become known in Europe as "Papa Klassiker," and foreign sales would exceed the figure of one billion.[33]

For the present, though, Albert Kanter, salesman and idealist, pursued his novel dream of using the same scorned medium to lead young comic-book readers to discover more substantial superheroes in d'Artagnan, Ivanhoe, Hawkeye, and Robin Hood. To keep them hooked, he needed consistently good art and reliable adaptations. He would soon have both, thanks to another energetic entrepreneur named Jerry Iger.

Opposite: **An early Australian edition of** *Kidnapped*, **with a redrawn cover by an unknown artist.**

II

Classical Interlude:
Classics Abroad

The shoestring operation that began in 1941 as *Classic Comics* evolved during the next two decades into an international publishing phenomenon. By 1962, when the Gilberton Company ended original-title production in the United States, *Classics Illustrated* was well-established in more than two dozen other countries, where growth continued for some time to come.[1]

Foreign publication had begun in the 1940s with a

series in Canada (April 1946), Australia (July 1947), and Brazil (July 1948). Within a few years, *Classics* would find a profitable foothold in the Netherlands (October 1948), Greece (March 1951), Great Britain (October 1951), Mexico (December 1951), and elsewhere.

For two years, from 1948 to 1950, the Australian series featured unusual-looking issues that were printed in an oblong, horizontal format. The interiors were black-and-white reductions of U.S. editions, while the covers sported redrawn variants of American artwork, a practice later common in the Mexican *Clásicos Ilustrados*. Home-grown Australian covers continued to appear until the line merged with the British *Classics Illustrated*.

Although the Brazilian series, *Edicão Maravilhosa*, began by issuing Portuguese-language editions of Gilberton titles, in 1950 it expanded its reach to include comic-book adaptations of works of Brazilian literature by José de Alencar, Jorge Amado, and others. Similarly, *Klassika Eikonographimena*, the Greek series, published ninety sequential-art renderings of Greek mythology, drama, and history, in addition to most of the original U.S. and European titles. The emphasis on national culture and her-itage served both the Brazilian and Greek *Classics Illustrated* offspring well in terms of reader interest and loyalty.

The British line, which initially had tracked the U.S. issue-numbering sequence, abruptly changed to its own rather eccentric system in 1956. For example, former No. 116, *The Bottle Imp*, became No. 45, though No. 46, *Kidnapped*, remained No. 46. Meanwhile, *The Octopus* (U.S. No. 159), *The Food of the Gods* (U.S. No. 160), and *Cleopatra* (U.S. No. 161) were catalogued as Nos. 139, 139A, and 139B, respectively. More than 20 new painted covers were introduced in the British series to replace U.S. line-drawing or painted covers.

In 1962, Albert Kanter's son William—who had served as *Classics Illustrated* editor and business manager and was listed with his father and uncle Maurice as one of the owners in annual publisher's statements—moved to England, where he supervised the publication of 13 new titles that were never issued in the American series. Subsequently, the Joint European Series covered the continent and beyond, reaching millions of readers in 24 countries and publishing 230 titles from 1956 to 1976.

III

Of Musketeers and Mohicans: The Jacquet Shop

When detractors in the comics field speak disparagingly of *Classics Illustrated*, what they generally have in mind are the earliest issues. Perhaps the kindest thing that can be said of some of the artwork that appeared in *Classic Comics* between 1941 and 1944 is that it aspired to mediocrity. A few of the cartoonists who illustrated the first issues produced work that was considered inferior even under the minimal standards of the developing comics industry.

A probable reason was the low pay artists and inkers received. Lloyd Jacquet, whose Funnies, Inc., shop had packaged the original *Marvel Comics* in 1939, apparently contracted with Kanter to launch *Classic Comics* but supplied only his second-string artists, presumably because of the fledgling publisher's inability to pay premium rates for the first few titles.[1] The situation evidently had improved by the fifth issue, when freelancer Louis Zansky arrived. His widow recalls that her husband, who came from an impoverished Bronx background, considered Gilberton's payment of between $400 and $600 per 64- or 56-page book more than adequate.[2] In any case, an artist, whether working independently or through a shop, would naturally have been tempted to rush through one project in order to get to another.

Comics art historian Hames Ware has pointed out that, in the infancy of comic books, nearly everyone working seemed to be either youngsters developing their stylistic identities or old timers finishing out their careers in a new medium.[3] The groundbreaking group of *Classic Comics* artists conformed to the pattern, and the unevenness of the product may have resulted from this inexperience or exhaustion.

Yet as bad as some of the early work was, it was really not much worse—and in some instances was actually better—than the now celebrated kitsch produced by other "Golden Age" artists. Not everyone employed elsewhere was a Reed Crandall or a Jack Kirby, both of whom would eventually illustrate *Classics*. Then, too, there was always the intrinsic appeal of the stories and Albert Kanter's dogged sense of what the publication could become.

MALCOLM KILDALE

Malcolm Kildale (d. 1971) of the Jacquet shop adapted and illustrated issue No. 1, *The Three Musketeers* (October 1941), and was listed as art director and editor through issue No. 2, *Ivanhoe*. In the view of comics historian Hames Ware, "Kildale probably would be one of your last choices you'd make to start off a new line of comics."[4] His work, though competent and even engaging, lacked polish.

Here and there, barren backgrounds and wooden figures offer evidence of fast work for low pay. Ware has spotted the styles of other illustrators, including Jacquet stalwart Ken Battefield, in various panels. "The final product is erratic, a true shop job," he observed, "with somebody doing the backgrounds and somebody else doing the inking and lettering."[5] Kildale, however, produced the vast bulk of the character drawings.

Yet what he lacked in refined technique, Kildale more than made up for in visual narrative energy. The pages leading up to and containing the initial swordplay are filled with a jaunty period swagger. Some of the artist's connecting panels, such as those depicting M. de Tréville's major domo and Madame Bonacieux, are quite striking. Kildale created distinctive physical presences for the story's Gascon protagonist and each member of the title trio, striking a balance between the iconic and the strictly representational. D'Artagnan is an unqualified success, animated with the naive, boisterous charm of Dumas's most appealing character.

If the *Musketeers* artwork was uneven, the adaptation was faithful, down to the name of the street on which d'Artagnan confronts the Duke of Buckingham. Some of the original's verve was retained in the dialogue, and neither scriptwriter nor artist flinched in representing the troubling moral ambiguity of Milady's extralegal beheading near the end of the story. Kildale's stark image of the executioner raising his sword above the kneeling villainess, her exposed neck and dangling hair eliciting the viewer's pity, is one of the most memorable panels in the book. The reader was allowed to identify with the mixed emotions of d'Artagnan ("Oh! I cannot behold this frightful spectacle! I cannot consent that a woman should die thus!") as he witnesses summary justice done to the woman who has murdered his beloved Constance.

Albert Kanter had shown that a comic-book version of a classic tale could capture something of the spirit—and a hint of the depth—of the original.

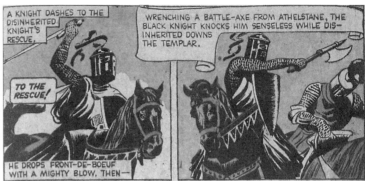

Edd Ashe, *Ivanhoe* (November 1941). The Black Knight to the rescue.

EDD ASHE AND OTHERS

The second *Classic Comics* title, *Ivanhoe* (December 1941), was a spirited but disappointing performance. Gilberton art director Malcolm Kildale supplied the cover, which was based on his design for the first *Classic Comics* issue. Edd Ashe, one of the better artists in the Jacquet shop, is generally credited with the artwork, although in a 1972 letter to Raymond S. True, a *Classics Illustrated* dealer and the founding editor of the *Classics Collectors Club Newsletter*, the artist recalled that "perhaps I only did a part of it" and that "the pay was lousey [*sic*]."[6] A page-by-page analysis by comics art expert Hames Ware confirmed that Ashe was responsible for a relatively small number of panels. Some of the work, including the impressive title-page splash, was done by Ray Ramsey.[7]

As in the *The Three Musketeers*, minimal backgrounds predominated. A heavy emphasis on brush rather than pen inks gave the issue a distinctive look. While the jousting panels and battle scenes had a certain vitality, one need only compare any episode with its counterpart in Norman Nodel's 1957 revision to understand why the 1941 edition was replaced. In other respects, the generally faithful script occasionally lacked continuity, and the three Norman villains never achieved individual identities, perhaps because they were drawn by different hands at different times.

Years later, Ashe contributed some outstanding pages to various titles in the Gilberton subsidiary series *The World Around Us* and *Classics Illustrated Special Issues*, including *The Crusades*, No. W16 (December 1959); *American Presidents*, No. W21 (May 1960); and *The War Between the States*, No. 162A (June 1961). By then, the artist had arrived at a richer, more complex style. In particular, he captured human figures and animals in motion especially well in the "Holy Lance" chapter of *The Crusades* and the "Chattanooga" section of *The War Between the States*.

Malcolm Kildale, *The Three Musketeers* (October 1941). Milady's execution. This scene was played "offstage" in the 1959 revision.

RAY RAMSEY

If the first two issues had their share of redeeming qualities, the third, *The Count of Monte Cristo* (March 1942), had almost none. The adaptation of the enthralling Alexandre Dumas revenge melodrama featured some of the weakest illustrations published under the *Classic Comics* banner. To compound matters, the uncredited scriptwriter sacrificed coherence by squeezing too many subplots into 62 pages.

The best thing about the book, the cover by Jacquet artist Ray Ramsey, was based on a painting by Mead Schaeffer for a 1929 Dodd, Mead edition of the novel.

Ramsey drew the protagonist Edmond Dantes throughout the issue, as former *Classics Reader* editor Bill Briggs has conclusively demonstrated in comparisons with panels from the artist's *Last of the Mohicans*.[8] The hand of Allen Simon is also evident, along with that of Vivian Lipman (Berg), who subsequently illustrated Longfellow's "Children's Hour" as a filler item for *Classic Comics* No. 15. (Years later, Lipman recalled having worked on a full-scale Gilberton project in 1942.)[9]

It is likely that Ramsey, a veteran of Funnies, Inc., initially received the assignment; hence his cover and the interior drawings of the Count. Perhaps because he was also scheduled to illustrate the fourth issue, Jacquet—or Kanter—turned other pages and characters over to Simon and Lipman. The resulting assembly-line product featured an average of eight small, mostly rectangular panels per page, filled with crowded, unimaginative collections of stiffly posed characters.

The Last of the Mohicans, No. 4 (August 1942), was the last Jacquet job and the first not to be parceled out among several artists. The title belonged exclusively to Ramsey, whose specialty was western art. Though he was more at home with 19th-century cowboys, he adapted well to 18th-century Indians and redcoats (though he gave the French commander Montcalm an ahistorical mustache and goatee, perhaps assuming that he looked more Gallic with one).

Ramsey's *Mohicans* is filled with greater energy, fluidity of movement, and attention to detail than any of the preceding titles. The final struggle between the nominal hero Uncas and the evil Magua, depicted on one of the most striking covers in the series, conveys the strengths of Ramsey's interpretation. In keeping with the rigid dualism of Cooper's novel, not to mention the lingering attitudes in the 1940s toward "savages," noble or otherwise, Uncas and Magua are drawn as types rather than individuals. Uncas embodies a natural aristocratic grace while Magua recalls Milton's fallen and degraded Satan. (See color section.)

After drawing *Roy Rogers Comics* for Dell Publishing Company for a number of years, Ramsey left the comics

Ray Ramsey, *The Count of Monte Cristo* (March 1942). Ramsey's Edmond Dantes—the best of a bad shop job.

THE LAST OF THE MOHICANS

by JAMES FENIMORE COOPER

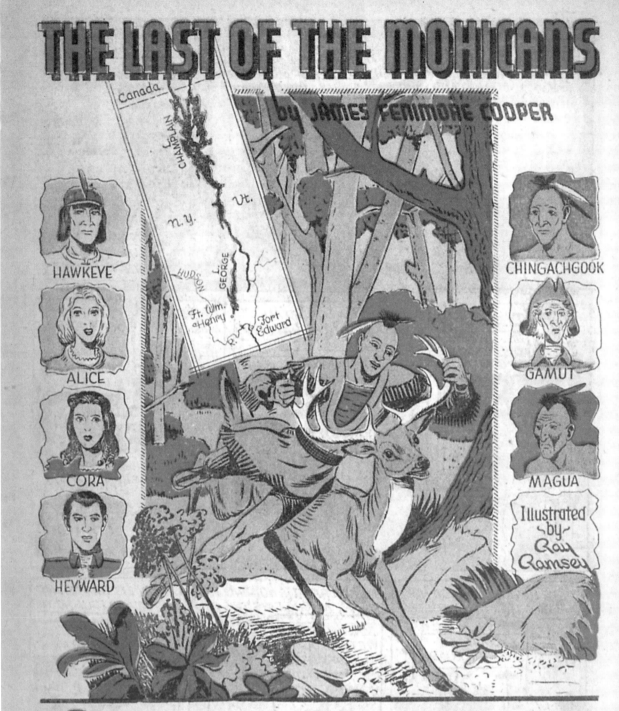

HAWKEYE

ALICE

CORA

HEYWARD

CHINGACHGOOK

GAMUT

MAGUA

Illustrated by Ray Ramsey

THERE IS GREAT ACTIVITY AROUND FORT EDWARD. WORD HAS JUST COME BY INDIAN RUNNER FROM COLONEL MUNRO, COMMANDANT AT FORT WILLIAM HENRY, OF IMPENDING DANGER. MONTCALM, WITH AN ARMY OF FRENCH AND INDIANS, "NUMEROUS AS THE LEAVES ON THE TREES." IS MOVING DOWN LAKE CHAMPLAIN TO ATTACK HIM.

GENERAL WEBB, IN COMMAND AT FORT EDWARD, HAS ORDERED A BODY OF SOLDIERS TO MARCH THE TWENTY MILES SEPARATING THE TWO FORTS, TO THE RELIEF OF COLONEL MUNRO.

IT IS 1757, THE THIRD YEAR OF THE FRENCH AND INDIAN WAR. SINCE BRADDOCK'S DEFEAT IN 1755, THINGS HAVE GONE BADLY FOR THE ENGLISH AND THEIR COLONISTS.

field altogether but returned to Gilberton in the late 1950s. He supplied illustrations for sections of *World Around Us* issues No. W6, *The FBI* (February 1959), and No. W9, *Army* (May 1959). His chapter "Manhunt!" for *Classics Illustrated Special Issue* No. 150A, *Royal Canadian Mounted Police* (June 1959), was a striking performance in which the artist employed different visual perspectives and light-dark contrasts to heighten the drama of a life-or-death struggle between the Mounties and a man they almost didn't get.

By that point, Ramsey's *Mohicans* had vanished, like the tribe in Cooper's book, replaced by a handsome revision by John P. Severin and Stephen L. Addeo.

ALLEN SIMON

Allen Simon, who contributed to *The Count of Monte Cristo*, has the dubious distinction of being regarded as the purest hack among all the *Classic Comics* illustrators. For sheer crudeness in rendering the human form, he couldn't be topped. Simon's characters seem to have stepped out of 17th-century broadsheets or chapbooks and are either outrageously wooden or impossibly elastic. Still, in his contorted, outlandish figures, the artist created a self-contained world that offered its own skewed visual charm.

Simon's first complete work as a freelancer for Gilberton, an adaptation of Charles Kingsley's Elizabethan adventure *Westward Ho!*, No. 14 (September 1943), was also his best. Panels were inventively shaped (a spyglass motif figured prominently), illustrations were well composed, and point-of-view followed narrative flow. The

strongest panel, depicting the blinding of the protagonist, Amyas Leigh, suggested the woodcut-style influence of Rockwell Kent or Lynd Ward. For the period in which it was published, Dan Kushner's adaptation was unusually faithful to the original.

The same could not be said for Simon's next credit. The future EC artist found a truly congenial subject in *The Hunchback of Notre Dame* (No. 18,

Allen Simon, *Westward Ho!* (September 1943). The hero, Amyas Leigh, loses his sight and regains his vision.

Right: Allen Simon, *The Hunchback of Notre Dame* (March 1944). Adolf Hitler flaunts his funny mustache at the Feast of Fools.

FACE AFTER FACE CONVULSES THE AUDIENCE. AFTER DOZENS OF THEM . . .

Opposite: Ray Ramsey, *The Last of the Mohicans* (August 1942): Uncas in action.

March 1944). But the adaptation by Evelyn Goodman, a great believer in textual liberty, owed more to the 1939 film starring Charles Laughton than to Victor Hugo's novel and anticipated the Disney cartoon with its happy ending and brave Captain Phoebus. Simon's natural bent was toward the grotesque, and his cover—the campiest in the series—showed an outsized Quasimodo wreaking havoc among soldiers attacking the Cathedral. (See color section.)

He clearly relished the Feast of Fools scenes, which included some wartime satire, with Adolf Hitler making a cameo appearance as one of the contestants mugging for the title of Fools' Pope. The *Führer* surfaces later in the guise of a mean-spirited magistrate who sentences Quasimodo to the pillory. The plight of the poet Gringoire, who is saved from hanging in the Court of Miracles by Esmeralda, is another comical high point in a largely successful issue.

Simon also did reasonably well with *The Corsican Brothers*, No. 20 (June 1944), a melodramatic novel about sympathetic twins by Alexandre Dumas. The original cover design, which featured a skeletal creature threatening the heroes, was withdrawn before publication, and a more restrained line drawing showing the pair on horseback was substituted. The title was discontinued in 1954 and was never revised or reissued.

A short piece, *The Flayed Hand*, attributed to Guy de Maupassant and included in *3 Famous Mysteries*, No. 21 (July 1944), gave the artist scope to indulge his affinity for bizarre characters and situations. *The Flayed Hand* was a ghoulish tale about the vengeful severed hand of a homicidal madman. Simon's splash page for the story points the way toward the horror comics of the late 1940s and early 1950s, while the script by Evelyn Goodman features such improvements on Maupassant as "Die! All my enemies die! Ha! Ha! Ha!" More than anything Gilberton had pub-

Allen Simon, "The Flayed Hand" in *3 Famous Mysteries* (July 1944). *Classic Comics* pushes the "horror" envelope.

lished before, *The Flayed Hand* simultaneously tested the middlebrow boundaries of what could be considered a "classic" and affirmed the lowbrow status of a series that, after all, included "comics" in its name.

IV

Classical Interlude:
The Mystique of the Reorder List

A source of profound confusion to the uninitiated, the *Classics Illustrated* reorder list enabled readers to check off by issue number the titles they had already obtained or those they wished to order directly from the publisher. For collectors, the lists have long provided the most accurate method of dating an edition.

More than 1,200 reprinted editions of 164 titles rolled off the presses between 1943 and 1971. Until 1963, Gilberton did not date its reprints but instead reproduced the original publication indicia inside the front covers. A (usually) current title list, however, was placed on the back or inside covers of all but a few reprinted editions, along with a coupon addressed to the publisher. The last title listed came to be known among collectors as the highest reorder number (HRN).

Thus, if the title list on your copy of No. 128, *Macbeth* (September 1955), ended at HRN 128 and had a "Coming Next" ad for No. 129, *Davy Crockett*, on the inside front cover, you knew you had an original edition. If the HRN was 143, the book was a reprint, issued around March 1958, when No. 143, *Kim*, was added to the series. A *Macbeth* with a list ending at HRN 158 dated from the fall of 1960. And so on until the spring of 1970, when the eighth printing appeared with the terminal HRN of 169.

If the example sounds confusing, in practice it wasn't. One's frame of reference was pictorial; the colorful lists spotlighted reproductions of different issue covers. When introduced at HRN 10 in 1943, each of the *Classic Comics* titles was depicted, but after the first 20 began crowding each other, representative issues were displayed. After 1953, only a single title, or at most two, were shown.

A 1950 *Classics Illustrated* reorder list.

READ THE BEST IN THE "WORLD'S FINEST JUVENILE PUBLICATION"

CLASSICS Illustrated

THERE HAVE BEEN NO GREATER STORY-TELLERS THAN THESE IMMORTAL AUTHORS

ALEXANDRE DUMAS
SIR WALTER SCOTT
JAMES FENIMORE COOPER
HERMAN MELVILLE
CHARLES DICKENS
VICTOR HUGO
DANIEL DE FOE
MIGUEL CERVANTES
WASHINGTON IRVING
ROBERT LOUIS STEVENSON
CHARLES KINGSLEY
HARRIET BEECHER STOWE
JONATHAN SWIFT
MARK TWAIN
EDGAR ALLAN POE
SIR ARTHUR CONAN DOYLE
GUY DE MAUPASSANT
RICHARD HENRY DANA, JR.
MARY W. SHELLEY
JULES VERNE
WILLIAM WILKIE COLLINS
RICHARD D. BLACKMORE
EDWARD BULWER-LYTTON
CHARLOTTE BRONTE
JONATHAN WYSS
EUGENE SUE
THOMAS HUGHES
LEWIS CARROLL
NATHANIEL HAWTHORNE
GEORGE ELIOT
HENRY WADSWORTH LONGFELLOW
EMILY BRONTE
ANNA SEWELL
BRET HARTE
EDWARD EVERETT HALE
JANE PORTER
WILLIAM SHAKESPEARE
FRANCIS PARKMAN
FREDERICK MARRYAT
ANTHONY HOPE
HOMER
JACK LONDON

THEY'RE ONLY 10¢ EACH POSTPAID
15¢ IN CANADA AND FOREIGN
*SEND JUST 10¢ EXTRA WITH YOUR ORDER TO COVER COST OF HANDLING

FOR YOUR CONVENIENCE FILL OUT COUPON OR A FACSIMILE AND MAIL NOW!

All of the great titles in the CLASSICS *Illustrated* series will give you the most memorable reading treat of your life. They're exciting, informative, thrilling, educational. Each title contains a complete adaptation — plus factual, enjoyable and educational featurettes.

HERE ARE THEIR UNFORGETTABLE STORIES

1. THE THREE MUSKETEERS
2. IVANHOE
3. THE COUNT OF MONTE CRISTO
4. THE LAST OF THE MOHICANS
5. MOBY DICK
6. A TALE OF TWO CITIES
7. ROBIN HOOD
8. ARABIAN NIGHTS
9. LES MISERABLES
10. ROBINSON CRUSOE
11. DON QUIXOTE
12. RIP VAN WINKLE
13. DR. JEKYLL AND MR. HYDE
14. WESTWARD HO!
15. UNCLE TOM'S CABIN
16. GULLIVER'S TRAVELS
17. THE DEERSLAYER
18. THE HUNCHBACK OF NOTRE DAME
19. HUCKLEBERRY FINN
20. CORSICAN BROTHERS
21. 3 FAMOUS MYSTERIES
22. THE PATHFINDER
23. OLIVER TWIST
24. A CONNECTICUT YANKEE IN KING ARTHUR'S COURT
25. TWO YEARS BEFORE THE MAST
26. FRANKENSTEIN
27. ADVENTURES OF MARCO POLO
28. THE PRINCE AND THE PAUPER
29. THE MOONSTONE
30. THE BLACK ARROW
31. LORNA DOONE
32. SHERLOCK HOLMES
33. MYSTERIOUS ISLAND
34. TYPEE
35. THE PIONEERS
36. JANE EYRE
40. MYSTERIES
41. TWENTY YEARS AFTER
42. SWISS FAMILY ROBINSON
43. GREAT EXPECTATIONS
44. MYSTERIES OF PARIS
45. TOM BROWN'S SCHOOL DAYS
46. KIDNAPPED
47. TWENTY THOUSAND LEAGUES UNDER THE SEA
48. DAVID COPPERFIELD
49. ALICE IN WONDERLAND
50. THE ADVENTURES OF TOM SAWYER
51. THE SPY
52. THE HOUSE OF THE SEVEN GABLES
53. A CHRISTMAS CAROL
54. THE MAN IN THE IRON MASK
55. SILAS MARNER
56. THE SONG OF HIAWATHA
57. THE PRAIRIE
58. WUTHERING HEIGHTS
59. BLACK BEAUTY
61. THE WOMAN IN WHITE
62. BRET HARTE'S WESTERN STORIES
63. THE MAN WITHOUT A COUNTRY
65. BENJAMIN FRANKLIN
66. THE CLOISTER AND THE HEARTH
67. THE SCOTTISH CHIEFS
68. JULIUS CAESAR
69. AROUND THE WORLD IN 80 DAYS
70. THE PILOT
71. THE MAN WHO LAUGHS
72. THE OREGON TRAIL
73. THE BLACK TULIP
74. MR. MIDSHIPMAN EASY
75. THE LADY OF THE LAKE

GET ANY ONE OR ALL OF THE ABOVE NUMBERED TITLES. ON SALE AT YOUR FAVORITE NEWSDEALER OR VARIETY STORE. IF THEY'RE OUT OF STOCK, ORDER DIRECT FROM US.

GILBERTON CO., INC., DEPT. 51, 826 BROADWAY, N.Y. 3, N.Y.

I am sending $_____ for_____ issues of CLASSICS *Illustrated* as circled below:

1 2 3 4 5 6 7 8 9 10 12 13 14 15 16 17 18 19 20 21 22 23 24 25 26 27 29 30 31 32 33 34 36 37 39 40 41 42 43 44 45 46 47 48 49 50 51 52 53 54 55 57 58 59 60 61 62 63 64 65 66 67 68 69 70 71 72 73 74 75

Name_____
Address_____
City_____ Zone No._____ State_____

Eight-year-olds could easily distinguish between reprints from the mid–1950s (showing *Don Quixote* against a red background), the late '50s (*Caesar's Conquests* on light blue), and the '60s (*Off on a Comet* on blue or white). Ten-year-old experts could explain why you should be wary of HRN 149 in guessing a book's age. (An HRN 149 surfaced in 1961, with the cover of No. 149 instead of No. 130 shown as the representative book, two years after No. 149 appeared.)

For obsessive personalities in the making, the reorder lists provided ideal training. Why was No. 43, *Great Expectations*, a frequently assigned school text, deleted in 1952 after a second printing, never to return to the *Classics* catalogue? Why was No. 11, *Don Quixote*, discontinued in 1949, reissued in 1953 with a painted cover that was given pride of place as the representative issue on reorder lists for nearly three years, and dropped again in 1956? Why were Nos. 68 and 82 available on coupons between 1955 and 1960 but not included on the actual title lists? Pity the young collector whose faith in an ordered universe might have been shaken by coming upon a British *Classics Illustrated* edition in which the renumbered list showed *Huckleberry Finn* rather than *The Three Musketeers* as issue No. 1.

The real source of fascination was in the older lists, where subsequently discontinued titles offered tantalizing bits of information and raised assorted conundrums: Was *Westward Ho!* about cowboys? Who were *The Corsican Brothers*? What was *The Black Tulip*? And how about *Mr. Midshipman Easy* or those *Forty-Five Guardsmen*? But most intriguing of all, what would you find in *Mysteries*, *3 Famous Mysteries*, and *Mysteries of Paris*?

V

The Painter's Touch:
Louis Zansky

During the publication's first four years, no artist left a greater imprint on *Classic Comics* than an irrepressible red-haired New Yorker named Louis Zansky (1921–1978). Recalled by his wife Jeanette as a natural charmer with an "impish" personality,[1] the young artist infused each of his Gilberton books with his own exuberance. To turn to Zansky's first title, *Moby Dick*, No. 5 (September 1942), from the occasionally leaden Jacquet issues that preceded it is to experience a refreshing expansiveness in the looser, flowing lines and the economical character studies.

The Great Depression had an impact on the artist's development. From his preadolescent years, young Louis drew—"sometimes," Mrs. Zansky related, "on smoothed-out paper grocery bags when there were no coins with which to buy unlined white paper"—and experimented "with water coloring and painting when oils were available."[2] Attending DeWitt Clinton High School in the Bronx, the aspiring artist produced black-and-white illustrations for the students' literary-art magazine, to which schoolmate and future screenwriter Paddy Chayefsky also contributed.[3]

After school, Zansky, who couldn't afford the five-cent subway fare, walked for miles to attend the Art Students League (where he was deeply influenced by teacher John Corbino), the National Academy, and Cooper Union. Upon graduation, he was awarded a full scholarship to New York University's School of Art and Architecture but was unable to accept because, said Mrs. Zansky, "he had to bring in money to the household. Which brought him to *Classic Comics*."[4]

Golden Age publishers offered a decent, steady, if not spectacular, income for New York's overpopulated art community. Albert Kanter was paying between $400 and $600 per book, a substantial if not extravagant sum.[5] Thus, in 1942, Zansky began working for Gilberton, where, according to a 1976 autobiographical statement, he became art director.[6] He was only 23 when he submitted his last pages to *Classic Comics* in 1944.

Before Zansky's departure, however, he left his mark on the Gilberton organization in an altogether different fashion. As Mrs. Zansky recounts the tale: "Lou had again been paid with a check which bounced. He fumed throughout the subway ride from the Bronx to the publisher's Manhattan office. He rushed in past the other bilked artists patiently waiting in the ante-room, past the receptionist's vain attempt to stop him, through [the business manager's] office door—which he theatrically slammed behind him. He emerged within minutes, waving real money. The artists and writers crowded around him, wanting to know the secret of his success, which was almost unheard of. Lou's response: 'I went in, grabbed his collar, shoved him to the window, and threatened to throw him out. But—it won't work unless, one, you're mad enough to say it, and, two, you're bigger than he is.' Obviously, Lou Zansky was both."[7]

The artist entered the army in March 1944. Even then, however, he could not leave *Classic Comics* behind. His best friend, etcher Jack Bilander, was serving at the time in North Africa. He reported that one day, while driving a Jeep along a dusty road, he noticed an Arab in the distance, sitting by the side of the road. The man was reading a magazine that somehow looked familiar. As the Jeep moved closer, Bilander could make out the English words on the cover—*Classic Comics Presents Moby Dick*—Zansky's first Gilberton title. He knew that, by some measure at least, his friend had arrived.[8]

Louis Zansky in Austria, 1946. (Courtesy of Jeanette Zansky.)

After the war and a stint as an art instructor for the United States Information Service in Vienna, Zansky returned to New York and continued to freelance as a comic-book artist, tackling a Western hero, the "Cross-Draw Kid," for Ace and using his wife as a model for a Fox cover that was "banned in Boston."[9] But, although he never disavowed his comics work, his artistic fulfillment lay elsewhere, and he continued with his work in watercolor, oils, and acrylics. By the 1960s, Zansky had created an impressive body of work as an award-winning painter and watercolorist, retaining the playful quality of his earlier figurative efforts and exploring new, more abstract treatments of color and space.

Always a superb visual storyteller in his Gilberton titles, he never lost the narrative impulse or his love for literary and historical themes. Mrs. Zansky noted that her husband returned to Don Quixote and Huckleberry Finn, two of his favorite *Classic Comics* subjects, in later years. A painting with a Revolutionary War theme, *And Called It Macaroni—II*, was accepted by the White House

Opposite: Louis Zansky, *Moby Dick* (September 1942). Ahab confronts his nemesis in the artist's favorite *Classic Comics* assignment.

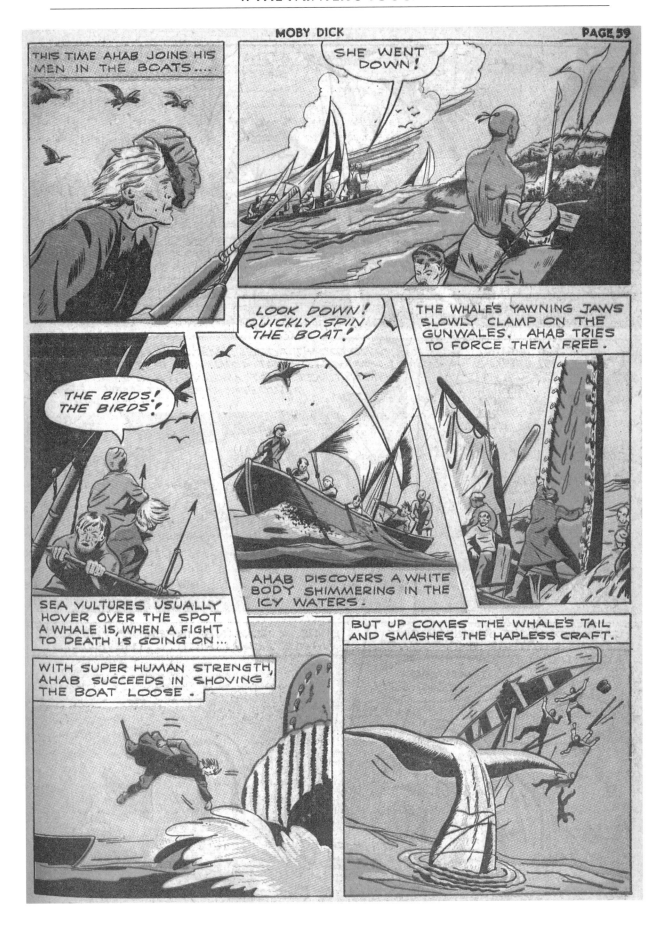

in 1976 for the Bicentennial collection, and the artist proudly posed for a photograph on the occasion of its presentation in Washington, D.C. Two years later, at the peak of his professional achievement, Louis Zansky died of a heart attack. Mrs. Zansky recalled her husband's pleasure in spotting in *House Calls*, the last film they saw together, several of his paintings on the set.[10]

As a *Classic Comics* illustrator, Zansky generally gave his panels an open, spacious look, emphasizing the characters at the expense of the backgrounds. In his first three assignments—*Moby Dick*, No. 5 (September 1942); *Robin Hood*, No. 7 (December 1942); *Adventures of Sherlock Holmes*, No. 33 (completed in 1943; issued in January 1947)—the artist worked with inker Fred Eng. Mrs. Zan-

sky remembers him as a financially harried man with a large family who "came to Lou in desperation a couple of times for inking and lettering work."[11] Such a division of labor inevitably resulted in lower fees for the artist, but Zansky was always willing to help his friend. The collaborative efforts produced a lighter line than the nascent painter would employ in his later Gilberton projects.

Moby Dick was Zansky's favorite *Classic*, and he provided not only the illustrations but also the adaptation of Melville's masterpiece. Although Zansky's abridgment was cast in the third person and paraphrased much of the dialogue and narration ("Call me Ishmael" becomes "Out of the bleak December dusk, walks the lone figure of Ishmael, looking for a night's lodging…"), it remained faithful to the spirit of the novel. His Ahab is a powerful conception, and a portrait of the captain, framed by a life preserver and linked to images of the *Pequod* and the doomed ship's route, telegraphs the essence of his character and obsession. In a kind of visual counterpart to the chapters devoted to the mechanics of whaling, the young artist supplied drawings and descriptions of right and sperm whales and a detailed side view of the sailing vessel, down to the "Booby Hatch" and the "Blubber Room."

What is evident in *Moby Dick*, and elsewhere in Zansky's work for Gilberton, is the artist's keen awareness of his medium. He was not striving to produce a reverent tribute to the genius of Herman Melville; instead, he was attempting to engage young readers in a medium that had its own conventions and resources—and he succeeded handsomely. When Acclaim Books began reissuing *Classics Illustrated* in 1997, editor Madeleine Robins chose Zansky's spirited *Moby Dick* for inclusion in the new line rather than its 1956 replacement.

The next project, *Robin Hood*, under the auspices of art director Gail Hillson, featured a surprisingly text-heavy script by Evelyn Goodman (who, contrary to later speculation on the part of some *Classics* collectors, was not Zansky's wife). In her adaptations, Goodman never let source material stand in the way of her concept of a story, and her treatment of *Robin Hood* borrowed several plot components from the 1938 Warner Brothers film, interpolated a jousting scene from *Ivanhoe*, and, on the whole, emphasized the humorous elements of the outlaw's legend. The scriptwriter evidently

Louis Zansky, *Robin Hood* (December 1942). Robin stands tall.

decided that Maid Marian would slow down the action, so the outlaw's love interest had to wait until the 1957 *Classics Illustrated* revision for her Gilberton debut.

Zansky obviously enjoyed himself with *Robin Hood*, creating an eccentric cast of Merry Men and a comically unhinged-looking Prince John. Despite the broad cultural impact of Errol Flynn's recent portrayal of the hero, the artist made an effort to give the title character his own identity, shortening his hair and trimming his Van Dyke goatee back to a simple sliver beneath the lower lip. Zansky's best panels show Robin in action, trading blows with Little John, crossing swords with Friar Tuck, and drawing his bow on the villains. His cover, featuring Robin in profile, sounding his horn to rally the Merry Men in their battle against the forces of tyranny, undoubtedly had a certain wartime resonance. A wrap-around cover that Zansky designed for a Saks Christmas 1942 giveaway is now among the rarest and most prized of *Classics* collectibles.

Another rarity is the displaced *Adventures of Sherlock Holmes* issue—scheduled as No. 9 and released as No. 33—in which Gilberton paired *A Study in Scarlet* and *The Hound of the Baskervilles* by Sir Arthur Conan Doyle. The former mystery, a 17-page adaptation, was the weaker script of the two (the resolution of the story was packed into a 26-line speech balloon in the final panel) and was dropped when the issue was reduced to 48 pages in 1948; it was reintroduced in 1953 as the lead story in *Classics Illustrated* No. 110, with artwork by Seymour Moskowitz.

Zansky's Holmes is all angularity and coiled energy. The inevitable deerstalker cap makes its appearance but doesn't obscure the artist's older-and-leaner-than-usual conception of the character. Watson stands on his own, an intelligent companion rather than mere comic foil. As he would later in another Sherlock Holmes mystery, *The Sign of the* [*sic*] *Four* in *3 Famous Mysteries*, No. 21 (July 1944), the artist employed shading and shadows to good effect.

The Sign of the Four, though drawn after *The Hound of the Baskervilles* and *A Study in Scarlet*, marked Sherlock Holmes's debut in the comic-book medium.[12] Despite its heavier, brushed inking style, it has a lighter, jauntier air than its predecessors, thanks to the comic interplay between Holmes and Watson, who is smitten with a young female client.

Zansky's most delightful work, for which his whimsical style was perfectly suited, was Samuel H. Abramson's adaptation of Miguel de Cervantes's *Don Quixote*. The affection the artist felt for the hapless, idealistic knight and his faithful, commonsensical squire is evi-

Louis Zansky, "A Study in Scarlet" in *The Adventures of Sherlock Holmes* (1943/January 1947). **Sherlock pieces the puzzle together.**

dent, and the pair's exchanges build character and set the tone of the comic book. Each panel exhibits a swift, impressionistic touch, and Zansky excels in such comic sequences as the knighting at the inn, the battle with the windmills, the freeing of the convicts, and the routing of the barber.

Two of the artist's finest Gilberton titles, in which his distinctive brushwork is pronounced, are a pair from James Fenimore Cooper's "Leatherstocking" series, *The Deerslayer*, No. 17 (January 1944), and *The Pathfinder*, No. 22 (October 1944). Both remained in print until the demise of the American series in 1971. In the two books, the central figure of Natty Bumppo is presented as the embodiment of the frontier myth, and the two covers Zansky designed amount to a kind of pop-culture apotheosis of the self-reliant, trailblazing frontiersman. The

Left: Louis Zansky, *Don Quixote* (May 1943). The Man of La Mancha meets the windmills. *Above:* Louis Zansky, *Huckleberry Finn* (April 1944). Huck and Jim, rollin' on the river.

cover for *The Deerslayer*, depicting the young protagonist surrounded by tomahawk-wielding Indians and swinging his rifle, could serve as a text for understanding the way most Americans perceived the conquest of the wilderness in 1944. (See color section.)

Mark Twain's masterpiece, *Huckleberry Finn*, No. 19 (April 1944), occasioned some of the artist's liveliest efforts. Huck himself is part Mickey Rooney and part Lou Zansky, an unrepentant scamp with sound instincts. Nowhere in his *Classic Comics* illustrations did the artist come closer to rendering a self-portrait. The title-page splash depicting Huck, arms akimbo and pipe firmly in mouth, captures the essence of Zansky's self-assured, mis-

chievous spirit. Although the dramatic cover illustration of men firing on Huck and Jim had nothing whatever to do with the novel, Evelyn Goodman's script was better than usual, and the artist obviously relished the project.

With a war beckoning overseas, Lou Zansky was just beginning to find his style, experimenting on his own with the liberal inking of *Classic Comics* boards. His widow recalled her husband working "with the tip of his brush in his mouth as he inked, poisoning himself without knowing it."[13] The freely brushed lines were the work of an artist who was ready to move beyond the strictly representational limitations of the comics formula of the time. And move he did, with the energy that filled every aspect of his life.

VI

The War Years:
Early Freelancers

The year 1942 brought stimulating change to *Classic Comics*: the arrival of Louis Zansky, the move to new quarters at 510 Sixth Avenue, and the adoption of the Gilberton Company name. Albert Kanter, under the pseudonym Albert W. Raymond (a combination of the co-owners' first names), served as editor and briefly as art director. He was assisted by family member and future editor Meyer A. Kaplan, a New York University graduate with a literature background.[1] Gail Hillson acted as art director for a single issue, No. 7, *Robin Hood* (December 1942), and became managing editor for issues 8 through 17 between February 1943 and January 1944.[2] During this period, Louis Zansky assumed the duties of art director, and Evelyn Goodman and other scriptwriters produced a string of loose adaptations that tarnished the reputation of the series in some quarters for decades to come.

STANLEY MAXWELL ZUCKERBERG

Born on 13 September 1919, native New Yorker Stanley Maxwell Zuckerberg had studied at the Pratt Institute and the Art Students League. His teachers included George Bridgman and Norman Rockwell. Ahead of him lay a fulfilling career as a prizewinnning painter of marine life, but in the early 1940s Zuckerberg was a freelance artist who picked up two *Classic Comics* titles.[3]

The first, *A Tale of Two Cities*, No. 6 (October 1942), already had a significant strike against it in the form of a howler of a script by Evelyn Goodman, who must have

carried a high-school grudge against Charles Dickens. "Put your head on the block, Evremonde!" says the executioner to Sydney Carton, in a supreme moment of anticlimax, immediately after the abridged "far, far better" speech. A priest stands by in the unlikely, ahistorical role of French Revolutionary minister to the condemned. The 1956 *Classics Illustrated* revision, probably adapted by Annete Rubinstein with art by Joe Orlando, did better justice to the ending.

Zuckerberg, who used the name Stanley Maxwell for his *Classics* pieces, aggravated matters with his complete indifference to historical detail. The principal male characters, Charles Darnay and Sydney Carton, are coiffed and clad as Regency dandies, while Mr. Lorry is costumed as a mid–Victorian swell. Lucie Manette fares better, actually landing in the 18th century, though in costumes a mere four or five decades out of date; by the final panel (depicting a postexecution scene invented by Goodman), she seems to have added an 1840s-style dress to her wardrobe.

The painter was already evident in the panels Zuckerberg sketched for *A Tale of Two Cities*. His style was elliptical, to say the least: backgrounds are often nonexistent and merely suggested by the colorist. Human figures occasionally begin to vanish toward the bottoms of panels, giving the reader the impression of torsos floating in air. Even the guillotine partially disappears under the priest's right elbow. A handful of illustrations, however, such as the title-page splash depicting the attack on the Bastille, gave a more favorable indication of the artist's abilities.

Robinson Crusoe, No. 10 (April 1943), showed some improvement for comic-book purposes; there, Zuckerberg

A TALE OF TWO CITIES   PAGE 63

IT IS A FAR, FAR BETTER THING I DO, THAN I HAVE EVER DONE; IT'S A FAR BETTER REST I GO TO THAN I HAVE EVER KNOWN.

PUT YOUR HEAD ON THE BLOCK, EVREMONDE!

Stanley Maxwell Zuckerberg, *A Tale of Two Cities* (October 1942). Sydney Carton comes to a far, far worse end in Evelyn Goodman's adaptation of the Dickens classic.

actually finished his panels, not only drawing complete, if still sketchy, bodies in all but two instances, but also filling in the backgrounds more often than not. Anachronisms still surfaced, though not as frequently as in *A Tale of Two Cities*. A 17th-century sailor is given a 19th-century cap with bill, and Robinson Crusoe fires a six-shooter. The "savages," who are accorded great prominence, seem to be derived from 1930s Tarzan films rather than from the pages of Daniel Defoe, whose work more or less served as the source for this popular *Classic*. A better-illustrated 1957 revision, narrated in the manner of the novel in the first person, was much closer to the mark.

LILLIAN CHESTNEY

Although the talents of Stanley Maxwell Zuckerberg were ill suited to the comics medium, his wife, Lillian Chestney, carved a small but memorable niche for herself at Gilberton. As a female cartoonist in the 1940s, she was a rarity in the overwhelmingly male-dominated world of shop production. Like her husband, Chestney illustrated two *Classics* titles, her only signed comics efforts.[4] But her work, in this context, was superior.

Chestney's first freelance assignment was *Arabian Nights*, No. 8 (February 1943), the first of many titles

added to the catalogue with an eye to capitalizing on a recently released Hollywood B-movie of the same name, which had next to nothing to do with the *Thousand and One Nights*.

For *Arabian Nights*, Chestney designed the most unusual cover in the history of the series. She placed the *Classic Comics* logo, which had not yet achieved the instantly recognizable yellow-banner form, in an ornamented black oval. (See color section.) A bare-chested jinn looms over two smaller figures, wearing an extremely low-cut loincloth. Generations of readers and collectors have debated whether Chestney or inker Fred Eng had meant to suggest a shadow beneath the navel or pubic hair. The Gilberton editorial staff had its own ideas, and the black blotch disappeared from the cover when the book was reprinted in 1944.

In the view of comics historian Hames Ware, "It was refreshing to have a woman render the narrative of Scheherazade."[5] The illustrations for *Arabian Nights* display a charmingly naive quality that is augmented by assorted rococo embellishments, such as emroidered panel borders, twinkling stars, and bejewelled turbans. Perhaps the childlike mystique was too precious for the boys who comprised so much of the readership; at any rate, Chestney's *Arabian Nights* was last reissued in 1950, and a single-printing revision of the title, with new art by Charles Berger, did not appear until 1961.

The second Chestney *Classic*, Jonathan Swift's *Gulliver's Travels*, No. 16 (December 1943), features another collection of beguiling drawings. However, adapter Dan Kushner, in limiting the tale to the "Voyage to Lilliput" and allowing himself more than a few textual liberties, entirely missed the "savage indignation" of Swift's satire—there was no colloquy with the King of Brodingnag, no encounter with the Struldbrugs, no discourses on truth and "the thing which was not" by talking horses. But then, it is difficult to imagine the fanciful Chestney of the early 1940s decorating panels devoted to Houhynyms and Yahoos.

In 1954, *Gulliver's Travels* was dropped from the *Classics Illustrated* reorder list. Almost two years later, a *Dell Junior Treasury* edition of the "Voyage to Lilliput" (January 1956) was published; the script stuck much closer to the original than Kushner's Swiftian improvisations, while the artwork by Alberto Giolitti aimed at a more realistic representation. Unfortunately, when Gilberton reissued No. 16 in 1960 with a painted cover (in response to the release that year of a film titled *The Three Worlds of Gulliver*), editor Roberta Strauss Feuerlicht didn't demand a more faithful and literate script from the gifted staff writer Alfred Sundel and a darker

GULLIVER'S TRAVELS

UNDISTURBED BY A HAIL OF ARROWS FROM THE SHORE, GULLIVER JOINS THE ROPES TOGETHER AND HEADS BACK TOWARD LILLIPUT, TAKING THE ENTIRE BLEFUSCU FLEET WITH HIM!

Lillian Chestney, *Gulliver's Travels* **(December 1943). Gulliver wins the war for Lilliput.**

set of illustrations that Norman Nodel could have provided with such elegant ease.

Chestney spent only a couple of years in the comics field. She turned to commercial art and soon distinguished herself with an award for Best Advertisement of 1948. Later, she received honors as a book and magazine illustrator, earning the Citation for Merit from the Society for Illustrators in 1961 and 1965.[6]

ROLLAND H. LIVINGSTONE

One of the most interesting of the early *Classics* artists, Rolland H. Livingstone foreshadowed Henry C. Kiefer with his beguilingly antiquated style. Livingstone's panels for *Les Miserables*, No. 9 (March 1943), *Rip Van*

Winkle and the Headless Horseman, No. 12 (June 1943), and *Uncle Tom's Cabin*, No. 15 (November 1943), bore a greater resemblance to early 19th-century illustrations than to mid 20th-century comic-book drawings.

The unpolished awkwardness that permeated the work of so many other early *Classics* artists is particularly evident in *Les Miserables*, where stiff-limbed figures and odd perspectives occasionally defeat the artist's evident intentions. But Livingstone is a natural visual storyteller, and his treatment of Victor Hugo's masterpiece, though far surpassed by Norman Nodel's 1961 revision, remains compelling. In particular, he makes effective use of atmospheric linework to enhance the suspense of Jean Valjean's rooftop escape and his flight through the sewers.

Washington Irving's *Sketch-Book* tales provided Livingstone ample opportunity to exhibit his skills as a caricaturist and his eye for period detail in the artist's most accomplished work for Gilberton. Rip Van Winkle's encounter with Henry Hudson's crew, his return to the village and ensuing confusion, Ichabod Crane's efforts at courtship, and his fateful meeting with the Headless Horseman are all engaging illustrations that successfully blend cartoonish figures and realistic backgrounds.

The adaptations by Dan Levin are typical of early *Classic Comics* retellings. Though faithful to the spirit of Irving's sketches, they contain interpolated material to which the author might have been reluctant to sign his name. Where, for example, Irving writes that Rip told the village children "long stories of ghosts, witches and Indians,"[7] the scriptwriter expands the general statement to a two-page account of single-handed combat with and capture by "the redskins." Levin also adds a shot cow and a menacing boulder to Rip's adventures.

Uncle Tom's Cabin was seriously marred by the racial stereotyping of the period. Amazingly, given the changing social and political currents between the first printing in 1943 and the 19th in 1970, the book was neither discontinued nor redrawn. It received a new painted cover in 1954, the year the United States Supreme Court handed down *Brown v. Board of Education*, and was the only title illustrated by Livingstone to remain on the active list until the series shut down. *Uncle Tom's Cabin* was, in fact, one of the 12 best-selling *Classics*.[8]

A few efforts were made in the painted-cover reissue to tone down some of the more overtly racist depictions of black characters. In a retouched panel showing the eye-popping, wide-mouthed Sambo and Quimbo

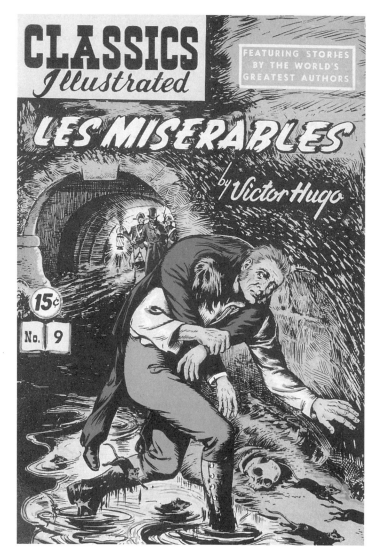

Left: Rolland H. Livingstone, *Les Miserables* (March 1943; 1951 *Classics Illustrated* reprint). Jean Valjean savors the sewers. *Above:* Rolland H. Livingstone, *Rip Van Winkle* (June 1943). Rip settles his brains for a 20 years' nap.

teeth, hairy arms, and raised fists. The big bad overseer inhabits the realm of camp and almost redeems this curious artifact.

ARNOLD L. HICKS

Arnold Lorne Hicks is a transitional figure in the early history of *Classic Illustrated*. An older artist who was producing pulp covers as early as 1920, he was the only Iger Shop affiliate to provide artwork for Gilberton before and after Jerry Iger assumed artistic control in 1945. Hicks began badly but in the end produced one of the finest *Classic Comics* issues.

His initial title for the series, Robert Louis Stevenson's *Dr. Jekyll and Mr. Hyde*, No. 13 (August 1943), has considerable historical significance as the first example of what would becomic a major genre—horror comics.[9] Unfortunately, despite its popular-culture credentials, the issue was an overstated clunker afflicted with the endemic crudeness of the early issues. In Stevenson's story, the doctor describes the projection of the "evil side of my nature" as "smaller, slighter, and younger than Henry Jekyll."[10] Elsewhere, Hyde is said to be "pale and dwarfish," giving "an impression of deformity without any namable malformation…."[11] Nothing if not obvious, Hicks's stocky, "unbridled, monster-like" Hyde came

fleeing from sheet-draped figures, the grotesquely enlarged eye and lip sizes were reduced and quivering speech balloons were eliminated. Yet the offensive drawing remained, even with its cosmetic enhancements, an inexplicable lapse in editorial judgment. A grave marker bearing the name "Uncle Tom" also disappeared. Otherwise, except for a more assertive Tom on a second painted cover in 1969, the artwork was never revised, even after Livingstone's better efforts in *Rip Van Winkle* were axed.

If Topsy is a minstrel-show embarrassment ("I didn' steal nuffin', I didn'"), Tom himself is allowed a measure of dignity, though in a rather patronizing sort of way ("My soul is myself, so you can't really harm me"). Little Eva's deathbed ascension is rendered with enough sentimentality ("The … angels … are … coming … for … me") to satisfy the most maudlin Victorian tastes. The good white folks—the Shelbys and the St. Clares—all but wear halos. Simon Legree, shown slavehunting on the original cover and in various states of rage in the interior, exudes sheer malevolence with his flaring nostrils, bared

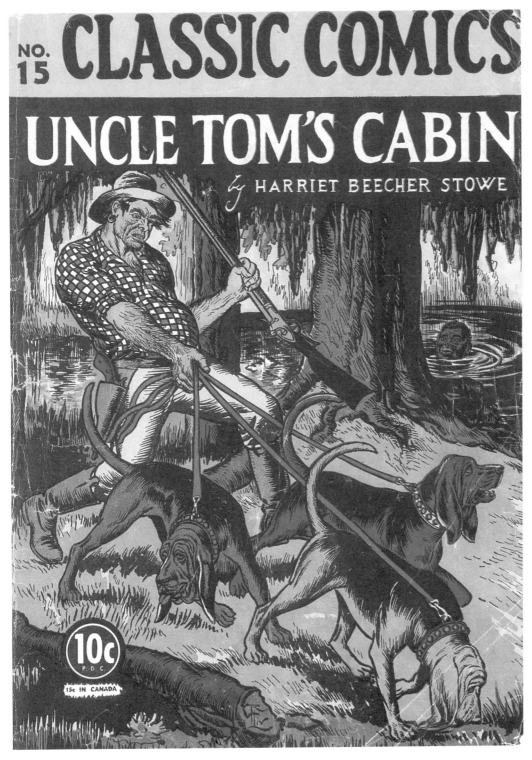

upon memories of the 1931 Rouben Mamoulian film or the more recent 1941 Spencer Tracy vehicle to flesh out their conceptions of the tale. As in the movie versions, a love interest unknown to Stevenson appears. Goodman begins the *Classic Comic* with a wholly invented party scene in which the fun-loving, debonair Jekyll (obviously no relation to his literary progenitor) exclaims, "To life! To laughter! To a gay evening!" The adaptation ends with another example of the unintentional humor that Goodman excelled in providing. Commenting on his friend Jekyll's fate, Dr. Lanyon sagely counsels, "[E]vil becomes a habit-forming drug. My advice is *stay away from that first taste!*" Beneath the speech balloon, Hicks helpfully drew a devil's head and pitchfork.

Dr. Jekyll and Mr. Hyde proved problematic for Gilberton as the company endeavored to distance itself from the perceived excesses of the comics industry. In 1949, one year before William Gaines raised the bar for horror with the first issue of *The Haunt of Fear*, Hicks's original *Classic Comics* cover, which displayed a rampaging Hyde scattering panic-stricken

Rolland H. Livingstone, *Uncle Tom's Cabin* (November 1943). Simon Legree living up to his name.

equipped with fangs, the better to scare you with. The script, another Evelyn Goodman atrocity, had even less to do with Stevenson's study of human duality than the Spencer Tracy movie of that approximate vintage.

In fact, Goodman and Hicks both may have called

Londoners, was suppressed, and a tamer, more respectable version drawn by Henry C. Kiefer was substituted in the renamed *Classics Illustrated* series. By 1953, however, it was obvious that the issue itself no longer had a place in the series, and managing editor Meyer A. Kaplan

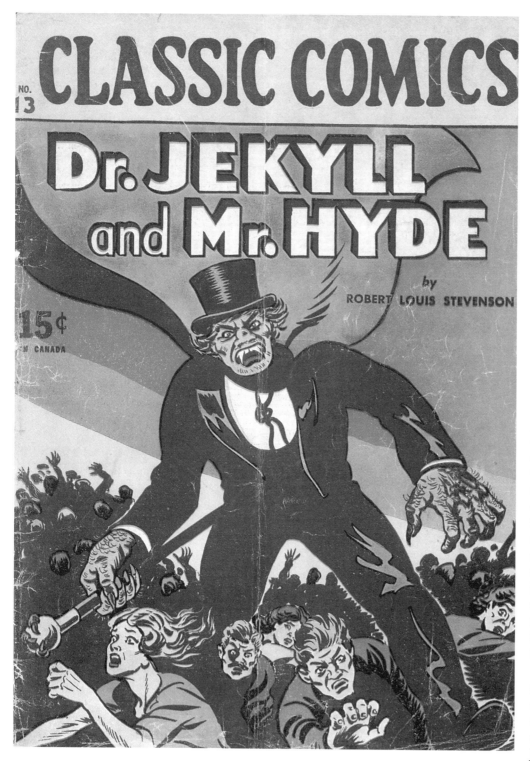

Arnold L. Hicks, *Dr. Jekyll and Mr. Hyde* (August 1943). Mr. Hyde takes an evening stroll.

A second pre–Iger piece, Edgar Allan Poe's "The Murders in the Rue Morgue" in *3 Famous Mysteries*, No. 21 (July 1944), evidenced only modest improvements on the part of both the artist and the adapter. With its panels depicting a bright-red pool of blood and a woman wedged upside down in a chimney, the story appeared to be Gilberton's rather awkward attempt to capitalize on the popularity of Lev Gleason's sanguinary *Crime Does Not Pay* series. The artist spoiled the resolution of the mystery by filling the title-page splash with the looming shadow of an ape.

Hicks truly came into his own when he received the first assignment of the Iger era, *Oliver Twist* , No. 23 (July 1945). Only Henry C. Kiefer equaled him in his affinity for Dickens, and his drawings of Oliver, the Artful Dodger, Fagin, Nancy, and Sikes catch some of the robustness of Cruikshank's original illustrations without imitating them. *Oliver Twist* represented a decisive step forward for the series with its faithful adaptation by Georgina Campbell.

Hicks's heavily inked, and at times brushed, *Michael Strogoff: A Courier of the Czar*, No. 28 (June 1946), adapted by Pat Adam from Jules Verne's novel (Albert Kanter's favorite), kept the action flowing from panel to panel with cinematic momentum. A departure from the author's usual science-fiction fare, the early espionage tale moves rapidly through the hero's dangerous mission to Siberia and his efforts to foil the nefarious schemes of the wily traitor Ivan Ogareff. The *Classic Comics* version was an exciting union of pictures and words and one of the

authorized a new adaptation, new interior art, and a painted cover, which showed a contemplative, fangless Hyde rising from Jekyll's green formula. A victim of the midfifties anti-comics hysteria, No. 13 was withdrawn in November 1955; when it returned to the reorder list in November 1959, it quickly became one of Gilberton's best-sellers.

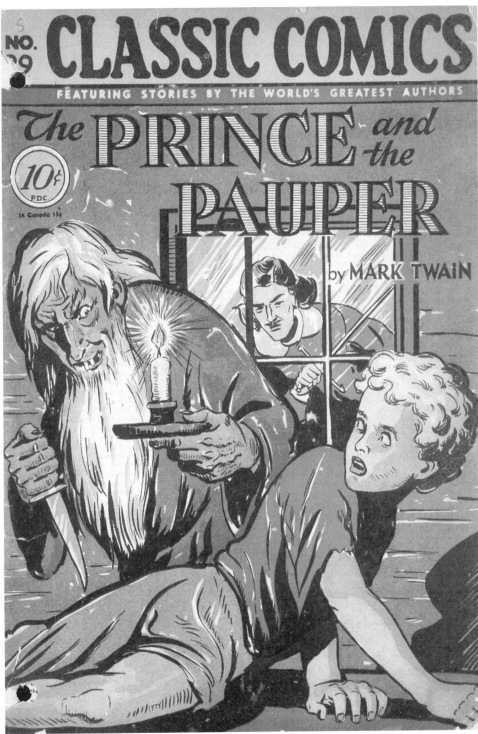

Above: Arnold L. Hicks, *Michael Strogoff* (June 1946). Villain Ivan Ogareff behaves badly and gets the hero's attention. *Right:* Arnold L. Hicks, *The Prince and the Pauper* (July 1946). The prince in peril. This controversial "child abuse" cover was never reprinted.

most artistically successful issues in the early Gilberton series, but the story's violence (stabbings, shootings, flogging, blinding) made it a target of critics, and it appeared erratically on the re-order lists until a painted-cover edition was published in 1954.

Three further works, *The Prince and the Pauper*, No. 29 (July 1946), *The Spy*, No. 51 (September 1948), and *Silas Marner*, No. 55 (January 1949), represented a return to the lighter-inked caricature style of *Oliver Twist.* Both *The Spy* and *Silas Marner* had originally been issued in longer *Illustrated Classics* newspaper editions in 1947.

Mark Twain's Tudor-era historical fantasy of switched identities generated controversy with its "horror" cover depicting the young prince in the clutches of a mad hermit. The offending cover was withdrawn after a single printing, but the popular title earned 14 addi-

tional printings with two replacement covers. Hicks supplied some of his best period drawings for *The Prince and the Pauper.*

For *The Spy*, James Fenimore Cooper's Revolutionary War tale of double agent Harvey Birch, the artist produced a thoughtful study of the complex central character. One of the interesting aspects of *The Spy* was Hicks's success in making the actions of the titular hero,

Arnold L. Hicks, *The Spy* (September 1948). Spanking the Skinners.

drawn as an older man, compelling to young readers. The Cooper issue also featured the most overt nudity in the series, in the episode of Captain Lawton's whipping of the "Skinners," where bare-bottomed men were shown strung up by their wrists, receiving punishment. It was indeed a different era—the illustration never attracted the attention of comics censors, presumably because the figures in question were male, and the title never went out of print.

The *Classics* edition of *Silas Marner*, George Eliot's story of the redemption of a cataleptic miser by golden-haired foundling Eppie, proved a perennial favorite with

high-school students whose efforts to dodge the original saw the abridgment through 12 printings. Hicks infused the relationship between the weaver and the little girl with a grace note of gentle sympathy, deeper than the comic books of the period demanded. The artist's depictions of Marner's parallel discoveries that his fortune has been stolen and that an unknown child sleeps on his hearth are among his best efforts.

Previously, Hicks had illustrated what Jerry Iger considered one of the finest of the earlier books in the series—a skillful if occasionally loose adaptation by Ruth A. Roche and Thomas T. Scott of Robert Louis

Stevenson's exercise in Lancastrian-Yorkist "tushery," *The Black Arrow*, No. 31 (October 1946).[12] The details of costuming and backgrounds indicate that the artist spent a respectable amount of time in period research, with more than a casual glance at N.C. Wyeth's paintings for the 1916 Scribner's edition of the book. Some coherence was lost when the book was reduced to a 48-page format in 1948; the moral ambiguities of the tale were softened with the excision of two pages depicting hero Dick Shelton, while cloaked as a monk, stabbing and disposing of the body of an enemy spy.

Most striking, however, are the emphatically individualized characters, from the "crafty and ambitious nobleman," Sir Daniel Brackley, to the "best maid and bravest under heaven," Joan Sedley—the latter being a rare achievement in 1940s comic books, where women were most often either sultry vixens or vapid ciphers. Gestures, expressions, bearing, and movement not only breathed life into the figures but also served to drive the script, so that, unlike some of the more static *Classics* in the pre–Iger era, the illustrations carried more than their share of the narrative burden. *The Black Arrow* was worlds apart from Hicks's previous Stevensonian excursion, *Dr. Jekyll and Mr. Hyde*, and the artist's transformation seemed to symbolize the new day at Gilberton.

Arnold L. Hicks, *The Black Arrow* (October 1946). A page of original art, showing Hicks's penciling, inking, and white-out marks. Note the Iger shop address in the upper left corner. (Collection of author.)

VII

Classical Interlude:
A Fan's Notes on the 1940s

Classics fans differ considerably in their attitudes toward the evolving artistic identity of the series. Those whose first encounters with the yellow rectangle occurred in the 1940s tend to prefer the earlier line-drawing covers and the less regimented art of that era. Toronto resident Bill Briggs, the second editor of *The Classics Reader*, a pioneering fanzine of the 1970s and '80s, offers the following musings:

> *Classics Illustrated* always had, for me, a note of magic. I was five years old, sickly, with no brothers or sisters. *Classics* kept appearing magically: inside a folded evening newspaper, at the foot of my bed in the morning, in a desk drawer. You get the picture.
>
> It was 1948 in Atlantic Canada…. A new issue appeared every two weeks. The covers were the first "hook"; filled with heroic figures and lavishly coloured, they invited the reader to enter worlds of wonder and romance not to be found in the humdrum of every day.
>
> The interiors of the *Classics* did not disappoint. I loved Zansky's larger-than-life heroes: Captain Ahab, Robin Hood, the Don of La Mancha, Pathfinder, the Sleuth of Baker Street. I have always imagined these mythic figures as I saw them for the first time, as Zansky drew them….

(I see Zansky as a fast, risk-taking, lyrical draftsman with a flair for action….)

Action was the byword in those early *Classics* issues. Mme. Thenardier throwing the boulder in *Les Miserables.* (What was it doing in the garret?) The Horseman throwing the pumpkin at Ichabod's head. (Was the Horseman really Brom Bones?) Rolland Livingstone, I presume!

I loved Lillian Chestney's jinn in *Arabian Nights* and her Lilliputians in *Gulliver's Travels*, so exotic with their curls and fingernails, all embellished with Chestney's filigreed art panels.

Oh, I know that Allen Simon's efforts are the butt of jokes of those who are in the know and that his *Hunchback* and *Flayed Hand* are editorial nightmares, but really now! This was the period when *Classics* stalwartly refused to take themselves too seriously, when *Classics* were just comic books. When *Classics* were, well, charming!

The Iger Shop's regime from 1945 to 1953 represents, for me, a backward step, an expulsion from Eden, an increasingly self-conscious period when *Classics* sought elevation from the status of "comics" to "the best in the world's finest juvenile publication"—the Iger era of the potted book reports. *Classics* had gained the world but had lost its soul.[1]

VIII

Enter Iger

Cartoonist and writer Samuel Maxwell "Jerry" Iger (1910–1990) was a major player in the comics field from the 1930s through the 1950s. In 1937, he and Will Eisner formed a shop that offered publishers ready-made original stories and artwork to meet the demands of the booming market. The next year, they approached Thomas T. Scott of Fiction House, a leading pulp publisher, with a proposal for a monthly comic-book series to be called *Jumbo Comics*, featuring a pin-up-style jungle queen named Sheena. Scott signed on, and Sheena began a lengthy, well-endowed existence on newsstands and in dreams.[1]

Jumbo Comics begat Fiction House's *Jungle Comics*. Other packaged creations from Iger and Eisner were *Planet Comics*, *Hit Comics*, and *Wonderworld Comics*; popular characters included the Blue Beetle, Wonder Boy, and the Flame.[2] Eisner left the partnership in 1940 to win a place in the comics pantheon as the creator of *The Spirit*, an innovative Sunday comics newspaper insert.[3]

Iger continued running what was then the pre-eminent comic-book shop, producing a variety of series for Fiction House, Fox Features Syndicate, and Quality Comics Group, and employing a diverse group of artists, including Rafael Astarita, Alex A. Blum, Reed Crandall, Lou Fine, Joe Kubert, and Henry C. Kiefer.[4] The Iger shop became particularly identified with "Good Girl Art," drawings of pouting-lipped, ample-bosomed, minimally clothed heroines, which staffers Matt Baker and John Forte supplied for Fiction House and Fox.

In November 1943, Jerry Iger met Albert Kanter, and the fortunes of both men changed. Kanter was well aware of the uneven quality of the artwork in the early *Classic Comics*, and Iger, who was impressed with the idea of publishing adaptations of great literature in comic-book form, introduced himself and offered the resources of his shop to produce other titles and, incidentally, improve the product.[5]

Having secured additional paper supplies, Kanter first engaged the services of the Iger shop to produce, between June and December 1944, three war-related comics: the single-issue *Story of the Commandos*, three issues of *Bomber Comics*, and two issues of *Spitfire Comics*.[6] The following year, using an allotment of book paper obtained through a friend, Kanter published a 12-volume set of children's books designed to compete with the popular Little Golden Books. Inside-cover ads for the "Little Folks" line (*Pee Wee and the Sneezing Elephant*, *Tickle Tickle Tickle*, *The Grasshopper Man*, among other titles) appeared in various *Classic Comics* issues. Iger's assistant editor, Ruth A. Roche, oversaw the unsuccessful project, which proved to be no match for Golden's Poky Little Puppy.[7]

Louis Zansky, who had been acting as de facto art director for Gilberton, entered the armed forces in 1944; simultaneously, the impact of paper rations began to be felt, defeating even Kanter's ingenuity. *Classic Comics* suspended publication in October 1944 with No. 22, *The Pathfinder*, Zansky's last title for Gilberton. Iger turned his attention to the line in the spring of 1945 and began assigning new titles to his shop artists, who were paid salaries rather than per-page rates.[8] Gilberton retained final control under the joint direction of managing editor Harry M. Adler (1944–1951) and editor William E. Kanter (1946–1956), the founder's son.

The first issue in the series under the new arrangement was *Oliver Twist*, No. 23 (July 1945), illustrated by Arnold Hicks. Iger's and Kanter's relationship would last for the next nine years, would cover nearly 100 issues, and would result in some of the finest editions published under the yellow banner. A "house style" would develop that would make *Classics Illustrated* immediately identifiable.

Not only the artwork but the adaptations also

dramatically improved—gone were the days of unrecognizable variations on themes by Stevenson and Hugo. The change for the better was due to Ruth A. Roche (1921–1983), who began scripting for Iger in 1940 and later became his coeditor and business partner. She wrote such Fiction House jungle features as "Sheena," "Kaanga," "Camilla," and "Wambi," as well as Matt Baker's syndicated *Flamingo* strip.[9]

Roche was also the single most important person in Iger's life—in a personal as well as professional sense. As his friend Ron Prager recalled, "Ruth Roche was the love of Jerry Iger's life. He loved her till the day she died, and he loved her till his own death several years later."[10] The romantic and creative electricity generated between the two fueled the Fiction House dynamics that made it one of the strongest contenders in the late 1940s comics field. The Gilberton Company was a third-party beneficiary.

The young writer displayed a command of narrative pacing in her scripts for *Classic Comics* and a willingness to trust the authors whose works she adapted. Fewer liberties would be taken with the originals on Roche's watch, and the textual matter would assume increasing importance during the Iger years, as the educational role of *Classics Illustrated* grew more prominent.

In the end, however, Iger decided that the large-scale adaptations demanded too much time and effort for the amount of compensation.[11] He and Kanter reached an amicable parting in 1953, and one of his principal artists, Alex A. Blum, remained with Gilberton as art director. Iger bowed out of the comic-book business in 1955 when the Comics Code effectively shut down his remaining publishing outlets.

JACK R. HEARNE

With Jack R. Hearne's cover and interior art for *A Connecticut Yankee in King Arthur's Court*, No. 24 (September 1945), *Classic Comics*

attained a higher level of technical achievement. The artist used skillful shading to convey atmosphere and character. Highly individualized facial features that border on the eccentric lift the protagonist, Hank Morgan, almost out of the comic-book realm. Throughout *Yankee*, Hearne employed unusual vantage points to maintain visual interest. Ruth A. Roche's adaptation of Mark Twain's novel was in some respects closer to the darker intent of the original than the 1957 *Classics* revision,

Jack R. Hearne, *A Connecticut Yankee in King Arthur's Court* (September 1945). Sir Boss takes charge.

where Morgan awakens in the final panel safe at home in Connecticut.

A Connecticut Yankee was Hearne's only title for Gilberton. Years later, he told comic-book artist Alex Toth that he had been paid $500 for the book.[12] Hearne, who had been active in the Binder and Jacquet shops earlier in the decade and had made a name for himself for his work with Novelty, a Curtis comics imprint, apparently had a brief connection with the Iger operation in the mid–Forties. Subsequently, he became a well-established magazine and juvenile-book illustrator, providing art for an Alfred Hitchcock line in the 1960s.[13]

ROBERT HAYWARD WEBB, DAVID HEAMES, ANN BREWSTER, AND ED WALDMAN

A man who seemed more content on the waves than under an illustrator's lamp, Robert Hayward Webb charged his illustrations with his own robust virility. Comics historian Hames Ware describes him as a good-humored man with a hearty laugh. Webb went to work for Jerry Iger in 1940 and spent the rest of his career with him, drawing such features as *Sheena, Queen of the Jungle* for Fiction House. At his retirement in the 1960s, he held the record as the shop's longest-tenured artist.[14]

Webb's greatest passion was ships and boats, and he drew them with obsessive enthusiasm for *Classics* in *Two Years Before the Mast*, No. 25 (October 1945); *Mysterious Island*, No. 34 (February 1947); *Kidnapped*, No. 46 (April 1948); and *The Dark Frigate*, No. 132 (May 1956). After leaving the comics field, he turned to boatbuilding and later roared with laughter as he told Hames Ware, "I used to *draw* boats, and now I *build* them."[15]

Webb generally inked his own pencils but occasionally worked with collaborators. His favorite was David Heames, a younger artist who ably assisted him on Richard Henry Dana's *Two Years Before the Mast* and Jules Verne's *Mysterious Island*. The antithesis of Webb's *Sheena* illustrations, the images in the Dana and Verne books were as macho as *Classic Comics* ever got, with their muscular he-men exerting themselves in panel after panel.

Two Years Before the Mast ran afoul of comic-book censors in the 1950s for its portrayal of brutal conditions aboard the good ship *Pilgrim*. The title page had warned readers that what followed was "A voice from the forecastle … presenting such shocking evidence of the seaman's life that it revolutionized the entire administration of maritime law!" But the educational disclaimer failed to convince critics that the artists weren't enjoying

the effects of Captain Thompson's whip just a little too much, and the title was withdrawn from 1955 to 1960.

The only instance of Gilberton issuing a sequel before the work that preceded it, *Mysterious Island* appeared a year before *20,000 Leagues Under the Sea* was added to the *Classics* list. The artwork emphasizes one exciting incident after another. Webb lavished attention on the cover illustration of a boat under sail, and the heavily inked panels of the interior show the castaways strenuously contending with the sea, wild animals, and pirates.

For his last *Classics* title, *The Dark Frigate*, an adaptation of Charles Boardman Hawes's Newbery Award-winning historical novel, Ed Waldman provided support, but the panels for the most part lacked the brio of Webb's earlier work. (There were, however, as always, plenty of hairy chests and forearms to go around.) Nestled between issues illustrated by representatives of a newer style,

Robert Hayward Webb, *Two Years Before the Mast* **(October 1945). Captain Thompson cracks the whip.**

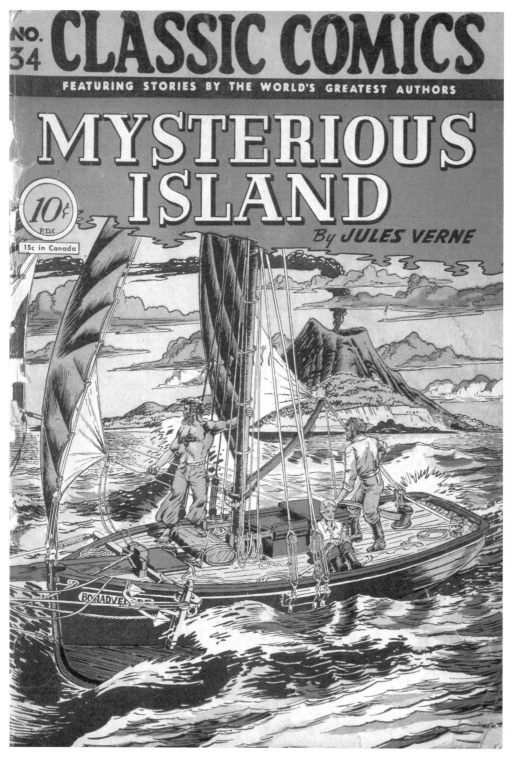

Robert Hayward Webb, *Mysterious Island* (February 1947). Forget Sheena—for the artist, the boat was the thing.

the Iger shop in the mid–Forties after an apprenticeship with Jack Binder, she inked the *Jane Martin* and *Hawk* strips and later gained recognition for her work in the "true crime" genre.[16] Between 1958 and 1960, Brewster's work appeared in assorted *World Around Us* issues. Her best work for that Gilberton series included the cleanly rendered "Caesar's Revenge" in *Pirates*, No. W7 (March 1959), the richly detailed "Rise of Napoleon" in *The French Revolution*, No. W14 (October 1959), and the crisply inked "Cursed Trick" in *Magic*, No. W25 (September 1960). Later, Brewster won several fine arts awards.

One of the plum assignments of the series, Ruth A. Roche's adaptation of Mary Shelley's gothic parable remained one of Gilberton's most popular titles, going through nineteen printings between 1945 and 1971. Comics authority Mike Benton lauded the *Classic Comics* edition of *Frankenstein* as "probably the most faithful adaptation of the original novel—movies included."[17] Comic-book writer Donald F. Glut singled out Ruth A. Roche's script for praise: "Her breakdown as interpreted by the artists remains as a veritable storyboard for the definitive movie version…, if it is ever filmed."[18]

Glut also noted the similarity between Boris Karloff's monster and Webb's and Brewster's creature, who was given bare feet and dark-gray skin coloring to avoid legal problems with Universal Pictures.[19] Webb and Brewster, like film director James Whale, got the period wrong, garbing the characters in something like Regency style rather than in clothing appropriate to the novel's 18th-

Norman Nodel and Lou Cameron, *The Dark Frigate* seemed a visual anachronism.

The artist joined forces on *Frankenstein*, No. 26 (December 1945), with Ann Brewster, an Iger inker capable of holding her own with the Good Girl boys. Arriving at

Robert Hayward Webb, *Frankenstein* (December 1945). The big guy in a bad mood.

tine were rendered in Webb's and Brewster's familiar erotically charged "Good Girl" style. Despite Elizabeth's plunging neckline and strategically uncovered leg and Justine's bared shoulder and prominent breast, the issue somehow escaped the scrutiny of the self-appointed upholders of decency in the 1950s, who evidently found the whip in *Two Years Before the Mast* more offensive. In any event, *Frankenstein* was neither withdrawn nor redrawn.

Perhaps Webb's finest effort for Gilberton was Robert Louis Stevenson's *Kidnapped*, on which he worked alone. Although the manly artist evidently had qualms about giving David Balfour, the red-blooded Scottish Lowland protagonist, 18th-century-style ribboned hair, he caught the dark, mythic overtones of the first section of the *bildungsroman,* creating a memorable sequence of panels depicting the young hero's ascent of the unfinished tower. Webb was equally up to the task of swashing buckles with Alan Breck Stewart in the siege of the Round-House. The only disappointing aspect of the issue was John O'Rourke's adaptation, which, though faithful to the plot, sacrificed an entire layer of

century setting. But most film costumers and, for that matter, book illustrators (Lynd Ward is a notable exception) have made the same mistake.

By the standards of the mid–Forties, *Frankenstein* featured the most shocking mixture of sex and violence to appear in *Classic Comics.* The murder of Victor's bride Elizabeth and the hanging of the innocent servant Jus-

meaning by abandoning the novel's first-person narrative voice.

Given his long association with the Iger Shop, it seems a pity that Webb was not assigned more *Classics* titles. His approaches to *Treasure Island, The Pilot, Mr. Midshipman Easy,* and *The Sea Wolf* would have given each of those stories an injection of high spirits and

Robert Hayward Webb, *Kidnapped* (April 1948). David Balfour runs a great danger in the House of Shaws.

nautical authenticity. But at the time, the artist's prolific Fiction House work took precedence.

HOMER FLEMING

An older artist, Homer Fleming (1883–1967) was drawing cartoons as early as 1912.[20] By the late 1930s, when the comics boom was underway, he was supplying artwork for Malcolm Wheeler-Nicholson's *More Fun*.[21] Fleming was a respected cartoonist and magazine illustrator whose style linked the Gibson Girl era and the Golden Age of comic books. In 1946, under Jerry Iger's auspices, he tackled the first nominally nonfiction *Classic Comics* title, *The Adventures of Marco Polo*, No. 27 (April 1946).

The factual basis of portions of the *Travels* has been a matter of dispute for centuries, though Marco Polo's (if

not his collaborator Rustichello's) credibility is in the main now generally conceded. In the *Classics* version, however, distinctions between legend and fact were of no moment; the first page announced that "[g]aps in narration have been filled in to make this a dramatic presentation of the travels of the world's most talked of explorer." Some episodes may have been suggested by Donn Byrne's popular novel, *Messer Marco Polo* (1921).

Marco's romance with a Princess Silver Bells (Golden Bells in Byrne's book), the distinctly Caucasian-featured daughter of Kublai Khan, and, worse, a victory orchestrated by the hero over "Japanese cannibals" (World War II was less than a year in the past) were not only interpolations but also among the most egregious examples of racial stereotyping in a publication that later stood so firmly against such practices. "I have seen many strange people," Marco Polo muses, "but never have I hated any except these sneaky men of Japan."

Fleming's second Gilberton title, *Tom Brown's School Days*, No. 45 (January 1948), was a beautifully old-

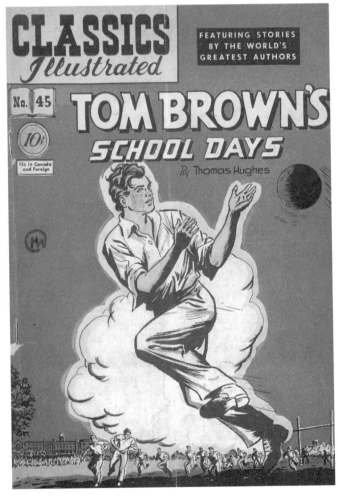

Homer Fleming, *Tom Brown's School Days* (January 1948). Our plucky hero in action.

Homer Fleming, *The Adventures of Marco Polo* **(April 1946). Those "sneaky men of Japan" at it again.**

tique charm of Fleming's work is evident in the cover illustration, where Tom is shown in a rugby match as a worthy exemplar of gentlemanly "good form."

DON RICO

Donato Francisco (Don) Rico (1918–1985) was a multi-talented artist and writer whose sole *Classic Comics* title, *The Moonstone*, No. 30 (September 1946), showed him working at less than his full capacity. Trained at Cooper Union and influenced by Lynd Ward's and Rockwell Kent's woodcut techniques, Rico worked for the Chesler, Binder, Jacquet, and Iger shops in the 1940s. During that period, he supplied art for *Target Comics* and produced a syndicated comic strip called "Johnny Jones."[22] While working for Timely, he substituted for Jack Kirby, who had enlisted to fight in the Second World War. In the late forties, he provided illustrations for *Murder Incorporated*, a crime-comics series published by Fox Feature Syndicate.[23] Later, his paintings found homes in private collections and museums, and the artist taught at UCLA. Rico became the first president of the Cartoon Arts Professionals Society in Los Angeles.[24] The artist's interest in writing led to his authoring about 50 novels and screenplays, including scripts for *Adam-12* and other television series.[25]

fashioned production. The drawings of Thomas Arnold's Rugby seemed to belong more to a 19th-century illustrated boys' book than to a mid–20th-century comic book. Tom Brown is portrayed as the paragon of Victorian boyhood, while the bully Flashman, with his wild shock of hair, is a comically effective caricature. The an-

Rico's illustrations for *The Moonstone* strike the right note of alien mystery, but neither they nor Dan Levin's severely truncated adaptation do justice to Wilkie Collins's novel of detection, with its mixture of suspense and wit. The artist evidently was given no guidance on

Don Rico, *The Moonstone* (September 1946). The fatal jewel shines brightly.

ness and promises of richer wonders in the original.

MATT BAKER

Among the most gifted of Iger's artists was Matt Baker, who, though chiefly recalled for his curvaceously drawn females, was a superb all-around artist. He was admired and respected by his comics industry peers and others who knew him in his all-too-short life. As his brief experience with Gilberton showed, there was much more to his art than the Good Girls who made and, in a sense, circumscribed his reputation.

An African-American, Baker was born in Homestead, Pennsylvania, a black community in the Pittsburgh area.[26] Like many of his contemporaries in the comics trade, he received his training at New York's Cooper Union. By the mid–1940s, when he was barely into his twenties, the handsome, dapper young artist arrived at Jerry Iger's studio and said simply, "Looking for a job." After he submitted a color sketch of, naturally, a beautiful woman, Iger, on the recommendation of Ruth Roche, signed him on. Beginning as a background artist, Baker was soon receiving major assignments.[27]

His Fiction House resume included the skimpily clad and frequently bound *Phantom Lady*, the alluring *Tiger Girl*, and the seductive *South Sea Girl*.[28] Apparently not wishing to divert the artist's attention from his lucrative Good Girls, Iger gave him only one *Classic Comics* project, but it was a beauty—Ruth A. Roche's skillful adaptation of R.D. Blackmore's historical romance, *Lorna Doone*, No. 32 (December 1946).

Baker seemed right at home in 17th-century Exmoor, with the broad-shouldered hero John Ridd and

character descriptions or period costuming. An unevenness runs from panel to panel, where well-executed homages to Ward and Kent alternate with stiff-limbed figures. The women appear to be afterthoughts, as do the stylized, minimalist backgrounds. Yet, with all its shortcomings, Rico's work offered an otherworldly strange-

jackbooted villain Carver Doone. The royal officer Jeremy Stickles is, in particular, a well-realized character study. Of course, the Good Girl artist couldn't resist giving the virginal heroine Lorna pouting lips and, on the title-page splash, a plunging neckline. The original splash was replaced in 1957 with the line-drawing-cover illustration when a painted cover was substituted and the interior artwork recolored. (See color section.)

Fine sequences of visual storytelling fill Baker's *Lorna Doone*: the abduction of the heroine as a child; John Ridd's ascent of the waterfall in Doone Glen; the outlaws' ambush of the troopers led by Jeremy Stickles; Ridd's arrest and near execution; the wounding of the heroine at her wedding; the hero's pursuit of Carver Doone into the Wizard's Slough. The artist emphasized action and yet supplied a host of arresting images that rewarded scrutiny. As well wrought as Roche's script is, not a single panel is subordinated to the text; word and picture are finely balanced in a way that would not be possible in some later issues where the verbal element impinged on the pictorial. Readers responded warmly and kept the *Classics* edition of *Lorna Doone* in print throughout the life of the series, even as the popularity of the novel on which it was based waned.

The artist continued drawing Good Girls for Iger, producing, from 1952 to 1956, the syndicated siren *Flamingo*. Others covered (or uncovered) the same territory, but Baker transcended the Good Girl genre, investing his female characters with strength as well as sex appeal. *Lorna Doone* showed a greater depth in the artist's work.

From the late 1940s through the 1950s, Baker demonstrated his versatility, supplying illustrations for such publications as Archer St. John's *Northwest Mounties*, *The Texan*, *Teen-Age Temptations*, and *True Love Pictorial*; Ajax-Farrell's *Voodoo*; and Dell's *Lassie* series and *Movie Classic* edition of *King Richard and the Crusaders*. In 1949, he assumed the duties of art director for St. John, where he remained until 1955.[29] The artist continued freelancing until his death a few years later. Comics art expert Jim Vadeboncoeur, Jr., spotted his hand in a publication dated as late as 1962.[30]

Novelist and former comics artist Lou Cameron knew Baker in the St. John days and wrote that "Matt was an agreeable handsome man who reminded one of the younger Harry Belafonte. Matt handled the race bit in a very comfortable manner. He never brought it up. The topic of the meeting was the assignment he had for you, and how you were going to manage it. I never met anyone in the field who didn't respect and like Matt.... I last saw Matt one cold December day [in 1959] when we were both shopping at Bloomingdales for Christmas.... The next thing I hear of Matt he was dead. All I know is that the causes were natural. Nobody admits they might be sick when they're free lancing. Who'd hire a dying swan?"[31]

Plagued by a rheumatic heart throughout his short life, and dying before he reached the age of 40, the artist never expected to live as long as he did. But Matt Baker left behind one of the richest legacies in the history of comics.

Matt Baker, *Lorna Doone* (December 1946). "Good Girl" Lorna as eighth-grade English teachers never imagined her.

EZRA WHITEMAN

Herman Melville's *Typee*, No. 36 (April 1947), was adapted by Harry Miller and signed by Ezra Whiteman, whose name appears nowhere else in comics annals. Hames Ware, whose trained eye is alert to the presence of different hands, suggests that "Ezra Whiteman" may have been a joint effort on the part of an African-American artist, Ezra Jackson, and his frequent collaborator, Maurice Whitman.[32]

The two artists are known to have played name games such as signing their joint ventures "Whit I. Jackson" (for "Whitman inked by Jackson"). Hence, Ware argues, it is possible that, for *Typee*, with its interracial themes, Jackson and Whitman combined their names in a more straightforward manner, adding the "e" to Whitman as an inside joke.[33]

More cartoonish than the art in other Iger-era *Classics*, the illustrations for the Melville adventure yarn are marked by bold lines and a simple, primitivist design. Forceful movement predominates, whether of hands, arms, or entire bodies, as most dramatically shown in the cover drawing of the narrator's friend Toby dodging a spear.

Typee was ripe for revision in the early 1960s. Gerald McCann had already provided a handsome painted cover for the 1960 reissue (the book had been out of print since 1952). Meanwhile, Luis Dominguez prepared a beautiful new interior that, unfortunately, was withdrawn when Gilberton halted new-title production in 1962. It remained for the British *Classics Illustrated* series, which outlasted its American parent, to issue the replacement.

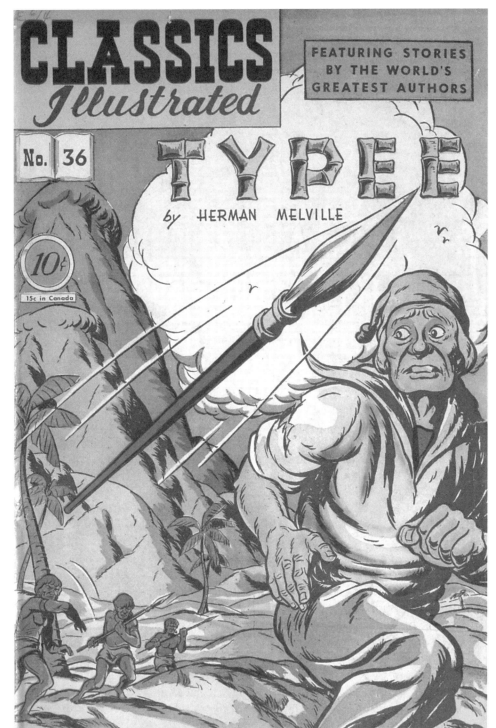

Ezra Whiteman, *Typee* (April 1947). Toby would "prefer not to."

Opposite: Matt Baker, *Lorna Doone* (December 1946; recolored 1957 reissue). Bad Boy Carver spoils Good Girl Lorna's wedding.

IX

Classical Interlude: "The World's Greatest Authors"

The cover of each *Classics Illustrated* issue boasted that the series featured "Stories by the World's Greatest Authors." Reorder lists in the early 1950s declared that "There Have Been No Greater Story Tellers Than These Immortal Authors" whose names were then catalogued. But who were they? And who weren't they?

A quick answer to both questions might be "The usual suspects." Most of the writers represented were European or American males. With ten books adapted in the series, Jules Verne was the most popular author followed by Alexandre Dumas (nine); James Fenimore Cooper (eight); Robert Louis Stevenson (seven); a tie among Charles Dickens, Sir Walter Scott, William Shakespeare, Mark Twain, and H.G. Wells (five); and a tie among Sir Arthur Conan Doyle, G.A. Henty, Victor Hugo, and co-authors Charles Nordhoff and James Norman Hall (four). Also-rans included Frank Buck, Rudyard Kipling, Jack London, and Edgar Allan Poe (three titles); and William Wilkie Collins, H. Rider Haggard, Charles Boardman Hawes, Homer, Henry Wadsworth Longfellow, Frederick Marryat, Herman Melville, Francis Parkman, and Ernest Thompson Seton (two titles).

Some of these were writers whose stories appealed primarily to boys, who, most industry analysts believed, bought most of the comic books in the 1940s, '50s, and '60s, although available data suggests a more even distribution. In any event, only eight women authors were represented in *Classics Illustrated*: Charlotte Brontë, Emily Brontë, George Eliot (Mary Ann or Marian Evans), Ouida (Marie Louise de la Ramée), Jane Porter, Anna Sewell, Mary Wollstonecraft Shelley, and Harriet Beecher Stowe.

If *Silas Marner* made the cut, why didn't *Little Women*? If there was room for the Brontës, why was Jane Austen excluded? Because, Gilberton's inventory control might have answered reflexively, where comic books were concerned, it was a boys' world (or thought to be so), and boys drew a distinction between women writers and what they perceived as girls' books. Then, too, there was the matter of the frequent appearance of the Brontë sisters and George Eliot on high school required-reading lists. Of the titles by the eight women authors, three—*Jane Eyre*, *Wuthering Heights*, and *Black Beauty*—were, at one time or another, dropped from the reorder list; these were more explicitly "girls' books."

Although written by women, *Uncle Tom's Cabin*, *Frankenstein*, *The Scottish Chiefs*, and *Under Two Flags* passed what might be called the "gender-neutral test." Some honorary "girls' books" by male authors, such as *Alice in Wonderland*, *The Woman in White*, and *The Cloister and the Hearth*, were out of print for long periods of time. Yet others, such as *Lorna Doone*, enjoyed continuous runs. For that matter, the best-selling biography published in the series was *Joan of Arc*.

No black authors appeared in the *Classics* catalogue, though, of course, at the time little attention was paid to African-American literature in either popular or academic culture. A well-intentioned effort to make amends in 1969 resulted in the final *Classics Illustrated* edition, *Negro Americans—The Early Years*. When it hit the newsstands a year after the assassination of Dr. Martin Luther King, Jr., the title was already an anachronism.

Classics Illustrated, in effect, established a literary canon for its young readership that to some degree mirrored the canon endorsed by high school and college English departments and that reflected the cultural

Left: Unidentified artist, *The Prince and the Pauper* (September 1955). Boys' books for a boys' world. *Right:* Sir Walter Scott's *Ivanhoe.* The most often reprinted title in the series.

assumptions of the period. *Ivanhoe, Moby Dick, A Tale of Two Cities, Huckleberry Finn, Jane Eyre, Silas Marner, Julius Caesar, The Red Badge of Courage,* and *Lord Jim* were among the most often-assigned works in postwar American schools, and *Classics Illustrated* ratified these and other pedagogical preferences. Sixty-six of the titles that appeared in the series were recommended in the 1957 Boy Scouts of America *Reading* manual (Merit Badge Series), including such relative obscurities as Henryk Sienkiewicz's *With Fire and Sword* and Frederick Marryat's *Mr. Midshipman Easy.*

At the same time, the series extended the shelf lives of second- or third-tier authors such as Charles Kingsley, R.D. Blackmore, Edward Bulwer-Lytton, Eugene Sue, Edward Everett Hale, Charles Reade, Jane Porter, Anthony Hope, Ouida, W.H. Hudson, Talbot Mundy, Richard Harding Davis, and G.A. Henty. By midcentury, these writers had largely receded from popular consciousness; they were introduced to another generation thanks to the childhood reading habits of Albert Kanter, Meyer Kaplan, and Ruth Roche—or the impending release of a Hollywood film.

X

Henry Carl Kiefer and the *Classics* House Style

No artist did more to define the *Classics Illustrated* house style in the late 1940s than Henry Carl Kiefer. A prolific illustrator, Kiefer produced artwork for a 1928 edition of Thomas Bailey Aldrich's *Story of a Bad Boy* and for more than sixty different comics series between 1935 and 1955. Before putting his stamp on Gilberton, he had drawn *Wing Brady* for Major Malcolm Wheeler-Nicholson's *New Fun* and *More Fun* (National/DC, 1935–1940) and was best known for *Wambi the Jungle Boy* (Fiction House, 1940–1948).[1]

Despite his involvement with nearly every major comics publisher at one point or another, little information is available about Kiefer's life. He was born in 1890, but his birthplace is unknown. According to comics historian Hames Ware, his contemporaries recalled a tall, imposing figure who affected aristocratic airs. A sometime Shakespearean actor who had married an actress, Kiefer sported a cape and declaimed rather than spoke. Although under contract to Jerry Iger, he considered himself above the drones who toiled in the rows of the shop's drafting tables. Kiefer worked at his own studio and made occasional dramatic appearances, delivering his completed pages with a theatrical flourish, tossing his cape over a shoulder. As Ware observed, "He would never have called himself a cartoonist; he would have considered himself an illustrator."[2]

Kiefer received his artistic training at the Atelier Julian in Paris and was engaged in the 1930s in supplying art for educational film strips, motion-picture promotional material, and pulp fiction.[3] From 1937 to 1940, he illustrated comics under the less-than-pleasant conditions prevailing in Harry "A" Chesler's shop, produc-

ing in 1937 an abridgment of *Oliver Twist*, in what might be seen as a dress rehearsal for *Classics Illustrated* a decade later. In 1940, Kiefer became affiliated with Jerry Iger's operation but freelanced for different publishers. Given his steady, reliable output, it is apparent that the flamboyant artist was a favored star in the Iger Shop. Unlike many other shop-system veterans, he both penciled and inked his own pictures, apparently not wishing to entrust his work to other hands.

After Iger assumed responsibility for Kanter's series, Kiefer quickly became, along with Alex A. Blum, one of the two dominant *Classics Illustrated* artists. He shaped the initial imaginative response of millions of young readers to such works as *20,000 Leagues Under the Sea*, *David Copperfield*, and *Wuthering Heights*. The artist's first work for Gilberton, in January 1947, was a rather lurid cover (see color section) and two splash pages for issue No. 33, *The Adventures of Sherlock Holmes*. Louis Zansky had illustrated the book, which included adaptations of *The Hound of the Baskervilles* and *A Study in Scarlet*, in 1943, but publication had been delayed because of difficulties with Sir Arthur Conan Doyle's estate.[4]

Kiefer landed the prestigious assignment of providing artwork for No. 35, *The Last Days of Pompeii* by Sir Edward Bulwer-Lytton, the first issue of the rechristened *Classics Illustrated*, in March 1947.[5] In retrospect, it seems rather symbolic. Between 1947 and 1953, Kiefer supplied covers and interior art for 24 titles and two special "educational" issues, *Shelter Through the Ages* and *The Westinghouse Story: The Dreams of a Man*, and covers alone for nine issues and one "Giants" (anthologies of earlier issues republished under the titles *An Illustrated Library of Great Adventure Stories*, consisting of

A Tale of Two Cities, Robin Hood, Arabian Nights, and *Robinson Crusoe*).

Yet, as closely identified with *Classics Illustrated* as he was, a major rift with Gilberton occurred in 1949. A new competitor in the literary-adaptation market, Seaboard Publishers, Inc., sought out the artist to illustrate their edition of Rafael Sabatini's *Captain Blood*, the second title in the recently launched *Fast Fiction* series. Of the 13 *Fast Fiction/Stories by Famous Authors Illustrated* issues between October 1949 and May 1951, when Albert Kanter bought the trademark and stopped production, Kiefer produced covers and interior art for seven titles and covers for two reprints at the same time he was drawing and inking five titles for *Classics Illustrated.*

The artist's relations with Gilberton were never again the same. A certain animus was evident during the fall 1951 reprint runs of No. 18, *The Hunchback of Notre Dame,* and No. 33, *The Adventures of Sherlock Holmes,* when the presses were stopped so that Kiefer's name could be stricken from the covers. (The name was restored in a 1954 reprint of No. 18.)[6] Gilberton offered no assignments in 1951 and only four titles (painted covers and interior art) and three additional painted covers in 1952 and 1953.

An old man by comics-industry standards, Kiefer continued working for another longtime account, Eastern Color Printing Company's *New Heroic Comics,* until 1955. He died in 1957.

Kiefer brought his acting experience and European training to bear in the period pieces he drew for Gilberton. As Hames Ware put it, "There wasn't anyone out there like him. Love his work or hate it, Henry C. Kiefer was an original, and whatever may be said about his efforts for other publishers, he and *Classics Illustrated* were a perfect match. As a world traveler blessed with an actor's insight, his style captivated young readers and kept them coming back for more."[7]

A certain alienness runs through Kiefer's work—a willful antiquity that set him apart from other illustrators of his time. It was a quality that some never understood or appreciated. He has been dismissed by such perceptive critics as Ron Goulart as "one of the busiest hacks of the forties."[8] Others have taken a different view: Hubert H. Crawford, in a discussion of the *Wambi* series, saluted Kiefer as a master of animal anatomy.[9] This aspect of the artist's work is best seen in *Swiss Family Robinson,* No. 42 (October 1947), with its dogs, cattle, monkeys, shark, lobster, kangaroos, sea turtle, sea gull, wild buffalo, donkey, and boa constrictor.

Whatever the opinions of others may have been, Kiefer was singlehandedly responsible for investing *Classics Illustrated* with an air of historical accuracy and almost metaphysical mystery not found in any other comic-

book line. This gift, according to Hames Ware, may have derived from his European training and theatrical approach to illustration.[10] Kiefer's illustrations appear to be less in the comics mold than a continuation of the tradition of 19th-century book illustration. His drawings for William Shakespeare's *Julius Caesar,* No. 68 (February 1950), for example, often suggest woodcuts, while the characters' dramatic attitudes recall Victorian stage poses, particularly in Mark Antony's funeral oration, delivered in the Henry Irving style.

It is equally arguable that Kiefer's compositional approach is largely based on the proscenium perspective, a natural point of reference for a stage actor. Rarely do the cinematic influences that are so evident in the work of younger contemporaries, such as Rudy Palais, appear in his panels.

If Kiefer was thus somewhat set apart from his contemporaries, it made him the ideal artist for costume pieces. He seemed most comfortable, and was clearly at his best, when working on Victorian-era stories charged with atmosphere. Of the five novels by Charles Dickens adapted in *Classics Illustrated,* three— *Great Expectations,* No. 43 (November 1947), *David Copperfield,* No. 48 (June 1948), and *A Christmas Carol,* No. 53 (November 1948)—were drawn by Kiefer. The artist's rendering of the graveyard scene at the beginning of *Great Expectations* was regarded as too intense for children by critics in the late 1940s. He effectively conveyed young David Copperfield's misery under the sadistic Murdstone and presented a vibrant Wilkins Micawber that was equally independent of the original renderings by "Phiz" (Hablôt K. Browne) and the celluloid impersonation by W.C. Fields. In *A Christmas Carol,* Kiefer's inking created a striking visual symbolism of darkness and light.

A less successful period piece was Emily Brontë's *Wuthering Heights,* No. 59 (May 1949), in which the artist simply got the period wrong. Donna Richardson has faulted Kiefer for failing to place the characters in the novel's 18th-century setting.[11] One can easily imagine the flamboyant *artiste* regarding even a glance at Brontë's book as beneath both his dignity and his contempt. In any event, Kiefer obviously had adopted the early–Victorian model of William Wyler's 1939 film version, basing his Heathcliff and Cathy on Laurence Olivier and Merle Oberon.

He was on more familiar ground with Mark Twain's antebellum thriller, *Pudd'nhead Wilson,* No. 93 (March 1952), and he offered a memorable character study of the villain's moral degeneration. For the cover, Kiefer painted the climactic scene in which the dissipated young master learns his true identity from his actual mother. The trial scene, in which lawyer Wilson introduces the novel

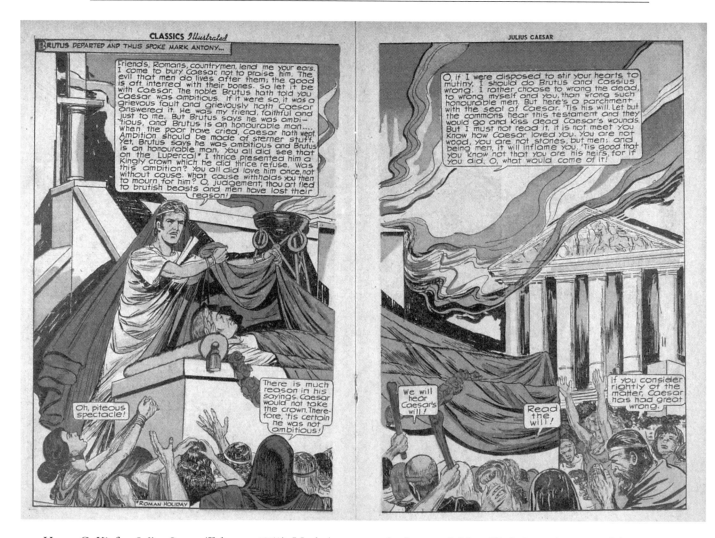

Henry C. Kiefer, *Julius Caesar* (February 1950). Mark Antony works the crowd. Note Kiefer's employment of the sequential-art strategy of telescoping time within a single large panel (here, two treated as one). The reader's eye moves from Antony as he begins his speech, through the text, and then to the reactions of his audience.

concept of fingerprinting, was dramatically effective in Kiefer's rendering.

Among the artist's attributes was a flair for the grotesque, which he shared with William Hogarth, James Gillray, Thomas Rowlandson, and other 18th-century caricaturists. Kiefer's illustrations for "The Adventure of Hans Pfall" by Edgar Allan Poe in *Mysteries*, No. 40 (August 1947), reveal a wry comic sensibility with their shooting stars, pipe-puffing Dutch burghers, and long-nosed inhabitants of the moon.[12]

On the other hand, his drawings of the hideous criminals Screech-Owl and the Schoolmaster in Eugene Sue's *Mysteries of Paris*, No. 44 (December 1947), and his line-drawing cover showing a corpse on the ground behind the hero and heroine were evidently so disturbing

to parents and teachers that they helped bring an end to the 1940s run of *Classics* "horror" issues. The artist's rendering of the novel's protagonist, Prince Rudolf, was the prototype for future square-jawed Kieferesque heroes.

Adventure yarns and swashbucklers came naturally to Kiefer. The artist brought a certain Sigmund Romberg flavor and Ronald Colman flair to Anthony Hope's *The Prisoner of Zenda*, No. 76 (October 1950). The Ruritanian fantasy of royal impersonation may well be the quintessential Kiefer *Classic*, with its dashing uniforms, clashing swords, and desperate rescue. Vivid characterizations of the hero Rudolf Rassendyll, the villain Black Michael, and the amoral schemer Rupert of Hentzau keep the visual style delightfully over the top.

Opposite: Henry C. Kiefer, *Swiss Family Robinson* (October 1947). A charging buffalo was one of many animals that made life interesting for the resourceful Robinsons.

Henry C. Kiefer, *Great Expectations* (November 1947). Pip and Magwitch get acquainted.

Haggard's description provides some basis for the illustrations.)

Two of the most popular *Classics* titles by the most popular *Classics* author—Jules Verne's *20,000 Leagues Under the Sea*, No. 47 (May 1948), and *Around the World in Eighty Days*, No. 69 (March 1950)—are among the artist's strongest works for Gilberton. Kiefer's theatricality served him well in his solid character interpretations of Captain Nemo, Ned Land, Phileas Fogg, Passepartout, and Detective Fix. The artist packed the Verne adaptations with rousing depictions of submarine attacks, battles with giant octopi and marauding Sioux, escapes from ice and flames, and wonders below and above the waves. On the second page of *20,000 Leagues Under the Sea*, a dramatic sense of shipboard urgency is conveyed as the crew of a doomed vessel attempts to discern what strange creature approaches.

Kiefer extended his range to the medieval realm in his illustrations for Sir Walter Scott's narrative poem *The Lady of the Lake*, No. 75 (September 1950)[13] and historical novel *The Talisman*, No. 111 (September 1953). The latter title was Kiefer's final Gilberton project (as Iger was closing its Gilberton account) and showed him still at the top of his form, fighting the Crusades with King Richard and Saladin.

The Cloister and the Hearth, No. 66 (December 1949), Charles Reade's account of the thwarted love between the parents of Erasmus, never appealed to young readers and was not reprinted. The comic book, however, is an interesting collection of some of

In H. Rider Haggard's *King Solomon's Mines*, No. 97 (July 1952), a charging elephant, an ancient witch, and a chamber of petrified corpses kept the reader turning pages. The racial climate of 1952 being what it was, Kiefer was obliged to compromise in depicting the interracial relationship in *King Solomon's Mines* between the white explorer John Good and the African woman Foulata, who was given vaguely Polynesian features and flowing tresses. (It should be noted, though, that Rider

the artist's best and worst work, from handsomely rendered, historically accurate figures and buildings to ludicrously scaled perspectives.

A good candidate for Kiefer's finest Gilberton effort is *Joan of Arc*, No. 78 (December 1950). The line-drawing cover, the artist's last of its kind for *Classics Illustrated*, is quite simply his strongest, with its charcoal shading and burst of brightness at the center where the Archangel Michael calls the Maid to her duty. (See color

Henry C. Kiefer, *Mysteries of Paris* **(December 1947). The last** *Classics Illustrated* **"horror" cover.**

the conventions of religious iconography. He leaves no doubt about his attitude toward the subject.

All-purpose artist that he was, Kiefer was also at home in the Wild West. His illustrations for "The Luck of Roaring Camp" and "The Outcasts of Poker Flat" in Bret Harte's *Western Stories*, No. 62 (August 1949), are as rough-and-tumble as the mining towns and wilderness they evoke. The tragic endings of the two stories are depicted with an almost classical austerity.

In Edward Everett Hale's *The Man Without a Country*, No. 63 (September 1949), Kiefer included a bare-breasted African woman in a slave-ship scene—the only female nudity in the series; somehow, the "headlights"-obsessed Dr. Fredric Wertham, comic-book nemesis, missed the panel. The colorist made an odd decision to outfit all the American soldiers (c. 1805) in red uniforms. Kiefer himself apparently had found it inconvenient to look at a portrait of Aaron Burr when drawing the political schemer.

A singular distinction held by the artist was the exclusion of dialogue balloons from an entire issue, Francis Parkman's *The Oregon Trail*, No. 72 (June 1950); speech was inserted in narrative boxes, instead, and surrounded with quotation marks. Although the issue went through 11 printings, the experiment was never repeated. Even so, it demonstrated the degree to which the artist saw himself as employed in the illustration of books rather than the drawing of comics.

Constantly in demand, Kiefer often showed the

section.) Throughout the biography, skillfully scripted by Sam Willinsky, the artist took obvious pains with the composition of both individual panels and full-page illustrations depicting battle scenes and Joan's martyrdom. If the Maid seems a bit too serene at the stake, it is worth remembering that Kiefer was self-consciously invoking

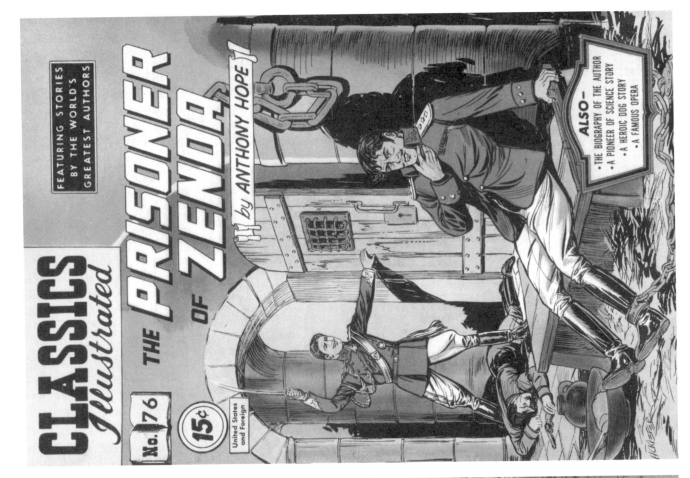

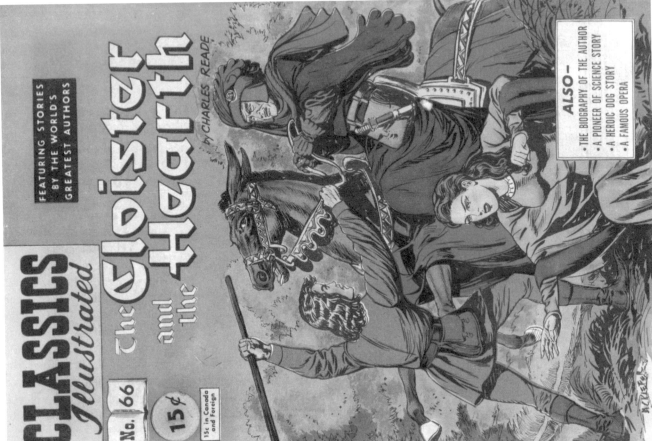

strain of a rapid production cycle. On one page of Bret Harte's "The Outcasts of Poker Flat," four panels display slight variations on one static scene. His figures are occasionally wooden, with stiff limbs and flat expressions. The protagonist in Frank Buck's *Bring 'Em Back Alive*, No. 104 (February 1953), does a considerable amount of jumping to avoid being mauled or bitten by the wild animals he traps, yet the artist seemed incapable of drawing a credible representation of a person bounding in the air, despite his convincing big cats and elephants. In certain books (notably *Mysteries of Paris* and *The Prisoner of Zenda*), Kiefer's men tend to look like Errol Flynn—and so, one might add, do his women.

This ambiguous, androgynous quality is evident in much of Kiefer's work. It is that aspect of his art, Hames Ware maintains, which is central to his achievement and "which probably accounts for why Kiefer's work appealed to younger children who had not yet formed clearly defined roles and likewise also would explain why older comics fans disliked his work for other publishers. But as for his *Classics* work, children did not have to take a very big leap from fairy-tale characters who undergo marvelous transformations to Kiefer's figures that achieved a universality that transcended gender."[14] Ware notes that a "Germanic darkness" permeated Kiefer's illustrations

Left: Henry C. Kiefer, *King Solomon's Mines* (July 1952). Allan Quatermain borrows a line from Charlie Brown. *Below:* Henry C. Kiefer, *The Oregon Trail* (June 1950). A balloonless comic book, in which dialogue appeared in the narrative boxes.

Opposite, left: Henry C. Kiefer, *The Cloister and the Hearth* (December 1949). Charles Reade's historical novel was one of several fading fixtures of the Victorian canon given a kind of extended life by *Classics Illustrated*. *Right:* Henry C. Kiefer, *The Prisoner of Zenda* (October 1950). Rassendyll rescues cousin Rudolf.

and observes that "[t]he difference between Blum and Kiefer is the difference between Hans Christian Andersen and the Brothers Grimm."[15]

His limitations were obvious, even to the children for whom his Captain Nemo, David Copperfield, Rudolf Rassendyll, and Joan of Arc were definitive. But at his best, Henry C. Kiefer could conjure the essential mood of a literary work as no contemporary could. He had the magic.

Henry C. Kiefer, *20,000 Leagues Under the Sea* (May 1948). A page of original art from Verne's submarine story.

XI

Classical Interlude: Promos and Premiums

Although the actual pages of *Classic Comics* and *Classics Illustrated* did not, with some early exceptions, contain advertising, the inside and back covers always displayed in-house promotional matter, from reorder lists for the various Gilberton series to inducements for subscribers. The ads evolved as the years progressed, reflecting the changing identity of the publication.

Featured on numerous back covers in the mid- to late 1940s were colorful pitches for "*Classic Comics* Gift Boxes," which contained five issues of sequentially numbered titles. Originally designed for mailing to World War II servicemen, the boxes never really caught on.

The problem was that the five issues were boxed together at a cost of 59 cents, while the buyer, who had no choice concerning the box's contents, could select five titles from the newsstand for only 50 cents, allowing change for a soft drink or a candy bar. Doing a little subtraction, most readers passed on the offer.

Simple math also doomed the three *Classics Illustrated* "Giant" editions, advertised on back covers and inside covers from 1949 to 1951. Each of the issues consisted of four previously published titles, collected under a single cover. The cost was 50 cents, which, until the cover price of the series increased from ten to 15 cents in March 1951, put the purchaser at a disadvantage.

A 1950s back-cover advertisement for *Classics Illustrated* binders: The phrase "Handsome, durable, permanent" taught many baby boomers that you can't believe everything you read.

In 1949, Gilberton introduced a subscription premium: "FREE! FREE! FREE! 40 of the World's Greatest Comic Strip Characters in TATTOOS (also known as Transfers or Decalcomanias) are yours FREE with a subscription for only 10 coming issues of *Classics Illustrated*." The same ad was printed on countless inside covers until 1959, when a *World Around Us* subscription solicitation took its place. Presumably, the same stock of "tattoos" lasted for a full decade.

Another long-running Gilberton promotion was for *Classics Illustrated* binders, which were introduced in 1951 and were advertised until the end in 1971. The supply more than exceeded the demand, and with good reason. According to the advertisement, "Each binder holds 12 books securely. Each is covered in beautiful, brown simulated leather and is richly imprinted with gold on both cover and backbone. Simple instructions make binding possible in a matter of minutes."

Unfortunately, "simulated" was the controlling descriptive term. Worse, binding was achieved with thick, remarkably unelastic rubber bands that tore the tops and bottoms of comic-book spines or that snapped when stretched too far to reach the opposing hook. Originally priced at $1.00, the cost had risen only to $1.50 when *Classics Illustrated* ceased publication, and the original inventory still served the purpose.

Responding to interest in the space race, Gilberton borrowed a promotional product and ad from its British subsidiary in the 1960s. "Now you can 'shoot the Moon'—land on Venus or Mars and perform many adventures in orbit with the sensational new Space Age Toy ORBITOP, 'Satellite on a string.'" A boy in distinctly English attire (school sweater and tie) was shown spinning what appeared to be a yo-yo with encapsulated back-to-back astronauts, strange creatures unknown to the GIs who had received *Classic Comics* Gift Boxes 20 years earlier.

Top left: The Three Musketeers (October 1941). Cover by Malcolm Kildale. *Top right: The Last of the Mohicans* (August 1942). Cover by Ray Ramsey. *Bottom left: Arabian Nights* (February 1943). Cover by Lillian Chestney. *Bottom right: The Deerslayer* (January 1944). Cover by Louis Zansky.

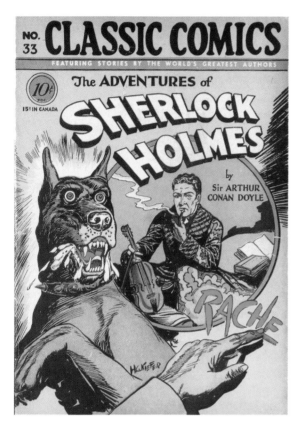
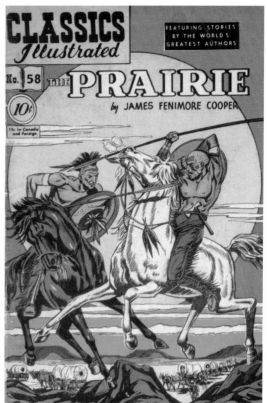

Above, top left: The Adventures of Sherlock Holmes (January 1947). Cover by Henry C. Kiefer. *Top right: The Prairie* (April 1949). Cover by Rudolph Palais. *Bottom left: The Man Who Laughs* (May 1950). Cover by Alex A. Blum. *Bottom right: Joan of Arc* (December 1950). Cover by Henry C. Kiefer.

Opposite, left: The Hunchback of Notre Dame (March 1944). Cover by Allen Simon. *Right: Lorna Doone* (December 1946). Cover by Matt Baker.

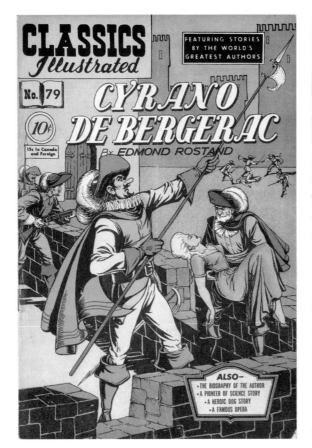

Top left: Cyrano de Bergerac (January 1951). Cover by Alex A. Blum. *Top right: The Bottle Imp* (February 1954). Cover by unidentified artist. *Bottom left: Rob Roy* (April 1954). Cover by unidentified artist. *Bottom right: The Hurricane* (June 1954). Cover by Lou Cameron.

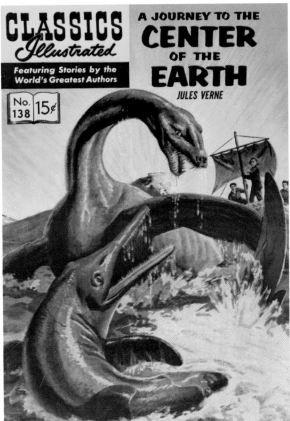
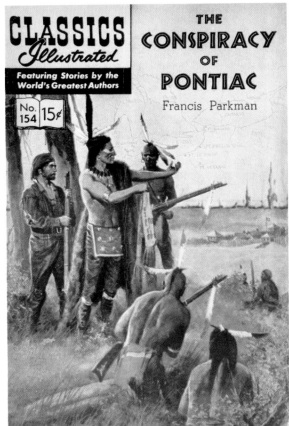

Top left: The War of the Worlds (January 1955). Cover by Lou Cameron. *Top right: A Journey to the Center of the Earth* (May 1957). Cover by unidentified artist. *Bottom left: The Conspiracy of Pontiac* (January 1960). Cover by Gerald McCann. *Bottom right: The Octopus* (November 1960). Cover by Leonard B. Cole.

CLASSICS Illustrated

Featuring Stories by the World's Greatest Authors

No. 161   15¢

CLEOPATRA

H. RIDER HAGGARD

CLASSICS Illustrated

Featuring Stories by the World's Greatest Authors

No. 160   15¢

The FOOD of the GODS

H. G. Wells

Above, top left: An Illustrated Library of Great Indian Stories (October 1949). Cover by Alex A. Blum. *Top right: The Wizard of Oz* (February 1957). Cover by Dik Browne. *Bottom left: The Ten Commandments* (December 1956). Cover by Norman Nodel. *Bottom right: The Illustrated Story of the French Revolution* (October 1959). Cover by unidentified artist.

Opposite, left: The Food of the Gods (January 1961). Cover by Gerald McCann. *Right: Cleopatra* (March 1961). Cover by "Poch."

The Jungle (June 1991). Cover by Peter Kuper.

XII

"A Prince of a Man": Alex A. Blum

Sharing with Henry C. Kiefer the honors for ubiquity at Gilberton in the late 1940s and early 1950s was Alex Anthony Blum (1889–1969), an artist whose training as an etcher left its unique stamp on more than 20 *Classics Illustrated* titles. Born in Budapest, Hungary, Blum studied at the National Academy of Design in New York and the Cincinnati Art Academy. While living in Philadelphia during the 1920s, he exhibited his dry-point etchings and won the Philadelphia Alliance Bronze Medal (1920) and an award from the National Academy of Design (1924).[1] Some of his works are included in the collections of the Metropolitan Museum of Art, Yale University, and the Boston Museum of Fine Arts.

Blum illustrated Mary Hazelton Wade's juvenile biographies of William Penn (1929) and Captain James Cook (1931), but by 1935, like many other marginally successful Depression-era artists, he was working in the rapidly growing comics industry. In that year, he illustrated part of a serialized adaptation of *Ivanhoe* for Major Malcolm Wheeler-Nicholson's *New Fun*.[2] Around 1938, Blum signed on with the Eisner-Iger shop; it was an association that lasted until 1954. The artist's daughter, Audrey ("Toni") Blum Bossert, also joined the team in 1938 as a scriptwriter.[3] One of Blum's earliest assignments was the Samson series for Victor Fox's *Fantastic Comics*.[4] He also produced drawings for Quality, Worth/Harvey, and Fawcett. In 1940, the artist introduced the popular Kaanga in Fiction House's *Jungle Comics*.

Although Iger had been supplying artists for *Classic Comics/Classics Illustrated* since 1945, Blum's first work for Gilberton did not appear until June 1947, when he provided a 63-page adaptation of Lewis Carroll's *Alice in Wonderland* for the short-lived *Illustrated Classics* newspaper series. In March 1948, the title was reduced to the standard 48-page format and issued as *Classics Illustrated* No. 49. Blum also penciled and inked an abbreviated *Illustrated Classics* newspaper version of Henry Wadsworth Longfellow's *Courtship of Miles Standish*, which appeared complete in a single Sunday section in March 1948. The narrative poem was paired with Blum's newly produced *Evangeline*, another Longfellow work, and was published in February 1952 as *Classics Illustrated* No. 92.

Soon Blum rivaled Henry C. Kiefer in output for the series; from 1948 to 1951, the two artists illustrated all but four of the titles between No. 57 and No. 80. (Those four—actually partial—exceptions to the Blum-Kiefer rule were No. 58, *The Prairie* [Rudolph Palais]; No. 60, *Black Beauty* [August M. Froehlich]; No. 65, *Benjamin Franklin* [Bob Hebberd, and Gustav Schrotter, with some interior art by Blum and a cover by Kiefer], and No. 74, *Mr. Midshipman Easy* [Bob Lamme, with cover by Blum].) The two very different artists established between themselves a Janus-faced *Classics Illustrated* house style.

Blum's work is as distinctively idiosyncratic as Kiefer's; both have a marked old-fashioned European quaintness about them. Yet Blum's etching experience translated into a clean, uncluttered style of linework (somewhat reminiscent of 18th-century engraver John Flaxman) that stood in marked contrast to the heavily scored, Hogarthian panels by Kiefer.

In Hames Ware's view, Blum was "essentially a miniaturist and worked best on a small scale."[5] Perhaps the most distinctive trademarks of Blum's illustrations are the rather angular bodies of his characters and their tapered, feminine hands. At his best, he invests his figures with an almost neoclassical grace. But at times his work appears half-finished and exhibits a startling lack of proportion and a disappointing lack of vitality.

The delicacy of Blum's technique made him especially well-suited for *Alice in Wonderland*, in which he preserved the flavor of John Tenniel's wood engravings while producing his own crisp, spare interpretation of the surreal proceedings at the bottom of the rabbit hole. A page depicting the courtroom tumult as a growing Alice upsets the jurybox derives its energy from the clean, controlled linework.

Perhaps because he had already drawn *The Courtship of Miles Standish*, Blum was handed another narrative poem by Henry Wadsworth Longfellow, *The Song of Hiawatha*, No. 57 (March 1949), as his third Gilberton project. The old schoolroom warhorse with its often-

Alex A. Blum, *Alice in Wonderland* (March 1948). Alice causes disorder in the court.

parodied trochaic meter proved congenial to the artist, who cloaked Longfellow's insistently rhythmic folk material with an otherworldly fairy-tale air that, at times, approaches what *Classics Reader* editor Bill Briggs termed "mythic grandeur."[6] The elevated, rather declamatory visual style of *Hiawatha* is conveyed in the cover illustration, where a wise and honorable chieftain (who would be at home on the French neoclassical stage) beneficently surveys his people.

Next came a Wilkie Collins mystery, *The Woman in White*, No. 61 (July 1949), which was marred either by Blum's evident unfamiliarity with the text of the original or scriptwriter John O'Rourke's failure to provide adequate character descriptions. The villainous Count Fosco, for instance, described in the novel as "immensely fat,"[7] was portrayed by the artist as a slender, insinuating figure; his fellow conspirator, Sir Percival Glyde, acquired some of the count's amplitude in Blum's rendering.

The inclusion of the title in the *Classics* line was probably due to two factors: the 1948 release of a film version that featured the rotund Sydney Greenstreet as Count Fosco (Blum apparently missed the movie, too) and the emergence in 1949 of romance comics as the industry's fastest-growing category. *The Woman in White* failed to catch on (it was out of print from 1952 to 1960) possibly because Blum rarely drew a woman whose face didn't call to mind the skull beneath the skin. The heroine Laura Fairlie was rendered as a walking *memento mori*.

A major assignment followed. Walt Disney was soon to release a film version of Robert Louis Stevenson's *Treasure Island*, and Gilberton, which, inexplicably, after eight years still had not added the boyhood favorite to the *Classics Illustrated* list, took advantage of the timing and issued an abridgment as No. 64 (October 1949). Kiefer was occupied with *Western Stories* and *The Man Without a Country*, so Blum, master of the refined line, stepped in.

The artist's Long John Silver is a leaner model of the buccaneer than N.C. Wyeth's or Norman Price's familiar depictions, to say nothing of Robert Newton's or Wallace Beery's cinematic portrayals. Stevenson described the pirate as "very tall and strong, with a face as big as a ham—plain and pale, but intelligent and smiling."[8] Blum's Long John may be tall, strong, and intelligent, but he has the lean and hungry features of a Cassius. Still, the artist caught something of the character's ambivalent charm.

Jim Hawkins, for his part, looks like a startled Vassar undergraduate, c. 1925, with a page-boy bob. Blum may have had at hand stills from the 1920 Maurice Tourneur film version of the story, in which actress Shirley Mason appeared as Jim. The white blouse, red waistcoat, and red knee-breeches in which the artist

sufficiently stout and obtuse, while Captain Smollett is abrasively forthright and resolute.

Throughout the book, Blum makes creative use of panel shapes to enhance visual interest. Many of the crucial sequences are dramatically potent—Black Dog's cutlass fight with Billy Bones, the pirates' search of the Admiral Benbow Inn, Silver's parley with Captain Smollett, Jim's shipboard confrontation with Israel Hands, and the treasure hunt itself. Other mythic scenes, however, such as Jim hiding in the apple barrel or the buccaneers storming the stockade, are disappointingly unimaginative in composition or point of view.

It is likely that another, more robust artist such as Robert Hayward Webb, who had brought Stevenson's *Kidnapped* dramatically to life for *Classics*, would have infused the pirate yarn with greater energy. Even so, Blum's interpretation held its own through fourteen printings between 1949 and 1969 and achieved a kind of iconic status with young readers. His *Treasure Island* illustrations inspired several imitations, the first of which was an anonymous set of drawings for a coloring book published in 1958 by James & Jonathan, Inc. The *Classics Illustrated* edition attained an afterlife in a 1989 painted-cover reprint that promoted the Long John Silver seafood-restaurant chain and the Charlton Heston television film based on the novel.

Alex A. Blum, *The Song of Hiawatha* (March 1949). One of the artist's most accomplished works, the Longfellow adaptation shows a strong classical influence.

outfitted Jim from start to finish of the comic book resemble the costume Mason wore in the silent movie.[9]

Blum had better success with secondary characters. The artist effectively conveyed the hollow bluster of Billy Bones, the embittered malice of Blind Pew, and the sneaking menace of Israel Hands. Squire Trelawney is

Having proved himself in an action tale, the artist went on to the historical romance, *The Scottish Chiefs*, No. 67 (January 1950), a skillful adaptation by John O'Rourke, shorn of what Donna Richardson termed "Jane Porter's florid prose."[10] Using N.C. Wyeth's illustrations of the novel as a guide, Blum created an equally idealized

Alex A. Blum, *Treasure Island* **(October 1949). "One more step, Mr. Hands...."**

the principal male characters appear with hair trimmed in the manner of the Napoleonic era. Whenever something resembling a peruke is seen, it ends in a prodigious ducktail with no ribbon to hold it together. (I recall wondering how much butchwax would be necessary to sustain such a challenge to the law of gravity.) Meanwhile, Blum gave Mr. Grey, the mysterious pilot of the title, the features of a rather prim, strongly disapproving John Wayne.

Two inspired treatments of a pair of lesser-known 19th-century French classics followed. A somewhat softened adaptation of Victor Hugo's *The Man Who Laughs*, No. 71 (May 1950), featured a less grotesque Gwynplaine than would appear in Norman Nodel's 1962 revision. Hugo's plea for downtrodden, "mutilated" humanity obviously moved the artist, whose inking was generally darker than usual in the book. An anachronistic 1890s Ferris wheel in the background of a scene set in the early 1700s failed to spoil one of Blum's finest covers, and *The Man Who Laughs* ranks among the artist's best works. (See color section.)

Equally impressive was *The Black Tulip*, No. 73 (July 1950). Alexandre Dumas's novel of political and personal intrigue set in 17th-century Holland highlighted Blum's predilection for working in miniature. Seldom are characters seen at close range; most of the panel composition is in midrange or at an even farther distance. The result is to heighten the reader's sense that greater forces are at work behind the scenes and that more is at stake than mere bulb envy.

Turning to Homeric epic, Blum offered a controlled, austere account of *The Iliad*, No. 77 (November 1950). Even if the armor is generic Greco-Roman and most of the details anachronistic, the tragedies of combat and the relations between gods and mortals unfold in understated panels. Especially effective are the sequences depicting

William Wallace, sword upraised and crying, "Liberty and Lord Mar!"

In *The Pilot*, No. 70 (April 1950), James Fenimore Cooper's Revolutionary War naval adventure, the artist revealed a prejudice (or blind spot) common to illustrators, film producers, and directors of his generation: a distaste for men's hairstyles of the 18th century. Most of

well-balanced panels echo the instructions of script-writer Ken W. Fitch and exhibit the artist's obvious enthusiasm for the material. The line-drawing cover was perhaps his best for the series. (See color section.) Blum's sketches of the swordsman-poet Cyrano, the inarticulate lover Christian, and the twice-beloved Roxane must be counted among his strongest character studies.

The artist was responsible for two of three novels by Jack London that were adapted for *Classics Illustrated*. Both *White Fang*, No. 80 (February 1951), which featured the last line-drawing cover, and *The Sea Wolf*, No. 85 (July 1951), were somewhat out of Blum's range. He was never at his best drawing animals, and his elegant linework was at odds with the brutality aboard Wolf Larsen's ship, although both books contained some stirring action sequences.

Rudyard Kipling's *The Jungle Book*, No. 83 (May 1951), a collaborative effort with son-in-law and fellow Iger artist William Bossert, was a striking, though uneven, venture into more exotic territory. The work was weakest in the wolf-pack scenes and strongest in "The King's Ankus," with its pair of gracefully interpreted snakes, Kaa the python and the white cobra.

Alex A. Blum, *The Black Tulip* (July 1950). Much ado about horticulture.

dialogue between the Olympians and their acts of intervention in battle. Nowhere else in the series is the artist's fundamentally classical vision more evident.

The following project, Edmond Rostand's *Cyrano de Bergerac*, No. 79 (January 1951), continued in the martial vein but with a baroque flavor. Blum's crowded but

Blum did a fair job on the title piece in Edgar Allan Poe's *The Gold Bug and Other Stories*, No. 84 (June 1951), but hit his stride again in an adaptation of William Shakespeare's *A Midsummer Night's Dream*, No. 87 (September 1951). While the confused pairs of vapid lovers were distinguishable only by the colorist's coding, the

Alex A. Blum, *The Iliad* (November 1950). Greeks and Trojans, gods and heroes introduced Homer to *Classics Illustrated*.

When painted covers were introduced in 1951, Blum supplied most of the first dozen. Because his specialty was the thin, supple line applied to paper, some of these works, such as the covers for *The Odyssey* and *The Sea Wolf*, seem uncharacteristically strained or indefinite. The artist's most successful efforts with brushes, such as the covers for *The Gold Bug* and *A Midsummer Night's Dream*, achieve a precision of execution similar to the best of his interior art.

Hames Ware has observed that Blum "responded well when text-heavy scripts were assigned, as in the Shakespeare adaptations."[11] The Bard elicited the artist's greatest single effort for *Classics Illustrated—Hamlet*, No. 99 (September 1952). Some of the characters, such as Claudius, Gertrude, and Polonius, were modeled on the actors in the 1948 film by Laurence Olivier. The Prince himself, however, was Blum's own concept, and was rendered with greater complexity than some stage performances of the role. Blum's instinct for pacing was unerring; he broke down short exchanges of dialogue into naturally flowing smaller panels, incorporated dramatic theatrical gestures in larger panels, and kept longer speeches, such as Hamlet's two soliloquies, intact in large balloons.

One can only wonder what Matt Baker might have done with W.H. Hudson's

forest antics of Puck and the theatrical effusions of Nick Bottom and his fellow rustics were charmingly wrought. The artist seemed to be enjoying himself, adding playful decorative motifs and experimenting with panel shapes and layout.

Green Mansions, No. 90 (December 1951), with its jungle heroine Rima, the Bird Girl. Blum's Rima was the closest the artist ever came to Iger shop Good Girl art; she was drawn as an ethereal, demurely erotic woman, though, of course, more demure than erotic. All the same,

Alex A. Blum (with William Bossert), *The Jungle Book* (May 1951). A sequence from "The King's Ankus."

she bears little resemblance to the artist's usual asexual, skeletal creatures.

For John Bakeless's biography, *Daniel Boone: Master of the Wilderness*, No. 96 (June 1952), Blum supplied vigorous drawings of frontier life (and more 18th-century ducktails). The adaptation by Ken W. Fitch was text-heavy even by *Classics Illustrated* standards, and the artist cleverly compressed panels in which the narrative voice supplanted dialogue, producing lively pictures on the miniature scale in which he worked so well.

A tale of 15th-century derring-do by Sir Arthur Conan Doyle, *The White Company*, No. 102 (December 1952), an outstanding adaptation by Fitch, and a cycle of Arthurian legends, *Knights of the Round Table*, No. 108 (June 1953), superbly scripted by John Cooney, demonstrated once again Blum's affinity for romanticized medieval settings. In both books, he drew and inked striking single-page or centerfold splashes of sword-wielding combatants against clean, uncluttered backgrounds.

The artist's single foray into the realm of science-fiction for Gilberton, Jules Verne's *From the Earth to the Moon*, No. 105 (March 1953), featured delightful caricatures of stovepipe-hatted, high-collared Victorian-era astronauts. The issue represented the first departure in the Iger era from the use of hand-lettered speech balloons and the introduction of Leroy lettering. *From the Earth to the Moon* proved to be the best-selling of all *Classics Illustrated* titles with a cover number higher than 100.

Valuing Blum's affability as well as his experience, Albert Kanter hired the veteran in 1953 as art director for *Classics Illustrated* and the newly launched *Classics Illustrated Junior* and *Picture Parade* series, just as the artist's former employer, Jerry Iger, was disengaging himself from the Gilberton account. Blum's duties limited his output; he illustrated the first *Junior*, *Snow White and the Seven Dwarfs*, No. 501 (October 1953); *Jack and the Beanstalk*, No. 507 (April 1954); *Macbeth*, No. 128 (September 1955); and, assisting William A. Walsh, backgrounds in *The Story of Jesus*, No. 129A (December 1955). From 1954 until his retirement in 1957, most of his drawing was confined to painting the odd cover, such as *Waterloo*, ornamenting filler material in *Classics Illustrated* and *Classics Illustrated Junior*, and sketching "Coming Next" ads for both series.

The artwork for Blum's final *Classics Illustrated* edition, Shakespeare's *Macbeth*, displayed continuity with his first in its emphasis on clean linework. By that point, the artist was 66—an old man, by the standards of the time, in a young man's game—and he devoted most of his energies to his duties as Gilberton's art director. In that role, he remained active, recruiting some of the most talented artists ever to work under the yellow banner, including Norman Nodel, Joe Orlando, and George Evans.

Alex A. Blum, *Green Mansions* (December 1951). Rima the Bird Girl in flight.

THE RED KNIGHT WASTED NO TIME ON PRELIMINARIES, AND THE BATTLE RAGED THROUGH MOST OF THE DAY...

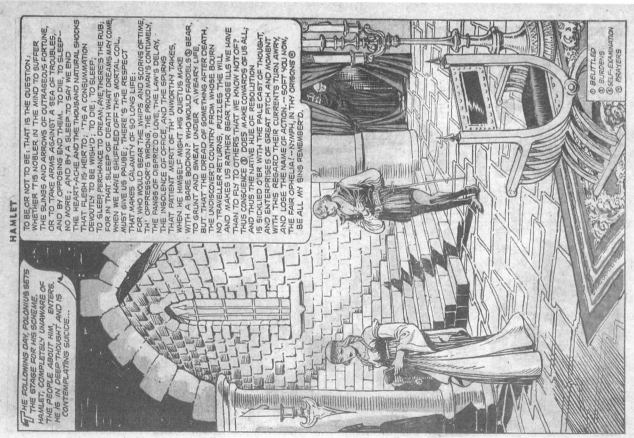

HAMLET

THE FOLLOWING DAY, POLONIUS SETS THE STAGE FOR HIS SCHEME. HAMLET, COMPLETELY UNAWARE OF THE PEOPLE ABOUT HIM, ENTERS. HE IS IN DEEP THOUGHT, AND IS CONTEMPLATING SUICIDE...

TO BE, OR NOT TO BE.: THAT IS THE QUESTION: WHETHER 'TIS NOBLER IN THE MIND TO SUFFER THE SLINGS AND ARROWS OF OUTRAGEOUS FORTUNE, OR TO TAKE ARMS AGAINST A SEA OF TROUBLES, AND BY OPPOSING END THEM. TO DIE, TO SLEEP-- NO MORE; AND BY A SLEEP TO SAY WE END THE HEART-ACHE AND THE THOUSAND NATURAL SHOCKS THAT FLESH IS HEIR TO; 'TIS A CONSUMMATION DEVOUTLY TO BE WISH'D; TO DIE; TO SLEEP; TO SLEEP: PERCHANCE TO DREAM; AYE, THERE'S THE RUB; FOR IN THAT SLEEP OF DEATH WHAT DREAMS MAY COME, WHEN WE HAVE SHUFFLED OFF THIS MORTAL COIL, MUST GIVE US PAUSE; THERE'S THE RESPECT THAT MAKES CALAMITY OF SO LONG LIFE; FOR WHO WOULD BEAR THE WHIPS AND SCORNS OF TIME, TH' OPPRESSOR'S WRONG, THE PROUD MAN'S CONTUMELY, THE PANGS OF DISPRIZ'D O LOVE, THE LAW'S DELAY, THE INSOLENCE OF OFFICE, AND THE SPURNS THAT PATIENT MERIT OF TH' UNWORTHY TAKES, WHEN HE HIMSELF MIGHT HIS QUIETUS MAKE WITH A BARE BODKIN? WHO WOULD FARDELS ② BEAR, TO GRUNT AND SWEAT UNDER A WEARY LIFE, BUT THAT THE DREAD OF SOMETHING AFTER DEATH, THE UNDISCOVER'D COUNTRY FROM WHOSE BOURN NO TRAVELLER RETURNS, PUZZLES THE WILL AND MAKES US RATHER BEAR THOSE ILLS WE HAVE THAN TO FLY TO OTHERS THAT WE KNOW NOT OF? THUS CONSCIENCE ③ DOES MAKE COWARDS OF US ALL; AND THUS THE NATIVE HUE OF RESOLUTION IS SICKLIED O'ER WITH THE PALE CAST OF THOUGHT, AND ENTERPRISES OF GREAT PITCH AND MOMENT WITH THIS REGARD THEIR CURRENTS TURN AWRY, AND LOSE THE NAME OF ACTION. -- SOFT YOU NOW, THE FAIR OPHELIA! -- NYMPH, IN THY ORISONS ④ BE ALL MY SINS REMEMBER'D.

① BELITTLED
② BURDENS
③ SELF-EXAMINATION
④ PRAYERS

Alex A. Blum, *From the Earth to the Moon* (March 1953). **A whimsical response to Verne's space-travel fantasy.**

Colleagues respected him and remembered him fondly. An old acquaintance and fellow Iger-shop alumnus, Rafael Astarita, described him as always impeccably dressed in a suit and tie.[12] George Evans "found [Blum] to be one of the nicest, gentlest, kindest people I had ever met. He was quite elderly, and if I were a movie director, I'd have had him play every charismatic older man in every film, even if only to show him as an 'extra.' He 'had it'— and those other artists I know who knew him all agreed with that assessment."[13] But the final assessment belongs to Norman Nodel, who lauded Blum as "a real gentleman, a prince of a man."[14]

Opposite, left: Alex A. Blum, *Hamlet* (September 1952). "Words, words, words." The Prince speaks his mind in a single panel within a single balloon. *Right:* Alex A. Blum, *Knights of the Round Table* (June 1953). An example of the artist's cleanly rendered figures and backgrounds.

XIII

Classical Interlude: Fillers and Features

In keeping with Albert Kanter's insistence on the educational role of *Classics Illustrated*, extra pages at the end of each issue were devoted to informative articles that, by the early 1950s, were often related to the subject matter of the book. During Roberta Strauss Feuerlicht's editorial tenure in the late 1950s and early 1960s, nearly all of the filler material had some thematic connection.

From issue No. 1 onward, a biography of the author accompanied the adaptation. Dumas, Scott, and Cooper, the first authors included in the series, received two-page profiles; later sketches were reduced to a single page. For the most part, the brief lives were accurate and occasionally entertaining. Sir Walter Scott's embarrassing and painful mishap with George IV's brandy glass was duly recorded, along with an anecdote about James Fenimore Cooper's impulsive decision to become a novelist while reading a book he disliked.

However, concessions to propriety were made in certain instances: the circumstances of Jack London's death and the marital status of Fanny Osbourne at the time she met Robert Louis Stevenson were treated with an excess of delicacy (Fanny was described as "an American widow"). In the 1941 edition of *The Three Musketeers*, readers were assured that, whatever his racial ancestry, Alexandre Dumas "had a fair skin, light hair and blue eyes."

Issue No. 3, *The Count of Monte Cristo*, contained the first actual filler item, a biography of Napoleon, whose fortunes set the plot of the Dumas novel in motion. During World War II, combat articles such as Michael Sullivan's "Flight Over Tokyo" or patriotic poems such as Ralph Waldo Emerson's "Concord Hymn"

frequently appeared. After the Iger shop began packaging *Classic Comics* in 1945, regular filler features were added. Heroic dog stories were an early and long-enduring staple.

"Pioneers of Science" was inaugurated in 1946 with an outline of Joseph Priestley's contributions; the feature continued until 1952, surveying the careers of 58 scientists, mathematicians, explorers, and inventors. In a 1989 article in the *Journal of Chemical Education*, Henry A. Carter praised the feature and other Gilberton publications for providing "a source of information on the lives of many famous chemists...."[1]

A feature titled "Great Lives" offered a biography in 1948 of Elizabeth Blackwell, the first American woman to receive a medical degree. American Indians and American rivers were studied in two-page spreads. "Famous Operas" introduced young readers to Mozart's *Don Giovanni*, Giuseppe Verdi's *Aida*, Richard Wagner's *Das Rheingold*, and Gilbert and Sullivan's *Iolanthe*. In "Stories From Early America," the capture of Ticonderoga and the California Gold Rush were among the many historical events recounted. Sports legends Babe Ruth, Lou Gehrig, and Knute Rockne were profiled, among others.

By the late 1950s, under Roberta Strauss Feuerlicht's direction, filler pieces bore some relation to the work adapted and supplied a broader context for the reader. Thus, a child who had just finished the *Classics* edition of G.A. Henty's *In the Reign of Terror* could read a biography of Robespierre—or, on completing Rudyard Kipling's *Kim*, could learn about the life of the Buddha. In the 1961 revised edition of *Tom Brown's School Days*, the article "Children of the Slums" revealed the other side of

Victorian England, while "A Mound of Ruins" juxtaposed the 1755 Lisbon earthquake with the devastation depicted in the 1961 revision of *The Last Days of Pompeii.*

An essay on the ancient Egyptian cult of the dead appeared in the 1961 edition of *Cleopatra*, along with an account of the ill-fated union of Antony and the Greco-Egyptian queen.

It was quite an education for 15 cents.

XIV

A "Newer, Truer Name": The Late Forties

Albert Kanter was proud of his publication, which was gaining increasing acceptance among parents and educators, some of whom wrote ringing endorsements for *Classic Comics*. But there was always that second half of the name, and comics were coming under increasing fire as postwar crime series attracted increasingly negative, and even hostile, publicity. Adults who approved of the publication and even some young readers sent letters to the editorial staff urging that Gilberton further distance its series from the "comics" stigma.

It was apparently Gilberton accountant Arthur Massin who hit upon the name *Classics Illustrated*. He contended that it would be more descriptive because the series had little in common with other comic books and offered instead illustrated versions of literary masterpieces. Kanter agreed, recognizing that the reputation of the line would be enhanced by the image makeover.[1] It would prove to be Gilberton's pivotal moment.

In January 1947, the following notice ran on the inside front cover of issue No. 33, *The Adventures of Sherlock Holmes*:

A NEW NAME BY POPULAR ACCLAIM!

Dear Reader:

1947 marks another milestone in the history of CLASSIC COMICS ... it is the sixth year that you've read and thrilled to these great stories. Because you have demanded the best in literature over these years, that's exactly what you have received ... the best that money can buy! Thanks to you for your splendid cooperation in making CLASSIC COMICS the acknowledged great publication that it is.

The stories that you will read this year have been selected for their thrills and excitement, their appeal to young and old, and their place in the world of literature. Just look at the list of coming titles and you'll see that we have picked just what you want.

Yes, there's another piece of news for you ... something important that you will want to know and remember! The name of CLASSIC COMICS is being changed. Starting in March, with issue number 35, the new name will be "CLASSICS *Illustrated*."

Why the change? Well, ever since our first issues, you have said that they really aren't "comics." We agree with you and so we're changing the name to "CLASSICS *Illustrated*."

Remember the date ... March, 1947 ... the issue, number 35, and the new name, "CLASSICS *Illustrated*." Ask for them by name, or ask for just plain "CLASSICS"; your dealer will know.

Yours truly,
The Editors

The next month, the new logo was unveiled, and another slogan was added to the announcement in issue No. 34, *Mysterious Island*, the last title to appear under the *Classic Comics* ribbon: "CLASSICS *Illustrated* ... A newer, truer name for CLASSIC COMICS ... IT'S NEW! IT'S TRUE! IT'S YOU!" Elaborating on the earlier blurb, the editors explained that

The name "CLASSICS *Illustrated*" is the better name for your favorite periodical. It really isn't a "comic" ... it's the illustrated, or picture, version of your favorite classics.

The name "CLASSICS *Illustrated*" is a name that you have suggested. We've had scores of letters from you readers, your parents, teachers and clergy urging us that CLASSIC COMICS needs a new name ... it's your idea!

A "Coming Next" ad heralded the imminent arrival of "the great first issue of CLASSICS *Illustrated*."

Then, in March 1947, with issue No. 35, Sir Edward Bulwer-Lytton's *The Last Days of Pompeii*, the "newer, truer" name appeared. The long yellow banner that filled the top of each cover was reduced to a yellow rectangle in the upper left-hand corner that remained a constant fixture (with some retooling of the logo lettering in December 1951) until 1971.

During the same month that Gilberton introduced the new series name, the company tried it out in reverse for a full year in newspaper comics supplements titled *Illustrated Classics*. Syndicated through the *New York Post*, the series ran from 30 March 1947 to 21 March 1948 and was carried, in whole or in part, by eight papers: the *Post*, the *Newark Star Ledger*, the *Queens Home News*, the *St. Louis Post-Dispatch*, the *Chicago Sun*, the *Indianapolis Star*, the *Milwaukee Journal*, and the *Dallas Home News*.[2]

Fourteen adaptations appeared in mostly four-week installments that generally amounted to the equivalent of 64-page books: *Kidnapped*, *20,000 Leagues Under the Sea*, *David Copperfield*, *Alice in Wonderland*, *The Spy*, *The Adventures of Tom Sawyer*, *The House of the Seven Gables*, *Julius Caesar*, *Silas Marner*, *A Christmas Carol*, *The Lady of the Lake*, *The Man in the Iron Mask*, *The Toilers of the Sea*, and *The Courtship of Miles Standish*. These were later added as *Classics Illustrated* titles in editions of reduced length to fit the 48-page format introduced with issue No. 45, *Tom Brown's School Days*, in January 1948.

Some friction developed between Jerry Iger and Albert Kanter concerning the newspaper serials. Iger believed that his shop was entitled to a share of the revenue from each of the papers running the weekly installments.

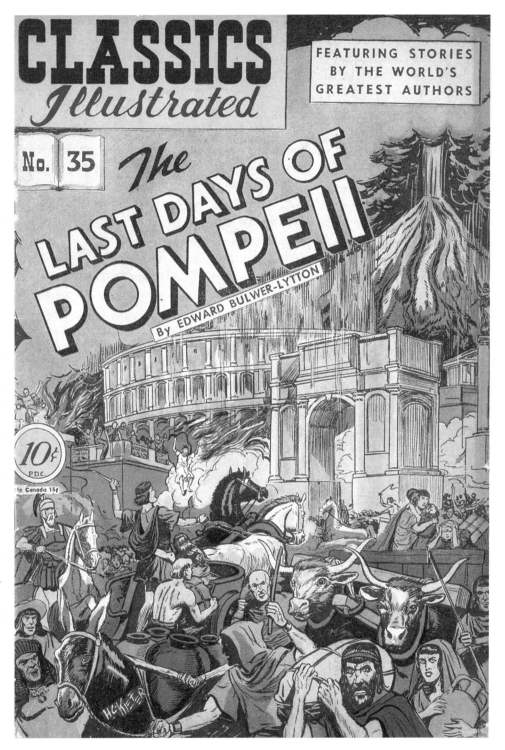

Henry C. Kiefer, *The Last Days of Pompeii* (March 1947). The first issue under the *Classics Illustrated* banner.

Kanter, however, insisted that Gilberton's standard contractual arrangement with Iger controlled. Although Iger briefly considered legal action, the dispute subsided, and cordial relations between publisher and art director were soon restored.[3]

Meanwhile, endorsements for the renamed *Classics*

Illustrated series came from parents and young readers alike, and some were printed on the inside front cover of No. 36, *Typee* (April 1947). From Selinsgrove, Pennsylvania, a "mother of a nine year old girl and a teacher in the elementary school" declared that "I cannot praise your CLASSICS too highly. Books of this type can be successfully used to build a better world, so please give us books that build better character, teach higher ideals and better morals."

The summer-camp contingent was represented by a writer from Chicago: "Your CLASSICS were by far the most popular books at our camp last year, and we are in the act of having them bound in books with hard covers for use at our camp, which should lengthen their life considerably. Your changing your name to CLASSICS ILLUSTRATED is excellent. They are in no class to be placed with the trashy so-called comics now on the market. Keep up the swell work."

A student from Smith Center, Kansas, sounded what would become an increasingly familiar note: "I like your adaptations of the CLASSICS very much. In school I have made book reports on nearly every one of these. Of course I read the book along with the CLASSIC magazine. [*Of course.*] It helped me to visualize the characters and scenes. I have had several compliments on my book reports by the teachers. Your magazine is really a great help."

Meanwhile, Jerry Iger was trying out a variety of hands on the rechristened *Classics Illustrated,* beginning with Henry C. Kiefer in No. 35. A visual identity for the series was evolving.

AUGUST M. FROEHLICH

Impressionistic linework, subtle character studies, and at-

tention to historical costuming characterize the contributions of August M. Froehlich, an older artist who died in 1949 shortly after completing his last *Classics Illustrated* assignment. A solo illustrator who penciled and inked his own work, Froehlich had drawn Captain Marvel, Jr., for Fawcett in the mid–1940s and had worked for Jack Binder's and Bernard Baily's shops before coming to

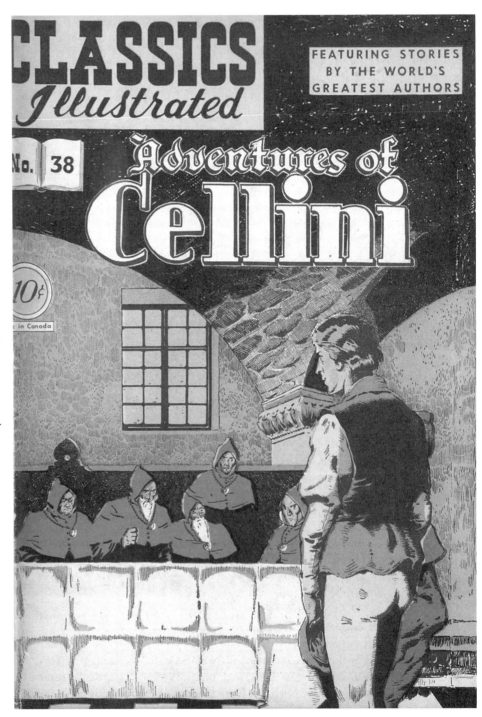

August M. Froehlich, *Adventures of Cellini* **(June 1947). A rare edition, discontinued two years after publication. Some religious authorities found the cover offensive.**

Iger.[4] Yet so consciously antiquated was his style, so Europeanized was his grounding, that it is difficult to imagine him being associated with any comics of the period other than *Classics*. The very nature of Gilberton's publication made what would have appeared hopelessly old-fashioned elsewhere ideally suited for the context.

Probably because of their anachronistic look, all of Froehlich's *Classics* titles were eventually redrawn or discontinued. An adaptation of Benvenuto Cellini's autobiography was dropped because of the less-than-flattering portrait it painted of the Renaissance Catholic Church.[5] Yet for the seven years or less that they remained in print, each offered what seemed a direct passage to another time. Quaintness, however, is only part of the charm of *Adventures of Cellini*, No. 38 (June 1947), "The Pit and the Pendulum" by Edgar Allan Poe in *Mysteries*, No. 40 (August 1947), *The Man in the Iron Mask* by Alexandre Dumas, No. 54 (December 1948), *The Toilers of the Sea* by Victor Hugo, No. 56 (February 1949), and *Black Beauty* by Anna Sewell, No. 60 (June 1949).

August M. Froehlich, *The Man in the Iron Mask* (December 1948). A delicate touch marked the artist's uniquely mannered style.

Froehlich produced striking line-drawing covers and evocative interiors for *Adventures of Cellini* and *The Toilers of the Sea*. The Cellini autobiography is the most concretely rendered of the artist's Gilberton efforts and provides a robust visual counterpart to the Florentine goldsmith's lively, self-aggrandizing memoir of life in Renaissance Italy. For the Victor Hugo title, the artist captured the starkness of the struggle of the protagonist, Gilliatt, to salvage an engine from a wrecked ship.

In Froehlich's hands, *The Man in the Iron Mask* became something more than a well-executed period piece; the *Classics Illustrated* version of Dumas's novel of dynastic intrigue suggests depths of motive beyond the capacity of most comic books in 1948. The artist's light touch, like a whisper, draws the reader into the panels and demands imaginative collaboration.

HARLEY M. GRIFFITHS

Few artists associated with *Classics Illustrated* seemed so perfectly matched with their material as Harley M. Griffiths. At home with the grotesque, he conjured fevered atmospheres for such gothic-tinged titles as Charlotte Brontë's *Jane Eyre*, No. 39 (July 1947), Edgar Allan Poe's "The Fall of the House of Usher" in *Mysteries*, No. 40 (August 1947), and Nathaniel Hawthorne's *The House of the Seven Gables*, No. 52 (October 1948). Griffiths also proved himself adept at handling classical matter, with a dash of strangeness, in his illustrations for *The Odyssey* of Homer, No. 81 (March 1951).

The artist completed all of his work for Gilberton

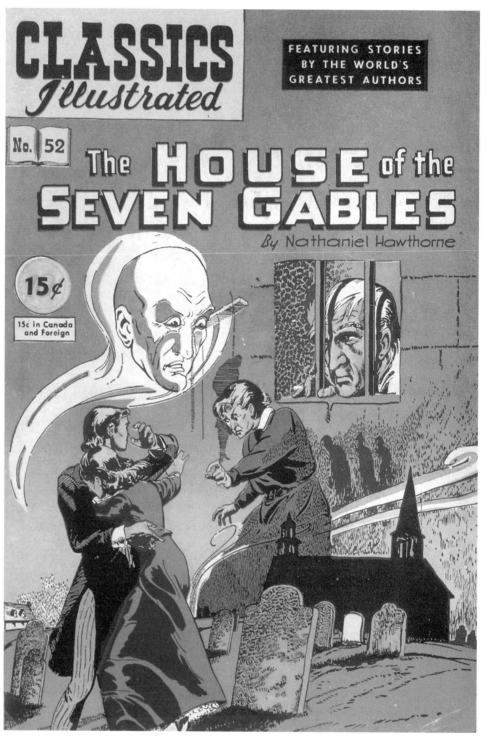

Harley M. Griffiths, *The House of the Seven Gables* (October 1948). **Extreme emotion was the artist's element.**

in 1947.[6] *The House of the Seven Gables* made its first appearance as an *Illustrated Classics* newspaper serial in September 1947; the pages for *The Odyssey* were held for nearly four years and apparently retouched by another hand.

Griffiths was born in June 1908 in Brooklyn, where

he graduated from St. Augustine's High School. He attended the Pratt Institute at night while working as a designer for a lighting manufacturer. Later, Griffiths attended the National Academy of Art while employed by Rambusch Liturgical Arts Co., designing art for their publications and religious statutes. This led to work as an illustrator for "Valiant Lives," a syndicated strip in Catholic newspapers.[7]

During World War II, Griffiths worked for General Dynamics in San Diego, rendering drawings of engineering plans for U.S. aircraft. In 1943, he married in New York, where he entered the comics field as a freelancer. Following a move with his family to Lac St. Joseph, Quebec, the artist submitted his completed assignments for *Classics Illustrated* by mail. At the same time, he was providing illustrations for *Picture Stories from the Bible*, a series published by Max Gaines's *Educational Comics* (soon to become notorious with its own change of name to *Entertaining Comics*, or just plain *EC*). That association lasted until Gaines's death in a freak boating accident.[8]

By the autumn of 1947, Griffiths was ready for a change of pace. He returned to New York to assume duties as an advertising art director for B. Altman and Company, where he worked until his retirement in 1973. Afterward, Griffiths found fulfillment as a watercolorist, and his art was shown in a number of one-man exhibits on Nantucket Island, where he spent his summers, in Westchester County, and in New York City. He was an active member of the National Arts Club, the Nantucket Artists Association, and the Hudson River Artists Association until his death in April 1986.[9]

In Griffiths's work for *Classics Illustrated* (with the excep-

tion of *The Odyssey*, which was probably inked by another hand), characters inhabit a realm of shadows in which forms continually threaten to dissolve or mutate into other, possibly sinister shapes. The covers for *Jane Eyre* and *The House of the Seven Gables* represent the most concentrated examples of the artist's unsettling vision.

Harley M. Griffiths, *Jane Eyre* (July 1947). Mad Bertha makes her point.

Harley M. Griffiths, "The Fall of the House of Usher" in *Mysteries* (August 1947). Roderick and Madeline, together at last.

Griffiths creates an atmosphere that suggests extreme emotion barely held in check. Averted eyes and bent or twisted figures are common. None of his men are conventionally handsome; none of his women are conventionally beautiful. Yet in *Jane Eyre*, the principals exude a barely suppressed sensuality, and in "The Fall of the House of Usher," the consummation of Roderick's obsession with his sister is memorably rendered.

It is significant that, when earlier *Classics* editions were being revamped in the late 1950s and early 1960s to conform to the new Gilberton house style, only one title by Griffiths—the atypical *Odyssey*—survived overhauling and deletion. Like Rochester's mad wife, Harley Griffiths's idiosyncratic art was removed to the attic, a reminder of a more undisciplined, unpredictable past.

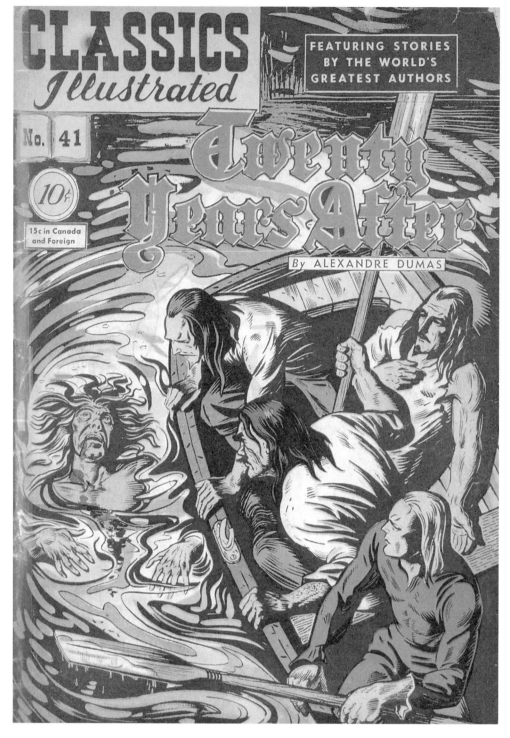

Robert C. Burns, *Twenty Years After* (September 1947). A soon-to-be-suppressed cover.

ROBERT C. BURNS

The most violent "horror" cover to appear in the *Classics* series graced Alexandre Dumas's *Twenty Years After*, No. 41 (September 1947), a sequel to *The Three Musketeers*. With its bloody image of the villain Mordaunt's corpse floating to the surface, it was a wonder that Albert Kanter, who had taken pains to disassociate his publication from "comics" by changing the line's name earlier in the year, allowed the controversial cover to be issued.

He didn't wait long, however, to correct what must have seemed at the time a major gaffe, and when the second printing of the title rolled off the presses in 1949, Henry C. Kiefer had dutifully supplied a soberly bland cover depicting Anne of Austria and the faithful Musketeers. The 1960 painted cover by Doug Roea was an improvement, showing d'Artagnan and the guys in action on horseback, clattering through a darkened street.

Nothing is known about Robert C. Burns, the artist who drew *Twenty Years After*. Hames Ware surmises that the name may have been a pseudonym.[10] At any rate, the style is a curious mixture of hurried, sketchy panels, swirling woodcut-style linework, and carefully rendered gore—as where, for example, the Executioner of Lille meets his end. Burns displays genuine enthusiasm for the story, faithfully adapted (if necessarily truncated) by Harry Miller, and a certain flair for crossed swords.

ALDO RUBANO

Aldo Rubano was highly regarded in the Iger organization for his backgrounds and inking. A lover of classical music, he played it continually at his desk in the shop, irritating some of his colleagues whose tastes inclined more toward Hit Parade fare.[11]

Iger assigned Rubano one *Classics Illustrated* title, *The Adventures of Tom Sawyer*, No. 50 (August 1948), which originally appeared in newspaper format in August-September 1947. Mark Twain's tale of growing up on the Mississippi was well served by Harry Miller's adaptation, and Rubano infused the illustrations with a rough-and-tumble, cartoonlike energy. Caricature predominates over

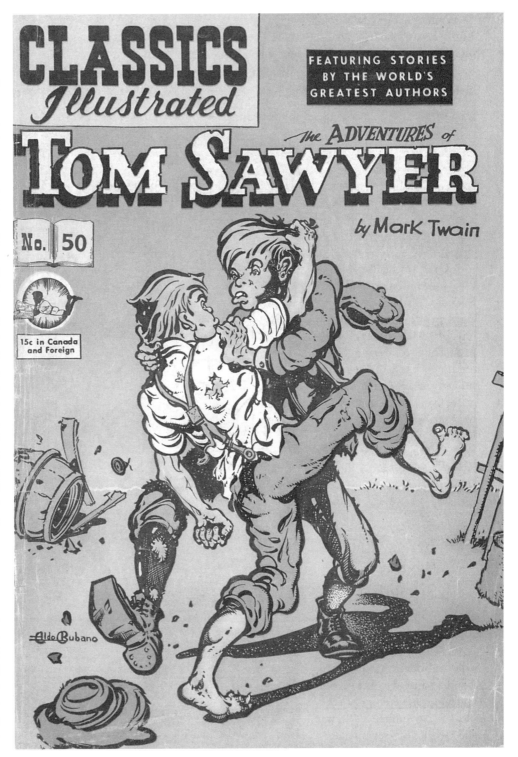

Aldo Rubano, *The Adventures of Tom Sawyer* (August 1948). Dr. Wertham was not amused.

realism, further boosting the high spirits of Tom's whitewashing scheme and schoolhouse heroics. The darker side of Twain's story was also well served by Rubano's evocative shading in the graveyard and cave episodes.

The cover illustration was singled out for its violence by Fredric Wertham in *Seduction of the Innocent*:

"An adaptation of one of Mark Twain's novels has the picture of two small boys in a fight, one tearing the other's hair—a scene not the keynote of Mark Twain's novel. Inside, three consecutive pictures show a fight between two boys ('In an instant both boys were gripped together like cats') and the last picture shows one boy with a finger almost in the other's eye (the injury-to-the-eye motif again)."[12]

One of the liveliest of the *Classics* issues, Rubano's splendid edition went through eight printings before it was replaced with a stupefyingly pedestrian rendering by an unknown hand in 1961. Fortunately, when Acclaim Comics revived the original *Classics* series in 1997, editor Madeleine Robins restored Rubano's unique *Tom Sawyer*, citing her fondness for its "loopy charm."[13]

BENJAMIN FRANKLIN: SHOP JOB

Winner of the Thomas Alva Edison Award for juvenile publications in 1956, when a painted-cover version appeared, *Benjamin Franklin*, No. 65 (November 1949), was the work of several Iger artists. Henry C. Kiefer produced the original line-drawing cover, while the styles of Robert Hebberd, Gustav Schrotter, and Alex A. Blum are evident in the interior art.[14] The anonymous script was derived in part from Franklin's *Autobiography* and possibly from Carl Van Doren's popular biography.

Despite its hodgepodge of styles that shift from

Henry C. Kiefer, *Benjamin Franklin* (November 1949). Kiefer, who contributed nothing to the interior stylistic jumble, was commissioned to provide a distinctively Gilberton identity for the cover.

panel to panel, the book holds together well with its uniform attention to costuming and period details. A substantial amount of cribbing from well-known portraits is evident. The artists convincingly rendered Franklin at different stages of his life; the boyhood and apprenticeship episodes were especially well managed, as well as the mission to France.

The Ben Franklin 5-10 variety-store chain and the Franklin Life Insurance Company, recognizing promotional opportunities in the book, distributed free editions in 1956. The giveaways, now collectors' items, sported a variation of the painted cover that was introduced that year.

XV

Classical Interlude:
The Horror! The Horror!

Lurid covers depicting horror themes became common comics fare in the late 1940s and early 1950s. The Gilberton Company paved the way in 1943 with a fanged Mr. Hyde bearing down on a panicked and fleeing London populace on the cover of No. 13, *Dr. Jekyll and Mr. Hyde*, the first actual "horror" comic book. A comically grotesque Quasimodo dominated the original cover of No. 18, *The Hunchback of Notre Dame*. A severed hand was featured on the cover of No. 21, *3 Famous Mysteries*, but the depiction of a skeletal figure on the cover of No. 20, *The Corsican Brothers*, was withdrawn before publication.

When the Iger shop took over production of *Classic Comics* in 1945, it promptly added more "horror" covers to the line. The first was a Boris Karloff knock-off on No. 26, *Frankenstein*, followed by a controversial "child abuse" scene gracing the front of No. 29, *The Prince and the Pauper*, which had actually been toned down from the mock-up that had appeared in the "Coming Next" ad. A blood-stained finger and rabid dog added to the newsstand appeal of No. 33, *The Adventures of Sherlock Holmes*.

The change of the series name to the more respectable *Classics Illustrated* seemed, paradoxically, to encourage the Iger artists to produce, for a brief period, even more horror subjects with even greater regularity. For the cover of No. 40, *Mysteries*, the

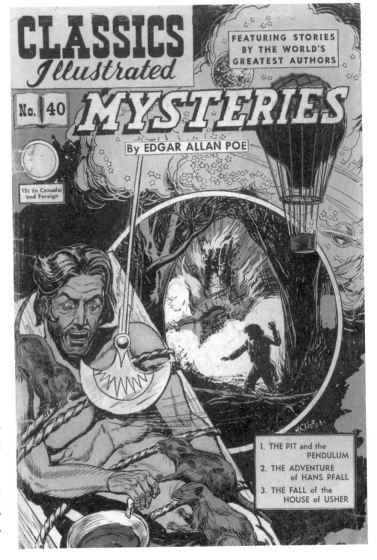

Henry C. Kiefer, *Mysteries* (August 1947). The original cover design had pictured rats gnawing on chains; between the appearance of the mock-up in a "Coming Next" ad and the publication of No. 40, someone apparently gave the matter further thought.

protagonist of "The Pit and the Pendulum" was shown directly beneath the menacing blade, covered by rats gnawing on his bonds. The floating corpse on the cover of No. 41, *Twenty Years After*, was perhaps the most notorious Gilberton cover and is highly prized by collectors.

By the standards of the day, even the substantially tamer covers of No. 43, *Great Expectations*, and No. 44, *Mysteries of Paris*, were controversial. After the appearance of the latter title in December 1947, Iger toned down the terror, and Henry C. Kiefer was assigned to render the worst offenders—Nos. 13, 18, 29, and 41—unobjectionable. Except for *Dr. Jekyll and Mr. Hyde*, he succeeded too well. The replacements were not only unobjectionable, they were emphatically uninspiring.

XVI

Blood, Sweat, and Rudy Palais

One of the most distinctive *Classics Illustrated* stylists, Rudolph ("Rudy" or "Rudi") Palais[1] filled such titles as *The Prairie*, *Crime and Punishment*, *David Balfour*, and *Pitcairn's Island* with characters seemingly always on the verge of springing into action or suffering agonies of suspense—muscles tensed, knuckles tightened, and sweat pouring. At his best, he brought a cinematic narrative sensibility to the eccentric, expressionistic panels he drew.

Palais came by it naturally—and early. "At the age of twelve," he wrote, "I joined a group of students selected by an art professor who had a radical approach to teaching art. Every Saturday morning, we the class would be lectured by the professor about developing the imagination of the student. By selecting a subject at random, we would then proceed to paint the subject strictly from our imagination—be it the rainy streets of a town or city—or a series of balloons in beautiful transparent colors. The professor disregarded the basic academic approach, stating that the development of the imagination was most important, and all else would follow in time." Traveling to various museums and art galleries in New York, the young Palais was captivated by the sunlight-drenched canvases of Georges Seurat.[2]

After attending the National Academy of Art and the Art Students' League, where he came under the influence of illustrators Norman Rockwell, J.F. Kernan, and Montgomery Flagg, among others, Palais spent a total of seven years in the 1930s producing "hundreds of full-color posters" for Warner Brothers and Columbia Pictures. His brother Walter, a comic-book artist, lured him to the East Coast and introduced him to Will Eisner and Jerry Iger, for whose shop he began working in 1941.[3]

By the mid–1940s, Palais was successfully negotiating his way in his new field, freelancing for a variety of comics publishers, including Fiction House, Quality,

Ace, Fox, and Harvey.[4] He produced artwork for the "Stormy Foster" series in *Hit Comics* and the "Deacon and Mickey" series in *Catman Comics*. In Lev Gleason's *Crime Does Not Pay*, Palais established his trademark style, wreathing his panels in smoke, bathing his bad guys in sweat, and clothing his loose women in as little as possible.[5] Later, the artist worked for EC, Fawcett, and Charlton. Among his influences in the realm of comics

Rudolph Palais, circa 1948. (Photo courtesy of Rudolph Palais.)

were Alex Raymond, Hal Foster, and associates Milt Caniff, Jack Cole, and Reed Crandall.[6]

In 1947, the artist began a seven-year association with *Classics Illustrated*. His first project for the series, James Fenimore Cooper's *The Pioneers*, No. 37 (May 1947), was among his finest efforts. The cover, showing Natty Bumppo being placed in the stocks while a dog nips at the heels of the petty official responsible for the indignity, concisely conveys the energy Palais invested in the adaptation. It was one of the last two line-drawing covers to be replaced by a painted cover in the American *Classics* series; along with Louis Zansky's cover art for *The Deerslayer*, another Cooper title, Palais's original cover for *The Pioneers* remained in print until 1968.

The artist did no work for Gilberton for nearly two years; then he was assigned the final Leatherstocking novel to be published in the series: *The Prairie*, No. 58 (April 1949). Although the book lacked the verve of *The Pioneers*, Palais designed a striking cover based on an illustration from a 19th-century edition of the novel. (See color section.) Both *The Pioneers* and *The Prairie* went through 11 printings, and one suspects that their success had more to do with the energy of the artist's images than the turgidness of Cooper's prose.

Returning to Western themes with *The Adventures of Kit Carson*, No. 112 (October 1953), a title issued to capitalize on the popularity of a current television series, Palais produced an abundance of sweating, bleeding, white-knuckled characters. One memorable full-page illustration depicts a hungrier-than-average bear shaking a sapling to which the perspiring hero clings.

The book was marred by the usually reliable Ken W. Fitch's surprisingly sanguinary script. "Drive this tack into your gun, Kit," a mountain man admonishes the young scout. "That's the way we keep count ... a brass tack for every Redskin we get!" For his part, the illustrator never quite got the locale or the period right.

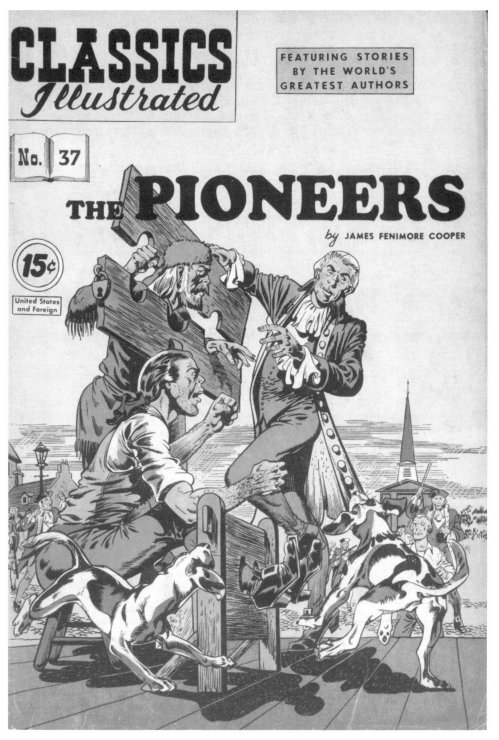

Rudolph Palais, *The Pioneers* (May 1947). Leatherstocking in the stocks. Note the Hogarthian energy of the artist's conception.

Rudolph Palais, *The Adventures of Kit Carson* (October 1953). The hero sweats out the situation.

Although Carson was born in 1809 and died in 1868, as the *Classics* edition informs the reader, vigilantes use six-shooters, which hadn't been invented yet, in an 1829 raid on a band of Mohawk-coiffed Apaches.

Lapses in *Kit Carson* notwithstanding, most of the artist's work for Gilberton revealed his close attention to historical setting. "Research was always a must," Palais recalled, singling out *David Balfour*, No. 94 (April 1952), as well as the Cooper books. Robert Louis Stevenson's sequel to *Kidnapped* (known as *Catriona*, after the heroine, in British editions of the novel) gave the artist a grounding in 18th-century costuming, which became something of a specialty for him. An almost tactile quality permeates his drawings of men and women in their 1750s clothing.

In *David Balfour*, Palais made excellent use of the comic-book panel's adaptability, skillfully de-ploying differently shaped frames and pushing characters outside them to accelerate the pacing and to achieve the desired atmospheric effect. The naive David's encounters with a fortune-telling hag and the cynical representatives of the Scottish judicial system are given an ominous edge through the constant relocation of the viewer's position. With the artist's inventive shifting of visual perspective and bold inking and adapter Ken W. Fitch's smooth streamlining of the morally complex tale, *David Balfour* remains one of the most interesting *Classics Illustrated* issues.

The artist's most characteristic—and memorable—work for Gilberton was *Crime and Punishment*, No. 89 (November 1951), a natural title for the Lev Gleason veteran. In his illustrations for Dostoevsky's study of moral ruin and regeneration, the artist was faithful to the intent of the severe and prudish abridgment, which presented the novel strictly as a psychological thriller and omitted entirely Sonya the prostitute, the agent of Raskolnikov's redemption. The protagonist bears an uncanny resemblance to the young Peter Lorre in Fritz Lang's *M*, and the murder scene proceeds with Hitchcock-style suspense, Welles-style angles and Palais-style perspiration.

The artist incorporated "angle shots" as "a ploy to heighten interest in the story telling—a method I employed to a great degree in horror and mystery stories."[7] Sweat-soaked protagonists served as another visual hook. The prominence given in *Crime and Punishment* to the pawnbroker's and Raskolnikov's hands was part of the same strategy. Indeed, hands are a central image in much of Palais's work; the artist stated that "Hands were always extremely important, and I tried to pay extra attention in rendering them. Hands expressed fright, anger, love, devotion, loyalty, etc., as one art instructor pointed out. Anatomically, I became very much aware of the potential...."[8]

Related to *Crime and Punishment* in tone is Palais's artwork for Edgar Allan Poe's "The Cask of Amontillado"

Rudolph Palais, *David Balfour* (April 1952). Hands—the more gnarled the better—figure prominently in the artist's work.

Left: Rudolph Palais, *Crime and Punishment* (November 1951). Raskolnikov acts on his theory. Note the artist's reliance on hands, sweat, and cinematic angles to build suspense. *Right:* Rudolph Palais, *Pitcairn's Island* (July 1953). Trouble in paradise — the violence depicted in the third *Bounty* adaptation led Gilberton to drop the title within two years.

in *The Gold Bug and Other Stories*, No. 84 (June 1951). The artist had established a solid reputation elsewhere with his horror illustrations, and the Poe story fell comfortably within the familiar genre.[9] Montressor sweats a storm as he walls up his old enemy Fortunato in the 14-page abridgment. The terror of the situation is depicted principally in the narrator's face. Adding vaporous streaks to augment the ambience in the catacombs and jutting, *Caligari*-style panels, Palais produced the most successful rendering of a Poe story in the *Classics Illustrated* catalogue.

An almost Düreresque obsession with linework is evident in *Men Against the Sea*, No. 103 (January 1953), the second title in the *Bounty* trilogy by Charles Nordhoff and James Norman Hall. The heavily scored waves, sails, and wood grain of the open boat — and even the folds in Bligh's coat — combine to convey the desperation of the

19 men set adrift by the mutineers. Palais's crowded, detailed panels endow the book, set mostly on the wide expanse of the sea, with the intensity of a radically narrowed world. Among the strongest sequences are those depicting a 36-hour storm in which Bligh, seated at the tiller, "seemed to have an exhilaration of mind that grew greater as our peril increased."

The final installment of Nordhoff and Hall's *Bounty* cycle, *Pitcairn's Island*, No. 109 (July 1953), pushes the emotional intensity of the tale of interracial passion and revenge to the boundaries of the grotesque. The artist depicted the English and Polynesian settlers hacking, clubbing, and shooting each other to death. With more than 30 panels devoted to some representation of violence, including the breaking of arms and the heaving of an enemy over a cliff, *Pitcairn's Island* was the most horrific of Palais's *Classics* efforts and an easy target for comics censors.

The issue was withdrawn in 1955, when Gilberton dropped several objectionable titles, and remained out of print until 1962.

Rob Roy, No. 118 (April 1954), one of Sir Walter Scott's "Waverley" novels, was added to the *Classics* list to capitalize on a current Walt Disney film of the same name. (A month earlier, Dell had issued, with a similar yellow cover, a handsome edition of the Disney *Rob Roy*, illustrated by Russ Manning.) The Gilberton book was Palais's final project for the publisher; it was interrupted midway by the illness of the artist.[10]

He turned the penciling and inking over to his brother and comics mentor, Walter Palais, whose attempt to duplicate Rudy's style resulted in a pallid imitation. All of the life goes out of the illustrations after a full-page duel between the hero, Francis Obaldistone, and his villainous cousin Rashleigh at the story's midpoint. Walter inked several of the pages penciled by his brother and improved none. About the time of *Rob Roy*, Gilberton began

exploring a new artistic direction, and Rudy Palais illustrated no more *Classics*. A new wave of talent would soon arrive.

"I was in the comic field for fifteen years," Palais wrote, "and I enjoyed every minute of it. The stories were assigned on a random basis at *Classic Comics* as well as throughout the industry. ... [I]t was always a three-month assignment, because the stories ... were approximately 50 pages long. We were usually paid one-third on the roughs, another one-third on the completed pencils, and finally one-third on the completed and inked page."[11] The sum amounted to about $100 a week, which, he said, "in those days was a lot."[12]

Rudi Palais earned every penny of it. Any nine-year-old who has anxiously perspired with Raskolnikov, nervously gripped a sword with David Balfour, or strained for a passing bird with Captain Bligh can attest to the indelible force of the artist's images.

XVII

Painted Covers and an Extra Nickel: The Early Fifties

The dawning of the 1950s saw the appearance of the first Shakespearean *Classics* title, *Julius Caesar*, No. 68 (February 1950), illustrated, appropriately enough, by the former thespian, Henry C. Kiefer. (The adaptation had actually run in Gilberton's newspaper format from 12 October to 2 November 1947.) For Albert Kanter, the inclusion of Shakespeare in the line offered incontrovertible evidence of the seriousness of his publication's purpose.

Even the *New York Times* found the news fit to print. The nation's newspaper of record reported that the "unexpurgated and unsimplified" comics adaptation had been prepared by Gilberton's "twenty man staff" with the cooperation of New York University at a cost of $11,000. The *Times* also quoted Kanter's estimate that 25,000 schools around the world used *Classics Illustrated*, which had sold 200,000,000 copies since the Gilberton Company began production.[1]

Not everyone, however, was impressed. In his polemical diatribe, *Seduction of the Innocent*, psychiatrist Fredric Wertham noted that

> David Dempsey, writing in the *New York Times Book Review*, has said of the comic book *Julius Caesar* that it has "a Brutus that looks astonishingly like Superman. 'Our course will seem too bloody to cut the head off and then hack the limbs...' says Brutus, in language that sounds like Captain Marvel..." and he notes that "Julius Caesar is followed by a story called 'Tippy, the Terrier.'"[2]

Of course, the language to which Dempsey and Wertham objected was Shakespeare's, slightly compressed, from Act II, scene i. The *Classics Illustrated* abridged line continues with the phrase "for Antony is but a limb of Cae-

sar." Both the critic and the doctor may have needed to brush up their Shakespeare; the original reads, in relevant part: "Our course will seem too bloody, Caius Cassius,/To cut the head off and then hack the limbs,/Like wrath in death and envy afterwards—/For Antony is but a limb of Caesar."[3]

Captain Marvel it wasn't, and, although "Tippy, the Terrier" indeed made his appearance in a "Dog Heroes" filler at page 47, Dempsey neglected to mention, and Wertham failed to discover, that the *Classics* adaptation of *Julius Caesar* was immediately followed, on page 45, by a biography of "The Bard of Avon." On page 46, opposite the offending "Tippy," Dempsey and Wertham would have found a "Pioneers of Science" biography of Blaise Pascal containing such violent language as "Pressure exerted anywhere upon the surface of a liquid enclosed in a vessel is transmitted equally in all directions, and acts with equal force upon all equal surfaces, and at right angles to the surfaces." Had either of the learned gentlemen bothered to turn to page 48, he would have been able to read a two-column plot summary of Jules Massenet's *Manon*. All in all, No. 68 was a typical issue of the period.

With Shakespeare enthroned on the reorder list, Kanter forged ahead to claim more of the literary high ground, issuing adaptations of the Homeric epics, *The Iliad*, No. 77 (November 1950) and *The Odyssey*, No. 81 (March 1951). *Classics Illustrated* versions of works by Caesar himself, Dostoevsky, Schiller, Zola, Conrad, Sienkiewicz, Gogol, and Goethe would eventually follow. Meanwhile, in April 1950, at the end of *The Pilot*, No. 70, Gilberton appended the high-minded tag line that would endure as long as the series itself: "Now that you have read the *Classics Illustrated* edition, don't miss the added enjoyment of reading the original, obtainable at your school or public library."

With that sort of plug, it was no wonder that the American educational establishment began to come to terms with the series. After all, if kids were going to read comic books anyway, they might as well read *The Black Arrow* rather than *Green Arrow*, *The Lady of the Lake* rather than *Phantom Lady*. Teachers began distributing *Classics Illustrated* editions of *Ivanhoe* and other assigned novels to encourage reluctant readers. In time, tens of thousands of schools in the United States, Canada, and other countries adopted Gilberton publications as supplementary instructional aids.[4]

In 1948, Kanter had signed on with the Curtis Circulation Company for distribution of *Classics Illustrated* in Canada. At the time, distribution in the United States was handled by P.D.C. and was concentrated in larger cities on the east coast. Pleased with Curtis's Canadian performance, Kanter awarded the company distribution rights for the United States in 1951.[5] The move gave Gilberton the display-space advantage of a nationwide system that stocked newsstands with *The Saturday Evening Post*, *Ladies' Home Journal*, *The Atlantic Monthly*, *Holiday*, and *Esquire*.

On the advice of the Curtis organization, Gilberton raised the issue price from ten to 15 cents in March 1951 with *The Odyssey*. The Homeric title proved to be a significant milestone in another respect, as well, inaugurating the painted covers that were to reshape the image of the series in the 1950s and boost its sales to spectacular levels. It is impossible to overstate the significance of the painted covers, which further set *Classics* apart from other comic books and, incidentally, served to justify the five-cent increase.[6] For many parents, the higher price seemed a guarantee of greater worth.

If imitation is the sincerest form of flattery, Albert Kanter should have felt flattered indeed by the appearance of Seaboard Publishers' *Fast Fiction* (soon to be renamed *Famous Authors Illustrated*), a 32-page competitor that began issuing titles such as *The Scarlet Pimpernel*, *Captain Blood*, and *She* in October 1949. Instead, of course, he was rather annoyed, particularly because the prolific Henry C. Kiefer, whose style was so closely identified with *Classics Illustrated*, was churning out artwork for the new series, illustrating Shakespeare's *Hamlet* and *Macbeth*, neither of which had been issued by Gilberton at that point.

Famous Authors was not, in fact, much in the way of

Albert Kanter (right) promoting *Classics Illustrated* on the air with Pat and Barbara Barnes (1952). (Courtesy of Hal Kanter and John Haufe.)

Henry C. Kiefer, *She* (*Fast Fiction* 1949/*Famous Authors Illustrated* 1950). The artist's work for Gilberton's chief rival caused hard feelings, but the competition proved beneficial to *Classics Illustrated.*

ber 1950). When *Classics Illustrated* got around to *Hamlet* in September 1952, adapter Sam Willinsky allowed the prince to use the words Shakespeare had given him.

Kanter's answer to the aggravation was to buy out the upstart and kill it, turning one of the unpublished titles in the series, *The Red Badge of Courage*, into a *Classics* issue, No. 98, in August 1952. A 15-page filler, "An Outline History of the Civil War," was added to bring the length into conformity with the 48-page Gilberton norm.

Seaboard's example had the salutary effect of weaning Gilberton from an exclusive dependence on public-domain material. The inclusion in the *Famous Authors* series of works still under copyright, such as John Buchan's *The 39 Steps*, Percival Christopher Wren's *Beau Geste*, and Rafael Sabatini's *Scaramouche*, spurred Kanter to take similar steps. In January 1951, a copyright-permissions notice appeared on the title page of No. 79, *Cyrano de Bergerac*. A proud declaration on the title page of *White Fang*, No. 80 (February 1951), informed the reader that the edition was "[p]ublished through special arrangement with CHARMIAN K. LONDON, sole and exclusive owner of copyright." During the next four years, *Classics Illustrated* would add to its catalogue authorized adaptations of books under copyright by Erich Maria Remarque, John Bakeless, Frank Buck, Talbot Mundy, Charles Boardman Hawes, Walter Van Tilburg Clark, and Charles Nordhoff and James Norman Hall.

With the publication flourishing, Kanter decided to vacate the crowded sixth-floor office and warehouse site at 826 Broadway. In September 1952, at the time the 99th *Classics* title, *Hamlet*, was issued, Gilberton relocated to its final home, 101 Fifth Avenue, a more prestigious business address. Kanter's brother Michael moved the warehouse to Brooklyn and later to Concord, New Hampshire, then finally to Passaic, New Jersey.[7]

Beginning in 1953, with *Dr. Jekyll and Mr. Hyde*, No. 13, and *Don Quixote*, No. 11, painted covers began to replace the old line-drawing covers. In the case of No. 13, a new, more faithful script and improved interior art were also introduced—a stylistic makeover that would accelerate from 1956 onward as Gilberton reaffirmed its commitment to its cultural and educational mission.

competition. Unlike *Classics Illustrated*, the would-be rival series sacrificed textual integrity for the sake of reader accessibility. As Seaboard Publishers proudly announced, "No longer is it necessary to wade through hundreds of pages of text to enjoy these great stories…. When you read FAMOUS AUTHORS ILLUSTRATED you, too, will know the great characters of literature. You, too, can quote the famous lines and impress your friends." The only problem was that some of the "famous lines" were inexactly rendered: "Oh, that this too, too solid flesh of mine would melt and release my soul from body," Hamlet moans in Dana E. Dutch's pastiche, No. FA8 (Octo-

Unidentified artist, *Don Quixote* (August 1953): The Don and his windmill get a painted-cover facelift.

BOB LAMME

During the period in which Iger was supplying artwork for Gilberton's rival, *Fast Fiction*, several unaffiliated artists of varying abilities worked briefly under the *Clas-* sics banner. Book illustrator Bob Lamme, a college friend of Hal Kanter's who had no comic-book credits elsewhere, was assigned Frederick Marryat's *Mr. Midshipman Easy*, No. 74 (August 1950).

In a 1977 letter to *Classics Index* author Charles Heffelfinger, Lamme, an artist for the *Miami Herald*, stated that he drew his one and only *Classics Illustrated* title in 1949. He noted that he didn't keep a copy of the book himself because he didn't believe he had done a good job on it.[8] Indeed, the interior art in *Mr. Midshipman Easy*, though not without its compensating naive charm, is often flat.

Captain Marryat's lively adventure tale was neatly compressed by scriptwriter Ken W. Fitch, but the novel's early chapters were dropped, resulting in a lack of context for the transformation of Jack Easy, the spoiled child of privilege and apostle of the theory of equality, on the decks of the warship *Harpy*. Perhaps under editorial direction, Lamme drew Mesty, the hero's black mentor and companion, as a white man.

Always more popular with a British audience, *Mr. Midshipman Easy* was not in great demand with American readers and was dropped from the reorder list in 1952. So few copies had been sold that it was possible to obtain first-and-only editions from the Gilberton warehouse as late as 1963. A European issue with an independently commissioned painted cover fared somewhat better abroad.

Bob Lamme, *Mr. Midshipman Easy* (August 1950). The artist's only Gilberton credit.

LAWRENCE DRESSER AND GUSTAV SCHROTTER

Known primarily as an illustrator of hardcover juvenile books, such as Augusta Stevenson's *George Washington: Boy Leader* (1942), Marguerite Henry's *Robert Fulton: Boy Craftsman* (1945), and Rita Halle Kleeman's *Young Franklin Roosevelt* (1946), Lawrence Dresser brought a decidedly different perspective to his comics assignments for *Classics Illustrated.* In *The Master of Ballantrae*, No. 82 (April 1951), the artist produced a well-researched costume piece, basing some of his drawings, including the first-page splash of a midnight duel, on William Hole's turn-of-the-century illustrations for Robert Louis Stevenson's tale of fratricidal hatred.

The murky moral atmosphere of the novel is well conveyed in the intelligent script by Ken W. Fitch, as well as by the contrast between Dresser's light linework and frequently heavy shading. A solid grasp of the complex psychological dimensions of the main characters—the manipulative charm of "The Master," the thwarted decency of the younger brother—on the part of both adapter and artist made *Ballantrae* one of the finest *Classics* titles. The only false note in Fitch's adaptation was his addition of a spoken line by the revived "week-old corpse" of James Durie on the final page.

Dresser, probably working with Gustav Schrotter and Harry Daugherty (brother of children's book illustrator James Daugherty), offered homage to author-illustrator Howard Pyle in *Men of Iron*, No. 88 (October 1951).[9] Yet the trio's work was by no means a mere derivative exercise. The *Classics Illustrated* retelling of the story of Myles Falworth's training as a squire and quest for honor is filled with fluid action scenes and carefully observed character development.

Schrotter, like Dresser, was a juvenile-book illustrator who also ventured into the comics field. Associated with Jerry Iger, he turned out *Nicholas Nickleby*, No. FA9 (November 1950), and *La Svengali* (*Trilby*), No. FA12 (February 1951) for *Famous Authors Illustrated.* While his contributions to Gilberton's *Benjamin Franklin* and *Men of Iron* were notable, his best—and only solo—work for *Classics* was *The Red Badge of Courage*, No. 98 (August 1952), a title originally scheduled for *Famous Authors Illustrated.*

Stephen Crane's masterpiece received less than its due from the unknown adapter, who, in *Famous Authors* fashion, invented dialogue when needed and ignored the author's ironic inflections. Still, Schrotter's drawings, based in part on the 1951 John Huston film, evoked to some extent the rush and confusion of battle and rout.

Lawrence Dresser, *The Master of Ballantrae* (April 1951). James and Henry settle their differences by candlelight.

After his episodic stint with Gilberton, Schrotter returned to juvenile books, illustrating such works as H.C. Thomas's *Noah Carr, Yankee Firebrand* (1957), A. Van der Loeff's *Avalanche!* (1958), and Esther Willard Bates's *Marilda and the Bird of Time* (1960).

JIM WILCOX

The identity of the artist who provided the unusual drawings for Edgar Allan Poe's "The Tell-Tale Heart" in *The Gold Bug and Other Stories*, No. 84 (June 1951), has been something of a mystery. Comics authority Hames Ware initially judged the work to be that of Jim Lavery

Jim Wilcox, "The Tell-Tale Heart" in *The Gold Bug and Other Stories* (June 1951). An artistic mystery solved by Bill Briggs and Hames Ware.

Gustav Schrotter, *The Red Badge of Courage* (August 1952). "The youth" improves his battlefield performance.

but was never comfortable with the tentative attribution, which subsequently appeared in Dan Malan's *Complete Guide to Classics Collectibles*.[10] In notes to himself, he had observed that "This artist resembles Jim Wilcox" of the Jacquet shop. Yet because the Iger shop was in charge of Gilberton's art in 1951, Ware assumed that it would have

been impossible for a Jacquet artist to receive an assignment.[11]

Meanwhile, *Classics* collector Bill Briggs discovered Wilcox's signature on an unpublished line-drawing cover for *The Odyssey*, the title that appeared as the first painted-cover issue in March 1951, a few months before "The Tell-Tale Heart." Ware reexamined the evidence and concluded that Jim Wilcox's was indeed the hand responsible for the Poe story.[12] It is possible that, although Wilcox was tied to the Jacquet operation, he may have subcontracted with Jerry Iger during the period when Henry C. Kiefer was busy supplying artwork for Gilberton's competitor, Seaboard's *Stories by Famous Authors Illustrated*.

In any event, Wilcox's illustrations for the macabre tale are among the most distinctive to appear in any *Classics Illustrated* issue. The spare linework and studied primitivism, which may seem at first glance a throwback to the awkward art of the early 1940s, succeed splendidly in conveying the narrator's mad obsession through the very strangeness, the "otherness," of the artist's style.

MAURICE DEL BOURGO

A superb illustrator who, in the words of Hames Ware, "never produced a disappointment," Maurice del Bourgo had worked for Ace, Hillman, and Prize.[13] At one point, he provided art for DC's *Green Arrow*. Although he was not associated with the Iger shop, he became a Gilberton regular between 1951 and 1953. Among the younger *Classics* artists of the early 1950s, only Rudy Palais equalled his dramatic energy; no one surpassed his pictorial narrative skill.

Like Robert Hayward Webb before and Lou Cameron after him, del Bourgo was a decisively masculine presence on the Gilberton roster. He was, in the words of *Classics Reader* editor Bill Briggs, an "outdoorsy, blow-by-blow, give-no-quarter, man's world artist."[14] His confidently inked work, whether set in the Alaskan wilderness or the North African desert, the trenches of the Western Front or the plains of the Wild West, seemed "all vigor, all struggle, all male bonding."[15]

But del Bourgo was also an intellectual among illustrators, an introspective artist who set high aesthetic standards for himself. He would never allow anyone else to do his inking, and he sought, unsuccessfully, to have some input in the coloring of his pages. As the artist observed in a written interview with *Classics Reader* editor Jim Sands, he "would ... agonize over things that ultimately didn't mean much of anything, but had a lot of significance for me."[16] Although he "deplored some of the illustrations" he saw in other *Classics Illustrated* issues,

he concluded that "the publisher wanted mass production with reasonable competence, and that's just what he got."[17]

Del Bourgo studied "sporadically" for six years at the Art Students League in New York under George Bridgman, who taught him anatomy, and Ivan Olinsky and William von Schlegell, two fine-arts painters. The artist's resources were limited, and he would from time to time "play saxophone with dance bands until I could get enough $$$ to resume my studies. This was possible at the ASL. After this I managed to latch on to some illustration and commercial art jobs with art studios, newspapers and ad agencies."[18] Meyer Kaplan recruited freelancer del Bourgo for Gilberton; editor and artist would later collaborate on a project for NBC, with Kaplan acting as agent.[19]

The first title assigned to del Bourgo was *Under Two Flags*, No. 86 (August 1951), an 1867 French Foreign Legion melodrama by Ouida (Maria Louisa de la Ramée), whose works have slipped from popular consciousness since Hollywood lost interest in them in the early 1960s. It is arguable that the overripe *Under Two Flags* was actually improved by scriptwriter Ken W. Fitch's pruning. As for the artist's contribution, his Cigarette was the most vibrant *Classics* heroine since Matt Baker's Lorna Doone. Her sacrificial intervention before the aristocratic English hero's firing squad broke many a preadolescent reader's heart.

Jack London's *The Call of the Wild*, No. 91 (January 1952), as adapted by Fitch, featured minimal dialogue and showcased del Bourgo's skill in creating character and conflict with animals. Buck's mortal combat with Spitz, his growing bond with John Thornton, and his ultimate transformation into the feared "ghost dog" are rendered without verbal or visual sentiment.

The devastation of war brought forth the artist's most harrowing work in Erich Maria Remarque's *All Quiet on the Western Front*, No. 95 (May 1952), published, interestingly enough, during the Korean War, in a year when war comics such as *War Adventures* (Atlas/Marvel) and *Star Spangled War Stories* (DC) were proliferating on newsstands.[20] The artist recalled that "I was delighted with the chance to do *All Quiet*. I had read Erich Maria Remarque and had been tremendously moved by it. Once I got the script, I determined to pull out all the stops."[21]

So disturbingly true to the antiwar novel were Fitch's adaptation and del Bourgo's illustrations that the title was withdrawn in 1955, when several other "objectionable" issues were discontinued. It was not reprinted for another decade, when another, more divisive, war was beginning to capture the nation's attention.

If there was a single instance to disprove Hames Ware's dictum that del Bourgo never produced a disap-

Maurice del Bourgo, *Under Two Flags* **(August 1951). Cigarette gives all for love.**

chest and tilting his head backward as a rather simian John "Wilks" (a letterer's, not the artist's, mistake) Booth leaps to the stage.

Among the finest of del Bourgo's efforts, *William Tell*, No. 101 (November 1952), features consistently interesting panel composition, vivid character delineation, and striking background detail. Tell's escape from a storm-tossed boat and the assassination of the tyrant Gessler are dramatically executed tableaux. Most memorable, however, is the famous episode in which the hero is forced to shoot an arrow through an apple placed on his son's head. Del Bourgo placed it at the center of *William Tell*, spreading the scene across two pages and adding to the tension, as the arrow speeds on its way, by rendering the reactions of the gathered witnesses.

Shifting to a Western setting posed no problem for the artist in *Buffalo Bill*, No. 106 (April 1953), which remained one of the most popular titles in the series through the early 1970s. A centerfold illustration of William Cody earning his sobriquet is an epic-scale scene of cheerful mayhem among the bison. Del Bourgo made effective use of shading in close-up drawings of characters' faces, lending greater nuance and depth to the most extroverted of his Gilberton performances.

The artist's final title for *Classics Illustrated* was a beautifully drawn adaptation of Alexandre Dumas's relatively unknown historical novel, *The Forty-Five Guardsmen*, No. 113 (November 1953), part of the Valois cycle that included *Queen Margot* and *Chicot the Jester*. The abridgment itself was deftly achieved, but, with its emphasis on the dynastic struggle between Henri III and Henri of Navarre, the book demanded a better acquaintance with 16th-century French history than most young American readers could claim. In *The Forty-Five Guardsmen*, the artist presented a rich panoply of period costumes. At the same time, del Bourgo's compositional technique shifted toward the clean lines and uncluttered backgrounds that would characterize the Gilberton house style from the mid–1950s onward.

Standing always apart, the artist saw himself as a serious illustrator who understood but resisted the traditional, commercialized comic-book formula. Meyer Kaplan hired him for specific projects if he thought his style was "compatible with the story."[22] Del Bourgo worked in his home studio, devoting a month to six weeks to each

pointment, it was the artist's work on "An Outline History of the Civil War." The 15-page filler item for issue No. 98 could be said to have paved the way for the *Special Issues* and *World Around Us* series of the late 1950s and was the first of three *Classics Illustrated* treatments of the national conflict. Designed to extend the length of the issue containing the *Famous Authors* edition of *The Red Badge of Courage*, the "Outline History" suffers from uncharacteristic lapses, including a panel depicting Abraham Lincoln, alone in his box at Ford's Theatre, clutching his

Classics script while simultaneously engaged in other projects.

At the time, according to the artist, Gilberton's standard rate was $15 per page, a low pay scale in keeping with the company's policy of getting the most for the least. But there were compensating factors in terms of page layout (six panels on average rather than eight), book length (44 pages), and creative control. "We had total freedom in interpretation," del Bourgo declared. "We developed our own guidelines."[23] That state of affairs would change significantly within a few years, thanks to a young woman hired at about the time the artist finished his last *Classics Illustrated* assignment.

MORRIS WALDINGER

Issue No. 100, *Mutiny on the Bounty* (October 1952), was a prize for Albert Kanter. Not only had *Classics Illustrated* reached a publishing milestone, but Gilberton had acquired the rights to adapt the other two novels in Charles Nordhoff and James Norman Hall's *Bounty* trilogy, *Men Against the Sea* and *Pitcairn's Island*. Yet the choice for illustrator of the 100th issue was unusual, considering the availability of Kiefer (who provided the painted cover), Blum, Palais, and del Bourgo.

Morris Waldinger, who received the nod, had no previous Gilberton assignments to his credit. His principal work elsewhere consisted of filler material for DC.[24] In *Mutiny on the Bounty*, the artist was at his best depicting action sequences—Bligh's acts of brutality, Christian's seizing of the ship, and the suffering of the captured mutineers aboard the *Pandora*. These scenes are as powerful as anything that appeared in *Classics Illustrated* at the time.

Yet some of the work shows signs of haste, particularly in panels where one figure positioned partially behind another is missing a leg or a shoulder at the point where the rest of the body should appear again on the other side of the foreground character. The narrator, midshipman Roger Byam, is not quite 18 years old when the story begins, but his apparent age changes from panel to panel—here he seems a callow youth and there a man well past his prime. Matters weren't helped by the colorist's decision to endow Byam and most of the other male characters with powdered hair, which gave the *Bounty* the appearance of a floating retirement community.

Top: **Maurice del Bourgo,** *The Call of the Wild* **(January 1952). The "dominant primordial beast" makes his kill.** *Bottom:* **Maurice del Bourgo,** *All Quiet on the Western Front* **(May 1952). The horrors of war on display in the artist's favorite** *Classics Illustrated* **assignment.**

Maurice del Bourgo, *William Tell* (November 1952). Grace under pressure.

Maurice del Bourgo, *The Forty-Five Guardsmen* (November 1953). Spare backgrounds predominated in the artist's last Gilberton project.

Waldinger was never assigned another *Classics* project. Rudi Palais was given the remaining *Bounty* stories. And Albert Kanter, whose fortunes had improved to the point that he was able to pay royalties for a best-selling trilogy of contemporary fiction, threw a party for Gilberton personnel to celebrate reaching the 100th issue.

SEYMOUR MOSKOWITZ

Seymour Moskowitz, a veteran of Atlas Comics, illustrated two *Classics Illustrated* titles in 1953: *King—of the Khyber Rifles*, No. 107 (May), and *A Study in Scarlet*, No. 110 (August). Had Fredric Wertham been aware of either book, he probably would have heaped abuse on them in his *Seduction of the Innocent*.

Talbot Mundy's *King—of the Khyber Rifles* was one of an increasing number of adaptations of works of marginal literary stature that were added to the *Classics* list during the mid- and late 1950s. A novel still under copyright that had recently been the basis of a motion picture, the tale of British imperial intrigue remained in print even during the peak of anti-comics hysteria in 1954 and 1955—despite the full-page drawing of the hero's discovery that he was holding his brother's severed head in his hands.

Like *King Solomon's Mines*, *King—of the Khyber Rifles* depicted a white man romantically involved with an exotic, dark-skinned woman. In this case, the woman not only lived, but she also got her man. It probably helped, in 1953, that she had blonde hair.

Two Sherlock Holmes stories were included in *A Study in Scarlet*—the title mystery and "The Adventure of the Speckled Band." The title story had originally appeared in the 1947 *Adventures of Sherlock Holmes* but had been cut when the 56-page issue was trimmed to the standard 48 pages in 1948. The new edition of *A Study in Scarlet* was criticized for its perceived anti–Mormon bias, a factor that may have resulted in its deletion from the reorder list in 1955. The macabre elements of the plot, with a bloody message inscribed on a wall and a force-fed poison pill, probably played a part, as well. A reprint surfaced in 1962 and soon disappeared. Despite the popularity of Sherlock Holmes, it was never again reissued.

Moskowitz was the first representative of a new, leaner technique of comics illustration that came to dominate the Gilberton house style in the mid- and later 1950s. The baroque amplitude of Henry C. Kiefer and Rudy Palais gave way to crisp linework and less ornately wrought panels.

Morris Waldinger, *Mutiny on the Bounty* (October 1952). Mr. Christian assumes command.

Seymour Moskowitz, *King—of the Khyber Rifles* (May 1953). The shock of recognition.

FAWCETT FUGITIVES: PETER COSTANZA AND KURT SCHAF-FENBERGER

As various comic-book publishers folded or shrank in the mid–1950s, succumbing either to the overburdened market or to the relentless anti-comics campaign, different groups of freelancers found themselves calling on the editorial offices at 101 Fifth Avenue. Among the first were Peter Costanza (1913–1984) and Kurt Schaffenberger (b. 1920), two talented fugitives from the 1953 Fawcett shutdown, occasioned by the publisher's decision not to engage in protracted copyright-infringement litigation with DC Comics concerning Fawcett's Superman-clone, Captain Marvel. Faster than you could say "Shazam," Fawcett abandoned not only superheroes but also the publication of comics.[25]

Costanza possessed one of the most individualistic styles of any artist whose work appeared in *Classics Illustrated*. A former pulp illustrator, he had assisted Charles Clarence Beck on *Captain Marvel* in Fawcett's *Whiz Comics* and on *Captain Tootsie* for Tootsie Rolls during the 1940s.[26] Fawcett artist Marc Swayze recalled Costanza as a "fast layout artist," a "great joker," and a "wonderful man to know," who, as Beck's assistant, never fully emerged from the older artist's shadow.[27]

Where Rudy Palais emphasized hands and sweaty brows, Costanza highlighted eyes and toothy mouths, bestowing on his characters a kind of cartoonlike cuteness that made him especially well suited to illustrate *Andy's Atomic Adventures* (September 1953) for the first *Picture Parade* issue, and *Cinderella,* No. 503 (December 1953), and *The Sleeping Beauty,* No. 505 (February 1954), for the newly inaugurated *Classics Illustrated Junior* series.

The artist illustrated three sea tales for the regular

THE MUTINEERS

By CHARLES BOARDMAN HAWES

HAVING BEEN BORN IN THE SEAFARING TOWN OF SALEM, MASSACHUSETTS, I, BEN LATHROP, HAD AS MY LIFE'S AMBITION THE DESIRE TO SHIP BEFORE THE MAST. I WAS A LAD OF SIXTEEN WHEN, IN THE YEAR 1809, MY FATHER TOOK ME TO SEE HIS GOOD FRIEND, CAPTAIN JOSEPH WHIDDEN, THE MASTER OF A SHIP CALLED THE ISLAND PRINCESS.

PETER COSTANZA

CAPTAINS COURAGEOUS

By Rudyard Kipling

PETER COSTANZA

Classics Illustrated line: James Fenimore Cooper's *The Red Rover*, No. 114 (December 1953), Rudyard Kipling's *Captains Courageous*, No. 117 (March 1954) and Charles Boardman Hawes's *The Mutineers*, No. 122 (September 1954). In each book, Costanza's light, almost comic touch seems occasionally at odds with the violent world depicted, though the tension between the competing elements makes the artist's efforts invariably compelling.

Captains Courageous, the strongest of the trio, presents a credible visual account of spoiled rich boy Harvey Cheyne's education and transformation, from his rescue at sea to his immersion in the fisherman's life. The artist also produced fine characterizations of Disko, Dan, Manuel, Penn, and others aboard the fishing vessel *We're Here*. In his work for Gilberton, Costanza always seemed most comfortable — and his art most natural — when his subjects were youthful protagonists. Ben Lathrop, the 16-year-old narrator of *The Mutineers*, is a less complex figure than Harvey Cheyne but an equally sympathetic figure in the artist's rendering of the novice seaman's experiences with pirates and other perils.

A charming pirate was the central character in *The Red Rover*; as drawn by Costanza, his appearance suggested a maritime Robin Hood. The issue's cover, which depicted a figure who in no way resembled the "Red Rover" of the story, was painted by Jo Polseno, who in 1958 illustrated a Grosset and Dunlap "Signature" biography of Robert Louis Stevenson and in the 1960s supplied artwork for *Kidnapped*, *The Adventures of Tom Sawyer*, and *The Merry Adventures of Robin Hood* in Grosset and Dunlap's *Companion Library* series. During the same period, Costanza illustrated Martha and Charles Shapp's *Let's Find Out About* (*Firemen, Houses*, and so on) children's books.

Another Fawcett veteran and Captain Marvel artist, Kurt Schaffenberger brought Beck's emphasis on humor and clarity of design to his one *Classics Illustrated* assignment, *Soldiers of Fortune*, No. 119 (May 1954), Richard Harding Davis's imperialistic potboiler about dashing gringos foiling a Latin American revolution to ensure that the benighted natives will enjoy the disinterested guidance of the benevolent North American mining interests that employ the mercenaries of the title. Schaffenberger portrayed the suave protagonist Robert Clay, "civil engineer and soldier of fortune," with wit and panache, and the drawings are distinguished by their vitality and economy of line.

Schaffenberger moved from Gilberton to DC, where he became the lead artist for the newly introduced *Lois Lane* series in 1958.[28] He later illustrated Patricia Relf's

Kurt Schaffenberger, *Soldiers of Fortune* (May 1954). The gringos make South America safe for iron mines.

Adventures of Superman (1982) for Golden Books and inked Curt Swan's pencils in Alan Moore's *Superman: Whatever Happened to the Man of Tomorrow?* (1997) for DC.

THE CHARLTON CONNECTION: SAL TRAPANI, MEDIO IORIO, AND SAL FINOCCHIARO

At about the time that Jerry Iger was finding Gilberton a less than satisfactory channel for his own shop's talents, various artists associated with Charlton Comics were brought on board to illustrate two titles, Sir Henry Morton Stanley's *How I Found Livingstone*, No. 115 (January 1954), and a western biography, *Wild Bill Hickok*, No. 121 (July 1954). Neither book had a distinctively *Classics Illustrated* look about them, and both seemed to suggest that Gilberton, which had recently launched its *Junior* line and the educational *Picture Parade* series for schools, was allowing its main product to drift toward a new, undefined post–Kiefer identity.

Sal Trapani (1927–1999) worked on both issues. He was assisted by other Charlton artists, including Sal Finocchiaro, on *How I Found Livingstone*. The comics

---

Opposite, left: Peter Costanza, *Captains Courageous* (March 1954). Harvey Cheyne grows up. *Right:* Peter Costanza, *The Mutineers* (September 1954): Bright-eyed heroes and villains populated Costanza's panels.

version of Stanley's journalistic quest for the missing missionary was all too often an unsatisfactory hodgepodge of derivative drawings, many of which, according to Hames Ware, had been "lifted in toto from the work of Dell artist Alberto Giolitti."[29] Some of the depictions of Africans are reflexively racist in the offhanded way of 1930s jungle movies, as in the case of an eye-popping medicine man who is given a whiff of ammonia. "Wah!" he cries, falling on the ground, "Medicine too strong! You keep! You keep!"

The adaptation, however, was fast-paced and filled with dramatic episodes, including a fierce sandstorm and the famous greeting itself. Despite other instances of racial stereotyping, the true hero of the tale proves to be Selim, Stanley's intelligent, multilingual African guide, who "can tell what kind of animal broke a leaf of grass, if only one hair of his body has fallen on it."

Sal Trapani and others, *How I Found Livingstone* (**January 1954**). Stanley and Selim weather the sandstorm.

Joining Trapani for *Wild Bill Hickok* was Medio Iorio—the pair gave the Western biography an unmistakable Charlton stamp. Published to capitalize on the popularity of the long-running television series starring Guy Madison and Andy Devine, the *Classics* version, like Mr. Clemens in *Tom Sawyer*, "mainly … told the truth." Still, the artists opted for a clean-shaven, short-haired hero somewhat like the one on TV rather than the mustachioed, hirsute gunslinger of history. (Gilberton later set the pictorial record straight in *Men, Guns and Cattle*, a 1959 *Special Issue* that revealed a more complex figure in fewer pages.) Although *Wild Bill Hickok* was one of the most popular of the later *Classics* titles, with eight printings between 1954 and 1969, the book always seemed a stylistic anomaly in the series.

ACE ARTIST: LIN STREETER

Lin Streeter, a veteran of the fading Ace Comics, came to Gilberton in the early 1950s. He had worked on the Marine comic strip, *Sergeant Stony Craig*, in 1946 and was known for his cartoonish style.[30] An affable man who supported a large family,[31] he drew Frank Buck's *Fang and Claw*, No. 123 (November 1954).

A brisk, sketchy technique brought a light-hearted energy to the adaptation of the famous animal collector's tales of tracking clouded leopards, wild boars, crocodiles, orangutans, and elephants. The artist's best drawings in the book were reserved for the larger panels that introduced each of the stories.

Streeter's finest, and most characteristic, work for Gilberton appeared in the *Classics Illustrated Junior* series: *Thumbelina*, No. 520 (November 1955); *The Frog Prince*, No. 526 (May 1956); *The Golden Bird*, No. 530 (September 1956); *Rapunzel*, No. 531 (October 1956); *The Three Fairies*, No. 537 (April 1957); *The Enchanted Fish*, No. 539 (June 1957); *The House in the Woods*, No. 543 (October 1957); and *The Wishing Table*, No. 547 (February 1958). Of these, *The Enchanted Fish* and *The Wishing Table* display the artist's abundant capacity for visual humor, with his portraits of the overreaching wife in the former title and the thieving innkeeper in the latter. Streeter also provided illustrations for *Picture Progress* that subsequently found their way into a couple of *Special Issues*—*The Story of America*, No. 132-A (June 1956), and *Adventures in Science*, No. 138-A (June 1957). He contributed two chapters to the first number of the *World Around Us* series, *The Illustrated Story of Dogs*, No. W1 (September 1958).

Like Costanza, Trapani, and others, Lin Streeter can be seen as playing a transitional role in the Gilber-

ton story as the publisher searched for a style in the aftermath of the severing of ties with the Iger shop. It remained for his fellow Ace colleagues, Lou Cameron and Norman Nodel, to transform *Classics Illustrated*.

Lin Streeter, *Fang and Claw* (November 1954). Catching a croc. The artist, however, found the fairy tales of *Classics Illustrated Junior* more congenial.

XVIII

Classical Interlude: Ken W. Fitch, Scriptwriter

From 1950 to 1953, Kenneth William Fitch (1908–1965) wrote more than 20 faithful, literate scripts for Gilberton, dramatically enhancing the quality of the series. Formerly a writer for Fox's *Murder Incorporated*, he brought a professional's skills to the task of presenting subject matter of a decidedly different stamp.

Fitch's standard practice was to read the book to be adapted and relevant reference works. The scriptwriter then took extensive notes on the plot, the characters, and the historical setting. In the case of *Daniel Boone: Master of the Wilderness*, he corresponded at some length with author John Bakeless. After outlining the book, drafting background memos that amounted to critical essays, and describing the characters for the benefit of the artist, Fitch would prepare a 40 to 45-page panel-by-panel breakdown.

For *Cyrano de Bergerac*, the scriptwriter offered atmospheric context with a discussion of "The Days of Cyrano": "Paris in the days of Savinien de Cyrano de Bergerac was a city teeming with people threading noisily through her narrow streets. Merchants vended their wares while nobles rode in sedan chairs carried on the shoulders of servants or hirelings. Urchins scampered through the streets between men of the church, the robe, or the guard. And among them all thieves and pickpockets thrived. ... A man who could not fight his own way in the world seldom lived past the first flush of youth."

Besides acting as project historian, Fitch played

Alex A. Blum, *The White Company* (December 1952). The artist follows (more or less) the scriptwriter's directions.

THE WHITE COMPANY

By A. CONAN DOYLE

ILLUSTRATED BY ALEX A. BLUM

When Alleyne Edricson went out into the world, he expected to find it as peaceful and quiet as Beaulieu Abbey, where he had been raised since babyhood by Cistercian monks. In place of peace and quiet, he found trials and tribulations, adventure and adversity, courage and cowardice, life and love. This is the story of Alleyne Edricson's journey into manhood.

104

the scriptwriter's usual role of film-director equivalent, providing, for example, the following detailed instructions for illustrating the page-one splash in *The White Company* by Sir Arthur Conan Doyle, referring the artist to N.C. Wyeth's treatment of the same scene: "The scene is the tilting yard of the Abbey of St. Andrews in Bordeaux, France, in the year 1366. High walls of the abbey close in three sides of the yard, while a swiftly flowing river borders the fourth side. Show trees and rough grass. Two men are dueling desperately. They are Alleyne Edricson and John Trantner. Refer to picture, p. 196. Alleyne's sword is being broken by Trantner's, but instead of showing position of men as they are shown in the illustration, place the men so that Trantner's back is to the river. Several squires stand about watching the fight. Wyeth's illustration of clothes of the period are authentic."

Fitch made extensive use of introductory and connecting rectangular spaces, which in other comics were often reserved for such terse explanations as "Later..." or "Then...," to include more of the story—and the authorial presence—than would have been possible otherwise. In *The Black Tulip*, for instance, the scriptwriter points up, in an adjacent narrative panel, the irony of the hero's situation as he is being marched to the executioner's block: "As Cornelius followed the guards to the scaffold, his mind dwelt bitterly on fate's sudden paradox; for where John and Cornelius de Witt had lost their lives for having thought too much of politics, he, Cornelius van Baerle, was about to lose his life for having thought too much of tulips." It was precisely this sort of emphasis on text that caused friends and foes of *Classics Illustrated* to revere or revile them as atypical comic books.

XIX

"If John Wayne Had Drawn Comic Books": Lou Cameron

"If John Wayne had drawn comic books," Hames Ware observed, "he would have been Lou Cameron."[1] There is, indeed, something larger than life about the artist turned writer, who won awards in both capacities. His drawings and painted covers for *Classics Illustrated* from 1953 to 1956 included some of the most vital artwork published in the series. In addition, the broad-smiling, hearty characters he drew reflected his own expansive personality.

Born in San Francisco on 20 June 1924, the son of actor Louis Arnold and Ziegfeld girl Ruth Marvin (through whom he was first cousin to actor Lee Marvin), Cameron studied at the California School of Fine Arts. Dropping out to join the army after the Japanese attack on Pearl Harbor, he served as an artillery scout and combat instructor in the European theater during World War II. He became a technical sergeant and won the Bronze Star, the Purple Heart, and three battle stars.[2]

At various times, the professed "Deathbed Catholic" worked as a movie extra, a private detective, a ranch hand, and a trucker. Between 1950 and 1960, Cameron free-lanced for magazines and comic books. For *The Man Who Discovered America*, a pictorial biography of Columbus that he drew for Gilberton's *Picture Progress* educational series, he received the Thomas Alva Edison Award in 1956.[3]

Abruptly turning his back on commercial art in 1957, Cameron began a successful career as the author of such novels as *The Block Busters*, *The Big Red Ball*, *The Dirty War of Sgt. Slade*, *The Amphorae Pirates*, *Cybernia*, *How the West Was Won*, *The Wilderness Seekers*, and *The Grass of Goodnight*. As he put it, "I went home and threw out my drawing board, set up the first typewriter I had ever bought, and announced I was a writer, period. I have never regretted the move."[4] In 1976, he won the Spur Award for his western novel, *The Spirit Horses*.

Cameron the author felt no warm nostalgia for his days as a comics artist. He wrote that "[N]one of us at the time thought we were doing all that much but paying the rent whilst we waited for Norman Rockwell to die and give us a crack at the real money. When a panel went well you smiled and inked it. When it came out a mess you considered what they were paying you and inked it."[5]

Several years after the end of World War II, Cameron, who "wanted to be an illustrator," had found himself "hand painting china lamps signed by the artist."[6] Deciding that comics "had to be an improvement," he broke into the field with publisher Billy Friedman, who paid $23 a page, "which was low, but, Lord, he was easy to please and always wrote you a check the day after you delivered."[7] Later, he did some work for DC and Timely (Atlas) before "finding a fairly steady niche with Ace," where the page rate was $32. Cameron became known in the early 1950s for his skull-strewn horror illustrations, which, however, were less overtly horrific than those of some of his contemporaries.[8]

In 1953, Ace and Gilberton both used the Bob MacLeod studio for Leroy-lettering penciled pages. Meyer A. Kaplan, managing editor of *Classics Illustrated*, recruited Cameron and Lin Streeter to freelance for the series. The rate was $5 less per page than Ace paid, but the 44 to 47 pages of artwork in a *Classics* issue more than compensated for the difference.

Kaplan evidently recognized and had confidence in Cameron's abilities. For his first assignment, the artist was given the task of completely redrawing a newly scripted edition of one of the most popular titles, Robert Louis Stevenson's *Dr. Jekyll and Mr. Hyde*, No. 13 (October 1953), which had been horribly adapted and crudely drawn in its original *Classic Comics* incarnation. This was the first of 30 earlier titles to be reissued with new illustrations and, with one exception, texts.

The revised *Dr. Jekyll and Mr. Hyde* remains one of the most compelling *Classics*. Eschewing the horror style employed by Arnold Hicks in 1943 (except for the trademark skull here and there), Cameron brought to the surface the internal conflict in Robert Louis Stevenson's parable of human duality, emphasizing the moral desperation in both the respected physician and his criminal alter ego through dramatic shading and imaginative angles.

Technically, Cameron's most interesting work for Gilberton was another Stevenson project—a pair of South Seas tales, "The Bottle Imp" and "The Beach of Falesa," issued together under the title, *The Bottle Imp*, No. 116 (February 1954). Harry Miller's adaptation of "Falesa," Stevenson's critique of colonial exploitation, softened the sexual and racial overtones and dispensed altogether with the distinctive first-person voice of the narrator, Wiltshire, and hence the author's carefully crafted irony. Still, it is to the publisher's credit that editor Meyer A. Kaplan recognized the neglected tale's merit at a time when both high school and university English departments largely ignored Stevenson's innovative later fiction.

Following the example of science-fiction illustrator Ed Cartier, the artist experimented with a Wolff carbon pencil instead of inking, which resulted in more textured panels in both "The Beach of Falesa" and "The Bottle Imp." The technique allowed Cameron, who excelled in rendering strenuous action, to experiment with shading

Left: Lou Cameron, *Dr. Jekyll and Mr. Hyde* (October 1953). Ten years after the misbegotten *Classic Comics* edition, *Classics Illustrated* revisits Stevenson's psychological fable. *Right:* Lou Cameron, "The Beach of Falesa" in *The Bottle Imp* (February 1954). The artist's Wolff carbon pencil in action.

and to achieve a dynamically fluid effect in three full-page illustrations in the Stevenson issue.

Another superbly drafted South Sea adventure followed—Charles Nordhoff and James Norman Hall's *The Hurricane*, No. 120 (June 1954), for which he supplied both the interior art and the painted cover. (See color section.) The 14-page sequence showing the storm building to its climax reaches a dramatic culmination in a splash page filled with streaked and swirled linework representing the deadly tempest. Of his illustrations in 1954, Cameron remarked, "I think some of my earlier work for *Classics* was better because I was simply allowed to draw it, hand it in, and cash the modest check."[9]

If any *Classics Illustrated* title has assured the artist a place in comics history, it is his spectacular rendering of H.G. Wells's *The War of the Worlds*, No. 124 (January 1955), for which he also painted the cover. (See color sec-

Lou Cameron, *The Hurricane* (June 1954). A tropical storm's intensity conveyed in the movement of lines.

tion.) Cameron's gripping visual narrative featured the definitive depiction of the deadly Martian tripods. A two-page splash portrayed the lethal effect of the aliens' attack in one of the most memorable drawings ever to appear in the series. Several decades later, when First Publishing attempted to revive *Classics Illustrated*, artist Ken Steacy was asked to provide artwork for a new edition of *The War of the Worlds*. He advised the editor simply to reprint Cameron's version. "There is no way I could do it any better," Steacy is reported as having said.[10]

Emile Zola's ironic novel of the Franco-Prussian War, *The Downfall* (*La Débâcle*), No. 126 (May 1955), was, with "The Beach of Falesa," one of the more mature literary adaptations that Cameron illustrated for Gilberton. It also featured Cameron's most polished work for the series. His one-page minidrama of Henriette Weiss's arrival at the scene of her husband's imminent execution and his two-page treatment of Jean Macquart mortally wounding his friend, Maurice Levasseur, are concise triumphs of sequential art.

Beginning in July 1955 with issue No. 127, *Classics Illustrated* ran a 12-part "Story of Great Britain" as a two-page, back-of-the-book spread. Cameron illustrated all of the installments and obviously relished working on the first seven ("The Celtic Invasion" through "The Elizabethan Age"), lavishing attention upon Roman, Saxon, Norse, Norman, and Tudor arms, armor, and costumes.

Davy Crockett, No. 129 (November 1955), was issued by Gilberton in an effort to capitalize on the coonskin-cap craze sparked by Walt Disney's three-part *Disneyland* television production (1954–1955) loosely based on the Tennessee congressman and Alamo martyr's life. Based in part on David Crockett's 1834 *Autobiography*, the *Classics Illustrated* version offered young readers a reasonably faithful account of the colorful frontiersman's life.

Unfortunately, the bimonthly *Classics* publication schedule didn't accommodate fads very well, and the Crockett phenomenon, which had peaked in the early spring of 1955, had played itself out by autumn. The first printing was available until 1961 and then temporarily withdrawn; a second, and final, printing appeared in 1966.

At about the time that Cameron was given *Davy Crockett*, his disagreements with then untitled editorial assistant Roberta Strauss about "alterations," which had been accelerating since *The Hurricane*, were coming to a head. Strauss, who would later become editor-in-chief, had a passion for historical accuracy, textual fidelity, and pictorial continuity. Cameron, who had his own sense of historical accuracy, textual fidelity, and pictorial continuity, found her editorial directives meddlesome and an infringement upon the artist's creative sphere.

The result was a halfhearted effort in *Davy Crockett*.

24   CLASSICS *Illustrated*

"THE NEXT MOMENT, OUR BIG GUN EXPLODED, THE AMMUNITION BLEW UP, AND THERE WAS FIRE AND DEATH ALL AROUND ME."

Lou Cameron, *The War of the Worlds* (January 1955). Mars attacks! The artist's conception of the original alien invasion story is regarded by many as definitive.

"I tried to cope," Cameron wrote, "leaving a few things roughly drawn so I could 'Alterate' in a way that didn't matter. You can see how steamed I was...."[11] Some of the panels seem rushed, and the characteristic Cameron brio gleams only intermittently. Yet when it does, as in a hunting episode or at the Alamo, the legendary hero (who bears more than a passing resemblance to the artist) leaps to life.

For H.G. Wells's *The Time Machine*, No. 133 (July 1956), Cameron "perked up ... because it was fun, or would have been."[12] The artist's Morlocks remind the reader of Swift's Yahoos, while his time machine is an elegant contraption that resembles, as Robert Franks has noted, electrons orbiting an atom, a potent symbol in the 1950s.

But the text was flawed by scriptwriter Lorenz Graham's sentimental unwillingness to follow the novel's ending. Moreover, editorial demands that the artist alter the Time Traveller's features to conform to the figure on the painted cover resulted in his most frustrating *Classics Illustrated* assignment. Cameron "made dumb changes to 'Suit The Original Mss' and get my damned money," but his distaste for Gilberton had reached critical mass.[13]

Then, just when it appeared that things couldn't get worse, they did. As Cameron tells the story, his Christopher Columbus book, *The Man Who Discovered America*, which originally appeared in the *Picture Progress* series (September 1955) and was subsequently included in *Classics Illustrated Special Issue* No. 132A, *The Story of America* (June 1956), "won a prize off the Thomas Edison Foundation, do gooders who cited it as an outstanding educational comic book for kiddies blah blah. They threw a dinner at a swank New York hotel and handed out various citations to various swell guys like me. Only I never got the invitation reserving places for me and my then current lady. The first I heard I had won in the comix category was by phone, from friends who'd read it in the trades. This inspired me to call Gilberton. Without so

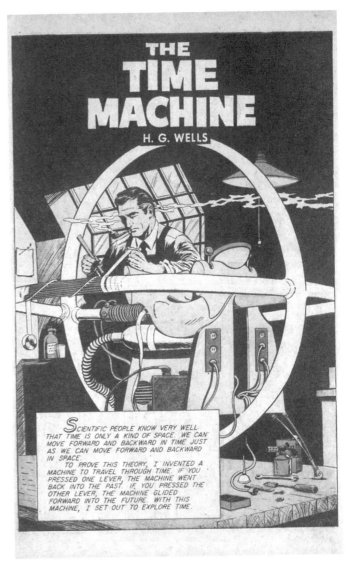

Left: Lou Cameron, *The Downfall* (May 1955). Henriette Weiss witnesses her husband's execution. *Right:* Lou Cameron, *The Time Machine* (July 1956). The artist was obliged to redraw the Time Traveller's head in 172 panels to match the face on the subsequently painted cover.

much as a hangdog grin I was given my citation from the Edison guys and told they hadn't forwarded my invitation because members of the staff had wanted to go to the dinner. I mean, they didn't even know this was not nice!"[14]

A final *Classics* project, a revision of Alexandre Dumas's epic of revenge, *The Count of Monte Cristo*, No. 3 (November 1956), afforded Cameron the opportunity to even the score with Gilberton. While the artist's illustrations included some interesting, if often spare, panel compositions, such as Edmond Dantes's shrouded escape from Château d'If, much of the book was filled with half-hearted, shortcut efforts. Cameron obviously had lost interest in the job, and his vented his distaste for the script by rewriting the speech balloons. In one panel, he has the

Count making a homosexual overture to another character, saying, "After ten years in prison, anything looks good." Later, speaking to Danglars, Dantes declares, "I condemn you also to die of boredom, as this is almost the end of the story."[15] The editorial staff was not amused, and after Leroy lettering restored the original script, the artist was offered no further *Classics Illustrated* assignments.

"I would like to say I quit," Cameron wrote. "But they never gave any of us the chance. ... I wasn't there when *Classics* went down the tube but I wasn't surprised. The hell of it was, ... it began as one of the best ideas in the field. Say what you like about Stan Lee and his ego trips, sensible management and consistent art work did keep the tight-underwear Comix going."[16]

XX

"A Certain Integrity": Norman Nodel

During the late 1950s and early 1960s, the prolific and accomplished Norman Nodel defined the increasingly polished *Classics Illustrated* house style. The soft-spoken artist dominated Gilberton's stable of freelancers in much the same way that Henry C. Kiefer had a decade earlier. Indeed, in terms of output, if any artist deserves to be called, as Kiefer was, "Mr. *Classics Illustrated*," it is Norman Nodel. In his quiet, unassuming way, he managed to outdraw and outlast them all.

Nodel has been described by former editor and scriptwriter Al Sundel as "a gentleman [of] the jacket-and-tie type, with a pleasing politeness";[1] his praises have been sung both as illustrator and man by artists as different in temperament as Lou Cameron and George Evans. A protégé of Alex A. Blum, the veteran art director, he was a favorite, along with Evans and Gray Morrow, of Roberta Strauss Feuerlicht, the young, energetic editor who entrusted him with various major projects.

Among Nodel's strengths were a good compositional eye, a realistic approach to his subjects, an instinct for appropriate atmosphere, close attention to period detail, and an ability to create convincing caricatures and fantastic figures within a solidly representational context. These qualities enabled him to produce some of the finest and most memorable books in the series.

Born in Phoebus, Virginia, near Hampton Roads, in 1922, Nodel spent his formative years in St. Louis, Missouri, where he developed an early interest in singing. At 15, he auditioned for the St. Louis Opera Chorus, impressing the conductor, Laslo Halasz, with his youthful bass voice. Nodel performed with the chorus through the season and was sponsored by the company and a contributor to study in New York.

"One of the roles I studied," he wrote, "was Mephistopheles in *Faust*. When I drew the artwork for the *Classics* edition of *Faust*, some of the mannerisms and the way that I depicted Mephisto were very much influenced by the way I had studied the role and the tutoring I had received from the dramatic coach."[2]

While his musical career was taking shape, Nodel explored another creative passion, drawing and painting constantly. "At that time," he recalled, "I was offered two scholarships; one to the National Academy of Design and one to Juilliard to study composition. I was forced to decline both by my sponsors, my voice coach, my voice teacher, and my dramatic instructor."[3]

Nodel served in the European Theater in the Second World War, winning the Bronze Star as a combat artist. In 1945, he was asked to perform at the celebration of the meeting of the American and Russian armies, where "top American brass and top Russian brass joined me in singing the 'Volga Boatmen.'"[4]

After the war, Nodel became the art director for an advertising agency. There he specialized in tight renderings using airbrush and scratchboard, techniques that would be put to use later in *Classics Illustrated*. After a year of producing ads for the Tourneau watch, William Wise, and others, the artist decided to "go free lance."[5] Among his accounts was Ace Comics, which also employed *Classics* artists Lou Cameron, Lin Streeter, and Louis Zansky.

Norman Nodel's association with the Gilberton Company began in 1954. "When I first went there," the artist recalled, "I submitted a portfolio to [art director] Alex Blum, who told me that *The Ox-Bow Incident* was scheduled for publication and asked me to work up a

Norman Nodel, *The Ox-Bow Incident* (March 1955). Powerful character studies in the artist's first assignment led to the
longest freelance association in the history of the publication.

page for it. I did and then was hired."[6] Nodel's illustrations for issue No. 125 (March 1955) caught the stark,
somber mood of Walter Van Tilburg Clark's tragic study
of mob justice in the waning days of the Wild West.
From the disillusioned narrator Croft with his dangling
cigarette to the implacable self-appointed executioner
Tetly with his unforgiving profile, from the earnest de-
fender of the rule of law, Davies, to the anguished innocent victim Martin, the artist tellingly conveyed the
essence of the novel's characters.

During the same period, Nodel also worked on
Gilberton's *Picture Progress* educational series, earning
the respect of the editorial staff for his reliability. His
next *Classics* assignment was an adaptation of *The King
of the Mountains*, No. 127 (July 1955), a little-known

French satirical work based on author Edmond About's
experiences among Greek bandits. The title allowed the
artist scope for his gift for caricature, and he applied
it gleefully to such types as the pedantic German narrator and the snobbish English hostages. Nodel returned
to Western terrain for Emerson Hough's combination of
morality play and romantic triangle, *The Covered
Wagon*, No. 131 (March 1956), but the drawings—and
particularly the inking—lacked the subtlety of his previous efforts.

In short order, the Gilberton editorial staff recognized the artist's merits and assigned him the task of illustrating revamped editions of significant earlier titles,
beginning with the two most popular books in the history of the series, *Moby Dick*, No. 5 (revised edition,
March 1956), and *Ivanhoe*, No. 2 (revised edition, January 1957). For the new adaptation of *Moby Dick*, issued
in the same year as John Huston's film, Nodel avoided
turning Captain Ahab into Gregory Peck and Ishmael
into Richard Basehart; instead, he chose to model his
characters' features on Louis Zansky's familiar 1942 *Classic Comics* drawings. But where Zansky's panels were
clearly in the comics tradition, Nodel's obviously belonged to the family of book illustration. (In addition, a
more accurate script restored some of Herman Melville's
language, including the famous opening line, "Call me
Ishmael.") The artist devoted particular attention to giving visual expression to the inner torment of Ahab as he
harangues or mesmerizes his crew.

Nodel's work on *Ivanhoe* also bore some resemblance
to the Jacquet shop's 1941 interpretation of Sir Walter
Scott's medieval romance. Here, however, the artist, who
was light-years ahead in technique, invested the various
characters with well-observed personality distinctions,
animating even the rather passive nominal hero. In *Ivanhoe*, he perfected his closeup character studies and also
displayed his flair for historical detail, from weaponry to
falconry. The result was one of the most handsome issues
in the *Classics Illustrated* catalogue.

For *The Ten Commandments*, *Special Issue* No. 135A
(December 1956), Nodel's commitment to authenticity
was further evidenced. In addition to studying the ma-
terials provided by Gilberton's research staff, the artist
spent an afternoon with Dr. William C. Hayes, the curator of New York's Metropolitan Museum of Art, who
showed him various antiquities that found their way into
the book's illustrations.[7] Nodel noted that "I used the
scratchboard technique in *The Ten Commandments* and
Faust. This is a method in which the illustrations are
'scratched' out of a completely black surface."[8] The experiment allowed the artist to enhance the effect of the
interplay between darkness and light. His painted cover
for *The Ten Commandments*, on the other hand, is awash

Norman Nodel, *Moby Dick* (March 1956). Dramatic linework underscored the intensity of Ahab's address to the doomed crew of the *Pequod*.

in red and yellow as Moses receives the tablets of the law. (See color section.)

After *The Ten Commandments* and *Ivanhoe*, which had kept him occupied for a considerable length of time, Nodel turned his attention to Jules Verne's *A Journey to the Center of the Earth*, No. 138 (May 1957). One of the most popular titles in the *Classics Illustrated* series, the science-fiction tale offered the artist a small number of characters and great imaginative scope. Nodel seized the opportunity, adding depth to his portrayal of the trio of subterranean adventurers and providing exotic views of imagined landscapes and extinct creatures. Among his most effective sequences in *Journey* was a depiction of the terror experienced by the narrator as he realizes he is lost underground. The artist returned to Verne for one of his last Gilberton projects, *Tigers and Traitors*, No. 166 (May 1962).

Versatility was one of Nodel's most esteemed qualities, and he showed it in his animal illustrations for Frank Buck's *On Jungle Trails*, No. 140 (September 1957), Ernest Thompson Seton's *Lives of the Hunted*, No. 157 (July 1960), and Anna Sewell's *Black Beauty*, No. 60 (revised edition, Fall 1960). The Seton book is particularly noteworthy for its examples of the artist's sequential experimentation.

Although the quality of *Classics Illustrated* artwork had dramatically improved during the years Nodel was associated with Gilberton, it had been at the cost of a certain homogenization in the format of the series. This was particularly evident in the almost universal prescription of square or rectangular panels with straight-edged borders. These gave the pages a clean, crisp look but sacrificed much of the function of the panel as a narrative device as employed, for example, by Rudy Palais in *David Balfour*. Comics artist and theorist Will Eisner has noted that the very shape or absence of the panel can further the momentum of the story by conveying "something of the dimension of sound and emotional climate

in which the action occurs, as well as contributing to the atmosphere of the page as a whole."[9]

Breaks from the straight-lined box were rare in *Classics Illustrated* after 1957, but even within those constraints, Nodel showed his command of the medium. In *Lives of the Hunted*, he made the convention work in his favor in a sequence of four elongated panels on one page showing the stages of a hunted ram's leap for safety down the sides of a steep gorge. The artist retained the full-length frame on the next page but widened it to depict the ram's entire flock following his example. Half-length panels then revealed the fate of the pursuing dogs and the bafflement of the hunters.

The artist demonstrated his mastery of historical illustration in *Abraham Lincoln*, No. 142 (January 1958), G.A. Henty's *The Lion of the North*, No. 155

Norman Nodel, *Ivanhoe* (January 1957). One of the artist's favorite illustrations in one of his favorite books.

Norman Nodel, *A Journey to the Center of the Earth* **(May 1957). The artist partially conceals the narrator's face to focus the reader's attention on the eyes and the movement of the hand.**

(March 1960), H. Rider Haggard's *Cleopatra*, No. 161 (March 1961), and in various *Special Issues* and *World Around Us* titles. For the Lincoln biography, Nodel relied

on a variety of period photographs and portraits. The Henty adaptation contained well-researched drawings of the middle phase of the Thirty Years' War, while *Cleopatra* included a wealth of Hellenized Egyptian details. His depiction of the execution of Louis XVI, in *The French Revolution*, No. W14 (September 1959), revealed an acquaintance with documentary accounts of the event.

Two books issued in the spring of 1959 showed the artist moving toward a new range of expression. Both Owen Wister's *The Virginian*, No. 150 (May 1959), and Washington Irving's *Rip Van Winkle*, No. 12 (revised edition, May 1959), featured a greater emphasis on shading to set the tone of a particular sequence of panels. The latter title included "The Legend of Sleepy Hollow," which contains one of the most delightful renderings of the hapless, lanky schoolmaster Ichabod Crane, quaking with fear at the sight of the Headless Horseman. (These illustrations served the artist so well that he used them as models for another edition of the story in 1970.[10]) The

Norman Nodel, *Lives of the Hunted* **(July 1960). Vertical panels emphasize the breathtaking nature of a ram's escape.**

Norman Nodel, "The Legend of Sleepy Hollow" in *Rip Van Winkle* (May 1959). Ichabod Crane meets the Headless Horseman.

new adaptation, unlike the 1943 version, was faithful to Irving's sketches, incorporating the author's language and conveying his gently satirical tone of voice.

Regarding his technique, Nodel commented that "At first I did mostly outline work as Mr. Blum directed, but in the later period I was able to add stronger blacks to attain richer texture."[11] The shift in style became particularly pronounced in *The Invisible Man*, No. 153 (November 1959), where a striking scratchboard title-page splash and detailed drybrush strokes and pointillist dots in the opening pages immediately create a suspenseful atmosphere for the H.G. Wells "horror" title.

The finest examples of the artist's mature style are found in two Victor Hugo titles, *Les Miserables*, No. 9 (revised edition, March 1961), and *The Man Who Laughs*, No. 71 (revised edition, spring 1962), and Goethe's *Faust* (August 1962). Somber shadings underscore the social messages of the Hugo adaptations. Nodel's three-page sequence in *Les Miserables* showing Jean Valjean bearing Marius through the Paris sewers masterfully compresses the themes of degradation, aspiration, and renewal.

In *The Man Who Laughs*, the artist produced a more startling conception of the disfigured Gwynplaine than Alex Blum's 1950 rendering. Alfred Sundel's adaptation

passed over the happy ending that had been tacked on to the earlier edition, and Nodel invested Hugo's parable of oppression with tragic dignity and a sharply satirical thrust.

Editor Roberta Strauss Feuerlicht considered the artist's treatment of *Faust* the pinnacle of Gilberton's achievement. It ranked with the Hugo books and the Irving stories among Nodel's favorites. Alfred Sundel, who wrote the script, recalled that the Goethe title was "done at my insistence to impress the [American Library Association] and booksellers' and educational conventions. I wrote *Faust* in a blaze on a weekend and in a few evenings, quickly, while I was on staff. It may have been one of the toughest scripts ever for me. Roberta gave it to Norman Nodel, and it took off as our showroom Cadillac."[12] Indeed, the appearance of the book, which transcended the comics category, prompted William Kanter's wry remark that "We make Cadillacs and market them as Chevrolets."

In addition to the intelligent adaptation, *Faust* provides a visual feast, with Nodel adroitly moving from baroque profuseness in Part I to classical spareness in Part II. Part of the artist's inspiration came from the stage. When he was working on the book, a German theater company came to New York for a rare production of Goethe's drama. Gilberton purchased two tickets for the artist and his wife so that he would have a more complete frame of reference for his illustrations. "That was the sort of care that they took," Nodel said.[13]

The deadline for *Faust* was tight; a booksellers' convention was looming, and the book was to be the centerpiece of the Gilberton display. The artist returned to the scratchboard style that had worked so well for him in *The Ten Commandments*. Nodel discovered that no sooner had he completed a penciled sketch for the cover than it was colored in by art director Sidney Miller and used in place of the painting he had intended to provide. "That was my only regret about the book," the artist remarked. "It [the cover] looked so unfinished."[14]

The next project was, in fact, left unfinished. In 1962, Roberta Strauss Feuerlicht assigned Nodel a revision of *The Pathfinder*, No. 22, which he had partially completed when the domestic *Classics* operation abruptly came to a halt. The boards remained with the artist but were eventually discarded after sustaining water damage.[15]

Left: Norman Nodel, *The Invisible Man* (November 1959). Nodel's scratchboard technique immediately sets the mood for the science-fiction thriller. *Right:* Norman Nodel, *Les Miserables* (March 1961). Darkness and light provide thematic contrasts in the illustrations for Victor Hugo's masterpiece.

Turning elsewhere for employment, the artist produced a treatment of *Doctor No*, the first James Bond film, for DC's *Showcase* series. The artwork was censored for what were deemed racially insensitive portrayals, but before the toned-down American edition appeared, an unexpurgated edition surfaced as British *Classics Illustrated* No. 158A. Near the end of the decade, Gilberton's successor, Frawley, engaged Nodel to produce a variety of new painted covers, including *A Tale of Two Cities, Les Miserables, Jane Eyre,* and *20,000 Leagues Under the Sea*; to overhaul completely *The Jungle Book*; and to illustrate the final *Classics* title, *Negro Americans—The Early Years,* No. 169 (Spring 1969).

Working in his Long Island backyard when weather permitted, Nodel enjoyed the frequent visits of neighborhood high school students who "knew I was working on *Classics* and would come to see what I was doing to get ideas for book reports."[16] In the 1990s, he continued producing artwork for educational and religious publications aimed at younger readers, such as historical and Biblical coloring books and card games and a 12-book series of full-color paintings depicting favorite Biblical stories for Waldman–Creative Child Press and several comic books, including *The Story of Money* and *The Story of Inflation,* for the Federal Reserve.

"It was my good fortune," Nodel wrote, "to work with a visionary publisher, Mr. Albert Kanter, and a dedicated editor, Roberta Strauss Feuerlicht. We shared a common dream: to improve on an authentic American art form, the comic book, raising it to a high level of quality so that we could attract children who would otherwise never be introduced to the great world of literature. I was also very proud to share this goal with George Evans, Lou Cameron, and other outstanding artists."[17]

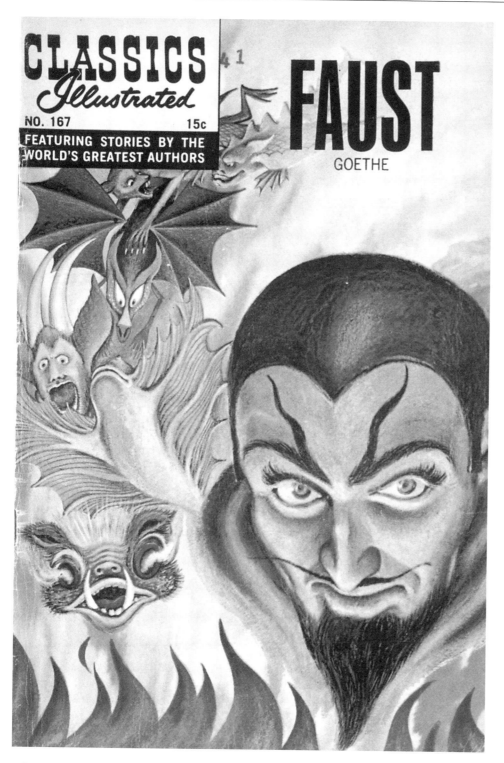

Norman Nodel, *Faust* (August 1962). A rush-order preliminary cover design became, to the artist's dismay, the real thing.

AN ARTIST'S NOTES

Norman Nodel on the creation of the artwork for a *Classics Illustrated* issue:

After conferring with Roberta [Strauss Feuerlicht] about the next story to be illustrated, I would often make sketches of characters and backgrounds. We would exchange ideas. I then proceeded to lay out the entire story, breaking the artwork into panels and lettering in the script so the letterer could gauge his or her spacing.

In illustrating a story, you, the artist, are like a movie director. You choose the cast, act as scenic designer, angle the dramatic shots, distant, close-up, down shots, up shots; whatever you feel adds interest and drama to the story. And let's not forget about research! Here is where you must avoid being sidetracked by some fascinating bit of historical information and lose valuable time. Sometimes *Classics* would provide me with some important reference.

Upon completion of pencils, Roberta and other editorial staff would "fine-tooth comb" every panel, making comments in blue pencil on the margins of the work, sometimes to your irritation. You often had to stand your ground about your interpretation.

After this procedure, the inking began. I used a Number 3 Windsor Newton Sable brush. In some stories, I used brush throughout, often employing a technique called 'feathering.' This required a very delicate touch to the tip of your brush where you made the brush spread gradually by increasing pressure. This was often repeated, one line next to another till you created an almost half-tone effect. It may also be done in reverse fashion. In other stories, I used pen first, then added brush.

—Letter to author, 25 July 1997

Illustrating 48-page books with an eye to authenticity was "tough work," the artist said, "but I enjoyed it, and I tried to keep a certain integrity in what I did."[18] Decades later, it still shows.

XXI

From the Crypt to the Classics: The EC Era

By 1954, the term "witch hunt" had gained great currency, thanks to Senator Joseph McCarthy, the Wisconsin Republican whose continually inflating demagoguery would soon be punctured by a few quietly spoken words. That year, the comics industry endured the climax of its own witch hunt, spearheaded by a rather unlikely figure, Dr. Fredric Wertham (1895–1981), a German-born psychiatrist and theorist aligned, like his friend Theodor Adorno, with the neo–Marxist Frankfurt School, which viewed American mass culture with a critical eye.[1]

Few people have had a greater impact on the history of the comic book and its place in popular culture than Wertham. Like Thomas Bowdler, Anthony Comstock, or, for that matter, Joe McCarthy, his name has become—in comics circles, at least—a byword for prudery, bigotry, and persecution. It was an ironic twist for one whose critique of comic books was grounded in passionately liberal, or even leftist, social concerns and was anything but a reactionary gesture. To the end, he protested (though perhaps too much) that his intentions had been misconstrued and, having rung the death knell for the Golden Age of comics in the mid–1950s, surprised many with a sympathetic study of comics fandom in *The World of Fanzines* (1973).

Born Frederic J. Wertheimer in Nuremberg on 20 March 1895, the future cultural lightning rod received his medical degree in Germany and furthered his education in France and England. In 1921, he began his career in psychiatry at Emile Kraepelin's clinic in Munich, where the importance of the patient's environment was emphasized. Wertheimer emigrated to the United States in 1922, settled in Baltimore, and joined the staff and eventually became director of the Phipps Psychiatric Clinic

at Johns Hopkins University. Five years later, on becoming a United States citizen, he changed his last name to Wertham. (In 1948, "Frederic" became "Fredric," to the everlasting confusion of bibliographers.)[2]

Wertham moved to New York City in 1932 to serve as senior psychiatrist in the New York City Department of Hospitals and to teach at New York University. Before his eternal link to comics was forged, he earned professional distinction as the author, with his wife Florence Hesketh Wertham, of the influential textbook, *The Brain as an Organ: Its Postmortem Study and Interpretation* (1934). From 1933 to 1939, Wertham held various positions at New York's Bellevue Hospital and in 1940 assumed the psychiatric-services directorship at Queens Hospital. Focusing on the link between mental health and violent crime, he established the first psychiatric facility to provide evaluations for convicted criminals. A proponent of racial equality, the psychiatrist in 1946 helped found the Lafargue Clinic for low-income and black patients in Harlem.[3]

Wertham entered the realm of popular culture with his best-selling *Dark Legend: A Study in Murder* (1941), an account of a teenager who killed his mother. Another work, the sensationally titled *The Show of Violence: A Psychiatrist Tells Why People Kill and How Murder Can Be Prevented* (1949), further solidified his standing as a popularizer of psychiatric research and purveyor of psychological speculation.

During the late 1940s, when the crime-comics wave was at its peak, Wertham, who had been working extensively with children, began focusing on comic books as a key to antisocial, abnormal behavior. In March 1948, while serving as president of the Association for the

Advancement of Psychotherapy, he chaired a symposium on "The Psychopathology of Comic Books." Wertham claimed that comic books promoted sex and violence, asserting that in each of his case studies of juvenile delinquents and disturbed children, the reading of comic books was a significant factor.[4]

The psychiatrist's critique of comic books touched a nerve at a time when what was termed "juvenile delinquency" aroused intense national concern. In 1948, *Time* magazine reported several "copycat" crimes—burglary, hanging, and poisoning—committed by youths who had been inspired by examples in comic books. In the same year, ABC radio presented a program titled "What's Wrong With Comics?"[5]

Despite dissenting opinions from the psychiatric community concerning Wertham's methodology, the anticomics crusade gathered increasing publicity and support in the late 1940s and early 1950s. The principal targets were crime and horror comic books such as Lev Gleason's *Crime Does Not Pay* and EC's *Haunt of Fear* that continued to multiply with each new wave of aroused indignation.[6]

Classics Illustrated was not exempted from the attacks. Earlier titles, including *Dr. Jekyll and Mr. Hyde*, *The Hunchback of Notre Dame*, *The Prince and the Pauper*, and *Twenty Years After*, had been criticized for covers depicting extreme violence, and Henry C. Kiefer was kept busy in 1949 supplying tepid replacements. Yet even Kiefer had contributed "horror" covers of his own to *The Adventures of Sherlock Holmes*, *Mysteries*, *Great Expectations*, and *Mysteries of Paris*. In 1952, when *Great Expectations* generated controversy because of the intensity of the cover depiction of two convicts struggling and the opening graveyard scene, the title was dropped from the U.S. series, though it remained in print abroad.

The New York Legislature was so exercised by the threat to decency posed by comic books that it created a Joint Legislative Committee to Study the Publication of Comics, which held hearings in New York City in December 1951. Among the authorities invited to appear was the increasingly ubiquitous Dr. Fredric Wertham, who declared that comic books caused the "psychological mutilation of children."[7]

Classics Illustrated managing editor Meyer A. Kaplan delivered a measured defense of the series in his concluding remarks:

> But in all humility, I suggest that the child who has no interest in good literature will never, of his own choice, read it. Forcible feeding of the classics will make no more impression on him than a visit to the Museum of Art will make on a child who has no interest in fine art. The taste for good literature and fine art must be cultivated in a child slowly. He must be made to understand it before he can like it. By forcing him to read the truly heavy and none too easily understood language of the classics while still too young to appreciate it, a dislike for good reading will be cultivated rather than an interest. But a pictorial rendering of the great stories of the world which can be easily understood and therefore more readily liked would tend to cultivate that interest. Then, when he grows older, if he has any appetite at all for these things, he will want to know more fully those bookish treasures merely suggested in this, his first acquaintance with them. He will more eagerly read them in the original form because he will already have a mind's eye picture of what the author was trying to portray in words. He will be able to visualize the protagonists: he will know how they looked and dressed and amidst what backgrounds and surroundings they worked, fought, loved and died. The names of d'Artagnan, Ivanhoe, Jean Valjean and other famous characters in the world of literature will be no strangers to him.[8]

The committee issued a report in 1955, finding Gilberton's *3 Famous Mysteries*, *The Pathfinder*, and *Two Years Before the Mast* especially reprehensible and declaring that "a quick examination readily reveals that the use of the word 'classics' is no guarantee against the presentation of brutality and violence."[9] In the fall of that year, *3 Famous Mysteries* and *Two Years Before the Mast* disappeared from the reorder list.

Meanwhile, the tireless Dr. Wertham had weighed in with his own condemnation of *Classics Illustrated*—and, for that matter, comic books in general. With the publication in 1954 of *Seduction of the Innocent*, he earned a species of immortality. The overwrought jeremiad was abstracted in the *Reader's Digest*, the popular conservative oracle, and was an alternate selection of the Book of the Month Club. It captured the reflexive public imagination and remains perhaps the single most important, and certainly the most influential, book ever written on comics.

Seduction of the Innocent amplified the themes sounded by Wertham since 1948. The author indiscriminately lumped a wide range of comics together, indicting crime, horror, and romance series for their dangerous influence on susceptible young minds. To underscore his concerns, he reproduced, out of context and apparently without obtaining copyright permissions, 16 pages of panels and covers from different publications. Although Wertham included examples of violence and horror, he seemed particularly obsessed with images of buxom, leggy, half-clad women, such as Matt Baker's bound and headlighted Phantom Lady. Evidently warming to the subject, the good doctor managed to detect a hidden image of a woman's pubic hair in an enlargement of triangular shading on a man's shoulder: "In ordinary comic books," he noted beneath the panel in question, "there are pictures within pictures for children who know how to look."[10] Or, one is tempted to add, for adults who try hard to find.

Naturally, *Classics Illustrated* attracted Wertham's attention and disapproval. The subjective, anecdotal character of *Seduction of the Innocent* is distilled in the following paragraph:

> Comic books adapted from classical literature are reportedly used in 25,000 schools in the United States. If this is true, then I have never heard a more serious indictment of American education, for they emasculate the classics, condense them (leaving out everything that makes the book great), are just as badly printed and inartistically drawn as other comic books and, as I have often found, do *not* reveal to children the world of good literature which has at all times been the mainstay of liberal and humanistic education. They conceal it. The folklorist, G. Legman, writes of comic books based on classics, "After being processed in this way, no classic, no matter who wrote it, is in any way distinguishable from the floppity-rabbit and crime comics it is supposed to replace."[11]

The authoritarian tone and broad brushstroke, evident throughout Wertham's book, foreclosed the possibility of serious debate. The judge had already pronounced the sentence: "here was a civilization poisoning its wellspring[.]"[12]

A generally sympathetic reader, *Commentary* associate editor Robert Warshow, noted Dr. Wertham's "humorless dedication" and pointed to his tendency to take anything said by a child at face value: "I suspect it would be a dull child indeed who could go to Dr. Wertham's clinic and not discover very quickly that most of his problematical behavior can be explained in terms of comic books."[13] Yet Warshow, the father of an 11-year-old EC fan, expressed a parent's concern: "I find it hard to accept the idea that there should be one area of his experience, apparently of considerable importance to him, which will have no important consequences. One comic book a week or ten, they *must* have an effect. How can I be expected to believe that it will be a good one?"[14]

With anxiety mounting, it was perhaps inevitable that the comics controversy should ascend to the exalted realm of the United States Senate. That august body, like the New York Legislature before it, dispatched its Subcommittee on the Judiciary to Manhattan, where, under the chairmanship of Senator Estes Kefauver, it held hearings on the connection between comic books and children behaving badly. EC publisher William M. Gaines bore the brunt of hostile questioning from Senator Kefauver concerning a *Crime SuspenStories* cover depicting a woman's severed head. The exchange, framed in unwinnable aesthetic rather than constitutional terms,

doomed EC's horror and crime comics—and, as it happened, other companies' publications as well.[15]

Although the Senate hearings resulted in no congressional action, the comic-book industry responded with its own policing agency, the Comics Code Authority, administered under the auspices of the Comics Magazine Association of America, which had been founded in September 1954.[16] Blandness became the order of the day.

In 1955, following the negative publicity generated by *Seduction of the Innocent* and the Kefauver hearings, William Gaines folded the EC comics lines, killing the popular *Tales from the Crypt* and other series and throwing some of the most talented comics artists out of work. DC and other publishers quickly embraced the newly devised content guidelines of the Comics Code Authority, and the former EC illustrators found themselves unemployed and, given the fearfulness permeating the industry, often unemployable.

Gilberton, like Dell (the home of *Walt Disney's Comics and Stories*, *Bugs Bunny*, *Woody Woodpecker*, *Dell Movie Classics*, and other mainstream comics), refused to adopt the Code, insisting that the quality of its self-regulated publications required no external review. Thus, where other comics publishers hesitated or simply refused to employ the "tainted" EC veterans, Albert Kanter simply declined to acknowledge such constraints.

Instead, he opened the door for the refugees.

JOE ORLANDO

The first of the EC artists to find a temporary home at 101 Fifth Avenue was Joe Orlando, one of the most innovative figures in the history of comics. From 1966 onward, the artist was active as editor, vice president, and creative director for DC Comics, where, among other things, he rehabilitated the horror genre, collaborated on the creation of *Swamp Thing*, and supervised the publication of the company's first graphic novel, *Star Raiders*, in 1983.[17] Following the death of his longtime friend William M. Gaines in 1995, Orlando assumed the mantle of associate publisher of *Mad Magazine*. In the 1950s, though, he was celebrated as one of the stars of Gaines's EC powerhouse roster.

Born on 4 April 1927 in Bari, Italy, Orlando was brought to the United States by his family in 1929. The young resident of East Harlem and aspiring artist received his initial training in art at New York's School of Industrial Arts.[18] After studying under John Groth at New York's Art Students League, he began illustrating comics under the auspices of Lloyd Jacquet in 1949, providing illustrations for *Treasure Chest*.[19]

Sharing studio space with Wally Wood and Harry Harrison, Orlando contributed to Fox, Fawcett, Avon, and other comics publishers until Fox's business reverses cost the trio $6,000 in unpaid work. For a brief period, the artist left the comics field, but Wood enlisted him in 1951 to assist on projects for EC, such as *Weird Fantasy*, *Tales From the Crypt*, and *Mad*. There he remained until 1956, establishing himself as a master of horror, science-fiction, and humor.[20]

With EC foundering, Orlando found a haven at Gilberton in late 1955. His first *Classics Illustrated* title, *Caesar's Conquests*, No. 130 (January 1956), was an adaptation of that bane of second-year Latin students, Caesar's *Gallic War*. (Curiously, Annete Rubinstein's script skipped over the notorious opening: "*Gallia est omnis divisa in partes tres....*")

Although Orlando easily made the transition from the EC realm to the Roman, producing a superb title-page splash and some splendid battle sequences, elsewhere the artwork is uneven and gives the impression that the artist was not fully engaged in the book. Comics art authority Jim Vadeboncoeur, Jr., spotted other hands that neither he nor fellow researcher Hames Ware could conclusively identify.[21]

Whoever may have been involved in *Caesar's Conquests*, they freely adapted artwork from other sources. At least one panel, at the top of page 30, was "swiped" (the refreshingly noneuphemistic comics term for a direct borrowing) from the 22 January 1939 installment of Hal Foster's *Prince Valiant*. But "swipes" have been common in comics from the beginning and, of course, are not unique to that particular art form.

In any event, the situation improved significantly in the artist's second *Classics* assignment. One of the most fortunate editorial decisions made at Gilberton was the choice of Orlando to draw the revised edition of *A Tale of Two Cities*, No. 6 (May 1956). This time, *Classics Illustrated* got it right, producing a faithful, literate adaptation of the Dickens novel of sacrificial friendship—and Orlando, assisted by his EC friend George Evans,[22] didn't try to get away with shortcuts or steals. He produced memorable character studies of Sydney Carton, Madame Defarge, Doctor Manette, Mr. Lorry, and Miss Pross, and even breathed life into the heavily starched Charles Darnay and saintly Lucie Manette.

Orlando's illustrations for Rudyard Kipling's *Kim*, No. 143 (March 1958), are superb examples of visual storytelling. The parallel plots of the Lama's quest for the River of the Arrow and Kim's search for his identity and participation in "The Great Game" are framed by beautifully realized backgrounds and costumes of late 19th-century British India. The characters of Kim, the Lama, the horse trader Mahbub Ali, and the English officer Colonel Creighton are delineated with subtle precision.

In anticipation of the following year's release of the wide-screen William Wyler blockbuster *Ben-Hur*, Gilberton commissioned the artist to illustrate a comics version of Lew Wallace's historical-religious novel, issued as No. 147 (November 1958) in the series. (Gustav Schrotter had produced an edition of the story for *Famous Authors* in 1951.) The most ornately wrought of Orlando's *Classics*, the book features generally busier panels and the frequent use of parallel lines to indicate shading or to suggest texture.

Besides the four *Classics Illustrated* titles, Orlando also provided artwork for sections of a *Special Issue*, *Crossing the Rockies*, No. 147A (December 1958), and two *World Around Us* issues, *The Army*, No. W9 (May 1959), and *The Marines*, No. W11 (July 1959). In none of these shorter projects, however, did the artist attain the same level he had set for himself in his earlier Gilberton books.

Whatever the case, Orlando was soon on his way to greater challenges, including a remarkable 1965 *Blazing Combat* (Warren) story titled "Landscape," which captured the moral ambivalence of America's engagement in Vietnam

Joe Orlando, *Caesar's Conquests* (January 1956). EC style conquers Gilberton.

Top, left: Joe Orlando, *A Tale of Two Cities* (March 1956): Sydney Carton makes a far, far better exit in Orlando's revised edition of the Dickens weeper. *Above:* Joe Orlando, *Kim* (March 1958). A high-spirited title-page splash invites the reader to enter a world of adventure and intrigue. *Bottom, left:* Joe Orlando, *Ben-Hur* (November 1958). Detailed linework enhances the panels depicting the climactic chariot race.

at a point before the war had fully taken hold of the American psyche.[23] *Classics Illustrated*, in the meantime, had helped pay the bills and further advance an outstanding artist's reputation. Universally respected, Joe Orlando died on 23 December 1998.

GRAHAM INGELS

The most extreme representative of the EC diaspora, Graham Ingels (1915–1991), who signed his experiments in terror "Ghastly," produced some surprisingly tame work for Gilberton. Whether the uncharacteristic restraint was the result of self-censorship or editorial direction is unknown, but, at least in the case of one

Classics Illustrated title, he made the limitations work for him.

Having begun his career as a freelancer in 1935, the artist moved to Fiction House in 1943 while serving in a Long Island navy desk assignment. After the war, Ingels became art director for Ned Pines's Better Publications. By the end of the decade, he had found his spiritual home at William Gaines's Entertaining Comics, where he supplied a story for the first issue of *War Against Crime*.[24]

With EC's shift to horror comics in 1950, Ingels achieved comics immortality as the creator of the "Old Witch" and as the lead artist for *The Haunt of Fear*. The bizarre, contorted features of his subjects and the detailed linework in his often shocking panels contributed to the outré image of the EC line and earned Ingels recognition as the leading horror-comics artist.[25]

Following the burial of the Old Witch and *The Haunt of Fear*, "Ghastly" Graham turned, in 1956, to the Code-defying Gilberton Company. Already plagued by the alcoholism that would eventually destroy his career and his family life, Ingels accepted a commission to illustrate an adaptation of Erckmann-Chatrain's *Waterloo*, No. 135 (November 1956), a historical sermon-as-novel on the follies of war and ambitious men.

Where William Gaines had promoted an atmosphere of friendly rivalry and unexampled creativity at EC, *Classics Illustrated* was a comparatively regimented operation in the days of Roberta Strauss's ascendancy. Although Alex Blum was art director and Meyer Kaplan managing editor, the young editorial assistant, who had already crossed swords with Lou Cameron, was unlikely to have been overawed by the industry reputation of the inimitable "Ghastly." Unwilling to compromise on period detail and internal consistency, Strauss insisted that Ingels keep track of the number of buttons on the Napoleonic-era uniforms from panel to panel.[26]

If the editorial demands wore on the artist, the strain didn't show in the finished product, which has been dismissed by some who admire the EC Ingels as "forgettable."[27] *Waterloo* is a disciplined performance, containing arresting contrasts between closeup individualized character studies and midrange to panoramic configurations of massed soldiers. Ingels drew what Emile Erckmann and Alexandre Chatrain wrote, conveying a different kind of terror—that of war and the annihilation of the individual—in images of inhumanly mechanical columns of uniformed troops who achieve separate identities only when killed or wounded. No EC overstatement was necessary.

Ingels also illustrated sections in seven *World Around Us* issues and the "Pony Soldiers" chapter in *Special Issue* No. 150A, *Royal Canadian Mounted Police*. Except for the

Graham Ingels, *Waterloo* (November 1958). Often underrated, the illustrations by "Ghastly" for Erckmann-Chatrain's historical novel convey an antiwar message in an atypical, understated way.

"Bloody Blackbeard" section in *Pirates*, No. W7 (March 1959) and the "Frontier Forts" section in *Army*, No. W9 (May 1959), which showed some sparks of energy, he seemed to be doing the minimum required to collect his check. In an effort to help Ingels, who, between his reputation as "Ghastly" Graham and his fondness for drink was having trouble getting work, George Evans passed along some penciled pages in *The French Revolution*, No. W14 (October 1959), which his friend inked, lending the pages something of his own style.[28]

The Evans and Ingels families were close friends and enjoyed sharing backyard cookouts. Evans recalls one such occasion when his young daughter "crawled into Graham's lap and started sipping beer from the can he was holding. I found them a little later, both asleep in the chair—and I didn't have a camera!"[29] Although Ingels was "a devout Catholic who was deeply disturbed by the work he had done for EC," Evans recalls a "playful man who could have fun with that image." One Halloween, Ingels, who lived in a wooded area, "rigged up a pulley that stretched for 90 feet from a tree to his house. He hung sheets from the line, and when kids came to his door, he flashed the lights and shook the line. The kids ran away screaming, and he was rolling on the floor. I told him, 'Graham, that probably did more harm than any of your comic books.'"[30]

Following his Gilberton years and a period spent as a Famous Artists School instructor, Ingels moved to Florida, where he led an increasingly reclusive life, estranged from his family and most of his former colleagues. Although he eventually reestablished a relationship with his daughter, he refused, with Salingeresque intensity, to entertain inquiries from anyone interested in his "Ghastly" career.[31]

GEORGE WOODBRIDGE

An artist whose work appeared in William Gaines's *Mad*, George Woodbridge was part of that circle of talented younger illustrators who toiled for *Classics* in the late 1950s. A fine draftsman who was fascinated by history, his light linework and rather sketchy figures foreshadowed Gilberton styles of the early sixties.

Woodbridge's drawings for the revised edition of *The House of the Seven Gables*, No. 52 (January 1958), have almost too airy a tone for Nathaniel Hawthorne's meditation on the workings of time and the expiation of Matthew Maule's curse. Still, certain panels, such as the procession of ghostly Pyncheons, are evocative compositions.

An interesting addition to the American *Classics Illustrated* series, Betty Jacobson's adaptation of *With Fire and Sword*, No. 146 (September 1958), the relatively unfamiliar first part of Henryk Sienkiewicz's Polish historical trilogy, occasioned Woodbridge's finest work for Gilberton. The artist's heavier brush strokes accentuated the dark atmosphere of the tale of the 17th-century Cossack revolt, particularly in a rendering of a battle fought in heavy rain.

But the title for which Woodbridge is best remembered by *Classics* collectors is H.G. Wells's *The First Men in the Moon*, No. 144 (May 1958), a collaborative effort with three EC alumni.

George Woodbridge, *With Fire and Sword* (September 1958). **A grim view of war from an EC veteran.**

MOON MEN: AL WILLIAMSON, ANGELO TORRES, ROY G. KRENKEL

A popular issue that went through seven printings, *The First Men in the Moon* was something of an EC homecoming event. Given the opportunity to explore the congenial terrain of science fiction, Woodbridge, who supplied most of the drawings of human characters, Al Williamson, Angelo Torres, and Roy G. Krenkel turned in imaginative drawings that stirred young baby boomers at the dawn of the space race.

Born in New York in 1931 and reared in Bogotá,

IT WAS UNREAL AND FANTASTIC. THE STRANGENESS OF WHAT WE DID, THE UNEARTHLINESS OF IT, WAS OVERWHELMING. THE WHOLE ENTERPRISE WAS MAD. AND IT COMES TO ME THAT MY PARTICIPATION IN THESE AMAZING ADVENTURES WAS, AFTER ALL, THE PUREST ACCIDENT.

Woodbridge, Williamson, Torres, and Krenkel, *The First Men in the Moon* (May 1958). *Weird Fantasy* meets *Classics Illustrated*.

western, and adventure genres for Atlas (later Marvel). Gilberton secured his services for *The First Men in the Moon*—where his talent for imagining alien worlds served the project well—and for two *World Around Us* titles, *Prehistoric Animals*, No. W15 (November 1959), and *Great Scientists*, No. 18 (February 1960).

Following his brief encounter with *Classics Illustrated*, Williamson, along with other former EC colleagues, contributed to the black-and-white magazines *Creepy* and *Eerie*. At the beginning of 1967, he took over the *Secret Agent Corrigan* comic strip (originally an Alex Raymond vehicle titled *Secret Agent X-9*). Williamson relinquished the strip to George Evans in the early 1980s.[34] At the behest of George Lucas, he also drew a *Star Wars* comic strip.

Ranking the *Classics* artists of the later years, scriptwriter and editor Alfred Sundel placed Angelo Torres among the top four regular freelancers—surpassed only by George Evans, Norman Nodel, and Gray Morrow. The young EC veteran provided some striking panels for *The First Men in the Moon*, but his finest work for Gilberton was the 1962 revision of issue No. 56, Victor Hugo's *The Toilers of the Sea*. Ably exploiting the medium's narrative (as opposed to merely illustrative) properties, Torres filled Gilliatt's singlehanded salvage operation and battle with an octopus with drama and suspense and, especially with the hero Gilliatt and the villain Clubin, revealed character through closely observed facial expressions.

Assisted by Stephen L. Addeo, who also worked on revisions of *The Last of the Mohicans* and *Black Beauty*, Torres produced an updated edition of *The Man Without a Country*, No. 63 (1962), that improved on Henry C. Kiefer's 1949 version in many respects. For one thing, the pair limned an Aaron Burr that more or less resembled the historical figure. The uniforms and hair styles belong to the correct period, and the colorist remembered not to put American soldiers of the early 19th century in red coats. But the lightly sketched drawings often appear unfinished, and the colorist filled in an average of one panel per page monochromatically.

Most of Torres's work for Gilberton appeared in short sections in various *Special Issues*—*The Atomic Age*, No. 156A (June 1960); *To the Stars!*, No. 165A (December 1961); *World War II*, No. 166A (Spring 1962); *Prehistoric World*, No. 167A (July 1962); and *The United Nations* (no number or date)—and *World Around Us* titles—*Great Scientists*, No. W18 (February 1960); *Through Time and*

Colombia, Al Williamson became one of the most revered figures in the comics field. Returning to New York in the 1940s, he studied under illustrator Burne Hogarth, whom he subsequently assisted on the *Tarzan* comic strip.[32] He also worked with John Prentice on the *Rip Kirby* strip originated by his childhood idol, Alex Raymond, whose style he emulated. Les Daniels has observed that "The subtle texture of his artwork was based on his ability to suggest shapes without a constant reliance on hard lines."[33]

In the early 1950s, Williamson rapidly rose to prominence with the refined, realistic style that he brought to such EC series as *Weird Science* and *Weird Fantasy*. Following EC's demise, he worked in the horror,

Angelo Torres, *The Toilers of the Sea* (Spring 1962). Gilliatt toils with the "devil fish."

Space: The Story of Communications, No. W20 (April 1960); *The Civil War*, No. W26 (October 1960); *Whaling*, No. W28 (December 1960); *Vikings*, No. W29 (January 1961); *Undersea Adventures*, No. W30 (February 1961); *Famous Teens*, No. W33 (May 1961); and *Fishing*, No. W34 (June 1961). According to Al Sundel, "The artists liked these shorter pieces, which meant more change in their pockets."[35]

Also assisting on the H.G. Wells title was Al Williamson's longtime friend and fellow EC émigré Roy G. Krenkel (1918–1983), a background specialist whose ability to create atmospheric settings was respected by his fellow artists. Always somewhat overshadowed by his col-

leagues, Krenkel achieved greater renown in the 1960s illustrating science-fiction and fantasy paperback covers.

George Evans recalled the artist as "a wild man with a wonderful sense of style and humor."[36] When Krenkel was dying of lung cancer (an irony that he, as a nonsmoker, was able to appreciate), he frequently found himself in the position of comforting his friends, telling them, "I'm anxious to see what's over there, if anything."[37]

JOHN P. SEVERIN

EC artist John Powers Severin (b. 1921) had a brief and ultimately unpleasant relationship with the Gilberton editorial department. Celebrated for the sophisticated simplicity that he had exploited to great effect in William Gaines's *Two-Fisted Tales*, Severin had developed by the late 1950s a technique at once ornately realistic and elegantly clean.

His first work for *Classics* was a pair of chapters, "Texas and the Alamo" and "The Mexican War," in *Special Issue* No. 144A, *Blazing the Trails West* (June 1958). The battle scenes are among the finest contributions to one of the strongest titles in the series and reflect the painstaking research that was part of Severin's legacy from *Two-Fisted Tales* editor (and *Mad* mentor) Harvey Kurtzman.

In 1959, art director L.B. Cole assigned Severin the art revision of *The Last of the Mohicans*, one of the best-selling *Classics Illustrated* titles. He completed only a dozen or so pages of pencils and then made his exit.[38] Like Lou Cameron, Severin didn't appreciate what might have been construed as editorial overinvolvement on the part of Roberta Strauss Feuerlicht.

The book was completed by Stephen L. Addeo, a competent illustrator who subsequently served as art assistant for the series in 1961 and 1962. Unfortunately, a dramatic loss of vitality is evident on the 13th page, and nothing in the rest of the adaptation lives up to the promise of the first dozen pages illustrated by Severin. Detailed drawings of British uniforms and frontier attire contribute to an atmosphere of authenticity. The artist's sketches of Hawkeye, Uncas, Chingachgook, Magua, Duncan, Cora, Alice, and David Gamut establish fundamental character traits. The animated composition draws the reader ever deeper into the forest drama.

John P. Severin, *The Last of the Mohicans* (May 1959). The EC artist brought historical realism to the few pages he contributed to the Cooper revision.

REED CRANDALL

A legendary figure in comics history, Reed Crandall collaborated with his friend and fellow EC artist George Evans on several of the most beautiful books published by Gilberton. Born in 1917 in Indiana, Crandall grew up in Kansas and received his training in the 1930s at the Cleveland School of Art. Among his influences were illustrators Howard Pyle, Joseph Clement Coll, and Henry C. Pitz. After moving to New York in 1940, he joined the comic-book shop run by Will Eisner and Jerry Iger and then drew a number of characters for Quality, including Stormy Foster, Captain Triumph, and Doll Man.[39]

Crandall's first specialty was military art, and in 1942 he found his métier in Quality's "Blackhawk" series, created by Will Eisner for *Military Comics.* Shifting gears and specialties in the 1950s, he explored the realms of science fiction, horror, and adventure at EC. Some of his best work in this period was for the short-lived *Piracy* series. When William Gaines's ship went down, Crandall, like the other outstanding EC illustrators, had difficulty finding work. Atlas (Marvel) provided some assignments, and, beginning in 1960, the Catholic Guild's *Treasure Chest* gave him steady employment drawing anti–Communist comics.

At about the same time, Al Williamson approached George Evans, who had established himself as one of the principal free-lancers for *Classics Illustrated.* Evans recalled that

Al asked if I had enough work to share some with Reed. I had, and did. We would work in whatever way time schedules allowed. I did all the layouts—breakdowns, and did faces pretty detailed so that likenesses were consistent. These I'd send to Reed, and he'd finish the stuff. Often he had better references than I'd found, and some delightful stuff would come back. He also did better Percheron horses than I ever did....

On those long adaptations, memory says I would lay out what Reed was to do—usually half the book—send them off and then go on to my half complete.[40]

The first Crandall and Evans collaboration was on a desperately needed revision of Victor Hugo's *The Hunchback of Notre Dame,* No. 18, which had been ineptly adapted by Evelyn Goodman and crudely drawn by Allen Simon in the original 1944 edition. The second time around, in the fall of 1960, was a charm for Gilberton. Evans's superbly rendered features of Quasimodo, Esmeralda, and Frollo were all but definitive and subsequently were shamelessly copied in a 1970s comics version. Crandall's exquisitely detailed historical framework made the redesigned *Hunchback* a handsome improvement and one of the best books in the series.

Lighter inking and a solidly realistic framework provided scope in the revised *Oliver Twist,* No. 23 (Fall 1961), for a brisk, modern approach to the Dickens novel. An occasional hint of caricature suggests a distant debt

Left: Reed Crandall and George Evans, *The Hunchback of Notre Dame* (Fall 1960). A toned-down Quasimodo replaced Allen Simon's bizarre 1944 conception. *Right:* Reed Crandall and George Evans, *Julius Caesar* (1962). A mobile, calculating Antony stirs the mob. (Compare with Kiefer's approach in the 1950 edition.)

to George Cruikshank, the novel's first illustrator. In a decisive rejection of stereotyping, Fagin is drawn without any specific ethnic identity. Once again, Crandall's fully realized historical context supplies a grace note.

Rising to, or even surpassing, the level of *The Hunchback of Notre Dame* was the revision by Crandall and Evans of *Julius Caesar*, No. 68 (1962). The artists offered incisive character studies of Brutus (replacing Henry C. Kiefer's somewhat Aryan model with an introspective Roman), Cassius (who looks lean, hungry, and sardonic), Antony (shown as a consummate political actor), and others. Blending classical gestures and backgrounds with Crandall's affinity for action, the pair brought Shakespeare's relatively static tragedy dramatically to life.

A final project, G.A. Henty's *In Freedom's Cause*, No. 168, was intended for publication in 1962; although a British edition was issued in 1963, the title did not appear in the American *Classics Illustrated* series until 1969. The tale of young Archie Forbes and William Wallace elicited some striking battle scenes, with intricately detailed backgrounds, from Crandall and Evans. Unfortunately, as George Evans recalled, after sending half the script to Crandall, "his section came back with five or six pages just as I'd sent them—undone. A brief letter said he 'couldn't finish them,' with no real reason given."[41]

During their tenure with Gilberton, the two artists also provided illustrations for Dell's movie edition of *Hercules Unchained* and *Twilight Zone* TV tie-ins (May 1961, April 1962). After the Kanter family shut down the American *Classics* line, Crandall and Evans found themselves back in EC territory, working in James Warren's noncode series *Creepy*, *Eerie*, and *Vampirella*.[42] One of Crandall's finest achievements was an eight-page adaptation of Bram Stoker's "The Squaw" for *Creepy*.[43]

The artist's technical proficiency fell victim to his losing battle with alcoholism, and he eventually stopped illustrating altogether. He lived for a time in Pennsylvania with Al Williamson but returned to Kansas, where he worked at various odd jobs, including night watchman, fast-food cook, and chain-restaurant janitor. After suffering several strokes, Crandall entered a Wichita nursing home, where he died of a heart attack in 1982. He was 65 years old.[44]

Reed Crandall and George Evans, *In Freedom's Cause* (1962/ 1969). The last collaborative effort for *Classics Illustrated* by the two former EC artists.

XXII

Classical Interlude: "Coming Next"

From the very first issue, *Classic Comics*—and then *Classics Illustrated*—previewed the next title with "Coming Next" ads. Back-cover, full-page color illustrations heralded subsequent editions through No. 14. In issue No. 15, the notice was moved to the inside back cover, where the short-lived "Klassic Komic Kid" (drawn by Lou Zansky), clutching a baseball bat and wearing a mortar board, an academic gown, and cleats, informed readers that "I've just seen the colored proofs of *Gulliver's Travels....* Gee ... it sure is exciting..." A few issues later, the Kid was exhorting readers not to miss "the mad story about *The Hunchback of Notre Dame* ... the homely little man who was brave enough to fight the whole population of Paris ... single-handed! Golly!" Despite these endorsements, the issues sold well.

A less goofy but no less restrained style soon took hold, and the "Coming Next" feature eventually moved to the inside front cover, displaying mock-ups of the forthcoming line-drawing covers. Breathless descriptions spoke of "*action—suspense—excitement in the next great issue of Classic Comics.*" Each successive issue was promoted in the language of testosterone. "*Never has there been a greater story than Kidnapped in the next great issue of Classics Illustrated,*" a January 1948 ad proclaimed. In April 1952, Gilberton announced the upcoming *All Quiet on the Western Front* as "*a story with the impact of an exploding bomb.*"

Two months later, in issue No. 96, the under-

"Coming Next...." The May 1958 ad for *Classics Illustrated* No. 145.

COMING NEXT

SWASHBUCKLING adventurer Jean Lafitte was a pirate king. In 1814, he and his men all but owned and ran New Orleans. But when the British offered him $30,000 and a commission to help them attack the city, he refused. Instead he gave his help to the struggling young republic, America. With courage and conviction he fought with General Andrew Jackson and the American army at the bloody Battle of New Orleans.

Be sure to read

THE BUCCANEER

NEXT IN

CLASSICS Illustrated

On sale at your favorite newsdealer or variety store.

CLASSICS Illustrated . . . MAY 1958 . . . Number 144 . . . Entered as second-class matter March 10, 1943. Reentered as second-class matter March 28, 1947, at the post office at New York, N.Y., under the Act of March 3, 1879. MEYER A. KAPLAN, Executive Editor; ROBERTA STRAUSS, Editor. Published bi-monthly, with special issues in June and December, by GILBERTON COMPANY, INC., 101 Fifth Avenue, New York 3, N.Y. . . . Subscription, $1.50 for 10 issues . . . Copyright by GILBERTON COMPANY, INC., 1958 in U.S.A. and all foreign countries. All rights reserved including the right to reproduce this publication or portions thereof in any form. Printed in U.S.A.

stated heading, "Coming Next Month," first appeared. It was replaced by "Coming" and finally "Coming Next" after *Classics Illustrated* shifted to a bimonthly publication schedule in 1954. Brief, descriptive paragraphs, written with increasingly greater skill, were appended. The style was adopted for *Classics Illustrated Junior* in 1953. Both series ran the ads in every new title until the final issues appeared—neither *CI* No. 168 nor No. 169 contained one, nor did *Junior* No. 577.

While the "Coming Next" ads in the line-drawing cover era generally provided an accurate representation in reduction of the following month's cover, painted covers were redrawn, usually by Alex Blum, with pen and ink. (Only *Crime and Punishment* was advertised using a photograph of the painted cover.) Generally, the line-drawing sketches of painted covers were reasonably accurate in terms of scale and physical features, but on some occasions, such as the promotions for *Davy Crockett* and *In the Reign of Terror*, Blum wasn't even close.

Then, too, there was the nonexistent No. 145, *The Buccaneer*, scheduled for July 1958, for which the artist created a cover that, as it turned out, had nothing to do with the delayed book. *The Buccaneer* was issued as No. 148 in January 1949 with a quite different painted-cover design by Norm Saunders; meanwhile, *The Crisis* had been substituted in the No. 145 slot, and the original edition of No. 144, with its erroneous "Coming Next" ad, became an instant collector's item.

XXIII

"The Professional": George R. Evans

No artist associated with *Classics Illustrated* was more highly respected than George R. Evans, whose exquisitely wrought panels were unsurpassed in the history of the publication. "As an illustrator," wrote scriptwriter and editor Alfred Sundel, "he had no weaknesses. He seemed the most professional [of the artists] in discussions. He was … a very determined sort of guy."[1]

Evans was born in Harwood, Pennsylvania, on 5 February 1920. His lifelong passions for airplanes and art—to say nothing of his determination—were evident early. "I have been an aviation nut since age seven—the 'Lindy' thing," he wrote.[2] (Charles Lindbergh made his celebrated nonstop flight from New York to Paris in 1927.) By the time he was 16, Evans was drawing airplanes for pulps. Three years of service in the Air Force followed a period of study at the Scranton Art School.[3]

In 1946, in the twilight of the Golden Age, Evans entered the comic-book field, working first for Fiction House and later for Fawcett. He resumed his studies at the Art Students League in New York in 1949. Comics immortality arrived in 1952, when he was hired by EC and began contributing to such titles as *Weird Science*, *The Haunt of Fear*, and *Frontline Combat*.[4]

Then came the fall—the EC debacle after Senate hearings—and Evans's rebirth as a *Classics* contributor. The artist recounted that

My stint with *CI* came as a result of the killing of the EC line by Kefauver and his politicians. Till then I'd just kept busy with other publishers, who paid a better page rate—and helpful as the digested versions of the great stories were, the art in [Gilberton's] earlier series led to the thought that they just weren't interested in illustration

George Evans, circa 1956. (Courtesy of George Evans.)

quality. When Bill Gaines ended his books except *MAD*, it was time to find other accounts (though I'd always kept other markets going, knowing how cyclical things tended to be). Naturally the "big" outfits were the ones I tried—and was astonished to find bitter resentment there over EC's success—then its failure. A couple of editors threw into my face the blunt charge, "You _____s brought on all the trouble with the ____ you did, now there's no way you'll get any work from here." (It turned out that that was personal animosity, for those outfits did, later, hire virtually all of the EC people [including Evans]—and swung toward what EC had done so well.)

Anyway, before pounding the streets for work in the fields of mag and book illustrating, which was my ambition, there came a call from Joe Orlando: could I help him finish up a long script [*A Tale of Two Cities*, 1956] he had taken from *Classics Illustrated*? I did that—evidently the *Classics* people liked what Joe turned in and offered him more work, and he suggested I go see Mr. Blum [then the Gilberton art director] on my own. Which I did—and found that man to be one of the nicest, gentlest, kindest people I have ever met. … I was sorry when he retired, for on every visit we would have some talk together.

L.B. Cole succeeded Mr. Blum, and we got on well from the first day. I hadn't known him, but knew his work. There was always another script waiting as soon as I turned in a finished job, right on till they erred in launching their digest-sized "slick" magazine to compete with the already-successful ones which evidently had a lock on the market.[5]

Evans's distinguished career continued with titles for Western and DC and ghost work on George Wunder's daily strips for the long-running *Terry and the Pirates*.[6] In the 1980s, he began drawing the enduring syndicated strip *Secret Agent Corrigan*, succeeding his friend and former EC colleague, Al Williamson.[7]

By any estimate, the books that Evans illustrated for Gilberton rank high among his achievements. His first *Classics* title, *Romeo and Juliet*, No. 134 (September 1956), displayed the artist's commitment to historical fidelity. As he wrote, "For a fact, I might be a richer man today if it weren't my problem that I busted myself in research on every story I illustrated."[8]

One of the great strengths of Evans's output for Gilberton was his ability to draw women who were neither Good Girl Art specimens nor Kieferesque androgynes. Juliet may be the finest example of the artist's skill in this regard. In her exchanges with Romeo, she is decidedly his equal, and she shows determination in her scenes with her nurse and Friar Laurence.

For the Shakespeare adaptation, Evans included handsomely drawn Italian Renaissance costumes and architecture, carefully observed principal characters, and an imaginatively fluid rendering of the six-page balcony

George Evans, *Romeo and Juliet* (September 1956). The balcony scene.

scene. The *Classics Illustrated* edition of *Romeo and Juliet* "won some sort of prize in Sweden, which they [the Gilberton staff] told me about," Evans recalled, "but if there were physical trophies, I never saw any."[9]

The next project, Joseph Conrad's *Lord Jim*, No. 136 (January 1957), was in some ways the most challenging, in part because the novel plumbed greater thematic depths than standard comic-book storylines—and in part because editor Strauss found Jim's act of self-sacrifice incomprehensible. "Roberta didn't think the ending was credible, and we debated it," Evans said. "She dismissed it as a grown-up boys' book. She just didn't get it."[10]

The title was one of the artist's favorites "though [it] had a tight deadline and I wish I'd had more time for the drawing."[11] (He had just completed *Romeo and Juliet* and was scheduled to illustrate *The Little Savage* for the next issue.) Conveying the hero's moral crises in comics

George Evans, *Lord Jim* (January 1957). Artist and editor argued the merits and meaning of Jim's moral choice.

form may have strained the resources of the medium, but Evans, working with a streamlined script that dispensed with Marlow's role as mediator of the narrative, nevertheless produced a stirring visual account of Jim's regeneration.

Adaptations of two boys' books followed. *The Little Savage*, No. 137 (March 1957), was a variation on the *Robinson Crusoe* theme by Frederick Marryat and showed the artist at ease with a straightforward adventure yarn. Evans produced several stirring action sequences, such as the boy hero's capture of a young seal, escape from attacking sharks, and struggle against a "violently agitated" sea.

In the Reign of Terror, No. 139 (July 1957), the first of several G.A. Henty we-were-there historical tales included in the *Classics Illustrated* series, was another of Evans's favorites. The plot-driven novel was well suited to standard comic-book pacing, and the artist skillfully sustained the action and suspense from panel to panel as the resourceful young hero contrives to rescue Robe-

spierre from footpads and the aristocratic heroine and her sister from one bloodthirsty revolutionary after another.

Cooperating with the Theodore Roosevelt Centennial Commission in the production of *The Rough Rider*, No. 141A (December 1957), Gilberton further established its growing reputation for serious educational publications. Evans illustrated the *Special Issue*, which was described by Commission Director Hermann Hagedorn in an introduction as "the first full length biography of a great American in this new and compelling medium." The book subsequently won the Thomas Alva Edison Award, but, according to the artist, "it was strictly on the subject matter." Evans had inherited the assignment, which turned into his least satisfactory *Classics* effort:

It had been given to another artist who sat on the script for an unconscionable time, then turned it back, so it was

George Evans, *The Little Savage* (March 1957). A shifting point of view contributes to the visual excitement of the sequence.

George Evans, *In the Reign of Terror* (July 1957). The English hero declines the blessings of liberty, equality, and fraternity.

an "emergency." I couldn't pencil and ink it, so they turned it over to an inker they knew. He was not a good inker—had a heavy hand as if using a trowel, so all detail stuff suffered. In addition, he appointed himself editor, too, and inked only what he thought was required in the panels and erased everything else. It led to a funny situation: I was ashamed of it, yet here it won a prize, indicating it was some of my best work. Ugh.[12]

Over the years, Evans worked on all but one of the remaining eleven *Special Issues*, notably *Blazing the Trails West*, No. 144A (June 1958), *Crossing the Rockies*, No. 147A (December 1958), *Men, Guns and Cattle*, No. 153A (December 1959), *To the Stars*, No. 165A (December

1961), *World War II*, No. 166A (1962), and *Prehistoric World*, No. 167A (June 1962). The artist also illustrated substantial sections of most of the issues in *The World Around Us* series, including *Flight*, No. W8 (April 1959), *The French Revolution*, No. W14 (October 1959) (inked in part by Graham Ingels), *Great Scientists*, No. W18 (February 1960), *Ghosts*, No. W24 (August 1960), *For Gold and Glory*, No. W32 (April 1961), and *Spies*, No. W35 (August 1961).

During 1958, Evans illustrated two titles for Gilberton's flagship *Classics Illustrated* line. The first was an adaptation of *The Crisis*, No. 145 (July 1958), a Civil War story by the now largely forgotten American historical novelist Winston Churchill (not related to the British prime minister). Like *In the Reign of Terror*, another popular work of marginal literary merit, *The Crisis* translated well into the comics medium, where the original's lack of complexity worked in favor of the imperatives of adaptation and sequential art. Central to the issue's success were Evans's realistic rendering of the steely Southern heroine, Virginia Carvel, who appears in 16 different period outfits, and his convincing character sketches of Lincoln, Sherman, and Grant.

Fortunately for Gilberton, the artist had already turned in the boards for *The Crisis* when another sort of crisis, involving deadlines, presented itself.

Albert Kanter's son, Hal Kanter, who had written for Bing Crosby on radio and had directed Elvis Presley in *Loving You* (1957), had been his father's eyes on Hollywood, giving Gilberton advance notice of forthcoming films based on classic literature to enable *Classics* to include the titles in the series production cycle. He had also been instrumental in arranging a movie tie-in with *The Ten Commandments* in 1956.

Hal Kanter scored a major coup for Gilberton in 1958, when he facilitated an arrangement for exclusive comic-book rights to another Cecil B. DeMille production, *The Buccaneer*, a first for the *Classics Illustrated* line. The Paramount script by Jeanie Macpherson was given to veteran comics artist Robert Jenney (b. 1914). A May 1958 "Coming Next" ad in *The First Men in the Moon* advertised *The Buccaneer*, complete with a line-drawing mock-up cover by Alex Blum, as issue No. 145.

Then Jenney found himself unable to complete the artwork on time. Editor Roberta Strauss called on Evans, who had rescued *The Rough Rider* under similar circum-

IT WAS THE WAR OF 1812. THE WEAK, NEW LAND, AMERICA, WAS STRUGGLING AGAINST ONE OF THE WORLD'S MAJOR POWERS, GREAT BRITAIN.
IN THE SOUTH, GENERAL ANDREW JACKSON HAD AN ARMY ILL-EQUIPPED TO FACE THE SUPERIOR FORCES OF THE BRITISH. THE TIME WAS LATE IN DECEMBER, 1814.

This book based on the CECIL B. DeMILLE presentation

YUL BRYNNER · CLAIRE BLOOM · CHARLES BOYER · *THE* BUCCANEER · co-starring INGER STEVENS HENRY HULL E G MARSHALL · also co-starring CHARLTON HESTON as Andrew Jackson

Produced by HENRY WILCOXON Directed by ANTHONY QUINN Screenplay by JESSE L. LASKY Jr. and BERENCE MOSX A Paramount Picture in VistaVision and color by Technicolor

George Evans, *The Buccaneer* **(January 1959). The book that ate a vacation.**

stances, to rush *The Buccaneer* to completion. Jenney had penciled about half of the book, and the July printing date was looming.

Unfortunately for the artist, the assignment came just before the "family of four plus dog" was to embark on its annual two-week vacation in Vermont, and the deadline fell during the first week of the Evanses' paid-for time:

> I begged for extra time, but, consulting her calendar, Roberta refused: Had to be in. So I worked on it that

week, got it mailed from Vermont, and had half a vacation, only to find when I went in for a new script that they had not even opened the package I'd sent. It was as hot an argument as we ever had—she explained about shifting things around, etc. And it got me a $5 a page raise in pay....[13]

The Crisis was substituted in the No. 145 slot, and *The Buccaneer* was held until January 1959.

In what was perhaps the ultimate vote of confidence in Evans as illustrator, Strauss gave him the choicest assignment of his association with Gilberton: redrawing issue No. 1, *The Three Musketeers*. Published around May 1959, the revised Dumas swashbuckler had symbolic significance as the first issue of the line. It was also one of the most popular titles, running eventually to 23 printings.

The original 62-page adaptation was rescripted and trimmed to 47 pages to fit the post–1948 *Classics* format. A painted cover based on Malcolm Kildale's 1941 interior art had replaced the old line-drawing cover in 1956, and Evans evidently used it as a general reference. He transposed physical characteristics, however, in an odd, if interesting, exercise in casting against type, assigning Porthos's portly physique to Aramis, Aramis's sleek figure to Athos, and Athos's mature frame to Porthos. In the case of Aramis, a few extra pounds provided greater potential for humor in the character development of the wavering candidate for holy orders; unfortunately, Porthos gained in *gravitas* as he lost weight, and the book lost its chief source of comic relief.

Notwithstanding these eccentricities, the 1959 *Three Musketeers* is one of the handsomest editions published in the 30-year history of *Classics Illustrated*. It is also one of the highlights of Evans's considerable body of work and, in its own right, a masterpiece of sequential art that fully realizes the potential of the medium. No panel is wasted; each carries narrative weight or delineates character. For example, in one-page episodes, Evans presents d'Artagnan's initial encounters with each of the Three Musketeers, concisely conveying Athos's pride, Porthos's vanity, and Aramis's carnal inclinations. D'Artagnan's high-spirited naivete is captured in a single panel as the impulsive Gascon volunteers to join the three men who

Left: George Evans, *The Three Musketeers* (May 1959). D'Artagnan chooses sides. *Right:* George Evans, *The Three Musketeers* (May 1959). Athos in his element.

will become his inseparable companions in their duel with five of the Cardinal's Guards.

The Three Musketeers occasioned an editorial skirmish with Roberta Strauss Feuerlicht, with whom the artist enjoyed a playful, bantering relationship: "We thrived on needling each other."[14] Evans recounted that

> When I brought it in with Athos plastered after being locked in the cellar with only *vin* to sustain him, Roberta [Strauss Feuerlicht] was kind of upset: "We can't print that! You'll have to change it" she protested. She agreed that of course he would be boozed up, but (rightly, probably) in comic-book form, we shouldn't show the hero drunk. I felt strongly enough about being true to the story to refuse making any changes.[15]

The artist had made his point and prevailed. Athos remained, as the dialogue balloon put it, "dead drunk."

Another, more significant, editorial battle was lost, however. Gilberton had published four of the South Seas novels by Charles Nordhoff and James Norman Hall and had the rights to *Falcons of France,* a World War I novel about the Lafayette Escadrille, in which the authors had served. Evans was born to illustrate the book—recognizing his expertise in matters aeronautical, William Gaines had created *Aces High* for him at EC in 1955.[16] Yet it was not to be:

> Roberta [Strauss Feuerlicht] evidently had the deciding vote on it and turned thumbs down because "It was a lot of hyped-up nonsense! People don't really believe in all that flag-waving, people don't *do* the crazy things [Nordhoff and Hall] wrote about." ... When I assured her it was truer than any other fiction they'd ever covered, she gave me a long look, suspecting I was needling her. Seeing I meant it, she shrugged, "Oh well, we have others to do. Maybe further along..." But it was one I would

have loved doing above all others—and it would have been totally authentic, for I had a library full of reference gathered through life.[17]

For the next few years with Gilberton, Evans kept busy on *Special Issues*, *The World Around Us*, and collaborations with Reed Crandall on *The Hunchback of Notre Dame*, *Oliver Twist*, *Julius Caesar*, and *In Freedom's Cause* (all of which are discussed in the preceding section on Crandall). The artist summed up his experience with *Classics Illustrated* as "enjoyable." Although the rates were far from top, Evans found adequate compensation in "the treat of working on scripts of substance, and, yes, dealing with bright, nice people like Roberta and a couple of assistants in the editorial area."[18] The end of the series merely marked the beginning of a new creative phase for the consummate professional and "very determined sort of guy." George Evans died on 22 June 2001.

XXIV

Roberta the Conqueror

For the last nine years of its existence, the driving intellectual force behind *Classics Illustrated* was a scrappy, diminutive editor named Roberta Strauss. (After her 1958 marriage to sculptor Herb Feuerlicht, she added her husband's name, a change not noted in the publication indicia until issue No. 154, in January 1960.) More than any other person, she was responsible for raising the artistic and textual standards of the series in the mid- to late 1950s. A perfectionist who demanded perfection in others, Feuerlicht caused controversy and earned respect.

In the 1960s and 1970s, she established a solid literary reputation with such nonfiction works as *The Desperate Act: The Assassination of Franz Ferdinand at Sarajevo* (1968), named by *The New York Times* as one of the ten best books of the year; *America's Reign of Terror: World War I, the Red Scare, and the Palmer Raids* (1971); *Joe McCarthy and McCarthyism: The Hate that Haunts America* (1972); and *Justice Crucified: The Story of Sacco and Vanzetti* (1977). Feuerlicht's 1983 book, *The Fate of the Jews: A People Torn Between Israeli Power and Jewish Ethics*, provoked both bitter attacks and impassioned defenses; its categorical insistence that Israel was not exempt from the standards that governed the conduct of other nations cost the author several friendships.

As her husband described her, "She was a placid person who ran from confrontations but would stand for principle."[1] In fact, "principled" is the descriptive term most often used by those who worked with her at Gilberton.

Born in New York on 23 November 1931, Roberta Strauss grew up in a Lower East Side cold-water tenement where, she later quipped, "We were so poor we had to take the garbage in at night."[2] A cleft palate, which was later surgically corrected, made her painfully shy as a child, a condition that she subsequently overcame with a vengeance.

After receiving a journalism degree from Hunter College in 1952, Strauss worked for a year as an associate editor for a Queens newspaper. In 1953, she came to the attention of Gilberton's William Kanter, who hired her as an editorial assistant at $55 a week.[3] Without a formal title or even so much as a masthead mention, Strauss quickly became indispensable, reviewing artwork and scripts for accuracy and continuity.[4]

The accounts of her attention to detail have assumed almost legendary proportions among *Classics* collectors. Lou Cameron's departure from the Gilberton circle of freelancers was occasioned by Strauss's insistence that he redraw the head of the Time Traveller to conform to the representation on the painted cover, which had been farmed out to a relative after the interior art had already been completed.[5] She counted buttons on soldiers' uniforms from panel to panel in Graham Ingels's *Waterloo*. Skirt folds came under scrutiny in Norman Nodel's *Cleopatra*. For *The Dark Frigate*, Strauss even sent an inquiry to the National Maritime Museum in Greenwich, England, regarding the procedure for 17th-century naval courts martial.

George Evans recounted an instance of the editor's obsession with accuracy:

> Roberta was, as she mentioned then, a "nut for folk dancing," and in something I did there was a scene for a "ballo"—a Latin American bash of a sort [for *Blazing the Trails West*]. Dancing was alien to me, and even how to research it and get the motions right. So I showed couples in Latin garb from the waist up. Even so, I got the hand gestures wrong, and she asked for another picture. With her help, I did produce one that she accepted, though she'd have preferred if the scripter had given a bigger space for that scene. It really wasn't key—just atmosphere. But, having interests of my own, I could understand her wish.[6]

Roberta Strauss Feuerlicht, book in hand, in the Maine woods (1958). (Courtesy of Herb Feuerlicht.)

Norman Nodel remarked that Feuerlicht was "a real stickler" on questions of historical authenticity. "She cared about the quality. She was a person of great integrity. She often had definite ideas about changes that she wanted made, but she had an open mind, and if you presented your case well, she would accept your point of view."[7]

Beginning with issue No. 139, *In the Reign of Terror* (July 1957), Strauss was listed on the masthead as editor. By the time she married in 1958, she was earning $125 a week and putting in long hours, from 8:00 A.M. to 6:00 P.M.[8] In 1961, as Roberta Strauss Feuerlicht, she was elevated to Editor-in-Chief and the next year became Managing Editor for the brief period in which Gilberton continued to issue new titles.

One of her most significant contributions to *Classics Illustrated* was in overseeing a massive facelift for the series through the upgrading of artwork in previously issued titles. The impetus for change came from Albert Kanter and Meyer Kaplan, but the implementation was often the responsibility of the young workhorse. During Feuerlicht's tenure as uncredited assistant or titled editor, revamped adaptations and upgraded interior art appeared in 28 earlier editions.[9] In the same period, new painted covers were commissioned to replace most of the line-drawing covers among the first 80 titles or unsatisfactory painted covers, such as No. 103, *Men Against the Sea*.[10]

Among Feuerlicht's most important decisions was to return a substantial number of formerly discontinued titles to print. As a result of both inventory constraints and Gilberton's commitment to replacing line-drawing covers with painted covers and interior art where required, a large number of the first 120 titles had been dropped from the catalogue by May 1959. When the last reduced reorder list, which extended to No. 150, was printed that month, 53 titles were unavailable.

Feuerlicht, however, had already begun what might be called the *Classics Illustrated* Great Revival in early 1958, ordering a redrawn edition of *The Man in the Iron Mask*, a popular title that had been out of print since 1955. A reissue of *Green Mansions* appeared in January 1959, followed by *Crime and Punishment* in September and *Dr. Jekyll and Mr. Hyde* in November. The floodgates opened in the first three months of 1960 with *Men of Iron*, *The Moonstone*, *Typee*, and *Alice in Wonderland*. Other rarities returned to circulation within the next two years, including *Les Miserables*, *Don Quixote*, *Two Years Before the Mast*, *The Last Days of Pompeii*, *Twenty Years After*, *Wuthering Heights*, *Black Beauty*, *Julius Caesar*, *Pudd'nhead Wilson*, *The White Company*, *A Study in Scarlet*, and *The Talisman*. More reissues would come in the wake of Gilberton's decision in 1962 to stop publishing new titles, and some, such as *Gulliver's Travels*, were among the best-sellers of the series.

Each of the 36 issues of *The World Around Us* bore Feuerlicht's name as editor. Her editorship of *Classics Illustrated Special Issue* No. 141A, *The Rough Rider*, brought her recognition in the *Congressional Record* as a "gifted editor with a passion for accuracy."[11] Feuerlicht also had a passion for her work. While resting in the hospital after the birth of her son Ira in March 1962, she called an editorial meeting in her room.[12]

When Gilberton terminated its juvenile lines in 1962, Feuerlicht assumed the editorship of *This Month*, a short-lived digest intended to replace Curtis's defunct *Coronet*. The magazine shut down after six months, and its last issue was printed but was never put on the stands.[13] Feuerlicht brought distinction to *This Month*, publishing fiction in English by her longtime friend Isaac Bashevis Singer. Of the future Nobel Prize winner, she wrote in a notebook: "I frequently have lunch with Isaac Bashevis Singer. I bring him news of this world, he brings me news of the next."[14]

Feuerlicht's departure from Gilberton coincided with the demise of *This Month*. When it became evident that the digest was foundering, she was instructed by the management to dismiss her staff. Rather than do so, she resigned. The employees were subsequently terminated with two weeks' notice.[15] Feuerlicht, meanwhile, moved on to a new career as a writer of acclaimed children's books and adult nonfiction.

A mugging in Spain in 1982 left the lively author with a triple fracture of the skull, 13 rib fractures, damage to the inner ear, and impaired health for the rest of her life. She continued writing but was no longer able to pursue

her first love, folk dancing. By 1990, she had great difficulty in walking but "kept her sense of humor and refused to be treated as crippled."[16] Feuerlicht was hospitalized with pneumonia in September 1991 and died of congestive heart failure on 2 October 1991.[17]

Unidentified artist, *Crime and Punishment* (reissued September 1959). One of the titles reclaimed for *Classics* fans in the "Great Revival."

Her husband's assessment of her work for Gilberton is seconded by most of those who were associated with her: "Roberta took a despised medium and elevated it. She insisted on accuracy, decency, and the treatment of characters as human beings rather than cartoon stereo-types. She succeeded in gaining respect for *Classics Illustrated* from other publishers and the educational community."[18]

Sadly, when the *New York Times* ran her obituary, no mention was made of her work at 101 Fifth Avenue.

XXV

Classical Interlude: "Who Am I?"

One of the most popular and enduring features in *Classics Illustrated* was the "Who Am I?" quiz that appeared inside the front covers of hundreds of original editions and reprints between 1951 and 1961. The literary trivia game not only tested the reader's knowledge of characters in stories adapted for *Classics Illustrated*, but also promoted the series. For ten years, the format never changed—five clues gave information that amounted to plot summaries, and the name of the character was printed upside down at the end.

The following are the first and last "Who Am I?" quizzes, as printed in issue No. 86, *Under Two Flags* (August 1951), and issue No. 163, *Master of the World* (July 1961). The same rules prefaced both:

I am a famous literary character. Can you guess my name from the clues below? Rate your familiarity with me as follows: If you can identify me from CLUE I, your score is superior; from CLUE II—excellent; from CLUE III—very good; from CLUE IV—good; from CLUE V—fair. If after CLUE V you still cannot identify me, I suggest you read the exciting story in which I appear.

From No. 86:

CLUE I: I was known as the greatest swordsman in France during the reign of Louis XIV.

CLUE II: A series of comic misunderstandings brought about a challenge to a duel with three men who soon afterwards became my closest companions.

CLUE III: On one of my many adventures, I was able to save the Queen of France from a conspiracy against her. This involved a dangerous journey to England during which I had to either elude or fight the Queen's powerful enemies.

CLUE IV: I wore the uniform of the Musketeers and with my gay, carefree companions, Aramis, Porthos, and Athos, served France. Our slogan was "One for all and all for one!"

CLUE V: My thrilling career, with my adventure-seeking companions, saw me through exciting duels, battles and the intrigues of the Court. I am the main character in the famous story, "The Three Musketeers" by Alexandre Dumas.

[D'Artagnan]

From No. 163:

CLUE I: I was the only daughter of an Italian nobleman who was engaged in a terrible feud with another noble.

CLUE II: One night at a large ball, I met the son of my father's enemy. From the moment I saw him, I loved him. He came to me that night and told me that he loved me too.

CLUE III: The next day, we were married in secret by a sympathetic friar. Then, to defend my honor, my husband was forced to kill my cousin. For this, he was banished from the city. Frantically, I sought a way to join him.

CLUE IV: My father, who did not know of my secret marriage to his enemy's son, insisted that I marry another man. The wedding was two days away.

CLUE V: Desperate, I went to the friar, who gave me strange advice. The exciting climax of my story can be found in the play by William Shakespeare which bears my husband's name and mine.

[Juliet]

XXVI

High Tide and Greenbacks: The Late Fifties

By 1956, Roberta Strauss's influence in the Gilberton editorial office was unquestioned. With the encouragement of both Albert and William Kanter, the hard-working assistant was on her way to an editorship. Her championing of better adaptations, better artwork, and revisions of early numbers coincided with and were partly responsible for the boom years that *Classics Illustrated* enjoyed in the late 1950s.

This was also the period in which the former EC artists made their contributions to *Classics Illustrated*. They were joined by other first-rate illustrators who found refuge at 101 Fifth Avenue at a time when it didn't always pay to draw comic books.

MIKE SEKOWSKY

In the spring of 1956, the first redrawn and newly adapted *Classics* editions since 1953's *Dr. Jekyll and Mr. Hyde* appeared. Roberta Strauss, whose influence vastly exceeded her still unacknowledged editorial status, selected the first two titles with an eye toward symbolism: Herman Melville's *Moby Dick* and Mark Twain's *Adventures of Huckleberry Finn*, midcentury rivals for designation as The Great American Novel.

While the reliable Norman Nodel landed the tragic *Moby Dick*, the supposedly lighter *Huckleberry Finn*, No. 19 (revised edition March 1956), went to the fast-working penciler Mike Sekowsky (d. 1989), who had supplied art for Fiction House, Lev Gleason, and other publishers and who later was celebrated for his contributions to the *Justice League of America* issues in the DC series *The Brave and the Bold*. [1] Sekowsky also later illustrated *The*

Mike Sekowsky, *Huckleberry Finn* (March 1956). Huck and Jim meet the Duke and the King.

Rebel (1960–1961) for Dell. Assisting on the Twain title was the respected inker Frank Giacoia (1925–1989), an Italian-born artist best known for his DC collaborations (*Strange Adventures*, *Mystery in Space*) with Carmine Infantino and his work on *Batman*, *Flash*, and *Green Lantern*.[2]

At the time, Sekowsky and Giacoia were penciling and inking a Sherlock Holmes comic-strip serial (1954–1956), and the pair seemed an ideal team for a *Classics Illustrated* project. They had recently displayed a decidedly comic bent in the *Classics Illustrated Junior* treatments of *The Golden Goose*, No. 518 (September 1955), *Paul Bunyan*, No. 519 (October 1955), John Ruskin's *King of the Golden River*, No. 521 (December 1955), and *The Gallant Tailor*, No. 523 (February 1956). Sekowsky had produced painted covers for *The King of the Golden River* and *The Gallant Tailor*; he would later supply another one, for *The Magic Fountain*, No. 533 (December 1956), on which he again collaborated with Giacoia on the interior art. Subsequently, Sekowsky joined forces with inker Mike Peppe for *The Wizard of Oz*, No. 535 (February 1957), and *Silly Willy*, No. 557 (December 1958).[3]

The Twain adaptation restored the first person to Huck's narrative, and Sekowsky's brisk, humorous style served the story especially well in the portions concerning the doings of the rascally Duke and King. But Roberta Strauss's primary concern was to see that the humanity of Jim, Huck's African-American companion and mentor, was fully acknowledged in the character's portrayal.[4] Sekowsky complied with the editor's instructions; he accorded the runaway slave a measure of dignity and some complexity, treating him not as a comic foil but as a mature mentor.

Jack Sparling, *Robin Hood* (January 1957). Robin gathers his Merry Men.

he returned to newspaper strips with *Buck Rogers in the 25th Century*.[5]

Ron Goulart has noted of Sparling that his best work was characterized by a "realistic brush style" and "odd and unusual angle shots."[6] These qualities are in evidence in Sparling's two *Classics Illustrated* titles, where a foreground Robin addresses his Merry Men in *Robin Hood* and where a deep-focus Hank Morgan makes his terms with an anxious King Arthur in *A Connecticut Yankee*.

SAM CITRON OR CHARLES SULTAN

One of the major early titles to be revamped in 1957 was Daniel Defoe's *Robinson Crusoe*, No. 10. The much improved adaptation appeared around September of that year. Only a tentative identification of the artist has been made. Comics authority Hames Ware suggests the possibility that lookalike artists Sam Citron and Charles Sultan, brother-in-law of the legendary Lou Fine, may have drawn the book in tandem or, perhaps, singly. Both men illustrated romance comics as a team or individually in the 1950s, and both favored a detailed, realistic style.[7]

Whether Citron or Sultan or both were responsible for the book, the result was a considerable improvement over Stanley Maxwell Zuckerberg's 1943 version. In the 1957 edition, Defoe's narrative was closely followed, and the "savages" were presented in a less sensationalized, almost anthropological manner. The redrawn *Crusoe* went

JACK SPARLING

Long associated with the Jacquet shop, Jack Sparling (b. 1916) provided new illustrations for two popular early *Classics* titles, *Robin Hood*, No. 7 (revised edition January 1957), and Mark Twain's *A Connecticut Yankee in King Arthur's Court*, No. 24 (revised edition September 1957). A native of New Orleans, the artist began his career there as a newspaper editorial and sports cartoonist. After moving to Washington, D.C., in 1940, Sparling drew syndicated comic strips, including *Claire Voyant* (1943–1948), and produced illustrations for the educational *True Comics* and the rather less educational *Nyoka, The Jungle Girl*. Later, he worked for DC (*Green Lantern*), Marvel (*X-Men*), and Dell (*Mission Impossible*). In 1982,

HE CAME NEARER AND KNELT IN TOKEN OF ACKNOWLEDGEMENT FOR MY SAVING HIS LIFE.

Sam Citron or Charles Sultan or both, *Robinson Crusoe* **(September 1957). Crusoe saves Friday and gains a friend and servant.**

through nine printings at 100,000 to 250,000 copies each before the series ceased publication in 1971.

STAN CAMPBELL

Castle Dangerous, No. 141 (November 1957), an account of an early 14th-century siege of an English-held Scottish stronghold, was the last of Sir Walter Scott's *Waverley* novels and the last adapted for *Classics Illustrated.* An inferior example of the author's fiction, in which his imaginative powers frequently appeared to fail him, the book nevertheless translated exceptionally well into the stripped-down comics medium, demonstrating once again the principle that lesser works had less to lose in 45-page adaptations.

Stan Campbell, a Charlton artist, drew and inked *Castle Dangerous.* His superbly rendered character studies of the disguised heroine, her minstrel protector, and the "Black Douglas," as well as his carefully wrought depictions of armor, mail, and arms, made this one of the handsomest of the later *Classics* titles. Campbell also illustrated two *Juniors*—*The Donkey's Tale*, No. 542 (September 1957), and *The Singing Donkey*, No. 550 (May 1958)—which featured delightfully cartoonish character sketches of the "Bremen Town Musicians" and the terrified robbers, along with sections of two *Classics Illustrated Special Issues*, *Royal Canadian Mounted Police*, No. 150A (June 1959), and *The War Between the States*, No. 162A (June 1961), and several *World Around Us* issues, including the cover and the interior art for *Flight*, No. W8 (April 1959), and interior art for *Marines*, No. W11 (July 1959), and *Famous Teens*, No. W33 (May 1961).

KEN BATTEFIELD

The third part of the d'Artagnan trilogy by Alexandre Dumas, *The Man in the Iron Mask*, No. 54, had been missing from the *Classics* reorder list since 1955. Baby boomers who expected solid linework and postwar real-

Castle Dangerous
Sir Walter Scott

IN 1307, THE SCOTS WERE IN THE MIDST OF A BLOODY STRUGGLE TO FREE THEMSELVES FROM ENGLAND. AMONG THE POSSESSIONS HELD BY THE ENGLISH WAS DOUGLAS CASTLE, WHICH OCCUPIED A STRATEGIC POSITION ON THE SCOTTISH BORDER.
DOUGLAS CASTLE WAS GALLANTLY BESIEGED BY THE SCOTS AND DEFENDED WITH EQUAL BRAVERY BY THE ENGLISH. THE CONFLICT FOR CONTROL OF THE CASTLE WAS PRESSED UNDER SUCH CIRCUMSTANCES OF VALOUR AND CRUELTY THAT IT SOON CAME TO BE KNOWN AS CASTLE DANGEROUS.

Stan Campbell, *Castle Dangerous* **(November 1957). A handsomely drawn exercise in medievalism, with traces of Batman in the "Black Douglas."**

ism in their comics apparently found it difficult to respond to August M. Froehlich's old-fashioned impressionism. Curiously enough, the revision of Dumas's tale of royal intrigue, issued in January 1958, is believed to have been assigned to an artist whose arrival at Gilberton had predated that of Froehlich's by six years. Ken Battefield (d. 1967) had assisted Malcolm Kildale in 1941 with the first *Classic Comic*, Dumas's *The Three Musketeers*, supplying panels here and there.

Although he is generally considered an illustrator of modest abilities, Battefield surpassed himself in *The Man in the Iron Mask*, spurred, no doubt, by Roberta Strauss's exacting eye. A few characters, including the central schemer Aramis and his accomplice Porthos, are awkwardly drawn. But the mid–17th-century costuming and settings are faithfully reproduced, the young Louis XIV and his fictional twin actually resemble the young Louis XIV, and the story's claustrophobic atmosphere of

THE MAN IN THE IRON MASK 35

AH, YOUR EYES ARE BECOMING WILD. I SHALL HAVE TO TAKE AWAY YOUR KNIFE.

THE JAILER LEFT. NOW THE KING'S RAGE AND FRENZY KNEW NO BOUNDS.

HE TORE AT THE DOOR WITH HIS NAILS AND UTTERED WILD AND FEARFUL CRIES.

TWO HOURS AFTERWARD, LOUIS XIV COULD NOT BE RECOGNIZED AS A KING—A GENTLEMAN—A HUMAN BEING.

Ken Battefield, *The Man in the Iron Mask* (January 1958). Louis loses his temper.

intrigue is effectively conveyed in crowded panels, contorted forms, and striking perspectives.

GERALD McCANN

Considered one of the top five "regulars" among the *Classics* freelancers of the later years,[8] Gerald McCann (b. 1916) produced some of the handsomest painted covers in the entire run of the series. His only rival in terms of quality was L.B. Cole. As for quantity, McCann outpaced everyone: he supplied painted covers or interior artwork for more than 40 *Classics Illustrated, Special Issues,* and *World Around Us* titles.

Best known as an illustrator of juvenile books, the artist's distinctive style, with its elongated, dry-brushed figures, graced many works of the period, such as Edesse Peery Smith's award-winning *Pokes of Gold* (1958), Enid Lamonte Meadowcroft's *We Were There at the Opening of the Erie Canal* (1958), and Anne Colver's *Florence Nightingale: War Nurse* (1961). McCann also illustrated other comic books, such as the Dell *Movie Classic* edition of *Morgan the Pirate* (September 1961). Soon after Gilberton shut down its American operations in 1962, he turned his attention to *Treasure Island, Robinson Crusoe,* and *Tom Sawyer Detective* for Grosset and Dunlap's *Companion Library* series.

McCann was remembered by George Evans as a "witty man" who worked well with the editorial staff and never missed a deadline. Unlike Evans, he had more contacts with the business end of 101 Fifth Avenue, about which he remarked: "If you ever have to deal with those people in management, you'll need embalming fluid."[9]

The artist's background was in pulp-fiction illustration, and he brought to the Gilberton publications the dry-brush and split-brush techniques associated with the genre. McCann's panels are painterly, marked by a broad-stroked linework that suggests rather than details; his backgrounds and costumes are generally sketchy, while the primary figurative emphasis is upon plasticity of expression and gesture.

While he had already provided painted covers for two *Classics, The First Men in the Moon* and *Ben-Hur,* and interior sections of *Horses, Space,* and *The FBI* for the newly inaugurated *World Around Us* in 1958, McCann's first complete book for Gilberton was Jules Verne's *Off on a Comet,* No. 149 (March 1959), a title that was destined to become a *Classics Illustrated* icon through reproduction of the cover (actually, a line-drawing mock-up) on reorder lists from 1959 to 1970. The science-fiction tale of two rivals whose duel is postponed when they and other inhabitants of the Mediterranean rim are swept into space is rendered with visual economy and wit.

During the rest of 1959, McCann was occupied with illustrating portions of every *World Around Us* edition that appeared on a monthly basis during the year. The artist's historical eye served him well in such issues as *Pirates,* No. W7 (March 1959), *The French Revolution,* No. W14 (October 1959), and *The Crusades,* No. W16 (December 1959), for which he painted one of the series' most striking covers.

Gerald McCann, *Off on a Comet* (March 1959). The artist's dry-brush style made his illustrations the most readily recognizable in the Gilberton publications of the late 1950s and early 1960s.

The following year brought two beautifully rendered *Classics Illustrated* titles: Francis Parkman's *The Conspiracy of Pontiac*, No. 154 (January 1960), and Alexandre Dumas's *The Conspirators*, No. 158 (September 1960), both seamlessly adapted by Al Sundel. McCann's illustrations bring the two relatively obscure works vibrantly to life, and the painted covers he produced are among the most compelling of Gilberton's later years. *Pontiac*, in particular, is a strikingly textured composition, with its finely observed French and Indian foreground figures and a background map filling the sky. (See color section.)

For another cover from that year, *The Lion of the North*, No. 155 (March 1960), the artist produced a dark scene of Gustavus Adolphus directing cannon fire. Despite the heroic posture of the king on horseback, the painting, with its midnight-blue sky and fallen soldier, seems a commentary on false glory and a dramatic foreshadowing of the Swedish monarch's fate.

Like Louis Zansky before him, McCann was obviously a painter barely at home in the comics medium. Unlike his predecessor, however, he was often able to leave pencil and ink behind on assignments. Between 1960 and 1962, McCann made his greatest contribution to *Classics Illustrated* with the covers he painted for *The Conspiracy of Pontiac*, *The Conspirators*, *The Lion of the North*, *Typee*, *The Man Without a Country*, *The Pilot*, *The Hunchback of Notre Dame*, *The Food of the Gods* (see color section), *Les Miserables*, *Tom Brown's School Days*, and

Gerald McCann, *The Conspirators* (September 1960). A title for which the artist produced both the painted cover and interior art.

Pudd'nhead Wilson, as well as those he produced for *Special Issues* and *The World Around Us*. If covers establish a newsstand identity, then Gerald McCann was as much the embodiment of Gilberton publications in the early 1960s as Norman Nodel or, earlier, Henry C. Kiefer and Alex Blum.

JOHN TARTAGLIONE

A romance-comics artist for Atlas (Marvel), John Tartaglione (b. 1921) might not have seemed a logical choice as illustrator of two red-blooded boys' books. Still, his interiors for G.A. Henty's *Won By the Sword*, No. 151 (July 1959), and the revision of Thomas Hughes's *Tom Brown's School Days*, No. 45 (March 1961), were lively exercises, and the latter title in particular was an unqualified success.

John Tartaglione, *Tom Brown's School Days* (March 1961). A perfect union of style and subject. Note the heavily scored linework, reminiscent of Victorian illustrations.

With their open-featured, plucky young heroes and delicate linework, Tartaglione's *Classics* exhibited an appealing playfulness. *Won By the Sword* follows the fortunes of young Hector Campbell in the Thirty Years War and is rendered as an extended adolescent daydream, the operative mode of most Henty novels. The artist depicts violence in so stylized a manner that even being pinned beneath a horse on a battlefield seems of little consequence to the indomitable principal character. (In contrast, Norman Nodel's illustrations for Henty's *Lion of the North*, No. 155, another story about a Scottish boy's adventures in the same conflict, present a darker,

less romantic view of the 17th-century bloodbath.)

Tom Brown's School Days is Tartaglione's Gilberton masterpiece—a handsomely drawn, beautifully inked depiction of life at Dr. Arnold's Rugby and the ongoing battle of wills between Brown, his friend East, and the archetypal bully Flashman. The artist's distinctive hatch marks lend an air of antiquity to Al Sundel's adaptation, creating a visual and even physical texture for this Victorian precursor of the Harry Potter novels. All of the characters are presented in such lifelike, natural poses that the panels seem invested with a nearly cinematic verisimilitude. The book ranks among the most perfectly achieved issues in the *Classics Illustrated* catalogue.

Most of Tartaglione's output for Gilberton appeared in three *Special Issues* and 19 *World Around Us* editions. An eight-page chapter on John Hunt Morgan's Kentucky raid in *The War Between the States*, a 1961 *Special Issue*, was among his more memorable contributions. Tartaglione later illustrated Marvel biographies of Pope John Paul II (1982) and Mother Teresa (1984) and inked Marie Severin's *Dragonslayer* series.

LEONARD B. COLE

Leonard Brandt Cole (1918–1995) arrived at Gilberton after a stint at St. John Publishing and served as art director from November 1958 to January 1961, succeeding the retired Alex A. Blum. Cole's friend Norman Nodel told him about the opening, and the already well-respected artist phoned executive editor Meyer A. Kaplan, who immediately hired him.[10]

Described by scriptwriter Al Sundel as a man "of Falstaffian girth,"[11] the ebullient, amiable Cole had illustrated Bible stories and had been the editor of Star Comics, where he inaugurated *School-Day Romances* (subsequently renamed *Popular Teenagers*).[12] At Gilberton, he presided over the assembly of a stable of talented artists driven to Kanter's lower-paying enterprise by the implosion of Atlas and other comics publishers. McCann, Tartaglione, Norman Saunders, Jack Kirby, and other Cole-era freelancers filled the quotas for the four series in production. In an interview toward the end of his life, Cole confessed that he had found it difficult to keep track of the multitude of editions in print and subject to revision.[13]

The art director's first Gilberton assignment had

Left: Leonard B. Cole, *Wild Animals I Have Known* (September 1959): Cole was unsurpassed in drawing animals in action. *Right:* Leonard B. Cole, *Lives of the Hunted* (July 1960). The artist's second Ernest Thompson Seton cover.

been a painted cover and a four-page section in an early *World Around Us* issue, *Horses*, No. 3 (November 1958), the only *Classics*-related piece he signed, and the only work he kept for himself.[14] As a teenager, Cole became infatuated with horses after seeing the racehorse legend Man o' War, and he drew them obsessively for a couple of years. He also had a passion for dogs.[15]

Although Cole was an extraordinarily versatile artist, animals remained his specialty, and his best work featured them prominently: the painted cover (see color section) and interior art for Ernest Thompson Seton's *Wild Animals I Have Known*, No. 152 (September 1959); the painted cover for Ernest Thompson Seton's *Lives of the Hunted*, No. 157 (July 1960); the painted cover for Frank Norris's *The Octopus*, No. 159 (November 1960) (see color section); and the painted cover and partial interior art for the late 1960 reissue of Anna Sewell's *Black Beauty*, No. 60. The cover, showing the horse galloping through a field, is a magnificent expression of the artist's love for the subject and an indelible icon.

Part of Cole's editorial duties involved supplying painted covers for the *Classics Illustrated Junior* series, and he did so for every issue from *The Magic Dish*, No. 558 (February 1959), to *The Happy Hedgehog*, No. 568 (October 1960). The artist also produced new covers for various *Classics Illustrated* reissues, including *Green Mansions*, No. 90 (second painted cover, January 1959), *The Moonstone*, No. 30 (painted cover, March 1960), and *Julius Caesar*, No. 68 (painted cover, Summer 1960).

Unfortunately, questions concerning Cole's handling of freelancer accounts, including alleged self-dealing, reputedly led to his abrupt departure from Gilberton.[16] The axe fell when *Black Beauty* was in progress, and Norman Nodel and Stephen L. Addeo (who had played a similar role in *The Last of the Mohicans*) stepped in to complete the revision. Years later, Cole insisted that he had walked away from Gilberton strictly as a matter of money and the changing state of the comics business.[17]

The year 1961 was, in fact, unkind to Albert Kanter's enterprise, with external pressures applied by the

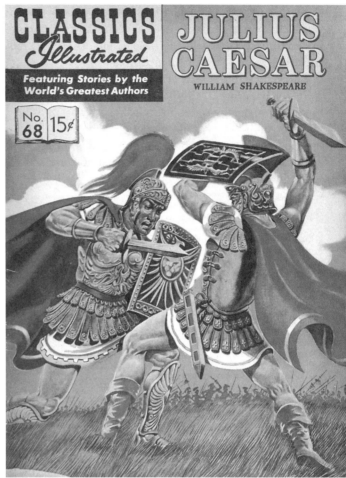

Left: Leonard B. Cole, *Black Beauty* (Fall 1960). The artist's last work for Gilberton; the subject, appropriately, was a horse. *Right:* Leonard B. Cole, *Julius Caesar* (May 1960). Roman faces Roman on the plains of Philippi.

postal authorities and the distribution network. Internally, a war of wills had been intensifying between two factions: the Old Guard, represented by longtime editor Meyer Kaplan and his chosen art director L.B. Cole, and the Young Turks, comprising Roberta Strauss Feuerlicht and scriptwriter Alfred Sundel. Feuerlicht and Sundel shared a vision of the future direction of the publications that gave greater emphasis to the educational content and, in view of Gilberton's expanding world market, greater prominence to Central and Eastern European, Latin American, and Asian history and literature. Once Feuerlicht gained Albert Kanter's confidence, the days of Kaplan and Cole were undoubtedly numbered, and whatever the precipitating incident might have been, the exit of the two friends and allies was probably inevitable.

Cole went on to work as art director for Dell Comics, which would soon face major internal changes of its own. And at 101 Fifth Avenue, under the less-is-more influence of the new Gilberton art director, Sidney Miller, *Classics Illustrated* never quite regained its artistic bearings, while the quality of the *Junior* line, which Cole had elevated, took a nosedive. Veterans such as Norman Nodel, George Evans, and Gray Morrow continued to produce outstanding work for Al Sundel's expertly crafted scripts, but the fallen art director's successor was unable to enlist new recruits of comparable talent.

Classics collector and researcher John Haufe, who befriended Cole, regards him as "in some ways a tragic figure." Yet, he maintains, the artist "brought so much to [Gilberton] in the late Fifties. He deserves to be remembered for his positive contributions—and all those wonderful animal covers."[18]

NORMAN B. SAUNDERS

He never drew a book for *Classics Illustrated*, but Norman B. Saunders (1907–1989) painted two of the most memorable covers of the 1950s—*Frankenstein*, No. 26 (September 1958), and *The Buccaneer*, No. 148 (January 1959). The former, a study in shades of icy gray and blue, shows the monster pursued by his creator in a frozen wasteland, while the latter depicts Jean Lafitte (or, more precisely, a costumed Yul Brynner), against a vivid red backdrop, primed for swashbuckling.

A veteran pulp cover artist, Saunders also produced work for paperbacks and other comics. In 1961, Topps hired him to paint a series of Civil War trading cards notable for their gory details of soldiers being impaled on bayonets or blown apart by cannon. Saunders stayed with Topps until his retirement in 1981, producing a *Batman* set in 1966 after achieving pop-culture apotheosis in 1962 with the card series *Mars Attacks*.[19]

DOUG ROEA AND GEOFFREY BIGGS

Two outstanding artists who provided painted covers for *Classics Illustrated* in an era otherwise dominated by Gerald McCann and L.B. Cole were Doug Roea and Geoffrey Biggs (b. 1908). Both produced their most evocative works for the series in 1959—Roea's cover for *The Virginian*, No. 150, showing a pair of gunmen facing each other on a darkened Western street, and Biggs's cover for *The Invisible Man*, No. 153, depicting the title character racing down a London street with eyeglasses resting on his unseen face.

Roea's first contribution to a Gilberton publication was the cover for a 1958 *World Around Us* issue devoted to the army. After *The Virginian*, which was given a dark-green cast, the artist painted striking studies dominated by darker colors for reissued editions of *Twenty Years*

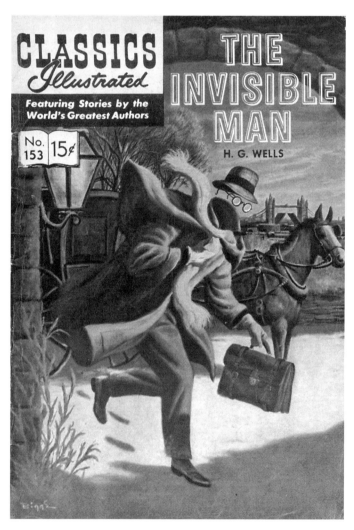

Left: **Norman B. Saunders,** *Frankenstein* **(September 1958). The monster redux.** *Right:* **Geoffrey Biggs,** *The Invisible Man* **(November 1959). A classic** *Classics* **cover.**

After, No. 41 (May 1960), and *The Woman in White*, No. 61 (May 1960). The artist employed sharp contrasts to good effect on the Wilkie Collins title.

Like Roea, Biggs started with a *World Around Us* cover, *Prehistoric Animals*, No. W15 (November 1959). Following his success with *The Invisible Man* during the same month, the artist depicted Cathy and Heathcliff on the moors under a stunning black sky for the reissued *Wuthering Heights* (May 1960). A pair of determined Union infantrymen were the focal point for Biggs's last Gilberton cover, *The War Between the States*, No. 162A (June 1961).

XXVII

Classical Interlude:
A Fan's Notes on the 1950s

The most devoted *Classics Illustrated* readers in the late 1950s lived on a bimonthly schedule, eagerly awaiting the arrival of the newest issue—or reissue—at their neighborhood variety, grocery, or drug stores. Among the ranks of the faithful was John Haufe of Kettering, Ohio, a future assistant editor of *The Classics Collector*. Writing about the pleasures of collecting the series in its heyday, Haufe recalled the most exciting moments:

1. Anticipating the Original issues as they came out between November 1953 and August 1962—it was very exciting to see the new covers. My S.S. Kresge *CI* spinner usually had two or three pockets of the current issue at the top of the rack. Also equally exciting for me was the thrill of discovering what was forthcoming in the series through the "Coming Next" ads. This feature was rather unique with *CI* as the other comic series were more predictable with their themes and characters.

2. Ordering hard-to-find numbers directly from Gilberton in New York and then receiving the copies in a large manila envelope. These "scarce" *Classics* not found at my local Kresge's outlet included such issues as Nos. 40 [*Mysteries*], 44 [*Mysteries of Paris*], 53 [*A Christmas Carol*], 66 [*The Cloister and the Hearth*], 73 [*The Black Tulip*], 74 [*Mr. Midshipman Easy*], 113 [*The Forty-Five Guardsmen*], 114 [*The Red Rover*], 116 [*The Bottle Imp*], 120 [*The Hurricane*], and 129 [*Davy Crockett*].

3. Seeing *Classics* away from my home town while vacationing every summer in the east. They could be found in the Howard Johnson gift shops along the Pennsylvania/New Jersey turnpikes and prominently displayed on the newsstands of New York City.[1]

Multiply variations of those experiences by tens of thousands, and a composite picture of the hardcore baby-boomer *Classics Illustrated* fan begins to emerge.

XXVIII

"Roberta's Reforms": The Early Sixties

By the early 1960s, Roberta Strauss Feuerlicht had recharted the direction of *Classics Illustrated*. On board were Alfred Sundel, the gifted scriptwriter who suggested many of the later titles, and editorial assistant Helene Lecar, who spent hours at the New York Public Library researching period costumes and artifacts. It was the heyday of Norman Nodel, George Evans, Angelo Torres, Gerald McCann, and Gray Morrow—and was dubbed by Sundel the era of "Roberta's Reforms."[1]

Perhaps the golden year was 1960, when three outstanding new titles—*The Conspiracy of Pontiac, The Conquest of Mexico,* and *The Octopus*—were published and 13 books long out of print—*Don Quixote, Gulliver's Travels, Two Years Before the Mast, The Moonstone, Typee, Twenty Years After, Alice in Wonderland, Wuthering Heights, Black Beauty, The Woman in White, The Man Without a Country, Julius Caesar,* and *Men of Iron*—were restored to the line. The "Great Revival" continued in 1961: *Arabian Nights, Les Miserables, The Last Days of Pompeii, Adventures of Cellini, Tom Brown's School Days,* and *A Midsummer Night's Dream,* all formerly discontinued titles, surfaced again, the first five in completely new editions. Four different publications appeared on a regular schedule and were earning the respect of teachers and parents, many of whom had grown up on *Classic Comics* and *Classics Illustrated.* Better art and more reissues had become the order of the day.

Meanwhile, Gilberton, which had been fighting with the Post Office to retain its second-class mailing permit, lost the legal battle in 1961. The immediate result was the abrupt cancellation of *The World Around Us* series and the termination of the *Classics Illustrated* bimonthly cycle. Issue No. 163 appeared in July 1961, but

No. 164 didn't appear until October; No. 165 was issued in January 1962.

More restored titles appeared in 1962: *The Man Who Laughs, The Courtship of Miles Standish, Pudd'nhead Wilson, The White Company, Knights of the Round Table, Pitcairn's Island, A Study in Scarlet,* and *The Talisman.* Despite its now irregular schedule, *Classics Illustrated* also produced in 1962 what the editorial staff considered their crowning achievement and the finest single issue—Goethe's *Faust,* masterfully adapted by Al Sundel and beautifully rendered by Norman Nodel. But the end was already at hand.

GRAY MORROW

One of the Gilberton Company's greatest finds, Gray Morrow (b. 1934) signed on through the good offices of a friend, *Classics Illustrated* contributor Angelo Torres:

> I was recently discharged from the army after serving in Korea '56–'58. The comics publishing industry was in a kind of doldrums. My friend Angelo Torres took me around to a couple of his clients, one being "Classics," and I was given a script. One thing led to another and I was soon working on a regular basis.[2]

Scriptwriter Sundel recalled the artist as one who "typically wore a tan belted raincoat" and was "on the quiet side, slim. He may have been married but he always looked dashingly single. He was younger than Nodel and Evans, his only peers among the best of our comic-strip artists. He simply had great natural talent."[3]

Of his Gilberton days, Morrow recalled that

the page rate wasn't much for the accuracy and authenticity they expected, but it was a challenge to "do it right." Roberta and Len Cole were demanding but genial editors. One job … about whaling [for *World Around Us* issue No. W28, *Whaling* (December 1960)] got me in dutch with Roberta. My research indicated that many of the whalers were blacks—so that's what I drew. She had a fit and insisted they all be redrawn to "avoid controversy." Also, I must've been one of the first to draw in comics men with hairy chests and nipples. In those days characters in comics didn't sport such indications of their genders. Women may've had torpedo-shaped breasts but lacked nipples and never wore a navel.[4]

"The Long Voyage," the chapter for *Whaling* that caused such a problem for the artist with editor Feuerlicht, retained a respectable number of African-American whalemen and proved to be one of the most outstanding works of the artist's tenure with Gilberton.

Morrow's first pages for the publisher had appeared in another *World Around Us* issue, No. W15, *Prehistoric Animals* (November 1959), for which he drew such creatures as the dimetrodon and pterodactyl and recreated the drama of early 19th-century fossil discoveries. He soon became a regular contributor to the monthly educational series, providing illustrations for 13 issues, including the painted cover and interior art for *Magic*, No. W25 (September 1960), and sections in *Great Scientists*, No. W18 (February 1960). Others he worked on were *The Jungle*, No. W19 (March 1960); *American Presidents*, No. W21 (May 1960); *Boating*, No. W22 (June 1960); *Great Explorers*, No. W23 (July 1960); *Ghosts*, No. W24 (August 1960); *The Civil War*, No. W26 (October 1960); *High Adventure*, No. W27 (November 1960); *For Gold and Glory*, No. W32 (April 1961); and *Famous Teens*, No. W33 (May 1961).

The artist was also responsible for the "Seven for Space" chapter devoted to the Project Mercury astronauts in the timely *Rockets, Jets and Missiles, Special Issue* No. 159A (December 1960). His drawings provided a cross-section view of the space capsule, offered individual portraits of the first astronauts, and followed "their difficult training program" from the centrifuge to zero-gravity flights. "One will be chosen to orbit the earth," announced the text of the final panel, which displayed the artist's spectral rendering of the mystery astronaut. The suborbital flight of Alan Shepard in *Freedom 7* was five months away; John Glenn's triple orbit in *Friendship 7* was 14 months in the future. Public anticipation was building, and Gilberton was playing its role, simultaneously educating and capitalizing on the historical moment.

It was Morrow's sustained efforts in three *Classics Illustrated* editions that reveal the qualities that earned the admiration of the editorial staff at 101 Fifth Avenue. The first of these, *The Octopus*, No. 159 (November 1960), is, along with *The Conquest of Mexico* and *Faust*, one of the showpieces of the Feuerlicht era. Like its companions, *The Octopus* features an intelligent adaptation by Al Sundel, who deftly encapsulated the propagandistic fervor and strident symbolism of Frank Norris's naturalistic novel about the tragic struggle between wheat farmers and the railroad in California's San Joaquin Valley.

Either Sundel supplied Morrow with Norris's extensive character descriptions or Morrow read the novel with the attention of a bar candidate scrutinizing Article 9 of the Uniform Commercial Code. In any event, *The Octopus* boasts the most accurate rendering of characters of any issue in the *Classics Illustrated* line, capturing everything from the heroic Annixter's "lower lip thrust out, the chin large and deeply cleft" to the oily S. Behrman's "great tremulous jowl" and "protuberant stomach."[5]

Yet Morrow's treatment of the work goes beyond mere descriptive fidelity. Each panel is composed cinematically. The climactic confrontations between the ranchers and the United States marshal and his deputies is first shown, subjectively, at close range and then, objectively, with Olympian detachment, from above. Character is illuminated through facial expression and physical stance, as when Annixter coolly faces a drunken gun-wielding cowboy or S. Behrman realizes that he is about to be drowned in wheat.

The next *Classics Illustrated* title assigned to Morrow was Jules Verne's *Master of the World*, No. 163 (July 1961), the better-known sequel to the preceding issue, *Robur the Conqueror*, and a then current Vincent Price motion-picture vehicle. Tackling an adventure tale with comparatively little dialogue (37 panels employ thought bubbles rather than speech balloons and another 35 rely only on narrative boxes), the artist exploited the drama of the machinery and succeeded in making the *Terror*—a combination "automobile, boat, submarine, and airship"—a character in its own right.

Morrow's Robur, the "master of the world" himself, though based for the sake of continuity on Don Perlin's conception in issue No. 162, surpasses its model in monomaniacal grandeur. On the other hand, the dapper protagonist, John Strock, may have been one of the figures Al Sundel had in mind when he wrote that "Gray's flaw, if he had one, was to tend to draw men who looked a bit too English and a bit too alike from book to book, a little taller than Gray himself but built along the same slim lines."[6]

For Alexandre Dumas's *The Queen's Necklace*, No. 165 (January 1962), Morrow worked at top speed: "[I]t was done when I'd moved to California and I needed those checks badly so I was penciling and inking eight

Gray Morrow, *The Octopus* (November 1960). A two-page, self-contained dramatic episode that defines Annixter's character and foreshadows the violent climax of the story. Note Morrow's use of the cinematic montage effect.

pages a day. That's as fast as I've ever been able to go."[7] Given the pace at which the book was executed, it is a remarkable performance. The *ancien régime* period details, encompassing clothing, hair, posture, and backgrounds, are presented with delicate precision. Although the sketches of Marie Antoinette appear rather rushed and one-dimensional, other figures involved in the intrigue that undermined the French throne are rendered with the complexity of the characters in *The Octopus*, particularly the scheming Count Cagliostro and the hack journalist Reteau.

During his freelance involvement with *Classics Illustrated*, Morrow was busy illustrating volumes in the Bobbs-Merrill "Childhood of Famous Americans" series, to which other Gilberton artists had contributed. He continued working on the juvenile biographies after *Classics* new-title production ceased, providing artwork for Helen Albee Monsell's *Henry Clay: Young Kentucky Orator*

(1963) and Laura M. Long's *Douglas MacArthur: Young Protector* (1965). Morrow became better known in the 1960s for his covers for such science-fiction works as Andre Norton's *Night of Masks* (1965) and his black-and-white comics for Warren Publishing's *Creepy*. He remained active through the 1990s and was approached by

Gray Morrow, *Master of the World* (July 1961). Robur takes an ego trip.

The winter and spring of 1784 devoured half of France. About the middle of April, three hundred thousand miserable beings, dying from cold and hunger, groaned in Paris alone. Scarcely another city contained so many rich people, but nothing had been done to prevent the poor from perishing of wretchedness.

The frost prolonged the miseries of the people. The frozen streets became so dangerous that the people suffered from broken limbs and accidents of all kinds. Snow prevented the carriages from being heard, and the police had much to do, because of the reckless driving of the aristocracy, to preserve from the wheels those who were spared by cold and hunger.

Gray Morrow, *the Queen's Necklace* (January 1962). The artist completed his illustrations for the Dumas title in five days.

First Classics, Inc., with a proposal to illustrate an issue on wolves in a new *World Around Us* line, but the projected series folded when the revived *Classics Illustrated* line failed.

Bruno Premiani

A pet project of scriptwriter Al Sundel, *The Conquest of Mexico*, No. 156 (May 1960), was a landmark issue

that showed the Feuerlicht Era *Classics Illustrated* at its best. Sundel's sophisticated adaptation of Bernal Diaz del Castillo's 16th-century narrative manages to convey in small compass the sweep of the epic eyewitness work yet never condescends to the reader. Researcher Helene Lecar unearthed a wealth of material for artist Bruno Premiani, who made the most of it, recreating conquistador accoutrements and Aztec architecture with impressive authenticity.

Premiani, best known for his work between 1963 and 1968 on *Doom Patrol*,[8] painted a dramatic cover showing a mounted conquistador plunging into battle. He incorporated an Aztec pictograph on the title-page splash, and his swiftly moving panels echo the ancient art form throughout the 45-page abridgment. The artist's illustrations are perfectly wedded to the substantial text, establishing the principal characters and pushing the action from panel to panel with a visual excitement seldom matched in the series.

Although *The Conquest of Mexico* was Premiani's sole *Classics Illustrated* credit, he supplied sections for *Special Issues* No. 156A, *The Atomic Age* (June 1960), and the unnumbered, undated *United Nations*. He also provided artwork for six *World Around Us* editions: *The Crusades*, No. W16 (December 1959); *Festivals*, No. W17 (January 1960); *Great Scientists*, No. W18 (February 1960); *Communications*, No. W20 (April 1960); *Whaling*, No. W28 (December 1960); and *Vikings*, No. W29 (January 1961). "The Walled City," a chapter on the Siege of Antioch in *The Crusades*, features panels filled with mail-clad Crusaders and scimitar-wielding Muslims, all drawn with an attention to historical detail that rivals if not surpasses *The Conquest of Mexico*.

Tony Tallarico

While George Evans and Reed Crandall were occupied with *The Hunchback of Notre Dame*, Gray Morrow was completing *The Octopus*, and Norman Nodel was preparing *Cleopatra*, art director Leonard B. Cole, in his last assignment, handed Al Sundel's artfully edited script for H.G. Wells's *The Food of the Gods*, No. 160 (January

Left: Bruno Premiani, *The Conquest of Mexico* (May 1960). A wealth of historical detail filled the artist's panels. *Right:* Tony Tallarico, *The Food of the Gods* (January 1961). A subversively light touch for an ultimately unsettling tale.

1961), to Tony Tallarico (b. 1933), a former Charlton artist with a distinctively light touch who later drew television tie-ins such as *Bewitched* and *F-Troop* for Dell.[9] Over the years, the prolific artist wrote and illustrated hundreds of children's books. In the 1990s, he decorated puzzle books and illustrated the *I Can Draw* series, introducing aspiring young artists to techniques for rendering such things as monsters, spaceships, and animals.

The Food of the Gods was the only *Classics Illustrated* title drawn by Tallarico. The artist's childlike, cartoonish approach bore little resemblance to the EC brand of realism that had shaped the Gilberton house style in the late 1950s. Still, Tallarico's playful style gave visual expression to the satirical thrust of Wells's philosophical fantasy about a race of giants who embody the principle of the "growth that goes on forever." The artist subverts the reader's expectations with the lightly sketched, whimsical figures that inhabit the first half of the book. A tex-

tual shift in tone occurs midway, beginning a movement toward a quasi-tragic and ultimately prophetic mode, but the same caricaturelike effect persists. The resulting aesthetic disjunction is intentionally jarring and eerily effective.

Like Lin Streeter and Peter Costanza before him, Tallarico appeared as an artist to be ideally suited to the folk tales and fairy tales of *Classics Illustrated Junior*. His style perfectly complemented *How Fire Came to the Indians*, No. 571 (April 1961), an early foray into the field of multiculturalism and, in terms of script and art, one of the most satisfying issues in the series, and *Brightboots*, No. 574 (c. October 1961), a high-spirited tale of a resourceful soldier who unwittingly serves his king. Tallarico's decisive simplicity enhanced both books.

Other fine efforts appeared in *World Around Us* issues No. W27, *High Adventure* (November 1960); No. W29, *The Vikings* (January 1961); No. W30, *Undersea*

Adventures (February 1961); No. W33, *Famous Teens* (May 1961); and No. W36, *Fight for Life* (October 1961). Bold linework particularly distinguished "The Strongest of the Vikings," a chapter in No. W29 based on a saga about the Jomsvikings and their leader Sigvald's rash vow that led to a crushing defeat. After the Frawley organization assumed control and began issuing second painted covers in an effort to breathe life into the expiring series, the artist was commissioned to paint a Fess Parker lookalike for a new edition of *Daniel Boone*, No. 96 (Winter 1969) and a new, more menacing Cyclops to replace Alex A. Blum's rather contemplative Polyphemus on the cover of *The Odyssey* (Spring 1969).

JACK KIRBY

Among the distinguished freelancers who collected Gilberton paychecks in the early 1960s was comics legend Jack Kirby (1917–1994), whose influence on the medium was incalculable. Born Jacob Kurtzburg in New York's Lower East Side, he enrolled at the Pratt Institute at the age of 14.[10] The artist worked on *Popeye* cartoons for the animation studios of Max Fleischer and subsequently drew adventure and humor comic strips for Lincoln Features. At first, he signed his work "Jack Curtiss," but when he began producing another strip for a different syndicate, he adopted the name "Lance Kirby." Merging the two pseudonyms in 1940, Jacob Kurtzburg became forever Jack Kirby.[11]

In 1941, he illustrated the first issue of *Captain Marvel Adventures*. That same year, he collaborated with Timely (Marvel) editor Joe Simon to create a comic-book icon, Captain America. Kirby and Simon were a perfectly matched dynamic duo of the comic-book Golden Age. They grasped the distinctive narrative potential of comic books, and together invented, among other new methods of expression, the two-page splash illustration.[12] The centerspread splash became something of a trademark *Classics Illustrated* convention in 1952 and 1953.

Moving to DC Comics in 1942, the team—always billed as Simon and Kirby—worked on *Boy Commandos* and an early incarnation of the "Sandman" character. A year later, both artists received their greetings from Uncle Sam.[13] After World II, the pair produced a variety of comics for Prize, including westerns and, in a wildly successful effort to reach a more mature female audience, *Young Romance* (September 1947), the first "love" comic book.[14]

Buffeted by the mid–1950s anticomics uproar, the collaboration dissolved in 1956. Kirby returned to DC, where he helped to inaugurate the comic-book Silver Age with the "Challengers of the Unknown" series for *Showcase*.[15] After a couple of years, the artist was on his own again, drawing a syndicated comic strip and, in 1961, freelancing for the Gilberton Company.

His first assignments were for *The World Around Us*, and he eventually produced artwork for six issues: *Undersea Adventures*, No. W30 (February 1961); *Hunting*, No. W31 (March 1961); *For Gold and Glory*, No. W31 (March 1961); *Spies*, No. W35 (August 1961); and *Fight for Life*, No. W36 (October 1961). Of particular interest are the strikingly conceived panels Kirby drew for a section titled "Early Hunters" in *Hunting*, where dramatic perspectives enliven the educational text.

The artist also contributed to two *Classics Illustrated Special Issues*: *The War Between the States*, No. 162A (June 1961), and *To the Stars!*, No. 165A (December 1961). Another Gilberton Civil War book had already appeared in the *World Around Us* series, but so great was centennial-year enthusiasm for the conflict among 10- to 12-year-old boys that a *Special Issue* on the subject was deemed a commercial necessity. Kirby's finest work for Gilberton can be found in his cleanly executed title-page splash and individual sections for *The War Between the States* devoted to the bombardment of Fort Sumter, the Peninsula campaign, the siege of Vicksburg, and a Confederate attempt to terrorize New York. Despite the artist's anachronistic importation of gray Confederate uniforms, the Fort Sumter chapter is a particularly compelling rendering of the war's fateful first shots, with its focus dramatically concentrated on the determined defenders.[16]

The only actual *Classics Illustrated* issue drawn by Kirby was the March 1961 revision of No. 35, *The Last Days of Pompeii*, Edward Bulwer-Lytton's turgid tale of love among the soon-to-be ruins. The title, Henry C. Kiefer's first full-scale Gilberton assignment, had been off the reorder list since 1949; the religious element, which had made the original edition objectionable, was excluded from the new version, and the love interest reigned supreme. A 1960 Steve Reeves "sword and sandal" motion-picture epic based on the book inspired the unearthing of the long-buried title.

Kirby's work on the adapted Bulwer-Lytton novel is uneven. Here and there, a hint of the artist's celebrated originality is evident, as in the starkness of the panel showing only the villain Arbaces' head and raised hand with dagger, the elegant linearity of the depiction of Arbaces felling the hero Glaucus with a single blow, and the physical animation of the gladiatorial contests.

However, Kirby, as he later informed *Classics* collector and researcher Ron Prager, sped through the pencils for *Pompeii* in ten days.[17] Veteran inker Dick Ayers, who was teamed with Kirby on many projects during the

Officers dragged off the stunned and insensible gladiator. There were now four combatants. One, a retiarius, or netter, was matched with a swordsman. The retiarius cast his net, but a quick inflection of the other gladiator's body saved him.

The retiarius now fled with the swordsman in hot pursuit as the people laughed and shouted.

Their attention was then turned to the two Roman combatants, who were in heated and fierce encounter. Soon the sword of one had inflicted the death wound upon the other.

Meanwhile, the retiarius had again cast his net, this time successfully. The gladiator struggled against its meshes in vain as the trident descended.

Jack Kirby, *The Last Days of Pompeii* (March 1961). The legendary artist working at less than full capacity.

1960s, finished the pages.[18] Signs of haste are evident throughout the book, with the features of the principal characters (excepting the villain) changing from panel to panel and the backgrounds barely sketched in or nonexistent. Perhaps Kirby felt constrained by the formalistic regularity of Gilberton's uniform panel design. Or it may simply have been that the artist was less comfortable in recreating an ancient setting to Roberta Strauss Feuerlicht's specifications than he was in imagining parallel realities.

Whatever the case, with Kirby's return to Marvel later in 1961 came his most signal contribution to comics history. During the next few years, he, artist Steve Ditko,

and writer-editor Stan Lee created the superheroes that essentially reinvented the comics industry: the Fantastic Four (1961); the Incredible Hulk (1962); the Mighty Thor (1962); the Amazing Spider-Man (1962); and the X-Men (1963). The artist's sophisticated simplicity gave Marvel its own unique house style and a model for future comics artists.[19]

Subsequently, Kirby and Lee quarreled and parted company. The artist found himself again at DC, where his love of fantasy came to the fore in the creation of his own mythology in such short-lived but influential series as *The New Gods* (1971) and *The Forever People* (1971).[20] The brief encounter with Gilberton—a creative detour—was by then a fading memory. By the time of his death in 1994, Kirby had become the most emulated and revered figure in the history of comics.

DON PERLIN

A Gilberton one-timer, Don Perlin (b. 1929) had studied at the Pratt Institute and Cooper Union and had drawn horror comics at Atlas (Marvel) in the 1950s. He later supplied artwork for *Sick* and *Cracked*, two *Mad* competitors.[21] In the late 1970s and early 1980s, Perlin illustrated *Ghost Rider*. For an educational comics series about African-American historical figures, issued by Seattle's Baylor Publishing Company in 1983, the artist turned his attention to the lives of Martin Luther King, Jr., and Thurgood Marshall.

Perlin's sole *Classics Illustrated* title, Jules Verne's *Robur the Conqueror*, No. 162 (May 1961), suffers from the inevitable comparison to its sequel, *Master of the World*, No. 163 (July 1961), which included some of the same characters subsequently drawn by Gray Morrow. *Robur* is an aeronautical variation on the plot and theme of *20,000 Leagues Under the Sea*, with the nominal hero-villain standing in for Captain Nemo and Uncle Prudent for Professor Aronnax. The artist's title-page splash showing representatives of different cultures watching the skies sets the stage for the appearance of Robur's "flying apparatus." Perlin's illustrations capture the story's mixture of whimsy and madness well enough, yet they somehow lack the energy and inventiveness that Morrow brought to the next issue.

Don Perlin, *Robur the Conqueror* (May 1961). The whole world is watching.

SIDNEY MILLER

The first new *Classics Illustrated* issue to deviate from the bimonthly publication schedule, *The Cossack Chief*, No. 164 (October 1964), also marked the only probable contribution of art director Sidney Miller to the series. (This is a tentative attribution by comics historian Hames Ware, who has also spotted a Milleresque four-page section in the *World Around Us* issue on *Fishing*, No. W34 [June 1961].)[22] Al Sundel had adapted and retitled Nikolai Gogol's *Taras Bulba*, which he had discovered in "a Russian bookstore that the CIA must have been watching through binoculars from a nearby loft."[23] It was another of the more challenging books, such as *The Conquest of Mexico* and *Faust*, that Roberta Strauss Feuerlicht encouraged Sundel to add to the Vernes, Wellses, and Hentys that were so heavily represented in the later issues.

While Sundel's script was unsparing in conveying the brutality of the nominal hero and his violent world, the light linework and often indistinguishable characters attributed to Gilberton's art director dissipated the impact of the adaptation. Even the coloring was lackluster, emphasizing flat reds and blues. A few effective sequences, such as Bulba's execution of his son Andrey, provided some dramatic relief, but the artist generally succeeded in making an otherwise compelling work almost impenetrable. One can't help wondering wistfully what Reed Crandall and George Evans might have done with No. 164, but they were contemporaneously revising *Oliver Twist*, far from the steppes where the Cossacks "grew used to looking peril straight in the face and forgot there was such a thing as fear in the world."

Sidney Miller (?), *The Cossack Chief* (October 1961). The new Gilberton art director favored a minimalist style.

CHARLES BERGER

Dropped from the reorder list in 1952, No. 8, *Arabian Nights*, had been the poorest selling of the first ten *Classics Illustrated* titles. Perhaps the regular readership regarded it as geared toward the younger audience that would be targeted by *Classics Illustrated Junior* in 1953. In fact, one of the stories from the 1942 *Arabian Nights*, *Aladdin and His Lamp*, was published as *Junior* No. 516 in May 1955.

By 1961, Gilberton had made considerable headway in returning out-of-print *Classics* to the newsstands. *Arabian Nights* was revived, with new adaptations of "Aladdin," "Ali Baba and the Forty Thieves," and "Sinbad the Sailor." "The Magic Horse," which had been included in the original 64-page edition, was omitted from the 48-page revision.

The new model performed less satisfactorily than the old, which, even as a relatively weak performer, had

Charles Berger, *Arabian Nights* (October 1961). Where was Lillian Chestney when Gilberton needed her?

gone through seven printings in the ten years it was available; the 1961 version was never reprinted. Part of the problem may have been the result of uncertain distribution at an uncertain time for the Gilberton Company. *Arabian Nights* was reissued in the autumn of 1961, in the wake of the Post Office fiasco, and was difficult to find in circulation.

But part of the problem was the art itself.

Charles Berger had contributed noncomics text illustrations to two "World of Story" filler items in *World Around Us* issues Nos. W32 (April 1961) and No. W33 (May 1961)—"Two Merry Pranks of Till Eulenspiegel" and "The Knight of the Couchant Leopard" from Sir Walter Scott's novel of the Crusades, *The Talisman*. This combination of the whimsical and the historical (not to mention the Middle Eastern touch in the Scott piece) won Berger the *Arabian Nights* assignment.

In the new No. 8, the artist's lightly inked, indifferently executed panels were undoubtedly intended to suggest the influence of Persian art. Instead, they reflected the minimalism prevalent during the brief tenure of art director Sidney Miller, who was simultaneously promoting the style in misguided new editions of *Jane Eyre* and *The Adventures of Tom Sawyer*. These lamentable revisions demonstrated in the starkest terms the price paid for firing Leonard B. Cole.

Little of the charm of Lillian Chestney's earlier rendering of Scheherazade's tales remained in Berger's *Arabian Nights*. Indeed, it was often difficult to see the pictures because the coloring was heavier than the surrounding linework. In addition, the artist was working within the confining conventions of the Miller-era Gilberton page layout, and illustrations were squeezed into four or five panels per page. Other than the title page, no splashes were allowed for greater scope, and characters were confined to the monotonously regular rectangles.

H.J. KIHL

Illustrator of the visually appealing "Rockets Through Time" section of *Rockets, Jets and Missiles*, No. 159A (December 1960), and, from 1958 to 1961, contributor to 21 of 36 *World Around Us* issues, H.J. Kihl provided artwork for only one *Classics Illustrated* issue, a 1962 revision of No. 39, *Jane Eyre*. While the revised adaptation was an improvement over the 1947 abridgment, the new Gilberton bare-bones style was simply wrong for Charlotte Brontë's gothic-tinged masterpiece. Harley M. Griffiths's heavily brushed panels were replaced by Kihl's thin-lined drawings, spare backgrounds, and brightly lit atmosphere.

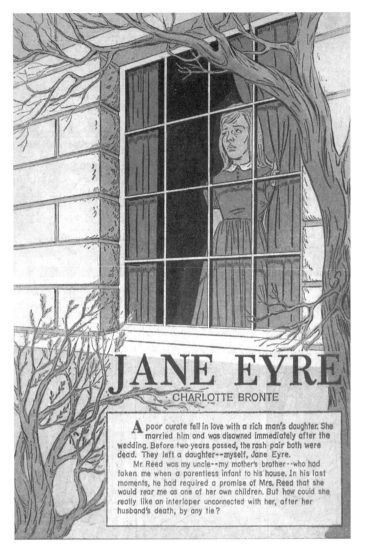

Left: **H.J. Kihl,** *Jane Eyre* **(1962). The antithesis of the Griffiths edition it replaced.**

The effect was strangely cheerful—a species of upbeat moroseness. When *Jane Eyre* was reprinted in 1997 as a *Classics Illustrated Study Guide*, Kihl's airy revision was rejected in favor of Griffiths's darker rendering.

UNIDENTIFIED ARTISTS

The artists who produced revamped *Classics* editions of *Adventures of Cellini*, No. 38 (October 1961), and *The Adventures of Tom Sawyer*, No. 50 (Fall 1961), have never been successfully identified. Norman Nodel was listed as illustrator for the second *Adventures of Cellini* in *The Complete Guide to Classics Collectibles*, but the artist explicitly rejected the attribution.[24] Alex Toth was erroneously named in a European website directory, despite the artist's statement in a letter to *The Classics Collector*

that he never worked for Gilberton.[25] The style, Hames Ware has suggested, is highly reminiscent of that of Bernie Krigstein.[26] But comics authority Jim Vadeboncoeur, Jr., who describes the mystery figure as a "very competent, even excellent, artist," notes that no one has been able to connect the work persuasively with any known American illustrator.[27]

In its revised state, *Adventures of Cellini* is one of the outstanding later editions published by Gilberton. Once again, adapter Al Sundel produced a miracle of compression, infusing each of the 45 pages with the spirit of Benvenuto Cellini's self-infatuated autobiography. The artist rose to the occasion, supplying visually active panels in which the delicate linework lends speed to the narrative, whether the hero is battling brigands in the street, contending with a storm on a lake, or escaping from a castle tower. Backgrounds are suggested rather than detailed, and the emphasis remains on the dramatically rendered foreground figures throughout the book.

Unidentified artist, *Adventures of Cellini* **(October 1961). The Mystery Artist remains a mystery.**

Efforts to connect a rather nondescript style with a particular artist in *The Adventures of Tom Sawyer* have been to no avail. The issue was perhaps the most misguided revision in the post–L.B. Cole era. Apart from the first-page splash featuring Samuel Clemens at a desk, the illustrations display little imagination or life, particularly when compared with Aldo Rubano's eccentric pencils and inks. If the effort was intended to make Mark Twain dull, the artist nearly succeeded. In selecting the inaugural issue for the new *Classics Illustrated Study Guides*, editor Madeleine Robins passed over the "improved" *Tom Sawyer* for the 1948 model.

END OF AN ERA

The plug was pulled in 1962, a little more than 20 years after Albert Kanter launched *Classic Comics* with *The Three Musketeers*. "Sociological and distribution patterns were changing," wrote Alfred Sundel. "Supermarkets were now coming into locales with the dramatic impact that Medical Centers have today. They were wiping out the old candy stores where the kids hung out. Americans were also … now edging into affluence. The government was soon to sponsor the purchase of juvenile books for libraries. Paperback juveniles were to appear in a year or so on new kinds of racks. The winds of change were blowing that would hurt CI, and nobody in the front office knew how to cope with it."[28]

In addition to the eclipse of five-and-dime stores and the increased availability of cheap juvenile paperback classics such as those published by Washington Square Press (Pocket Books), Dell, Signet, and Airmont,[29] another, perhaps decisive, factor came into play. Those children who, a few years earlier, might have read comic books for entertainment were now held in thrall to the unprecedented power of television. With its somewhat more rarefied appeal, *Classics Illustrated* stood to lose more ground than the superheroes or other comics genres.

In 1961, F.W. Woolworth, one of the principal circulation vehicles for *Classics Illustrated* nationwide, had commissioned a market study and concluded that because of declining sales, the chain would no longer carry comic books. At the same time, *Coronet*, the Curtis Circulation Company's *Reader's Digest* competitor, went under. Noting the Woolworth report and Gilberton's failure to win a renewal of its second-class postage permit, Curtis representatives persuaded Albert Kanter to discontinue new-title production and to publish, instead, a digest-sized *Coronet* replacement.[30]

The new magazine, *This Month*, was edited by Roberta Strauss Feuerlicht. Unfortunately, it was barely noticed and expired within six months of its March 1962 debut.[31] Gilberton had better success, however, with William Kanter's crossword-puzzle magazine, *Merit*, which lasted longer than the original *Classics Illustrated* series.[32]

Meanwhile, the comics lines chugged on with works in progress, the *Juniors* concluding in June 1962 with No. 576, *The Princess Who Saw Everything*, and *Classics Illustrated* and the *Special Issues* in July with No. 167, *Faust*, and No. 167A, *Prehistoric World*. New-title production shifted to England, where William Kanter moved to oversee the successful operation. Among the additions to the British series were Daniel Defoe's *Sail with the Devil (Captain Singleton)*, Oscar Wilde's *The Canterville Ghost*, R.M. Ballantyne's *The Dog Crusoe*, Alexander Pushkin's *Queen of Spades*, Leo Tolstoy's *Master and Man*, and Virgil's *Aeneid*. Al Sundel continued to write scripts for the European *Classics*, which were often illustrated by less than satisfactory artists.[33]

Given the choices made for the British and European lines and the literary tastes of Feuerlicht and Sundel, it is likely that, had the American series continued to issue new titles, classical Greek and Roman and 19th-century Russian authors would have been heavily represented, alternating with the usual reliable "boys' books." Historical works similar to *The Conspiracy of Pontiac* and *The Conquest of Mexico* probably would have appeared with greater frequency, especially after the loss of *The World Around Us* as a nonfiction venue.

As it turned out, for the next few years Gilberton continued reprinting existing editions and returning some retired titles—such as *The Master of Ballantrae*, *The Gold Bug*, and *All Quiet on the Western Front*—to active duty on the reorder list. It was a matter of going through the motions.

XXIX

Classical Interlude: A New Old Look

Master of the World marked the appearance of the final design change for *Classics Illustrated*. The familiar open-book device, which had first been used on issue No. 6 in 1942 and had been a standard cover emblem since issue No. 35 in 1947, disappeared, much to the dismay of many loyal readers. In a move evocative of the *Classic Comics* style, the issue number and price were shifted to the bottom of the yellow banner. Art director Sidney Miller's militant modernist minimalism, which had already asserted itself on *Classics Illustrated Junior* covers and a logo makeover for *The World Around Us*, was evident in the stylized depiction of Robur's airship, the *Terror*, struck by lightning.

Why the abandonment of the open book was viewed as an improvement is a puzzle. The issue number, squeezed into a fraction of the space it had occupied before, was hard to find, let alone read. The eye was accustomed to finding that particular space filled, and, initially, the open book's absence appeared to throw the cover's balance off. Still, ten years had passed since the introduction of painted covers, and, apart from the aberrations of Nos. 83–85, the same basic design had been in place for a decade. A change may have been due, but the compromise between the original banner style and the post–1947 reduced rectangle changed both too much and too little.

The end was still a year away, but for some young traditionalists it seemed already to have arrived.

A "new frontier" in cover design: *Master of the World* (July 1961).

XXX

Five Little Series and How They Grew: *Picture Progress; Classics Illustrated Junior; Classics Illustrated Special Issues; The World Around Us; The Best from Boys' Life Comics*

In addition to *Classics Illustrated*, the Gilberton Company published five other series for young readers. Each demonstrated the publisher's commitment to its Horatian goal of teaching while entertaining. Only one was an unqualified commercial success.

By the fall of 1953, with more than 110 titles issued, *Classics Illustrated* stood unchallenged in its field, having vanquished and absorbed its sole competitor, *Stories by Famous Authors*. The series was winning increasing, if grudging, respect from parents and teachers, and Gilberton emphasized its purpose in a 1953 promotional poster announcing that "CLASSICS ILLUSTRATED Will Help *YOU* OPEN THE DOOR TO GOOD LITERATURE."

At this point, the trademark had attained a degree of stature and success at home and abroad that enabled Albert Kanter to trade upon the value of the logo by developing new lines. An *Educational Series* under the *Classics* banner had produced two commercially sponsored titles in 1951 and 1953, *Shelter Through the Ages* (Rubberoid)

and *The Westinghouse Story: The Dreams of a Man* (Westinghouse), both illustrated by Henry C. Kiefer. But these 16-page comics had been little more than glorified advertising supplements. Now Gilberton was ready to expand its own educational mission.

PICTURE PROGRESS

In September 1953, aiming further to enhance Gilberton's prestige and profitability, Albert Kanter launched a line of comics aimed directly at schools, with a publication cycle tied to the academic year. *Picture Parade* focused on one topic per 24-page issue, beginning with the uplifting account of *Andy's Atomic Adventures*, illustrated by Peter Costanza, in which the young hero's dog Spot emerges uncontaminated from exposure to a nuclear test after chasing a rabbit onto the nearby Nevada proving grounds.

Historian William W. Savage, Jr., has commented on the "rather curious variety of folklore" that developed in the United States during the years following Hiroshima—"a mythic vision of the Bomb, intended to accommodate the thing to everyday life, to make it an unobtrusive engine of death, so to speak." The comic book played its part in sustaining the postwar myth, Savage contends, by "advancing the idea of a benign Bomb, a friendly Bomb, a Bomb that would never hurt anybody unless we willed it—and certainly it would never hurt us."[1] With a precarious cease-fire having brought the Korean War to an inconclusive conclusion as recently as July 27, 1953, and the anti–Communist campaign of Senator Joseph McCarthy still proceeding at ramming speed, *Picture Parade* did its duty. *Andy's Atomic Adventures* does nothing if not accentuate the positive.

Andy visits his quarantined pup at the proving-grounds laboratory, where he receives an upbeat lesson in nuclear fission (helpfully pronounced "*fish*-un"), complete with a matchhead demonstration of a chain reaction. He later learns that "Atomic energy will light cities … run big factories … and run my electric train." In the penultimate panel, Mr. Wilson, driving home with his son and the radioactive-free Spot, sagely explains, "We have to have [the Bomb] to protect us if we need it. I hope it will never again be used to destroy." "I hope not," Andy replies, going on to assure young readers that "This world is going to be even more wonderful when all that atomic energy is really put to work."

After the fourth issue, the name of the series was changed to *Picture Progress*. The range of subjects covered history (*Paul Revere's Ride, The Lewis and Clark Expedition*); science (*The Story of Flight, The Discoveries of Louis Pasteur*); geography (*The Hawaiian Islands, Alaska: The Great Land*); current events (*Around the World with the U.N., 1954: News in Review*); and entertainment (*Life in the Circus, Summer Fun*). As mentioned earlier, one of the later titles, *The Man Who Discovered America,* Vol. 3, No. 1 (September 1955), illustrated by Lou Cameron, won the Thomas Alva Edison Award in 1956.

Yet the recognition came too late. Despite a subscription price of 80 cents for nine issues—a bargain even by Eisenhower Era standards—and a publicity campaign

Norman Nodel, *The Lewis and Clark Expedition* (October 1955). *Picture Progress* **proved to be a trial run for** *Classics Illustrated Special Issues* **and** *The World Around Us.*

that included back-cover *Classics Illustrated* ads, *Picture Progress* could not attract enough interest from schools. The timing, undoubtedly, was unfortunate; the anti-comics campaign was at its apex. In the eyes of many parents and teachers, a *Classics* version of *Swiss Family Robinson* purchased at the neighborhood variety store might have been preferable to a copy of *Tales From the Crypt*, but comic books were still comic books, and the classroom was no place for them. So, after 18 issues in the 1953-1954 and 1954-1955 school years and two issues in the fall of 1955, *Picture Progress* abruptly came to an end, but not before setting the pattern for the more significant *Special Issues* and *World Around Us.*[2]

CLASSICS ILLUSTRATED JUNIOR

Next to *Classics Illustrated*, Albert Kanter's most successful venture was *Classics Illustrated Junior*, a line geared, as the name suggests, to younger readers. Debuting in October 1953, the 32-page comic books featured adaptations—or in some instances, such as *Goldilocks and the Three Bears*, No. 508 (May 1954), liberal expansions—of fairy and folk tales. Where all of Kanter's other publications were issued under the Gilberton imprint, *Classics Illustrated Junior* was produced by Famous Authors, Ltd., the former rival that was now a division of the thriving business housed at 101 Fifth Avenue.

Except for the last few months of 1954 and the first half of 1955, the *Juniors* were issued monthly through 1958, when a bimonthly schedule was established that remained in place until the tumultuous last half of 1961. The final Gilberton *Classics Illustrated Junior* was *The Princess Who Saw Everything*, No. 576 (June 1962), but *The Runaway Dumpling*, No. 577 (Winter 1969), was subsequently issued under Frawley ownership.

The *Junior* artwork emphasized visual simplicity for its kindergarten and elementary school audience; images were generally streamlined, though there were striking exceptions, such as the books by Mike Sekowsky and Frank Giacoia or the relatively intricate, unattributed illustrations for *Aladdin and His Lamp*, No. 516 May 1955. (The Aladdin story, which had been included in *Classic Comics* No. 8, *Arabian Nights*, fared better in its *Junior* incarnation, remaining in print for the life of the publication.) Artists such as Peter Costanza, Lin Streeter, and Tony Tallarico, whose drawings in *Classics Illustrated* often seemed too light or juvenile for the context, thrived in the *Juniors*.

Alex A. Blum illustrated the first issue, *Snow White and the Seven Dwarfs*, No. 501 (October 1953). His delicate linework was eminently suitable for the familiar story, though he seemed unable to invest the wicked queen and her wizened alter ego with much malevolence. Similarly, in Blum's *Jack and the Beanstalk*, No. 507 (April 1954), the giant looks more like a jolly farmer than a menacing ogre; rather than crashing into the ground, he falls into a lake. As art director for the *Junior* series, Blum appeared to take pains not to frighten young readers and evidently advised his freelancers to follow suit.

Managing editor Meyer A. Kaplan adopted the same policy for scripts. Early issues frequently soften the harsh or ambivalent endings of the original fairy tales. Thus, in *Little Red Riding Hood*, No. 510 (July 1954), the wolf, who has merely locked Grandma up in the closet, is chased away by the woodsman and is "never heard from again." The trespassing heroine of *Goldilocks and the Three Bears*, No. 508 (May 1954), writes a note of apology to her aggrieved hosts, and all is forgiven. The little man in *Rumpelstiltskin*, No. 512 (September 1958), stamps through the floor upon hearing his name but is rescued by two guards. He then goes "back to the woods to find that temper he lost so badly."

William A. Walsh, who scripted Mickey Mouse stories for Dell, illustrated more *Juniors*

Albert Kanter discusses *Classics Illustrated Junior* with ABC's Maggie McNellis (1953). (Courtesy of Hal Kanter and John Haufe.)

than any other artist—indeed, he might be called the Henry C. Kiefer of the series. His whimsical style and light touch in such titles as *The Ugly Duckling*, No. 502 (November 1953), *The Three Little Pigs*, No. 506 (March 1954), and *The Little Mermaid*, No. 525 (April 1956), connected with a younger readership than Gilberton had previously attracted. Yet his limited range is apparent in most of the two dozen or so issues he drew and inked, and the reputation the series has for uneven quality is chiefly due to his hit-and-miss efforts.

Certain titles, such as *Pinocchio*, No. 513 (November 1954), *The Dancing Princesses*, No. 532 (November 1956), *The Chimney Sweep*, No. 536 (March 1957), and *The Golden Fleece*, No. 544 (November 1957), show Walsh exceeding his usual self-imposed limitations. In the latter title, a retelling of the legend of the hero Jason, the artist was working in a more realistic mode; he avoided

the round-faced cuteness that had afflicted another foray into the realm of Greek myth, *The Golden Touch*, No. 534 (January 1957). Had *The Golden Fleece* been expanded to 48 pages and the tragic aspects of the story relating to Medea been developed, the book would have belonged on the *Classics Illustrated* list. (As it happened, *The Argonauts* was the last title published in the British *Classics Illustrated* series.)

Peter Costanza, who illustrated seafaring tales by Cooper, Kipling, and Hawes for the parent publication, seemed more at ease stylistically with the *Juniors*, for which he produced two exquisitely wrought titles: *Cinderella*, No. 503 (December 1953), and *The Sleeping Beauty*, No. 505 (February 1954). As elsewhere in the artist's work, great attention is devoted to the characters' eyes. The awakening scene in *The Sleeping Beauty* was scripted with a rather chaste climax, in which, without

Left: William A. Walsh, *The Little Mermaid* (April 1956). Walsh was the most frequent contributor to the *Junior* series. *Right:* Peter Costanza, *The Sleeping Beauty* (February 1954). No kiss needed.

the benefit of a kiss, the slumbering princess opens her eyes as soon as her deliverer enters her bedchamber.

An artist whose style was ideal for *Classics Illustrated Junior* was Dik Browne (1917–1989), best known as the creator of *Hi and Lois* and *Hagar the Horrible*. Many of the early *Junior* covers, including *Puss-in-Boots*, No. 511 (August 1954), *Thumbelina*, No. 520 (November 1955), and *The Nightingale*, No. 522 (January 1956), were painted by the artist. Although his so-called "primitivism" would have looked out of place in *Classics Illustrated*, it added an engaging sprightliness to the covers and interior art for *The Pied Piper*, No. 504 (January 1954), *Beauty and the Beast*, No. 509 (June 1954), and *The Steadfast Tin Soldier*, No. 514 (January 1955).

Browne's vibrant panels particularly enlivened *The Pied Piper*, based on Robert Browning's poem; the artist's portraits of the wily Piper and the venal burghers of Hamelin added a satiric dimension to the retelling. *The Steadfast Tin Soldier* is closer stylistically to Browne's

later comic strips and offers perhaps the finest example in the series of the artist's elastic simplicity—page after page, the artist demonstrates how much can be conveyed in a few decisive lines.

Some of the best illustrations in the *Juniors* came from the pencil of Mike Sekowsky, whose work was inked by Frank Giacoia or at times by Mike Peppe. In *The Golden Goose*, No. 518 (September 1955), *Paul Bunyan*, No. 519 (October 1955), *The Gallant Tailor*, No. 523 (February 1956), and *The Magic Fountain*, No. 533 (December 1956), Sekowsky and Giacoia set standards for the series that were seldom met by other artists.

Their treatment of John Ruskin's Victorian fairy tale, *The King of the Golden River*, No. 521 (December 1955), may be the most satisfying single issue in the line, with its delightfully eccentric title character, the kind-hearted young hero Gluck (in some ways a rehearsal for the artists' handling of Huck Finn a few months later), and the grasping, greedy older brothers, Hans and

Left: Dik Browne, *The Steadfast Tin Soldier* (January 1955). Browne was the king of the *Junior* covers. *Right:* Mike Sekowsky, *The King of the Golden River* (December 1955). Different perspectives lead to an explosive climax.

Schwartz. Throughout the book, Sekowsky and Giacoia shifted point-of-view angles for greater visual effect.

While not as well rendered as the Sekowsky-Giacoia collaborations, the titles by Sekowsky and Peppe are still engaging. Although the artists cut corners on the Yellow Brick Road and drew the cowardly lion with disappointing cartoonlike features in *The Wizard of Oz*, No. 535 (February 1957), they nevertheless made it clear that they were illustrating L. Frank Baum's book rather than the 1939 MGM movie. *Silly Willy*, No. 557 (December 1958), is, on the whole, a better executed performance of a tale from the Brothers Grimm that in some respects is the male companion to *Simple Kate*, No. 549 (April 1958) (possibly illustrated by Jerry Fasano), an earlier title with a similar theme—that of the "holy fool" who blunders his or her way into good fortune.

George Peltz's cartoonlike drawings proved appealing in such issues as *The Magic Dish*, No. 558 (February 1958), with its broadfaced hero and almost Disneyesque supporting cast of fish, ants, and ravens, and *Hans Humdrum*, No. 561 (August 1959), in which the illustrator's gifts for caricature found expression in the features of the freckled, chinless protagonist and the long-nosed troll farmer he outwits. A less successful effort was *The Japanese Lantern*, No. 559 (April 1959), where the artist attempted to fuse "orientalism" and realism with oddly wooden results. In *The Salt Mountain*, No. 564 (February 1960), Peltz produced a superbly balanced mixture of comically sketched characters and realistically rendered ships, buildings, and Russian costumes.

If Dik Browne's covers established a lighthearted newsstand identity for the early *Juniors*, those by Leonard B. Cole in 1959 and 1960 demonstrated the Gilberton art director's versatility, issue after issue. Some of Cole's *Junior* covers, such as *The Happy Hedgehog*, No. 568 (October 1960), showed the same playfulness that he had

Left: George Peltz, *The Magic Dish* (February 1958). An engaging cartoon style distinguished Peltz's *Junior* titles. *Right:* Leonard B. Cole, *The Japanese Lantern* (April 1959). The Gilberton art director painted 11 covers in different styles for the *Junior* series between 1958 and 1960.

brought to *Frisky Animals* in the late 1940s and early 1950s. Others, including *The Enchanted Pony*, No. 562 (October 1959), with their lovingly rendered horses or other animals, added a touch of magic. One of Cole's best nonanimal covers, for *The Japanese Lantern*, No. 559 (April 1959), was a gracefully balanced composition tinged with the exotic.

The majority of the *Junior* titles consisted of *Märchen* collected by Jacob and Wilhelm Grimm (*Rumpelstiltskin*) or fairy tales written by Hans Christian Andersen (*The Emperor's New Clothes*). The adaptations adhered to the three-part patterns of the originals but allowed room for character development, as in the case of the henpecked fisherman in *The Enchanted Fish*, No. 539 (June 1957), or the gullible Inga in *The Silly Princess*, No. 565 (April 1960). Scripts became more sophisticated as the line expanded its range.

In addition to European folk and fairy tales, the *Junior* series made available to young readers a wide range of stories from various sources, from Greco-Roman myths (usually filtered through Nathaniel Hawthorne's *Wonder Book*) such as *The Magic Pitcher*, No. 548 (March 1958) to American folklore such as *Johnny Appleseed*, No. 515 (March 1955). A Native American legend, *How Fire Came to the Indians*, No. 571 (April 1961), illustrated in a spare, modern style by Tony Tallarico, was a landmark early step in multicultural storytelling for children. The tale celebrates the virtues of cooperation and community within the framework of an origins myth.

Some of the stories were unavailable in any other version. When *The Runaway Dumpling*, No. 577, an adaptation of a Japanese tale by Lafcadio Hearn, appeared in 1969, no other edition was in print. Not until the publication in 1972 of *The Funny Little Woman*, a Caldecott Medal winner by Arlene Mosel and Blair Lent, did another retelling of the story reach a contemporary audience.

Beginning with issue No. 509 in June 1954 and continuing through No. 576 in 1962, two- to five-page retellings of "Aesop's Fables" ("The Ant and the Grasshopper") or other short folk parables ("Stone Soup") appeared as filler material. Adapters and artists devoted as much attention to these well-constructed *Classics* in miniature as they did to the title stories, and they produced some memorable work on a smaller scale, as in William A. Walsh's "The Fox and the Stork." Rounding out each issue were "The Animal World," a feature that profiled such creatures as the dingo, the armadillo, and the chinchilla, and nursery rhymes ("Sing a Song of Sixpence") or poems by Robert Louis Stevenson ("Windy Nights") or Edward Lear ("There Was an Old Man with a Beard").

Classics Illustrated Junior almost rivaled the parent publication in popularity. Comics historian Hubert H. Crawford has asserted that the series led all children's books, as opposed to comic books, in sales.[3] A December 1960 Famous Authors ownership statement declared an impressive average monthly circulation of 262,000.[4] The two best-selling issues, *Cinderella*, No. 503 (December 1953), and *Paul Bunyan*, No. 519 (October 1955), were both reprinted ten times—an indication that the series had equal appeal to girls and boys. Only the final issue, *The Runaway Dumpling*, had no reprints, but by the time it was published in 1969, the Frawley organization was only two years away from shutting the entire operation down.

One of the intriguing "what ifs" in Gilberton lore involves an abortive animated television series based on *Classics Illustrated Junior*. In 1958, Albert Kanter approached P.A.T., the production team that would soon become famous for *Rocky the Flying Squirrel*, and proposed a cartoon program based on *Junior* titles. Bill Scott, Jay Ward's partner and the voice of Bullwinkle, began to work up a script and storyboard adapted from the *Junior* edition of *Goldilocks and the Three Bears*. The project, however, was abandoned, and Ward and Scott would in short order offer their own "Fractured Fairy Tales."[5]

At about the same time, MGM Records released, on its budget Lion label, a 45-minute album of songs and stories adapted from twelve *Classics Illustrated Junior* issues, including *Pinocchio*, *The Pied Piper*, *The Wizard of Oz*, and *The Sleeping Beauty*, performed by radio and television personality Robert Q. Lewis. The record, like the projected cartoon series, was evidence of Kanter's faith in his product and his entrepreneurial determination to seek as many different media outlets for it as possible.

CLASSICS ILLUSTRATED
SPECIAL ISSUES

In December 1955, Gilberton issued a 96-page *Classics Illustrated Special Edition* titled *The Story of Jesus*. The timing was significant—and not merely because of the seasonal factor. *Classics Illustrated* was putting its best foot forward at a time when comic books were enduring sustained scrutiny and attack.

As further proof of its bona fides as an educational publisher, Gilberton had recently added *Macbeth* to its list and was preparing to include *Caesar's Conquests*. Having just scrapped *Picture Progress*, Albert Kanter was ready to produce an even more emphatic demonstration of the difference between *Classics* and other comics.

What better subject, then, than Jesus? How could even a Fredric Wertham take exception? The answer, of

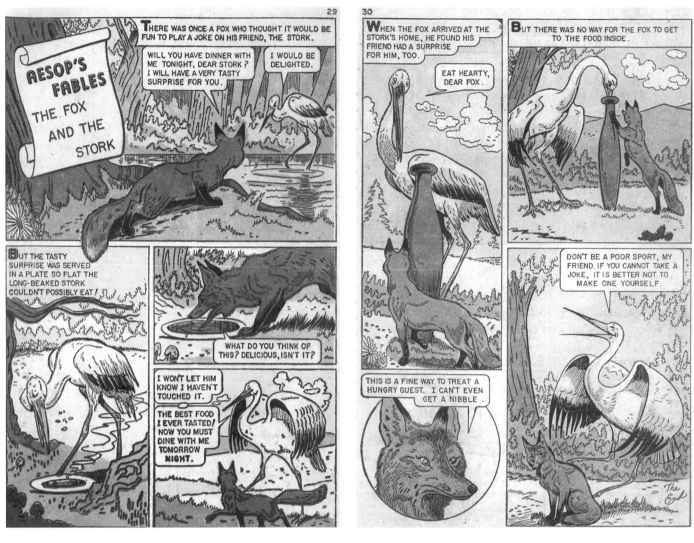

William A. Walsh, *Aesop's Fables*. "The Fox and the Stork" in *Junior* No. 511 (August 1954). A complete *Classics Illustrated Junior* feature.

course, was that critics might see it, as Wertham had viewed the comic-book versions of Shakespeare, as a vulgarization or even desecration of the source material. Anti-Semitic fundamentalists might even object to Kanter's credentials as publisher. Still, the potential for prestige and profit made the venture worth the risk.

The concept of biblical comics, like the concept of "classic" comics before it, was not new. In the 1940s, Max Gaines's seven-issue *Picture Stories from the Bible* had sold millions of copies.[6] Two of the New Testament numbers from the series had been reprinted in 1945 as a 96-page *Complete Life of Christ*. More recently, Atlas had published, from August 1953 to March 1954, five issues of *Bible Tales for Young People*, and Famous Funnies had begun a four-issue run of *Tales from the Great Book* in February 1955.

Convinced that Gilberton could improve on the formula, managing editor Meyer A. Kaplan hired an African-American former missionary, Lorenz Graham, to script the *Classics* book. His adaptation would have pleased the most rock-ribbed biblical literalist. Indeed, it satisfied the conservative Daniel A. Poling, editor of the *Christian Herald Magazine*, who delivered a back-cover endorsement expressing his happiness "that the manuscript follows the gospel texts in the classic King James vernacular, and that it tells that immortal story, the greatest story ever told, without distortion or interpretation." Representatives of the Roman Catholic Archbishopric of Mexico, the Canadian Council of Churches, and the Queens Federation of Churches also supplied testimonials. Gilberton marketed the book as "The Classic of Classics."

Not only was the adaptation faithful to the letter of the Authorized Version, the illustrations, by *Junior* workhorse William A. Walsh and *Classics* veteran Alex A. Blum, are stiffly reverent in the best tradition of Sunday

THE STORY OF JESUS

CLASSICS
Illustrated
Special Edition

35¢

The Story of Jesus (December 1955). **The ultimate bid for respectability.**

an *Edition. The Story of America*, No. 133A (June 1956), was simply a compilation of recycled *Picture Progress* stories: Lou Cameron's award-winning "The Man Who Discovered America," Lin Streeter's "The Birth of America," Peter Costanza's "Paul Revere's Ride," and Tom Hickey's "Star Spangled Banner."

The year ended with an Old Testament story to balance the 1955 *Story of Jesus. The Ten Commandments*, No. 135A (December 1956), illustrated by Norman Nodel, was the first of two Paramount movie tie-ins arranged with the assistance of Albert Kanter's son, Hollywood screenwriter and director Hal Kanter. An ad for the film gracing the inside back cover promised that "If you have enjoyed this book you are certain to enjoy this motion picture masterpiece."

Norman Nodel's well-researched illustrations, with their scratchboard effects and experiments in shading, stood in dramatic aesthetic contrast to the reverently inhibited panels in *The Story of Jesus*. Once again, Lorenz Graham provided an unobjectionable text, based, unlike the movie—or the competing Dell Giant *Moses and the Ten Commandments* (August 1957), illustrated by Mike Sekowsky—on the Book of Exodus.

Like *The Story of Jesus, The Ten Commandments* boasted back-cover blurbs from religious leaders. Daniel A. Poling returned, declaring that "Unqualifiedly I endorse this work." He was joined by spokesmen for the National Conference of Christians and Jews and, again, the Canadian Council of Churches, and a rabbi and a Methodist minister from New York City, the latter uttering the rather Delphic pronouncement: "We think in pictures and these are pictures which make us think."

School art. Perhaps some misgivings occurred with Victor Prezio's painted cover, showing Jesus giving the Sermon on the Mount. It was briefly replaced in a 1958 reprint with what collectors call the "Three Camels" cover, but the original returned in the final two printings.

In the summer of 1956, another 35-cent *Special* appeared, this time and henceforth as an *Issue* rather than

Running a close second to *The Story of Jesus* in sales

was *Adventures in Science*, No. 138A (June 1957), which enjoyed a total of three printings. Following the method employed in *The Story of America*, the editors merely assembled four *Picture Progress* features, "The Story of Flight," the redoubtable "Andy's Atomic Adventures," "The Discoveries of Louis Pasteur," and "From Tom-Tom to TV" (a subject that would be explored in greater depth in a 1960 *World Around Us* issue on communications). Peter Costanza illustrated the first three stories and Lin Streeter the last. The popularity of *Adventures in Science* may have been due both to the Cold War appeal of its missile-launcher cover and to the book's appearance on the threshold of the space race between the United State and the Soviet Union, when the very word "science" was invested with talismanic properties.

Gilberton's next *Special* proved to be the most honored of all the titles in the series. Published under the imprimatur of the Theodore Roosevelt Centennial Commission, *The Rough Rider*, No. 141A (December 1957),

The Rough Rider (December 1957). Gilberton's biography of Theodore Roosevelt won congressional plaudits.

was a factually accurate, if hagiographic, portrait of the energetic young president, presenting his various incarnations as cowboy, police commissioner, soldier, governor, and hunter. The book, penciled by George Evans, received congressional approbation, a ringing testimonial from the Director of the Centennial Commission, and the now standard praise from the dependable Daniel A. Poling and other worthies, including the Director of the President's Council on Youth Fitness and the First Vice-President of the General Federation of Women's Clubs.

All four of the *Special Issues* published in 1958 and 1959 were devoted to an impressive trilogy outlining the history of America's westward movement—and a related Canadian excursion. One of Roberta Strauss Feuerlicht's most ambitious projects, the well-researched, handsomely executed serial represented one of Gilberton's finest educational efforts. The editor's demand for accuracy led her to engage the services of Sylvester Vigilante, Bibliographer of the New York Historical Society, as series consultant.

Blazing the Trails West, No. 144A (June 1958), illustrated by George Evans and John Severin, began with an overview of colonial history, recounted the careers of Daniel Boone and Kit Carson (both of whom had starred in their own *Classics Illustrated* issues), followed the Lewis and Clark Expedition and the Santa Fe Trail, and concluded with chapters on the Alamo and the Mexican War. Although the issue of "Manifest Destiny" was taken at face value ("[M]any Americans were saying that the United States ought to include all of the Far West"), and nothing of the debate on the Mexican conflict was reflected, the book nevertheless offered young readers a compelling account of the nation's expansion.

The sequel, *Crossing the Rockies*, No. 147A (December 1958), was another visually strong installment, featuring cover artwork by Gerald McCann, and interior illustrations by Norman Nodel ("The Oregon Trail," "Death and the Donners," "This Is the Place"), by George Evans ("The Gold Rush"), and by Joe Orlando ("The Apache Wars," "The Overland Mail," "Pony Express," "Bound By Rails"). Most of the stories, however, lacked much of the dramatic conflict found in *Blazing the Trails West*, and the issue failed to attract a wide readership.

The final volume, *Men, Guns and Cattle*, No. 153A (December 1959), with its focus on the post–Civil War era of cattle drives, gunslingers and Indian wars, fared somewhat better at a time when cowboy programs such as *Gunsmoke* and *Maverick* dominated prime-time television. Artistically the least unified of the Western titles, the book included a cover painting and internal art by Gerald McCann and additional illustrations by Leonard B. Cole, George Evans, noted artist Everett Raymond Kinstler, Norman Nodel, and George Peltz (whose child-

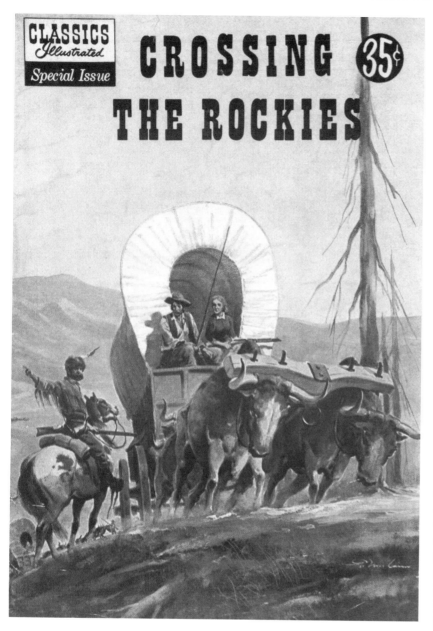

Crossing the Rockies (December 1958). The second of three *Special Issues* devoted to the settlement of the American West.

figure than the straight-shooter eulogized in *Classics Illustrated* No. 121.

Wedged in among these titles was a nod to the Western history of the north, *Royal Canadian Mounted Police*, No. 150A (June 1959), for which retired Mounties Superintendent J.C. Story served as consultant. Although the intent may have been not to slight young Canadian readers while the Western trilogy was under way, the result was the weakest of the *Special Issues*—the subject would have been more appropriate for the smaller-scale *World Around Us* series.

Further, the artwork for the Mounties book was of varying quality, with the best contributions by Graham Ingels ("Pony Soldiers") and Ray Ramsey ("Manhunt!"). If the former's tame drawings bore little resemblance to his inventive "Ghastly" creations for EC, the latter's style had grown more refined since his simpler Golden Age drawings for the 1942 *Classic Comics* version of *The Last of the Mohicans*.

Having covered a significant portion of the American past, editor Feuerlicht turned her attention to the more current matters of science and technology in *The Atomic Age*, No. 156A (June 1960), and *Rockets, Jets and Missiles*, No. 159A (December 1960). Both titles contained a mixture of good and indifferent art, the best represented by Norman Nodel, Bruno Premiani, George Evans, and Gray Morrow. Perhaps the finest section in either book was Premiani's beautifully rendered nine-page historical overview of atomic theory in No. 156A, extending from ancient India through the early 19th century.

The Atomic Age enlarged upon the optimism of "Andy's Atomic Adventures," looking forward to a time when, "[f]rom infancy to old age," thanks to the benefits of atomic research, "man will live with little fear of disease. He will live more easily and longer." The *Special* ended, however, on a cautionary note: "Whether the atom is used to build up a new world, or blow up the present one, is up to us."

Rockets, Jets and Missiles addressed the fascination of the space race and the anxieties of the Cold War. Airplane specialist George Evans lavished attention on a Flying Fortress, an F-51 Mustang, an F-80 Shooting Star, and the experimental X-1 in a superbly paced introductory section on Chuck Yeager's 1947 flight that

friendly rendering of the Pecos Bill legend would have been more appropriate for the *Classics Illustrated Junior* series in which most of his work appeared).

An attempt at an evenhanded treatment of Native Americans was made in the script's narration of the slaughter of the buffalo and the origin of the Ghost Dance; even so, Geronimo was depicted as the baddest of bad guys, and the massacre at Wounded Knee was rendered almost in terms of tragic necessity. The white man's perspective prevailed, and most of the book's 96 pages dealt with the exploits of Wild Bill Hickok, Billy the Kid, Bat Masterson, and the Earp brothers. A sketch of Wild Bill's career depicted a more complex, ambivalent

Rockets, Jets and Missiles (December 1960). A Cold War artifact, published at the dawn of the New Frontier.

rendered by Gerald McCann, who also illustrated biographical sketches of rocket and jet pioneers Robert Hutchings Goddard and Frank Whittle.

Individual planets were discussed on text pages, and the final third of the book, illustrated by Gray Morrow and others, centered on Project Mercury, the seven astronauts, and the future of the space program. John F. Kennedy had just been elected president, and a New Frontier in space beckoned. No issue published by Gilberton had been as timely, but the rapid movement of events within the next few months would make *Rockets, Jets and Missiles* seem suddenly dated. A sequel would be required.

Meanwhile, the year 1961 witnessed the beginning of the Civil War Centennial; marketing had been well under way in 1960. Not until the American Bicentennial 15 years later would there again be such public enthusiasm for a national historical epoch, and Gilberton took full advantage of the spirit of the times, issuing *The Civil War*, No. W26, in its *World Around Us* series in October 1960 and *The War Between the States* (adopting the Southern locution) as *Special Issue* No. 162A in June 1961.

Three artists overlapped—Norman Nodel, Sam Glanzman, and George Peltz—and so, inevitably, did some of the subject matter. Strong showings were made in the *Special Issue* in sections by Jack Kirby ("Fort Sumter," "The Peninsula," "Vicksburg," "New York City") and George Evans ("Shiloh," "Reconstruction"). However, some of the flatness that seems to have coincided with Sidney Miller's tenure as art director crept into the sections by Glanzman ("The Causes," "Gettysburg").

As history, *The War Between the States* was well-researched and impressive in its scope. A four-page section titled "The Causes" (marred slightly by artist Glanzman's misplacing of the Missouri Compromise Line on a map) succinctly covered such topics as the Compromise of 1850, the *Dred Scott* Decision, and the struggle between proslavery and abolitionist forces in Kansas. Strategic and tactical considerations were presented in sections on New Orleans, the Seven Days' Battles, Gettysburg, and Vicksburg.

A structural weakness was evident in *The War Between the States* in the extended attention devoted to the exploits of John Hunt Morgan's raiders in Kentucky or those of Confederate saboteurs in New York at the expense of the more significant battles of Antietam,

broke the sound barrier and served as a "stepping stone for faster flights to come as man reached for space." Gilberton anticipated Tom Wolfe's enshrinement of the laconic Yeager as the original exemplar of "the right stuff" by nearly two decades.

John Tartaglione's "Jets Around the World" offered sharply drafted examples of commercial (Boeing 707, Convair 880) and military (Saab-35 Draken, MIG-21) models; his "Rocket Engines" contained side-view diagrams of solid-fuel, liquid-fuel, and other rockets. Somewhat ominously, the editors surveyed the Polaris, Thor, SM-65 Atlas, and other missiles and rockets, accurately

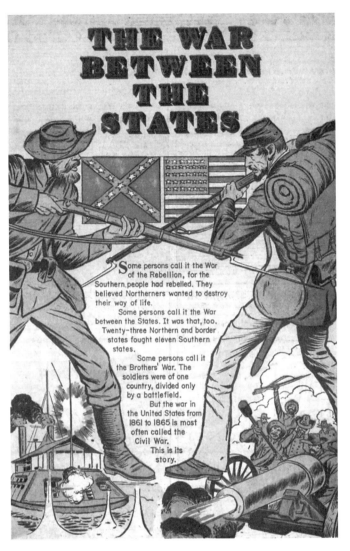

The War Between the States (June 1961). Jack Kirby drew the title-page splash and four chapters in Gilberton's second Civil War Centennial issue.

Fredericksburg, Chancellorsville, and the Wilderness, which received half-page summaries each. Still, the text dealing with Gettysburg provided a well-proportioned ten-page account of the campaign, including the behind-the-scenes conflict between Union generals, Henry Halleck and Joseph Hooker, that led to General George Meade's assumption of command, and the disagreement between Confederate generals, Robert E. Lee and James Longstreet, over the third-day disaster that would become known as "Pickett's Charge."

Exactly 100 years to the day after the firing on Fort Sumter, on 12 April 1961, Soviet cosmonaut Yuri A. Gagarin became the first person to reach outer space and to orbit the earth. The Civil War Centennial had been upstaged at its formal inception, and attention shifted again to the space race. By the end of 1961, two Americans had briefly entered outer space, and a third, John H.

Glenn, would soon achieve the status of national hero with his orbital flight on 20 February 1962.

Against that backdrop, Gilberton published *Special Issue* No. 165A, *To the Stars!* (December 1961). Up to the minute, the book covered the recent exploits of both Gagarin and Alan Shepard, the first American in space. As in all other science-oriented *Specials*, the script provided a historical perspective—in this instance, expertly drawn, thoroughly researched sections by Angelo Torres on the history of flight, and by George Evans on the changing concept of Earth's position in the universe, the evolution of the telescope, and William Herschel's discovery of Uranus.

A significant portion of *To the Stars!* abandoned the traditional panel format of comics in favor of illustrated text. Indeed, it may have been the most straightforwardly educational of any book issued by any of the Gilberton

To the Stars! (December 1961). Gilberton's response to the space race was part comic book and part illustrated textbook.

lines. In its comprehensive treatment of the sun, the planets, and the constellations, *To the Stars!* offers some indication of the direction Roberta Strauss Feuerlicht might have pursued with the *Special Issues* had new-title production not ceased in 1962.

At some point in the first half of 1962, when the Gilberton publication cycle had become increasingly erratic, *World War II*, No. 166A, landed on newsstands and drugstore racks. The recent popularity of William L. Shirer's *Rise and Fall of the Third Reich*, the box-office success of *Judgment at Nuremberg*, and the televised trial of Nazi war criminal Adolf Eichmann in Jerusalem made the subject a timely addition to the series.

The art in *World War II* was uniformly superior; the three contributors—Angelo Torres, George Evans, and Norman Nodel—were from the top tier of freelancers. An incisive, occasionally eloquent script also distinguished the issue, which surveyed such subjects as the origins of the conflict, the fall of Western Europe, the German invasion of the Soviet Union, the war in the Pacific, the Nazi death camps, and the Nuremberg war-crimes trials.

In July 1962, a final American *Special Issue*, No. 167A, *Prehistoric World*, appeared. The first 57 pages of artwork were by Angelo Torres, and the remaining 39 were divided among George Evans, Norman Nodel, Jo Albistur, and Gerald McCann. Fine scripting by Al Sundel complemented the carefully researched and wellwrought illustrations. The popular title was reprinted once.

Sixty of the book's 96 pages carried no speech balloons; instead, much of the issue offered half- or fullpage drawings (with appended pronunciations) of such dinosaurs as Tyrannosaurus, Brachiosaurus, Stegosaurus, Triceratops, and Plesiosaur, and sections on prehistoric mammals and early man, where minimal dialogue was introduced. A cleverly designed section, "The Wonderful Earth Movie," dramatically conveyed the concept of geological time. The principles of evolution were presented more thoroughly than in some school textbooks of the era, beginning with "The First Fishes," continuing with "Living on Land," and on through "The Dawn Men" to "Homo Sapiens."

An unnumbered *Special Issue* on the United Nations was published, according to Dan Malan's estimate, in 1966, but it was not part of the U.S. series.[7] Begun by George Evans, Angelo Torres, and Bruno Premiani before the Gilberton Company's new-title production was ended in 1962, the book was finished by European artists. The English-language edition was printed in Norway for sale at the United Nations headquarters in New York.

Under the guidance of Roberta Strauss Feuerlicht, *Classics Illustrated Special Issues* afforded young readers a wealth of educational material that exceeded in scope

anything attempted before in the comics medium. The best titles went beyond such popular noncomics series as *How and Why Wonder Books* and compared not unfavorably with Random House's *Landmark Books*. With the series, Albert Kanter saw his dream of using comic books as an educational medium exceed his original expectations. Yet, in a sense, the last three *Specials* were no longer comic books, and that perception, which would have been welcomed by the editorial staff in 1961, ultimately served to strand the series in a conceptual limbo between the dime store and the classroom, where its daring comprehensiveness and solid artistic merits remained, unfortunately, unsung.

THE WORLD AROUND US

Similar in format to *Classics Illustrated Special Issues* but priced a dime cheaper at 25 cents, *The World Around Us* covered a broader range of topics, from the Crusades to fishing, from pirates to medicine, from railroads to ghosts. Both series represented extensions of the *Picture Progress* concept. While two *Special Issues* reprinted several *Picture Progress* titles, *The World Around Us* incorporated four unpublished *Picture Progress* titles—featuring new scripts and art, *Through Time and Space: The Story of Communications*, *American Presidents*, and *Whaling* appeared as separate issues, and *Weather* did duty as filler material.[8]

The World Around Us, published under the slightly different corporate name of Gilberton World-Wide Publications, Inc., was a particular passion of editor Roberta Strauss Feuerlicht, who adopted from the outset a userfriendly approach for the series. Where the rather imposing *Story of Jesus* had launched the *Special Issues*, the humbler *Illustrated Story of Dogs*, No. W1 (September 1958), premiered the new line. Gilberton's top artist, George Evans, drew and inked the first section, "Heroic Dogs" (a throwback to the late 1940s and early 1950s "Heroic Dogs" *Classics* filler articles), which contained, among other canine biographies, the tale of the legendary Balto. The rest of the sections were competently, if uninspiringly, illustrated by Ernest H. Hart (who also painted the much more impressive cover), George Peltz, Lin Streeter, and William A. Walsh.

The unevenness of the artwork remained a constant problem for the series, as did the eclecticism that Feuerlicht envisioned as one of its chief merits. *Dogs* was followed the next month by *Indians*, No. W2 (October 1958), and then by *Horses*, No. W3 (November 1958), and *Railroads*, No. W4 (December 1958). A timely issue devoted to *Space*, No. W5 (January 1959), anticipated more extensive treatments of the topic in the *Special*

Issues. One of the most popular titles, *The FBI*, No. W6 (February 1959), appeared at a time when crimefighter dramas captured a large share of the television audience. *Pirates*, No. W7 (March 1959), was an impressively comprehensive historical survey of a favorite preadolescent subject. Expanding on a *Picture Progress* theme and setting the stage for a future *Special Issue* was *Flight*, No. W8 (April 1959). An armed forces miniseries allotting one recruitment-oriented title apiece to the United States Army, the Navy, the Marines, the Coast Guard, and the Air Force filled the prime enlistment months of late spring and summer.

Then suddenly, with a single issue, the character of *The World Around Us* changed dramatically. In October 1959, Gilberton published No. W14, *The French Revolution*, an exceptionally well-researched and well-organized

work. The 80-page book explained the three Estates of prerevolutionary France, discussed the economic crisis that led to the calling of the Estates-General, explained the Declaration of the Rights of Man, and offered visually gripping accounts of the fall of the Bastille, the march on Versailles, the royal family's abortive escape to Varennes, the attack on the Tuileries, the trials and executions of Louis XVI and Marie Antoinette, the birth and death of the Terror, and the rise of Napoleon. Biographical sketches of Danton, Robespierre, Saint-Just, and other leaders were provided.

The French Revolution was stronger artistically than

Left: The FBI (April 1959). Several early *World Around Us* issues were patriotically respectful tributes to the FBI, the U.S. Army, the Marines, and other defenders of the American Way of Life. *Right: The French Revolution* (October 1959). The execution of Louis XVI, drawn by Norman Nodel.

most *World Around Us* titles; more than 50 pages were illustrated by Gerald McCann, Norman Nodel, and George Evans. Ann Brewster, who had worked with Robert Hayward Webb on *Frankenstein* for *Classic Comics* in 1945, contributed a section on Napoleon's rise to power. The most comprehensive historical project undertaken by Gilberton, it demonstrated the comics medium's largely unacknowledged ability to address great themes without diluting or trivializing them. The book also paved the way for other complexly rendered historical studies on the Crusades, the American Civil War, and the Spanish conquest of America.

With the next title, *Prehistoric Animals*, No. W15 (November 1959), the series' page count dropped from 80 to 72. Like *Prehistoric World*, the *Special Issue* that followed it nearly three years later, most of the issue consisted of illustrated text. Sections outlining the origins and evolution of life on earth predominated. Sam Glanzman's detailed full-page renderings of dinosaurs were the artist's finest contribution to any Gilberton publication. Gerald McCann provided artwork for biographical sketches of William Smith, Baron Cuvier, and Charles Darwin, while Gray Morrow depicted the process of fossilization and the earliest discoveries of prehistoric "Tracks, Teeth and Bones." In "Death of the Dinosaur" and "Mammals, Men and Ice," Al Williamson created characteristic fusions of landscapes and figures for what proved to be visually the strongest sections of the book.

Attention then shifted to *The Crusades*, No. W16 (December 1959), an impressive overview that was as consistently well-illustrated—by Gerald McCann, Everett Raymond Kinstler, Bruno Premiani, Edd Ashe, and H.J. Kihl—as *The French Revolution*. Less successful was a multicultural survey of *Festivals*, No. W17 (January 1960), which, apart from sections on Christmas by George Evans and Thanksgiving and Chanukah by Norman Nodel, was an anthology of artistic disappointments. A who's who of Gilberton freelancers—George Evans, Al Williamson, John Tartaglione, Bruno Premiani, Gray Morrow, Norman Nodel, and Angelo Torres—contributed to the ambitious *Great Scientists*, No. W18 (February 1960), an edi-

Prehistoric Animals (November 1959). Dueling dinosaurs, painted by Geoffrey Biggs.

tion that reached back as far as Eratosthenes and concluded with Einstein. When the book appeared, American educators were emphasizing the need to strengthen and expand science courses in the nation's schools.

Issues devoted to *The Jungle*, No. W19 (March 1960), and *Communications*, No. W20 (April 1960) followed. As the 1960 presidential primary season headed toward the summer conventions, *The World Around Us* capitalized on the growing interest in the campaigns with

Great Scientists (February 1960). Gilberton does its part for scientific literacy.

plorers, No. W23 (July 1960), *Ghosts*, No. W24 (August 1960), and *Magic*, No. W25 (September 1960).

Ghosts was something of a departure for *The World Around Us*, which, even in its lighter moments, had focused only upon the factual and verifiable. Although some attention was given to research on extrasensory perception, most of the book was just plain fun. The best sections were the modern urban myths "The Hitch-Hiker," strikingly rendered by George Evans, and "Room for the Night," superbly drawn by Gray Morrow. Both Evans and Morrow understood the atmospheric imperatives of the tales they were recreating, and their rain-soaked, cross-hatched panels exude a delicious creepiness.

As publicity concerning the Civil War Centennial mounted during the fall of 1960, *The World Around Us* published a 64-page overview of the conflict. *The Civil War*, as noted earlier, was later complemented by a *Special Issue* No. 162A, *The War Between the States*. Norman Nodel depicted a battle scene in the cover painting, where the sword-borne officer's cap between the tattered Union and Confederate flags immediately drew the viewer into the action. Nodel also provided interior art, along with Gerald McCann, Angelo Torres, George Peltz, H.J. Kihl, Sam Glanzman, and Gray Morrow, whose "War Drums," an account of a Union drummer boy's battlefield initiation, was the best section in the book. A substantial amount of space was devoted to illustrated text (as opposed to panels), including "These Brave Fields," a Union lieutenant's account of the battle of Gettysburg, and biographical sketches of paired "War Leaders" such as Lincoln and Davis, Grant and Lee, and Meade and Jackson.

In *High Adventure: The Illustrated Story of Men Against Mountains*, No. W27 (November 1960), members of a "European Advisory Board" were listed for the

American Presidents, No. W21 (May 1960), which profiled each chief executive through Eisenhower, with sequential-art chapters on Washington, Jefferson, John Quincy Adams, Jackson, Lincoln, Theodore Roosevelt, and Franklin D. Roosevelt. A further reduction to 64 pages occurred in the issue. Summer reading included such varied subjects as *Boating*, No. W22 (June 1960), *Great Ex-*

Ghosts (August 1960). A page from "The Hitchhiker," illustrated by George Evans.

first time beneath the Gilberton editorial credits on the inside front cover. As a result of the publisher's struggles with the Post Office over the renewal of its second-class mailing permit, beginning with this issue, the editorial staff turned a hefty portion of the "back of the book" into a collection of separate and unrelated sections—"The World of Story" (a noncomics adaptation of Mark Twain's "Jumping Frog of Calaveras County"); serials ("D-Day" and "The Red Planet"); and "The World of Science," a continuing feature. As Dan Malan observed, "Gilberton had been so successful in marketing [*Classics Illustrated*] as books that they were unable to convince postal authorities of the periodical nature of their publications."[9] The continuing features began in issue No. W27, *High*

Adventure (November 1960), and new serials on the Salem Witch Trials and the Spanish Armada were under way when the series ended the following year.

Whaling, No. W28 (December 1960), featured some of the most impressive art in the entire series, particularly "The Long Voyage" by Gray Morrow. A cautionary note was sounded at the end: "No one knows what the future of whaling will be. There are signs that the whale population is getting smaller. Some whalemen believe that by the year 2000, whaling will be at an end. But others feel that the cry 'There she blows!' will sound for many years to come." The underlying attitude suggested by the title—*Whaling* rather than *Whales*—makes the book a curious artifact of the years just before a major shift in international public consciousness occurred.

For an issue devoted to *Vikings*, No. W29 (January 1961), Alfred Sundel supplied a solidly researched text that featured handsomely rendered sections by Evans, McCann, Nodel, Torres, Glanzman, Tallarico, and Premiani. The following month, *Undersea Adventures*, No. W30 (February 1961), covered frogmen, submarines, sea monsters, and sunken treasure. *Hunting*, No. W31 (March 1961), which introduced a new cover design that ran the *World Around Us* banner above the cover illustration, provided a historical perspective on "the excitement of the chase and the danger of the unexpected," from prehistoric times to the 20th century. Jack Kirby's strikingly conceived panels employed dramatic perspectives to enliven the educational text.

The best of the later issues was *For Gold and Glory*, No. W32 (April 1961), a sequel of sorts to the previous year's *Classics Illustrated* No. 156, *The Conquest of Mexico*. The new book, reflecting scriptwriter Alfred Sundel's sympathy for the subjugated Indians of the Americas, covered the Spanish conquest of the New World, with special attention devoted to Pizarro's destruction of the Inca empire of Peru. *For Gold and Glory* was the only Gilberton comic book to feature a cover photograph. Taken by Sundel, the image was "of a rare Zapotec urn (easily 100 pounds) that a husky [Museum of Natural History] curator had taken out of storage for the shot."[10]

Celebrating *Famous Teens* in issue No. W33 (May 1961), the series simultaneously courted its target audience and acknowledged its increasingly powerful role in the changing culture of John F. Kennedy's New Frontier. (That same year, Motown scored its first chart-topping hit, Bob Dylan released his first album, and a British group named the Beatles recorded their first sides in Germany.) In the next issue, *Fishing*, No. W34 (June 1961), only 16 out of 48 pages in the lead section contained panels with speech balloons, and the best efforts of the artists were reserved for a portrait of Izaak Walton and sketches of catfish, barracuda, and sturgeon. *Spies*, No. 35 (August

THE WORLD AROUND US

FOR GOLD AND GLORY

25¢

Also in this issue:
D-Day (part 6)
Desert Treasure (part 2)

For Gold and Glory (April 1961). Cover photograph by Alfred Sundel.

the necessary reader loyalty from month to month. Indeed, in the last two issues, a questionnaire occupied the inside back cover, asking readers "What made you buy this book?" and "Do you have trouble finding *The World Around Us* in stores?" Still, as the series evolved, it issued some of the most outstanding comics to appear under the Gilberton aegis, and it more than fulfilled the educational role that Albert Kanter and Roberta Strauss Feuerlicht envisioned for it.

THE BEST FROM BOYS' LIFE COMICS

A short-lived Gilberton series, *The Best from Boys' Life Comics* had a mere five-issue run. The quarterly debuted in October 1957 and expired in October 1958. Each of the 96-page editions consisted of material (none by Gilberton personnel) reprinted from the official Boy Scouts magazine, *Boys' Life*, which had introduced its own comics section in 1952.

Among the reruns were Dik Browne's "Tracy Twins," Mal Eaton's "Rocky Stoneaxe," Percy K. Fitzhugh's "Pee Wee Harris," Craig Flessel's "Stories from the Bible," Al Stenzel's "Scouts in Action" and "Space Conquerors," and Lee J. Ames's well-illustrated "Old Timer Tales of Kit Carson." Thirty-two pages of unimaginatively designed noncomics "Special Features" added dead weight at the back of the book and boosted the cover price to a comparatively expensive 35 cents, the cost of a *Special Issue*.

The handsome covers, painted in the *Classics Illustrated* style, proclaimed that the books had been "Published in Cooperation with the Boy Scouts of America." Respectability didn't get much more respectable than that. Prefacing the first issue was a message from Chief Scout Executive Arthur A. Schuck, who emphasized the educational purpose of the publication:

1961), had a Cold War resonance and a silly cover that was undoubtedly intended to look urbanely witty and uncompromisingly modern. The final issue, a history of medicine titled *Fight for Life*, No. W36 (October 1961), was the most poorly illustrated of the lot—not even a few lackluster sections by Jack Kirby could save it.

Moreover, Gilberton's best efforts couldn't save *The World Around Us*. In retrospect, it seems that, with its fragmented appeal to different audiences, the series never established a clearly defined identity and never secured

Comics, using pictures to tell stories, have become part of our literature. They have dramatized some of the greatest classics, including the Holy Bible. In the hands of imaginative artists and writers, they are more than just

PUBLISHED IN COOPERATION WITH THE BOY SCOUTS OF AMERICA

"funnies"; they are a vital way of communicating ideas…. The stories and articles in this collection open the doors to the world of great books. Read the comics, and if you enjoy the stories they tell, read books, too. Read them, enjoy them, for in them you will find information, adventure, and friendship. Books can be your life-long friends.

The credo could have served for *Classics Illustrated*, as well. Gilberton editor Meyer A. Kaplan, who had defended the cultural role of his publication in 1951 and now oversaw Gilberton's end of the joint venture with the BSA, added a note expressing his "hope that boys everywhere will read, enjoy and benefit from the articles and stories…."

Despite the noble intentions, the hybrid series had trouble finding its niche. The *Boys' Life* in the title may have initially attracted some Scouts, and the *Classics Illustrated* logo on the front cover and familiar reorder list on the back may have sold a few copies to budding collectors. But the former probably saw no point in paying for comics they had read long ago, while the latter most likely wondered what had happened to d'Artagnan and Ivanhoe.

The Best from Boys' Life Comics (October 1957). **A good idea that never quite worked.**

XXXI

"Frawley's Folly" (1967–1971)

Patrick Frawley (1923–1998), like Albert Kanter, was a successful entrepreneur. A colorful man "given," as his *New York Times* obituary put it, "to instant and excessive enthusiasms,"[1] he owned a variety of businesses at one time or another, including Schick, PaperMate, Technicolor—and *Classics Illustrated.*

Born in Nicaragua, the son of an Irish father and a Franco-Spanish mother, Frawley was educated in San Francisco. A high school dropout at 16, he returned to Nicaragua, where he learned the basics of business dealings while working with his father, a self-made man. Following service with the Royal Canadian Air Force during World War II, Frawley married, settled in San Francisco, became a United States citizen, and set about making and remaking his fortune with the companies he purchased.

Under his direction, PaperMate developed the leak-proof pen, Schick introduced the stainless-steel blade, and Technicolor pioneered a film-cartridge technology that foreshadowed the videocassette. A devout Roman Catholic, Frawley became renowned in the political arena as a staunch supporter of conservative candidates and organizations. The enterprise closest to his heart was the Schick Shadel chain of alcohol and drug treatment centers, which he founded.[2]

Where the Russian-born New Yorker Kanter had expressed the depth of his religious feeling in his fervent support of Israel, investing a substantial portion of his income in the country, the Irish-born Californian Frawley put his faith in practice by backing Dan Lyons, a Jesuit priest and journalist, in the founding of a national Catholic weekly newspaper called *Twin Circle.*[3]

In 1964, Frawley contacted Gilberton Vice-President and General Manager O.B. "Bernie" Stiskin and indicated his interest in buying the rights to *Classics Illustrated.*[4] According to a 1968 Curtis Circulation Company marketing brochure, the phone call was prompted by Frawley's enthusiastic reading of a *Classics* issue belonging to one of his children.[5] As negotiations proceeded, the prospective purchaser's plan for the series evolved. He hoped to accomplish twin objectives: first, to resuscitate the fading comic-book line, and secondly, to promote the new *Twin Circle* publication by offering a free *Classics Illustrated* title with each weekly edition.[6]

Although associates advised him against selling, Albert Kanter signed off on the deal in December 1967.[7] The purchase price, according to Albert Kanter's brother Mike, was $500,000.[8] The former owner received a five-year consultant's contract, while Bernie Stiskin remained as General Manager, with Mike Kanter continuing in charge of the warehouse.[9] But the main office, in effect, had shifted to the West Coast, and *Classics Illustrated* was now one part of the growing enterprise that would soon be known as the Frawley Corporation. Dan Lyons nominally supervised the new acquisition; he was succeeded in 1969 by Gladys Briggs, a former Technicolor regional sales manager.[10]

For a two-year period, Frawley did his best to restore *Classics Illustrated* to its former prominence among juvenile publications. Copies were included in *Twin Circle* issues, but postal regulations, which prohibited the inclusion of a separately sold item in a periodical, once again proved insurmountable.[11] *Twin Circle* then began printing the issues serially within the newspaper, reproducing 105 *Classics Illustrated* and *Classics Illustrated Junior* titles between 1968 and 1976.[12]

The Curtis Circulation Company, which still distributed the books, was optimistic and in 1968 offered a plan, modeled on its 1951 strategy, to enhance the shelf appeal of the series and to increase profits. Frawley would commission new painted covers for certain titles (two of which, *The Deerslayer* and *The Pioneers*, retained their original 1940s line-drawing covers), the new covers would be printed on a heavier paper stock, and the publisher would raise the retail price from 15 to 25 cents.[13]

To the great delight of collectors, new painted covers appeared on Frawley-era editions of *Moby Dick, A Tale of Two Cities, Les Miserables, Don Quixote, Rip Van Winkle, Uncle Tom's Cabin, The Deerslayer, Michael Strogoff, Lorna Doone, The Pioneers, Jane Eyre, 20,000 Leagues Under the Sea, Alice in Wonderland, Black Beauty, Western Stories, Joan of Arc, The Odyssey, The Master of Ballantrae, The Jungle Book, Daniel Boone, The Red Badge of Courage, Hamlet, Kit Carson, Romeo and Juliet, The First Men in the Moon, Ben-Hur,* and *Off on a Comet.* One of the reissued titles, *The Jungle Book,* featured entirely new external and interior art by Norman Nodel; it was the only instance in the history of the series when a revised *Classics* edition employed the original script.

Some of the covers, such as Nodel's *Tale of Two Cities* and *Les Miserables,* Albert Micale's *Black Beauty,* Edward Moritz's *Hamlet* and *Romeo and Juliet,* and Taylor Oughton's *Rip Van Winkle* and *Ben-Hur,* were striking conceptions. The spirit of the late 1960s was reflected in the proud black man who dominated the cover of *Uncle Tom's Cabin,* replacing the hunted slave on the 1954 exterior. Others, however, such as *Daniel Boone* and *Kit Carson,* were less potent than the covers they replaced. The worst example was the dreadful portrait of a smiling Scotsman of indefinite era on the cover of *The Master of Ballantrae.* The perpetrator, known only as "Siryk," evidently was unacquainted with Stevenson's dark tale of fraternal loathing and produced what appeared to be a sunny poster for a worse than usual community theater production of *Brigadoon.*

Then, too, there was the odd decision to ditch the relatively recent painted cover of *Off on a Comet* (March 1959). If any single cover in the history of *Classics Illustrated* had attained iconic status and talismanic significance, it was the dramatic depiction on No. 149 of a foreground figure clutching a fragment of Earth while hurtling

into space. The unknown artist's cover for the Jules Verne story had appeared on every reorder list on nearly every *Classics* edition issued since September 1959—including the Fall 1968 reprinting of *Off on a Comet* that introduced Edward Moritz's rather tepid painted cover showing two balloonists observing the planet.

As part of the effort to rejuvenate *Classics Illustrated,* Frawley briefly resumed the production of new titles in 1969. *In Freedom's Cause,* No. 168 (Winter 1969), with

Norman Nodel, *The Jungle Book* (1968). A Frawley era makeover.

artwork by Reed Crandall and George Evans, had been advertised as the next issue in *Faust*, seven years earlier, and had already appeared in the European series. It went through a single printing and is among the rarest of the later titles. (See color section.)

Rather than reprinting a European *Classic*, Frawley recruited Norman Nodel to illustrate No. 169, *Negro Americans: The Early Years* (Spring 1969). The book contained brief biographies of Crispus Attucks, Benjamin Banneker, Phillis Wheatley, James Beckwourth, Harriet Tubman, Frederick Douglass, Daniel Hale Williams, Booker T. Washington, George Washington Carver, and Matthew Henson. Aimed at schools, it did well enough at a time of increased interest in black history to warrant a reprinting. Still, its modest success failed to justify the addition of more *Classics*.

Printing and paper costs were rising, the market was shrinking, and dealers were returning shipments unopened at Frawley's expense. In 1970, Kanter suffered a stroke that left him unable to speak or to move his right side. With Bernie Stiskin's assistance, however, he recovered to a remarkable degree.[14] In the meantime, Frawley had reluctantly decided to cut his losses and shut down the operation that had come to be known as "Frawley's Folly." The end came on 21 April 1971, not quite a full 30 years after Albert Kanter published his comic-book abridgment of *The Three Musketeers* with the hopeful "No. 1" placed next to the *Classic Comics* banner. In a letter written that day to Ralph Yarrish, a Gilberton sales and marketing representative, Kanter ruefully remarked that "It should have been better. It could have been better."[15]

All of the *Classics Illustrated* plates were stored; much of the original artwork was sold. On 17 March 1973, less than two years after the demise of his dream child, Albert Lewis Kanter died.[16]

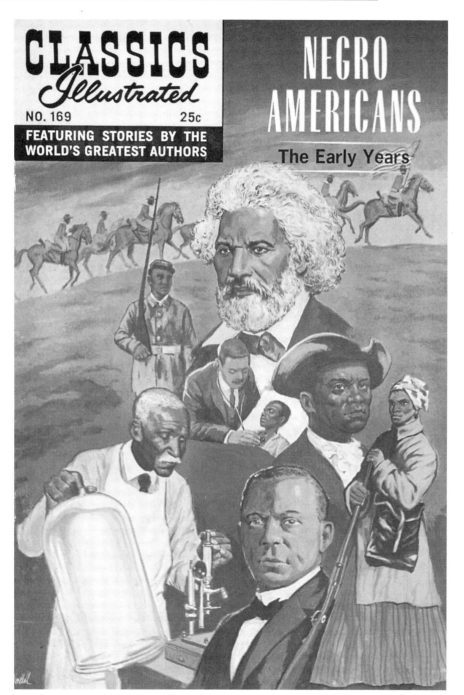

Norman Nodel, *Negro Americans—The Early Years* (1969). The last U.S. title.

XXXII

Classical Interlude: Copycats and Pirates

*C*lassics copycats had appeared as early as 1942, when Dell published *Treasure Island* and *Tom Sawyer* as *Famous Stories*. Dell tried again in the 1950s, with the irregularly issued *Rudyard Kipling's Mowgli: Jungle Book* (August 1953, August 1954, April 1955) and the *Dell Junior Treasury*, featuring *Aladdin and the Wonderful Lamp* (August 1955), *Gulliver's Travels* (January 1956), *The Wizard of Oz* (July 1956), and seven other titles. Then, of course, there was the *Classics* clone, *Fast Fiction/Stories by Famous Authors* (1949–1951), which Gilberton ultimately absorbed.

In the 1970s, while Frawley was serializing *Classics Illustrated* titles in *Twin Circle*, other publishers made efforts to fill the void left by the disappearance of the series. Distributor David Oliphant aimed at the educational market in 1972 with his authorized *Now Age Books Illustrated*, a set of 12 black-and-white repackaged *Classics Illustrated* and *Classics Illustrated Junior* editions. When sales proved disappointing, he discontinued the line and in 1973 began producing *Pendulum Classics*, which featured all new black-and-white art. By 1978, a total of 72 titles were in print, some of which, such as *Heidi*, *The Return of the Native*, and *The Turn of the Screw*, had not appeared in the Gilberton publication.

Stan Lee recycled a dozen colorized *Pendulum* issues in his *Marvel Classics Comics* (1976–1978) before introducing original art and adaptations "in the Mighty Marvel Manner" as the covers (many by Gil Kane) boasted. The series ran out of steam after 36 issues. It appeared that the classics weren't quite at home in the house that Spider-Man rebuilt: on the cover of *The Odyssey*, Polyphemus the Cyclops was depicted as a one-eyed, one-horned, purple people-eater; on the cover of *Frankenstein*, the author's last name was spelled "Shelly"; and on the cover of *The First Men in the Moon*, Jules Verne was credited with having written H.G. Wells's book. During the same period, from 1977 to 1979, King Features published 24 titles in the *King Classics* series, including *Five Weeks in a Balloon* and *Lawrence of Arabia*.

If imitation was the mode in the 1970s, outright illegality characterized the first half of the next decade. An unauthorized agent provided two publishers, Regents (1981) and the Cassette Book Company (1984), with *Classics Illustrated* art in violation of copyright law. Dumbed-down dialogue replaced the original speech balloons in the Cassette Book Company's reprints of *The Three Musketeers*, *The Count of Monte Cristo*, *Robinson Crusoe*, *Dr. Jekyll and Mr. Hyde*, *Two Years Before the Mast*, and *Treasure Island*. Legal action brought an injunction in 1986. Because the Regents product had an educational purpose, Frawley allowed its continued dissemination, subject to royalty payments. The Cassette Book Company, however, was ordered to destroy the six booklets and tapes it had produced.

XXXIII

Great Expectations:
First Publishing's *Classics* Revival

After nearly two decades of dormancy and several abortive attempts to resurrect the line or at least exploit the logo, including Sunn Classic made-for-television movies in the 1970s and negotiations between Frawley and Motown, *Classics Illustrated* returned—with a substantial difference.[1] First Publishing, a new Chicago comics company with attitude, had quickly established itself as an industry leader with such young-adult titles as *American Flagg!* (1983), *Grimjack* (1984), and *Nexus* (1985).[2] Although the publisher had also issued an adaptation of *Beowulf* (1984), it was perhaps best known for its *Teenage Mutant Ninja Turtles* series.

In 1990, First revived *Classics Illustrated*, creating a new logo and producing an ambitious, visually stunning collection of titles with completely new adaptations and artwork. Yet despite the participation of some of the most outstanding contemporary comics artists, the new line expired after the appearance of issue No. 27, *The Jungle* by Upton Sinclair (June 1991), the victim of an overabundance of corporate optimism and a changed commercial and cultural climate.

By the late 1980s and early 1990s, the Golden Age of comics was a distant memory. So, too, was the era dominated by EC-style realism. Instead, the comics industry of the period was under the spell of the "graphic novel," which brought a rather self-conscious sophistication to both the visual and textual elements of sequential storytelling. Encouraged by First's success in marketing "literary" comic books, publisher Rick Obadiah was convinced that the time was right for a return of the *Classics*, and he approached the Frawley Corporation.

With the support of Frawley Vice-President Kathryn Turpin, an exclusive licensing agreement was reached with First Publishing in 1988. Initially, the idea was to reprint the old *Classics*, and a feint was made in that direction with the photographic reproduction of No. 64, *Treasure Island*, as a promotional item for the Long John Silver restaurant chain in connection with a TNT television film of Robert Louis Stevenson's adventure tale. Partly as a result of disappointing sales of the reprinted book, First Publishing executives concluded that the better course would be to introduce a new line with fresh covers and contemporary interiors.

The decision was also supported by Obadiah's recognition that "[t]imes have changed, and the reading public has changed."[3] While the original series had been aimed primarily at the adolescent male comic-book fan who already had a frame of reference thanks to a popular culture awash in film adaptations of novels by Sir Walter Scott, Jules Verne, H.G. Wells, and Robert Louis Stevenson, the contemporary comic-book reader was often clueless about either the classics or *Classics Illustrated*.

Hence, the new series targeted a visually oriented young-adult audience that may have been adept at deconstructing the film mythos of David Lynch but was apparently incapable of deciphering *Moby Dick*. Citing, in a 1990 interview, studies that indicated a 20 to 25 percent illiteracy rate in the United States and a rising average age for bookstore customers, Obadiah saw *Classics Illustrated* as a means of attracting otherwise reluctant readers. First Publishing consulted with various literacy programs, and the books were intended to some extent for use as reading tools.[4]

Although the educational mission had not changed

substantially since Albert Kanter's day, the odds against success were greater. The cultural consensus that had given *Classics Illustrated* a certain authority in the 1940s and 1950s had dissolved, and comic books of whatever stripe were now fighting a rearguard action in the postliterate era.

Still, First Publishing was determined to fight the good fight. It was, Obadiah insisted, "a major labor of love."[5] Wade Roberts, the first editor of the resurrected series, hoped to create greater contemporary appeal by avoiding the house-style look that characterized *Classics Illustrated* in the Iger and Feuerlicht eras. Consequently, First Publishing contracted with artists known for their highly individualized approaches. When the first four titles appeared in February 1990, the distinctiveness of the artwork in each book was unmistakable.

Indeed, the prominence accorded each artist was among the most striking features of the new series. Apart from the occasional cover signature of a Henry C. Kiefer or the title-page splash acknowledgment of an Alex A. Blum, most of the artists who worked in the original *Classics* line contented themselves, as did Norman Nodel, with small signatures or no identifying mark whatsoever. By the 1990s, however, comics artists had become not merely stars in their field but, more significantly, *auteurs*—they were to the comic books they drew what film directors had become to the movies they made. Thus, John K. Snyder III's name was printed as large as Robert Louis Stevenson's on the cover of *Dr. Jekyll and Mr. Hyde* while Bill Sienkiewicz's name was actually larger than Herman Melville's on the cover of *Moby Dick.*

One of the most recognizable names and styles inaugurated the new series. Issue No. 1, *The Raven and Other Poems* by Edgar Allan Poe, spotlighted the macabre wit of Gahan Wilson, with such poems as "Annabel Lee" and "The Conquerer Worm" serving as springboards for the artist's clever variations on ghoulish themes. Wilson later adapted *The Devil's Dictionary and Other Works,* No. 18 (February 1991), for the series and found himself very much at home in the realm of Ambrose Bierce's waspish imagination.

An accomplished artist and the compiler and illustrator of *A Treasury of Victorian Murder* (1987), Rick Geary (b. 1946) may have seemed a logical candidate for the second title, *Great Expectations.* His drawings were

Gahan Wilson, *The Raven and Other Poems* (February 1990). The First Publishing series was launched with works by widely recognized graphic artists.

engaging on their own terms but less successful in capturing the atmosphere of Dickens's novel than Henry C. Kiefer's darkly oppressive 1947 illustrations. Rendered in the bubblefaced technique of 1960s underground comics (the artist's work had appeared in *National Lampoon, Heavy Metal,* and *Raw*), the bright, exaggerated panels often seemed to be working against the darker-hued Victorian text.

The same tensions are evident, though to a lesser degree, in the artist's treatment of Emily Brontë's *Wuthering Heights,* No. 13 (October 1990). His Heathcliff and

Cathy, however, are potent figures and a decided improvement on Kiefer's 1949 Olivier-Oberon stand-ins. In Geary's most successful work for First, *The Invisible Man*, No. 20 (March 1991), the artist's distinctive style proved an ideal match for the fantastic elements of H.G. Wells's science-fiction period piece.

Kyle Baker (b. 1965), a product of New York's School of Visual Arts, produced a superb postmodern rendering of Lewis Carroll's *Through the Looking Glass* in issue No. 3. The illustrations showed the influence of Milton Glaser, for whom Baker once worked, in their clean graphic style. A later issue illustrated by Baker, *Cyrano de Bergerac*, No. 21 (March 1991), captured the verve of Edmond Rostand's sword-and-pen-wielding hero and would-be lover.

Among the first four titles, the one that attracted the most attention was issue No. 4, the dark, brooding pictorial commentary on Herman Melville's *Moby Dick* by Bill Sienkiewicz (b. 1958). A powerful, stylized evocation of the novel rather than a traditional sequential narrative in the manner of Louis Zansky's and Norman Nodel's versions, the book was the clearest declaration that the new *Classics Illustrated* would be nothing like the old.

Sienkiewicz's *Moby Dick*, with its challenging blend of paintings and text, was one of the greatest artistic triumphs of the brief First Publishing era and an extraordinary achievement in its own right. Yet despite its disturbing beauty and interpretive genius, the demanding book baffled almost as many readers as it enthralled and may have served to alienate a segment of the audience that might have been drawn to the revived line simply on the strength of the White Whale's enduring appeal. Even so, it was one of the best-selling titles in the First series.

If *Moby Dick* perplexed some hesitating purchasers, John K. Snyder III's outstanding illustrations for *Dr. Jekyll and Mr. Hyde*, No. 8 (April 1990), enraged others—at least, those who were still expecting the new *Classics* to resemble in some fashion the old. A brilliant hallucinatory treatment of Robert Louis Stevenson's "fine bogey tale" of human duality, the artist's work owed an obvious debt to the German Expressionist film masterpiece, *The Cabinet of Dr. Caligari*, with its menacing buildings and distorted faces.

Snyder (b. 1961), whose comics credits included *Grendel*, *Grimjack*, and *Nexus*, produced an even stronger adaptation of *The Secret Agent*, No. 19 (February 1991), Joseph Conrad's prescient 1907 novel about modern ter-

John K. Snyder III, *Dr. Jekyll and Mr. Hyde* (April 1990). **An emphatic break with the past.**

rorism. Employing the same expressionistic visual vocabulary that he had used in *Dr. Jekyll and Mr. Hyde*, the artist effectively conveyed the moral limbo inhabited by Verloc and his fellow revolutionary conspirators through claustrophobic frames and recurring motifs such as eyes, skulls, and knives. Nowhere in the series were panels more inventively stretched, compressed, and exploded.

One of the finest *Classics* in the new series was the sole Shakespeare—*Hamlet*, No. 5 (March 1990). The adaptation by Steven Grant (b. 1953) improved upon Sam Willinsky's 1952 script, dispensing with connecting expository rectangles and employing more of the play's dialogue. Tom Mandrake (b. 1956), whose credits included *Batman*, *Captain Marvel*, and *Swamp Thing*, as well as First Publishing's *Grimjack*, conjured a splendidly menacing atmosphere with his crowded panels and alternating closeups. Hamlet and his father's ghost are rendered mostly in shades of gray, accented occasionally with purple or red; Ophelia is shown in white; Gertrude, Claudius, and the court at Elsinore provide contrasting patches of color.

Dean Motter's *The Rime of the Ancient Mariner*, No. 24 (May 1991), was an impressively evocative treatment of Samuel Taylor Coleridge's parable of sin and redemption. The entire poem was reproduced, and the artist's paintings of ghostly figures and the haunted ship could be "read" as well, offering an imaginative visual experience that enhanced the reader's encounter with the familiar Romantic text. Motter (b. 1953) was the creator and writer of the series *Mister X* and a collaborator on the graphic novel *The Sacred and the Profane*, and he brought a philosophical depth to his illustrations for the *Ancient Mariner* that transcended the comics category.

The final title in First Publishing's *Classics* catalogue, *The Jungle*, No. 27 (June 1991), adapted from Upton Sinclair's novel of social protest and illustrated by Peter Kuper (b. 1958), rivaled the books by Sienkiewicz, Snyder, and Motter in terms of originality and the appropriateness of the graphic design. The artist, who had served as cofounder, coeditor, and publisher of the political comic *World War 3 Illustrated*, adopted a stylized, geometrical approach somewhat reminiscent of early 20th-century Russian Constructivism. Kuper's *Jungle* represents a sophisticated union of art and text, hammering home the author's polemical intent, and serves as a fitting capstone for First's striving for excellence in the revived series. (See color section.)

While the more experimental books generally proved the most successful artistically among First Publishing's *Classics*, some of the more straightforward issues were also impressive. Perhaps the single most charming issue in the history of *Classics Illustrated*—old or new—was Mike Ploog's adaptation of *The Adventures of Tom Sawyer*, No. 9 (May 1990). The joyously playful illustrations show the influence of Will Eisner, with whom the artist had worked as an assistant before venturing into the comics and film industries.

Ploog (b. 1940) displays a mischievous affinity for Mark Twain's boyhood idyll, from the whitewashing episode to Tom and Huck's discovery of treasure in McDougal's cave. The artist's use of caricature serves to universalize the experience of the comic book; Tom becomes Everyboy, inviting reader identification.[6] An almost cinematic immediacy is present, testimony to the sharpening of Ploog's narrative skills as a storyboard artist, designer, writer, and editor for such films as *The Unbearable Lightness of Being*, *Little Shop of Horrors*, and *Melvin and Howard*.

For P. Craig Russell's adaptation of Nathaniel Hawthorne's *The Scarlet Letter*, No. 6 (March 1990), Jill Thompson (b. 1966) produced a beautifully textured work that made symbolic use of light and shading. The artist's subtle watercolors capture something of the characters' spiritual isolation and anguish against a lush colonial forest backdrop. Considered too mature for inclusion in the original *Classics Illustrated* series, *The Scarlet Letter* had become a staple of high school reading lists by 1990. The only shortcoming in Thompson's treatment of the familiar story is that in some respects it suggests a latter-day teenage romance movie, with Arthur Dimmesdale in particular looking a bit too "buff" for the austere 17th-century Puritan New England setting.

A newcomer to comics, children's book illustrator Jeffrey Busch (b. 1962) produced two quite different yet equally delectable titles for First Publishing's *Classics*. His adaptation of Washington Irving's *Rip Van Winkle*, No. 11 (July 1990), combined detailed character linework and simple backgrounds in a whimsical manner. His lush, green-dominated *Jungle Books*, No. 22 (April 1991), evoked the sense of mystery at the heart of Rudyard Kipling's Mowgli tales.

Another new *Classics* artist with a background in children's book illustration, Eric Vincent (b. 1953), was a 1984 Children's Choice Award winner for *Clovis Crawfish and the Orphan Zo-Zo*. In 1989, he inked Steven Grant's science-fiction tale, *Twilight Man*, a four-part First Publishing graphic novel. For the new *Classics Illustrated* series, Vincent delivered a chilling rendering of Grant's adaptation of *The Island of Dr. Moreau* by H.G. Wells, No. 12 (August 1990). The feverish drawings were marred only slightly by a rather excessive reliance on conventional comic-book sound effects ("Wap!" "Rrraaaaa-aarggh!" "Blam!"), which were rarely used in either the original Gilberton series or the First Publishing line. The artist also adapted and illustrated *25 Aesop's Fables*, No. 26 (June 1991), employing a range of period settings for his witty retellings.

With his attention to the most minute details of hair, clothing, and furnishings, Garry Gianni (b. 1954) evoked the "Gibson Girl" magazine style in his period drawings for O. Henry's *The Gift of the Magi and other Stories*, No. 15 (November 1990). The artist's work in the title story is tightly focused on the two principals, as attested by the substantial proportion of single "head shots." In "A Retrieved Reformation," on the other hand, Gianni offers an early 20th-century urban panorama with a splendidly realized cast of characters. His affectionate restatement of the Gibson manner encompassed both the

Left: Mike Ploog, *The Adventures of Tom Sawyer* (May 1990). Full circle—an Eisner-influenced work. *Right:* Jill Thompson, *The Scarlet Letter* (March 1990). The artist's watercolors captured the novel's rich imagery of darkness and light.

broad humor of "The Pimienta Pancakes" and the treacly sentiment of "The Last Leaf," and he delivered it all without affecting a knowing, ironic distance.

For *Ivanhoe*, No. 25 (May 1991), Ray Lago (b. 1958) used watercolors to add richness and depth to Sir Walter Scott's medieval pageant. Each panel is exquisitely composed, with colors and detailed or minimal backgrounds perfectly underscoring the accompanying text. The artist's characters are remarkably contemporary in appearance (though certainly no more so than the Troy Donahue–like Ivanhoe on the 1957 Gilberton painted cover), while the costuming, in keeping with the historical Romanticism of the novel, is solidly in the Romantic vein. Lago's neotraditionalist edition, along with Ploog's *Tom Sawyer*, became a favorite with older collectors.[7]

Other titles in the First Publishing series included

Dan Spiegle's *The Count of Monte Cristo*, No. 7 (April 1990), which, as drawn by the veteran Dell artist, harkened back to an older comics style; Ricardo Villagran's *The Call of the Wild*, No. 10 (June 1990), a visually compelling production; Jay Geldhof's *The Fall of the House of Usher*, No. 14 (September 1990), with its gripping renderings of inner torment; Joe Staton's *A Christmas Carol*, No. 16 (December 1990), a warmly nostalgic account of the Dickens perennial; and Pat Boyette's *Treasure Island*, No. 17 (January 1991), and *Robinson Crusoe*, No. 23 (April 1991), both packed with a rough vigor, though the Stevenson pirate saga featured a rather stocky Jim Hawkins and exhibited a certain indifference to period details such as the appearance of Captain Smollett, who looked more like a relative of the hirsute Robert Shaw in *Jaws* than a proper 18th-century naval officer.

Lapses notwithstanding, the artwork in each issue

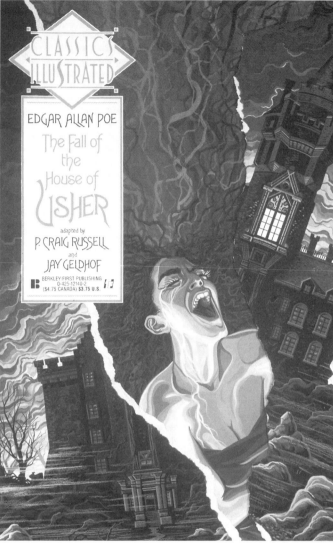

Left: Jeffrey K. Potter, *The Island of Dr. Moreau* (August 1990). An atmospheric blend of painting and photography. *Right:* Jay Geldhof, *The Fall of the House of Usher* (September 1990): She's b-a-a-ck (and so is Poe).

was never less than well matched to the demands of the specific narrative. First Publishing achieved one of its goals in bringing classic literature in comics form into the 1990s, 50 years after Albert L. Kanter's gamble on the appeal of Dumas, Scott, and Cooper. Further, eight of the First Publishing titles had never appeared in the Gilberton series, while a ninth, *The Rime of the Ancient Mariner*, had been printed in the 1940s as a *Classic Comics* filler.

Projected issues included *Kidnapped, Around the World in Eighty Days, The Last of the Mohicans, 20,000 Leagues Under the Sea, The Red Badge of Courage, Candide, Dracula, Adventures of Huckleberry Finn*, and, most ambitiously, John Milton's *Paradise Lost*. But publication of the new *Classics* ended abruptly after the 27th issue appeared in June 1991. A year later, Dark Horse Comics picked up the unpublished *20,000 Leagues Under the Sea* (art by Gary Gianni) and *The Last of the Mohicans* (art by

Jack Jackson), issuing the books in a black-and-white format.

The entire comics industry was enduring a sluggish period, and the downturn was reflected in the collectors' market, always a driving factor. Comics aficionados were simply not responding to the new series. It was reported that First Publishing had printed more than 200,000 copies of each book but had sold only about 50,000 per title.[8]

It was apparent that the new *Classics* had failed to build a cohesive audience. Some have argued that First's updated art was in some instances too radical a break with the Gilberton-Frawley *Classics* tradition. It is more likely, though, that the time had simply passed for a newly scripted reenactment of Albert Kanter's dream. No matter how many pictures accompany the text, the irreducible fact of a literary adaptation is the printed word.

Perhaps First's admirably stubborn insistence on the primacy of the author's individual, idiosyncratic language (the new *Classics* were more faithful to the originals than many of the old) proved too great a cultural barrier for many readers bred on images.

Meanwhile, internal turmoil at First Publishing was followed by restructuring under the new corporate name, Classics International Entertainment, Inc. (CIE), spurred by the energetic direction of Richard S. Berger. Although attempts to create a comic book store chain and a *Classics* book club collapsed, Berger remained determined,[9] and by the mid–1990s, that determination paid off.

XXXIV

Classical Interlude: *Classics* in the Movies

Classics Illustrated issues show up from time to time in motion pictures as period references, plot-related props, or visual jokes. Director Hal Kanter, as a playful act of homage to his father, included a copy of *The Gold Bug* in a couple of scenes in Elvis Presley's *Loving You* (1957). A newspaper photographer accompanying a Dallas reporter is shown reading the comic book. He then folds it and stuffs it in his jacket pocket, with the yellow logo plainly visible on the camera side.

Fast forward to 1985 and *Explorers*, Joe Dante's science-fiction children's fantasy, in which the aspiring young space voyagers discuss a copy of *The War of the Worlds* before setting off to encounter their own aliens. As Tom Hanks packs up his personal effects after quitting his oppressive job in John Patrick Shanley's *Joe Versus the Volcano* (1990), he holds up a vintage edition of *Robinson Crusoe*, a book that has some thematic relationship to the movie's subsequent plot development. A copy of *The Man in the Iron Mask* can be seen on a table in a scene with the card-playing Demi Moore in Dan Aykroyd's *Nothing but Trouble* (1991).

Classics Illustrated figured most prominently, though, in David S. Ward's *Major League* (1989). Seeking to win the approval of literate Rene Russo, ballplayer Tom Berenger is shown reading—anachronistically, given the time frame, and improbably, considering the relative rarity of the issue—a 1940s *Classic Comics* edition of *Moby Dick*. Berenger's absorption in the comic book is catching, and soon his teammates are gleefully tossing each other copies of the 1951 first printing of *Crime and Punishment* and the 1968 painted-cover edition of *The Deerslayer*.

XXXV

Recalled to Life:
Acclaim's *Study Guides*

Five years after the new *Classics Illustrated* series was terminated, the original series was, to borrow a phrase from Dickens, recalled to life. In May 1996, Acclaim Comics, a New York–based publisher, entered into a licensing agreement with First Classics, Inc., a CIE subsidiary, to republish the *Classics* properties.

The new line would be marketed as *Classics Illustrated Study Guides*, and the educational thrust would be underscored by the motto "Your Doorway to the Classics." Each issue would feature a back-of-the-book essay by an authority on the author in question or the work adapted.

Although Acclaim was authorized to reissue any title from either of the American series, editor Madeleine Robins discovered that the Gilberton-Frawley editions proved more suitable for reproduction and recoloring in the digest-size format adopted by the publisher than the complex page designs of the First Publishing *Classics*.[1] When given a choice between the original artwork or the Feuerlicht-era revisions, Robins tended to prefer the older drawings, such as those by Arnold Hicks for *Oliver Twist*, Rolland Livingstone for *The Legend of Sleepy Hollow*, and Henry C. Kiefer for *Julius Caesar*, for their strong "period" appeal.[2]

Unfortunately, even with the exclusive use of the older comics, the linework in the Acclaim books frequently suffered. Subtleties of expression in the work of George Evans, Joe Orlando, and Norman Nodel were lost in the heavily inked reproductions. The computer recoloring was also erratic. VanHook Studios supplied the most natural enhancements for the series in such titles as *Les Miserables* and *Treasure Island*. But Twilight Graphics produced dimly lit editions of *The Call of the Wild* and *The Last of the Mohicans* with day-for-night panels that obscured facial features and dark-tan narrative boxes that were all but unreadable.

The first four issues—*Tom Sawyer, Romeo and Juliet, A Tale of Two Cities*, and *Jane Eyre*—appeared in February 1997. The editor restored Aldo Rubano's 1948 artwork in the Twain title, which featured analysis by Clemens biographer Andrew Jay Hoffman. Robins, a Charlotte Brontë enthusiast and specialist for whom *Jane Eyre* was a "totemic" work, went back to Harley Griffiths's 1947 edition but rewrote a scene in Harry Miller's adaptation between the heroine and Rochester that, she said, "reeked of 1940s' women's movies."[3]

Four *Study Guides* were published each month through May 1997; the schedule increased to six monthly issues from June through September 1997. During the first few months, Robins included in each set of four one work apiece by Shakespeare, Dickens, and Twain. In July, four of the six releases were Jules Verne adaptations, the editor's nod to summer reading habits. Distribution became increasingly problematical as the year progressed, and Acclaim returned to the four-title cycle from October 1997 through February 1998. Another thematic grouping was packaged for Halloween—*Frankenstein, The Invisible Man, The Legend of Sleepy Hollow*, and *Dr. Jekyll and Mr. Hyde*—and *A Christmas Carol* was issued in December. Plans for issuing collected editions of Dickens, Shakespeare, Wells, and horror tales (similar to Gilberton's 1949 "Giants") were scrapped as the series foundered.

One of the benefits of editing the series, in Robins's view, was "the opportunity to reacquaint myself with classics that I hadn't read in years or that I hadn't read at all.

I doubt that I would have read a boy's book like *Captains Courageous* otherwise." Some of the works, she discovered, actually improved in the condensed comic-book versions. Recalling the "punitive experience" of reading George Eliot's *Silas Marner*, she concluded that the *Classics Illustrated* treatment, with its rapidly paced, plot-driven narrative, "made a better book." On the other hand, architectonically complex texts, such as Joseph Conrad's *Lord Jim*, suffered from the reductionism inherent in the comics medium.

In such books, Robins said, the critical supplements served to amplify the adaptations: "We try to put back in what was left out."[4] For example, in his essay on Dostoevsky's *Crime and Punishment*, Andrew Jay Hoffman noted that the *Classics* version includes only one "narrowly represented" plot line, the pawnbroker's murder, and misrepresents the character of Raskolnikov; he probed motivations and consequences, summarized the omitted portions of the novel, and explored such concerns as reality and duality. Beth Nachison of Southern Connecticut State University offered a penetrating examination of Stevenson's *Master of Ballantrae*, emphasizing the neglected masterpiece's thematic relationship to the author's better-known *Dr. Jekyll and Mr. Hyde*, and provided historical context in a discussion of the Jacobite rising of 1745.

Perhaps the most promising development with Acclaim was Robins's decision to commission scripts and art for previously unpublished *Classics Illustrated* titles. The "Original Editions" began appearing in February 1998 and included William Shakespeare's *Henry IV—Part One*, No. SG 59 (February 1998) (art by Patrick Broderick), Frederick Douglass's *Narrative of the Life of Frederick Douglass*, No. SG61 (March 1998) (art by Jamal Igle, Ravil Lopez, and Mike DeCarlo), and Baroness Emmuska Orczy's *The Scarlet Pimpernel*, No. SG62 (April 1998) (art by Patrick Broderick and Ralph Reese).

Unlike the bold First Publishing editions, however, the Acclaim new-title *Classics* featured artwork that was not only conventional but also, with the exception of a robust rendering of *The Scarlet Pimpernel*, downright dull. *Henry IV—Part One* was filled with too many closeup panels of talking heads. The artists who worked on the Frederick Douglass autobiography produced illustrations that were more inventively composed but that matched

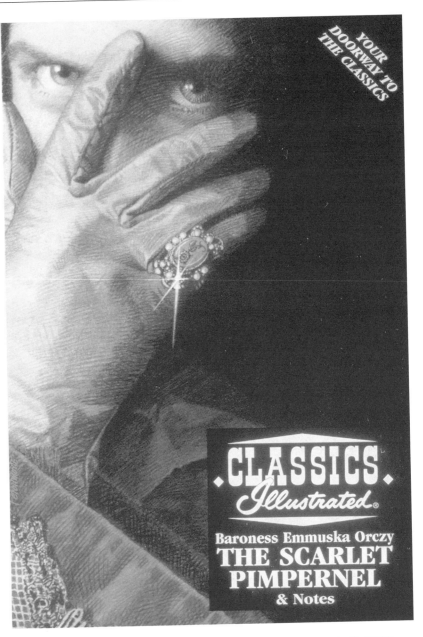

The Scarlet Pimpernel (April 1998). The last hurrah. (Copyright © 1997 by Acclaim Books, Inc.)

Stanley Maxwell Zuckerberg's drawings in the 1942 *Tale of Two Cities* for historical cluelessness—the *Narrative's* setting is the first half of the 19th century, yet most of the characters are garbed in late Victorian or even early 20th-century attire, while an 1830s slave master is given an 18th-century queue.

Still, Robins and her team were making an effort to turn the series into something more than a line of reprints. A new century was approaching, and Albert Kanter's dream continued to resonate. As if to bring matters full circle, Robins commissioned Norman Nodel to illustrate Shakespeare's *Much Ado About Nothing*. It seemed almost too good to be true. As it happened, it was.

Once again, a publisher had misjudged the market, and Acclaim suspended publication in April 1998 after issuing 62 titles. Unreleased were "Original Editions" of *Beowulf*, Shakespeare's *Henry IV—Part 2*, and Jane Austen's *Pride and Prejudice*. The digest size and the emphasis on "Study Guides" had effectively killed comic-book dealers' and collectors' interest in the series.[5] Meanwhile, bookstore chains seemed uncertain how to categorize the odd little volumes.

It was the old *Classics* marketing conundrum: were they comics? magazines? books? What, after all, were they?

The graying early readers had never troubled themselves with such fine distinctions. They had always known the answer—"good stories."

XXXVI

Classical Coda

Nostalgia is a seductive yet sterile trap, as I have frequently reminded myself while working on this book. I trust that on the whole, excepting the Introduction and this passage, I have maintained a reasonable distance from its snares and have avoided mistaking the personal dimension of remembered enjoyment for intimations of universal significance.

Sentiment is one thing, the record another. Evidence of the cultural role of *Classics Illustrated* is plentiful: the 1,343 printings in the United States of 169 *Classics Illustrated* titles and 432 editions of 77 *Juniors*; the millions of copies distributed worldwide; the adoption or approval of the series by thousands of schools; the imitations by other comics publishers; the continuing efforts to revive the line.

Equally important, however, is the controversial position of *Classics Illustrated* in the midcentury culture wars, which, unlike those at the end of the 20th century, were largely fought on terrain selected by an intellectual elite promoting a modernist literary canon and sensibility. As Bart Beaty has indicated, this mandarin class, including critic Leslie Fiedler and poet Delmore Schwartz, insisted on a particular way to read and disparaged perceived "middlebrow" attempts at diluting the proper response to Shakespeare, Hawthorne, Melville, and Dostoevsky.[1]

In the end, though, it comes back to the individual's experience, and it's futile to deny the appeal of anything that connects one to the fading Wordsworthian "visionary gleam" of childhood discovery—to that moment of revelation in the spring of 1959, that epiphany in the summer of 1960. So adults roam the eBay categories searching for some connecting thread, whether in the form of a Marx "Battle of the Blue and Gray" playset or a vintage Barbie doll or a 1955 Brooklyn Dodgers baseball card. It's a sad phenomenon, perhaps, the consequence

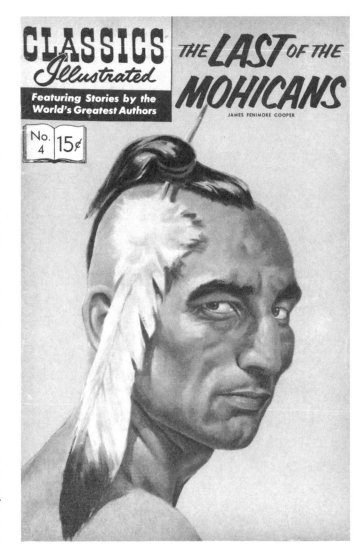

Unknown artist, *The Last of the Mohicans* (November 1956). "…and yet, before the night has come, have I lived to see the last warrior of the wise race of the Mohicans."—James Fenimore Cooper (1826)

of two centuries of post–Romantic idealization of the child or, as some might say today, the Inner Child.

Classics authority Jim McLoughlin offers a knowing corrective in his account of an evening spent with Mike Kanter, Albert Kanter's brother and Gilberton's warehouse manager. Unable to comprehend the strange promptings that drive collectors, Kanter and his wife "sat and shook their heads and laughed at the idea of grown men running around the country buying comic books, stationery, display racks, and anything else associated with *Classics Illustrated*."[2]

Yet the power of the yellow rectangle extends beyond the rarefied subculture of *Classics* collectors. Over the years, I've spoken to many adults who recall with animated affection particular titles—and the artwork—that continue to carry special meaning: for a journalist, it was Lou Cameron's *War of the Worlds*; for a university professor, August M. Froehlich's *Toilers of the Sea*; for a lawyer, Don Rico's *Moonstone*; for an interior designer, Matt Baker's *Lorna Doone*; for a doctor, Robert Hayward Webb's *Mysterious Island*; for a novelist, Rudy Palais's *Crime and Punishment*; for a U.S. Air Force colonel, Norman Nodel's *Ivanhoe*; for a voice-over artist, Lou Cameron's *Dr. Jekyll and Mr. Hyde*.

For this writer, several 48-page wonders still echo. George Evans's *Three Musketeers*, Joe Orlando's *Tale of Two Cities*, Norman Nodel's *Les Miserables*, Louis Zansky's *Don Quixote* and Rudy Palais's *David Balfour* taught unforgettable lessons about courage, loyalty, sacrifice, humor, and holding fast to one's ideals.

As children, we create our own mythologies as we reinvent the world. Although I was born a Presbyterian and confirmed an Episcopalian, the religion of my boyhood was *Classics Illustrated*; the creed of my young adulthood was the literature that the series had prepared me to embrace.

I know better now, I suppose—irony is an inescapable element of the postmodern human condition, and our culture has been deconstructed nearly to death. My frame of reference is, I hope, broader, but then the range of publications that juxtaposed Goethe and G.A. Henty, the Brothers Grimm and Native American myth, the sport of fishing and the lives of "famous teens" was broad enough.

"[W]hat we have been makes us what we are," wrote George Eliot,[3] whose pseudonym and real name I first encountered in *Classics Illustrated* No. 55 at the age of eight.

Thank you, Mr. Kanter. Thank you all.

Notes

INTRODUCTION: "GOOD STORIES"

1. Donna Richardson, "Classics Illustrated," *American Heritage* (June 1993), p. 78.
2. Anne Rice, "Giving 100%" (interview), *Comic Buyers Guide* # 1340 (23 July 1999), p. 40.
3. Pete Hamill, *A Drinking Life: A Memoir* (Boston: Little, Brown and Company, 1994), p. 101.
4. *Ibid.*
5. Mike Benton, *The Comic Book in America: An Illustrated History* (Dallas: Taylor Publishing Company, 1993), pp. 46, 48.
6. Nancy Mahler, Interview with author, 15 June 2000.

I. ALBERT KANTER'S DREAM

1. Dan Malan, *The Complete Guide to Classics Illustrated, Volume Two: Foreign Series and Related Collectibles* (St. Louis: Malan Classical Enterprises, 1993, rev. 1996), pp. 8, 10.
2. Hal Kanter, *So Far, So Funny: My Life in Show Business* (Jefferson, N.C.: McFarland & Company, Inc., Publishers, 1999), p. 1.
3. Michael Sawyer, "Albert Lewis Kanter and the Classics: The Man Behind the Gilberton Company," *Journal of Popular Culture*, 20:4 (Spring 1987), p. 1.
4. Dan Malan, *The Complete Guide to Classics Collectibles, Volume One: The U.S. Series of Classics Illustrated and Related Collectibles* (St. Louis: Malan Classical Enterprises, 1991), p. 16.
5. Sawyer, p. 2.
6. Roger Sabin, *Comics, Comix & Graphic Novels: A History of Comic Art* (London: Phaidon Press Limited, 1996), pp. 12, 15.
7. Robert L. Beerbohm and Richard D. Olson, Ph.D., "In the Beginning: New Discoveries Beyond the Platinum Age," in Robert M. Overstreet, *The Overstreet Comic Book Price Guide*, 30th Edition (New York: Gemstone Publishing, Inc./HarperCollins Publishers, Inc., 2000).
8. Les Daniels, *Comix: A History of Comic Books in America* (New York: Outerbridge & Dienstfrey, 1971), pp. 2–3.
9. Daniels, p. 6.

10. Robert C. Harvey, *The Art of the Comic Book: An Aesthetic History* (Jackson: University Press of Mississippi, 1996), p. 275. Harvey notes that *The Yellow Kid Magazine*, often said to have been the first comic book, merely displayed the attention-getting character on the cover and had no comics content.
11. Harvey, p. 16.
12. Mike Benton, *The Comic Book in America: An Illustrated History* (Dallas: Taylor Publishing Company, 1993), p. 14.
13. Benton, p. 14.
14. See Ron Goulart, *Ron Goulart's Great History of Comic Books* (Chicago: Contemporary Books, 1986), Chapters 1–2, 5–7; see also Benton, pp. 16–27.
15. Harvey, p. 23; see Jerry Bails and Hames Ware, *Who's Who of American Comic Books, Volume Four* (Detroit: Jerry Bails, 1976), pp. 335–340.
16. Goulart, pp. 199–200.
17. Goulart, pp. 200–201.
18. Ron Goulart, "Bobby Thatcher," *The Encyclopedia of American Comics*, ed. R. Goulart (New York, Oxford: Facts on File, 1990), pp. 40–41.
19. Goulart, *Great History of Comic Books*, pp. 56, 58, 66.
20. Sawyer, p. 2.
21. Malan, *Complete Guide to Classics Collectibles*, Vol. I, p. 18.
22. Sawyer, p. 2.
23. Malan, *Complete Guide to Classics Collectibles*, Vol. I, p. 22.
24. Sawyer, p. 3; Malan, *Complete Guide to Classics Collectibles*, Vol. I, p. 18.
25. Sawyer, p. 3.
26. Malan, *Complete Guide to Classics Collectibles*, Vol. I, p. 22.
27. Sawyer, pp. 3–4.
28. Sawyer, pp. 3, 6.
29. Sawyer, p. 4.
30. Malan, *Complete Guide to Classics Collectibles*, Vol. I, p. 22.
31. Harvey, *The Art of the Comic Book*, p. 16.
32. Malan, *Complete Guide to Classics Collectibes*, Vol. I, p. 22.
33. Malan, *Complete Guide to Classics Illustrated*, Vol. II, p. 8.

II. CLASSICAL INTERLUDE: *CLASSICS* ABROAD

1. A detailed, definitive survey of the worldwide dimensions of *Classics Illustrated*, which is outside the scope of this volume, can be found in Dan Malan's superbly researched reference work, *The Complete Guide to Classics Illustrated, Volume Two: Foreign Series of Classics and Related Collectibles* (St. Louis: Malan Classical Enterprises, 1993, 1996).

III. OF MUSKETEERS AND MOHICANS: THE JACQUET SHOP

1. Ron Goulart, *Ron Goulart's Great History of Comic Books*, pp. 100, 207.
2. Jeanette Zansky, Letter to author, 16 June 1997.
3. Hames Ware, interview with author, 7 July 2000. The more lucrative comic strips, on the other hand, were almost uniformly the work of veteran cartoonists. See Robert C. Harvey, *The Art of the Comic Book: An Aesthetic History* (Jackson: University Press of Mississippi), p. 25.
4. Hames Ware, interview with author, 21 July 1994.
5. *Ibid.*
6. Edd Ashe, letter to Raymond S. True, 17 February 1972.
7. Hames Ware, interview with author, 21 July 1994.
8. Bill Briggs, paired panels reproduced in letter to author, 30 June 2000.
9. Hames Ware, interview with author, 7 July 2000.

V. THE PAINTER'S TOUCH: LOUIS ZANSKY

1. Jeanette Zansky, interview with author, 25 July 1994.
2. J. Zansky, letter to author, 16 June 1997.
3. *Ibid.*
4. *Ibid.*
5. *Ibid.*
6. Louis Zansky, resume for art show, 1976.
7. J. Zansky, letter to author, 16 June 1997.
8. *Ibid.*
9. J. Zansky, interview with author, 25 July 1994.
10. *Ibid.*
11. *Ibid.*
12. Mike Benton, *Crime Comics: The Illustrated History* (Dallas: Taylor Publishing Company, 1993), p. 103.
13. J. Zansky, interview with author, 25 July 1994.

VI. THE WAR YEARS: EARLY FREELANCERS

1. Michael Sawyer, "Albert Lewis Kanter and the Classics: The Man Behind the Gilberton Company," *Journal of Popular Culture*, 20:4 (Spring 1987), p. 8.

2. Dan Malan, *The Complete Guide to Classics Collectibles, Volume One: The U.S. Series of Classics Illustrated and Related Collectibles* (St. Louis: Malan Classical Enterprises, 1991), p. 20.
3. *Who's Who in American Art: 1999–2000* (New Providence, N.J.: Marquis/Reed Elsevier Inc., 1999), p. 1365.
4. Trina Robbins and Catherine Yronwode, *Women and the Comics* (Eclipse Books, 1985), p. 55.
5. Hames Ware, Interview with author, 21 July 1994.
6. Robbins and Yronwode, p. 55.
7. Washington Irving, "Rip Van Winkle," *The Sketch Book of Geoffrey Crayon, Gent.*, in *History, Tales and Sketches* (New York: The Library of America, 1983), p. 770.
8. The adaptation of Stowe's novel tied with *Rip Van Winkle* and *Frankenstein* for tenth place; the other nine *Classics Illustrated* leaders, in order of sales ranking, were *Ivanhoe, Moby Dick, The Three Musketeers, The Count of Monte Cristo, Robin Hood, The Last of the Mohicans, A Tale of Two Cities, Robinson Crusoe,* and *Huckleberry Finn.*
9. Mike Benton, *Horror Comics: The Illustrated History* (Dallas: Taylor Publishing Company, 1991), p. 10.
10. Robert Louis Stevenson, *The Strange Case of Dr Jekyll and Mr Hyde* in *Dr Jekyll and Mr Hyde and Other Stories*, ed. Jenni Calder (Harmondsworth: Penguin Books, 1979), p. 84.
11. *Ibid.*, p. 40.
12. Ron Prager, "My Friend—Jerry Iger," *The Classics Collector*, No. 14 (December 1991), p. 18.

VII. CLASSICAL INTERLUDE: A FAN'S NOTES ON THE 1940s

1. Bill Briggs, letter to author, 30 June 2000.

VIII. ENTER IGER

1. Mike Benton, *The Comic Book in America: An Illustrated History* (Dallas: Taylor Publishing Company, 1993), p. 119.
2. Ron Goulart, "Jerry Iger," in *The Encyclopedia of American Comics: From 1897 to the Present*, ed. R. Goulart (New York, Oxford: Facts on File, 1990), p. 193.
3. Stanley Wiater and Stephen R. Bissette, *Comic Book Rebels* (New York: Donald I. Fine, Inc., 1993), p. 269.
4. Steve Duin and Mike Richardson, *Comics Between the Panels* (Milwaukie, Ore.: Dark Horse Comics, Inc., 1998), p. 233.
5. Ron Goulart, *Ron Goulart's Great History of Comic Books* (Chicago: Contemporary Books, 1986), p. 210.
6. Dan Malan, *The Complete Guide to Classics Collectibles, Volume One: The U.S. Series of Classics Illustrated and Related Collectibles* (St. Louis: Malan Classical Enterprises, 1991), p. 22.
7. Michael Sawyer, "Albert Lewis Kanter and the Classics: The Man Behind the Gilberton Company," *Journal of Popular Culture*, 20:4 (Spring 1987), p. 4.
8. Robert C. Harvey, *The Art of the Comic Book: An Aesthetic History* (Jackson: University Press of Mississippi, 1996), p. 25.
9 Trina Robbins and Catherine Yronwode, *Women and the Comics* (Eclipse Books, 1985), p. 52.

10. Ron Prager, interview with author, 31 May 2000.

11. Goulart, *Great History of Comic Books*, p. 210.

12. Alex Toth, letter to *The Classics Collector*, No. 14 (December 1991), p. 6.

13. Hames Ware, interview with author, 23 February 1997.

14. Ware, Interview with author, 7 July 2000.

15. *Ibid.*

16. Robbins and Yronwode, p. 56.

17. Mike Benton, *Horror Comics: The Illustrated History* (Dallas: Taylor Publishing Company, 1991), p. 10.

18. Donald F. Glut, "Frankenstein Meets the Comics," in *The Comic-Book Book*, ed. Don Thompson and Dick Lupoff (New Rochelle, N.Y.: Arlington House, 1973), p. 110.

19. *Ibid.*

20. Ware, interview with author, 23 February 1997.

21. Goulart, *Great History of Comic Books*, p. 64.

22. Ware, interview with author, 23 February 1997.

23. Duin and Richardson, p. 371.

24. *Ibid.*, at 370.

25. Ware, interview with author, 23 February 1997.

26. Duin and Richardson, p. 38.

27. Jerry Iger, "Jerry Iger Talks About Matt Baker," in *Jerry Iger's Famous Features*, Vol. 1, No. 1 (San Diego: Pacific Comics, July 1984), p. 9.

28. Goulart, *Great History of Comic Books*, p. 246.

29. Lou Cameron, letter to author, 4 November 1993; Ware, interview with author, 23 February 1997.

30. Jim Vadeboncoeur, Jr., e-mail to author, 21 March 2000.

31. Cameron, letter to author, 4 November 1993.

32. Ware, interview with author, 23 February 1997.

33. *Ibid.*

X. HENRY CARL KIEFER AND THE *CLASSICS* HOUSE STYLE

1. Dan Malan, *The Complete Guide to Classics Collectibles, Volume One: The U.S. Series of Classics Illustrated and Related Collectibles* (St. Louis: Malan Classical Enterprises, 1991), p. 107; Hubert H. Crawford, *Crawford's Encyclopedia of Comic Books* (Middle Village, N.Y.: Jonathan David Publishers, Inc., 1978), p. 145.

2. Hames Ware, interview with author, 27 January 1997.

3. Jerry Bails and Hames Ware, *The Who's Who of American Comic Books, Volume Two* (Detroit: Jerry Bails, 1974), p. 121.

4. Malan, p. 22.

5. *The Last Days of Pompeii* had a curious history with Gilberton. The title chosen to introduce the *Classics Illustrated* name was withdrawn in 1949 because of controversy over its explicitly religious content; the title reappeared 12 years later in a "secularized" adaptation by Alfred Sundel with art by comics legend Jack Kirby.

6. Raymond True, interview with author, 16 January 2000.

7. Hames Ware, interview with author, 7 July 2000.

8. Ron Goulart, *Ron Goulart's Great History of Comic Books* (Chicago: Contemporary Books, 1986), p. 210.

9. Crawford, p. 145.

10. Ware, interview with author, 7 July 2000.

11. Donna Richardson, "Classics Illustrated," *American Heritage* (June 1993), p. 83.

12. See M. Thomas Inge, "Edgar Allan Poe and the Comics Connection," *Comic Book Marketplace* (March 2000), p. 24.

13. A somewhat different version was originally published as an *Illustrated Classics* newspaper serial from 28 December 1947 to 18 January 1948.

14. Ware, interview with author, 7 July 2000.

15. Ware, interview with author, 27 January 1997.

XII. "A PRINCE OF A MAN": ALEX A. BLUM

1. Jerry Bails and Hames Ware, *The Who's Who of American Comic Books, Volume One* (Detroit: Jerry Bails, 1973), p. 15.

2. Ron Goulart, *Ron Goulart's Great History of Comic Books* (Chicago: Contemporary Books, 1986), p. 64.

3. Trina Robbins and Catherine Yronwode, *Women and the Comics* (Eclipse Books, 1985), p. 52.

4. Goulart, p. 127.

5. Hames Ware, interview with author, 20 February 1996.

6. Bill Briggs, letter to author, 30 June 2000.

7. William Wilkie Collins, *The Woman in White* (New York: Alfred A. Knopf/Everyman's Library, 1991), p. 193.

8. Robert Louis Stevenson, *Treasure Island* (New York: Charles Scribner's Sons, 1911), p. 60.

9. See, for a discussion of the Tourneur film and a photograph of Mason as Hawkins, Scott Allen Nollen, *Robert Louis Stevenson: Life, Literature and the Silver Screen* (Jefferson, N.C.: McFarland & Company, Inc., Publishers, 1994), pp. 93–94, 96.

10. Donna Richardson, "Classics Illustrated," *American Heritage*, 44:3 (June 1993), p. 84.

11. Ware, interview with author, 20 February 1996.

12. *Ibid.*

13. George Evans, letter to author, 17 February 1996.

14. Norman Nodel, interview with author, 22 November 1993.

XIII. CLASSICAL INTERLUDE: FILLERS AND FEATURES

1. Henry A. Carter, "Chemistry in the Comics: Part 2. Classic Chemistry," *Journal of Chemical Education*, 66:2 (February 1989), p. 119.

XIV. A "NEWER, TRUER NAME": THE LATE FORTIES

1. Michael Sawyer, "Albert Lewis Kanter and the Classics: The Man Behind the Gilberton Company," *Journal of Popular Culture*, 20:4 (1987), p. 5.

2. Dan Malan, *The Complete Guide to Classics Collectibles,*

Volume One: The U.S. Series of Classics Illustrated and Related Collectibles (St. Louis: Malan Classical Enterprises, 1991), p. 93.

3. Ron Prager, interview with author, 31 May 2000.

4. Jerry Bails and Hames Ware, *The Who's Who of American Comic Books*, Vol. I (1973), p. 66.

5. Malan, p. 26.

6. Harley M. Griffiths, Jr., letter to author, 30 May 1995.

7. *Ibid.*

8. *Ibid.*

9. *Ibid.*

10. Hames Ware, interview with author, 12 March 1997.

11. *Ibid.*

12. Fredric Wertham, *Seduction of the Innocent* (New York: Rinehart & Company, 1954), p. 37.

13. Madeleine Robins, interview with author, 4 April 1997.

14. Malan, p. 102.

XVI. Blood, Sweat, and Rudy Palais

1. The artist signed most of his work for *Classics Illustrated* "Rudolph Palais," but he used the nickname "Rudy" on three title pages; in later years, he preferred the variant spelling "Rudi."

2. Rudolph Palais, letter to author, 30 December 1993.

3. *Ibid.*

4. *Ibid.*

5. Mike Benton, *Crime Comics: The Illustrated History* (Dallas: Taylor Publishing Company, 1993), p. 32.

6. Palais, letter to author, 30 December 1993.

7. *Ibid.*

8. *Ibid.*

9. Mike Benton, *Horror Comics: The Illustrated History* (Dallas: Taylor Publishing Company, 1991), p. 26.

10. Rudolph Palais, interview with author, 1 November 1993.

11. Palais, letter to author, 30 December 1993.

12. Palais, interview with author, 1 November 1993.

XVII. Painted Covers and an Extra Nickel

1. "Shakespeare Bows to 'Comics' Public: Play Texts Will Be Produced in Picture Form to Interest World's Popular Audience," *New York Times* (9 March 1950), p. 24.

2. Fredric Wertham, *Seduction of the Innocent* (New York: Rinehart & Company, Inc., 1954), pp. 36–37.

3. William Shakespeare, *Julius Caesar*, Act 2, scene i, in *The Complete Works*, eds. Stanley Wells and Gary Taylor (New York: Oxford University Press, 1986), p. 682.

4. Hubert H. Crawford, *Crawford's Encyclopedia of Comic Books* (Middle Village, N.Y.: Jonathan David Publishers, Inc., 1978), p. 205.

5. Dan Malan, *The Complete Guide to Classics Collectibles, Volume One: The U.S. Series of Classics Illustrated and Related Collectibles* (St. Louis: Malan Classical Enterprises, 1991), p. 28.

6. Michael Sawyer, "Albert Lewis Kanter and the Classics: The Man Behind the Gilberton Company," *Journal of Popular Culture*, 20: 4 (Spring 1987), p. 9.

7. Michael Sawyer, p. 10.

8. Bob Lamme, letter to Charles Heffelfinger, 11 October 1977.

9. Hames Ware, interview with author, 7 July 2000.

10. Dan Malan, p. 102.

11. Hames Ware, letter to Mike Nicastre, March 1997.

12. Hames Ware, interview with author, 20 March 1997.

13. *Ibid.*

14. Bill Briggs, letter to author, 30 June 2000.

15. *Ibid.*

16. Maurice del Bourgo, interview with Jim Sands, "M.D.B.," in *The Classics Reader*, No. 5 (October 1975), p. 11.

17. *Ibid.*, pp. 11, 12.

18. *Ibid.*, p. 12.

19. *Ibid.*, p. 10.

20. See Mike Benton, *The Comic Book in America: An Illustrated History* (Dallas: Taylor Publishing Company, 1993), pp. 49–50.

21. Del Bourgo, p. 10.

22. Maurice del Bourgo, interview with Jim Sands, "Maurice del Bourgo," in *The Classics Reader*, No. 4 (August 1975), p. 8.

23. *Ibid.*

24. Ware, interview with author, 20 March 1997.

25. Benton, p. 119.

26. Ron Goulart, *Great History of Comic Books* (Chicago: Contemporary Books, 1986), p. 165.

27. Marc Swayze, interview with author, 1 June 2000.

28. Les Daniels, *DC Comics: Sixty Years of the World's Favorite Comic Book Heroes* (Boston: Little, Brown and Co., 1995), p. 118.

29. Hames Ware, interview with author, 31 March 1997.

30. Ron Goulart, "Sergeant Stony Craig," *Encyclopedia of American Comics*, ed. Ron Goulart (New York and Oxford: Facts on File, 1990), p. 328.

31. Ware, interview with author, 20 March 1997.

XIX: "If John Wayne Had Drawn Comic Books"

1. Hames Ware, interview with author, 22 July 1994.

2. Ann Evory, ed., *Contemporary Authors, New Revision Series*, Vol. 4 (Detroit: Gale Research Company, 1981), p. 107.

3. *Ibid.*

4. Lou Cameron, letter to author, 4 November 1993.

5. *Ibid.*

6. Cameron, letter to author, 20 November 1993.

7. *Ibid.*

8. Mike Benton, *Horror Comics: The Illustrated History* (Dallas: Taylor Publishing Company, 1993), p. 37.

9. Cameron, letter to author, 20 November 1993.

10. Dan Malan, "CI#124, *War of the Worlds* Model," in *The Classics Collector*, No. 17 (January 1996), p. 13.

11. Cameron, letter to author, 4 November 1993.

12. *Ibid.*

13. *Ibid.*

14. Cameron, letter to author, 20 November 1993.

15. George Hagenauer, "Cameron and the Count," in *The Classics Reader*, No. 10 (February 1978), p. 30.

16. Cameron, letter to author, 4 November 1993.

XX. "A Certain Integrity": Norman Nodel

1. Alfred Sundel, letter to author, 17 September 1994.

2. Norman Nodel, letter to author, 25 July 1997.

3. *Ibid.*

4. *Ibid.*

5. *Ibid.*

6. Nodel, interview with author, 22 November 1993.

7. *Ibid.*

8. Nodel, letter to author, 25 July 1997.

9. Will Eisner, *Comics and Sequential Art* (Tamarac, Florida: Poorhouse Press, 1985), p. 46.

10. [Washington Irving], *The Headless Horseman of Sleepy Hollow*, retold by Cherney Berg; illustrated by Norman Nodel (Mahwah, N.J.: Educational Reading Service, 1970).

11. Nodel, interview with author, 22 November 1993.

12. Alfred Sundel, letter to author, 21 August 1994.

13. Norman Nodel, interview with author, 12 May 1997.

14. Nodel, interview with author, 22 November 1993.

15. Nodel, interview with author, 12 May 1997.

16. Nodel, interview with author, 22 November 1993.

17. Nodel, letter to author, 25 July 1997.

18. Nodel, interview with author, 22 November 1993.

XXI. From the Crypt to the Classics: The EC Era

1. Amy Kiste Nyberg, *Seal of Approval: The History of the Comics Code* (Jackson: University Press of Mississippi, 1998), p. 86.

2. Nyberg, p. 87.

3. Nyberg, pp. 88–89; Ron Goulart, *The Encyclopedia of American Comics: From 1897 to the Present* (New York, Oxford: Facts on File, 1990), p. 382.

4. Ron Goulart, *Ron Goulart's Great History of Comic Books* (Chicago: Contemporary Books, 1986), p. 263.

5. Mike Benton, *The Comic Book in America: An Illustrated History* (Dallas: Taylor Publishing Company, 1993), p. 45.

6. Les Daniels, *Comix: A History of Comic Books in America* (New York: Outerbridge & Dienstfrey, 1971), p. 86; Goulart, *Great History of Comic Books*, p. 266.

7. Mike Benton, *Horror Comics: The Illustrated History* (Dallas: Taylor Publishing Company, 1991), p. 41.

8. *Minutes*, State of New York Joint Legislative Committee to Study the Publication of Comics (December 3–4, 1951), pp. 861–862, quoted in Michael Sawyer, "Albert Lewis Kanter and the Classics: The Man Behind the Gilberton Company," *Journal of Popular Culture* (Spring 1987), 20: 4, p. 8.

9. *Report of the New York State Joint Legislative Committee to Study the Publication of Comics* (1955), p. 95, quoted in Sawyer, "Albert Lewis Kanter and the Classics," p. 9.

10. Fredric Wertham, *Seduction of the Innocent* (New York: Rhinehart & Company, Inc., 1954), illustrated insert, p. viii.

11. Wertham, p. 36 (emphasis in original).

12. Wertham, p. 389.

13. Robert Warshow, "Paul, the Horror Comics, and Dr. Wertham," *Commentary*, 17: 596–604, at 601 (June 1954).

14. Warshow, p. 600.

15. Les Daniels, p. 86.

16. Goulart, *Great History of Comic Books*, p. 272.

17. Les Daniels, *DC Comics: Sixty Years of the World's Favorite Comic Book Heroes* (Boston, New York: A Bulfinch Press Book, Little, Brown and Company, 1995), pp. 150, 158, 160, 208.

18. Steve Duin, Mike Richardson, *Comics Between the Panels* (Milwaukie, Ore.: Dark Horse Comics, Inc., 1998), p. 339.

19. Duin, Richardson, p. 340.

20. Ron Goulart, *The Encyclopedia of American Comics*, p. 280.

21. Hames Ware, interview with author, 7 July 2000.

22. George Evans, interview with author, 31 May 1997.

23. For a reproduction and analysis of Orlando's "Landscape," see Daniels, *Comix: A History of Comic Books in America*, pp. 102–103, 111–114.

24. Duin, Richardson, p. 238.

25. Mike Benton, *Horror Comics: The Illustrated History*, p. 16.

26. Herb Feuerlicht, interview with author, June 1997.

27. Duin, Richardson, p. 239.

28. George Evans, interview with author, 30 January 2000.

29. *Ibid.*

30. *Ibid.*

31. Duin, Richardson, p. 239.

32. Ron Goulart, *Encyclopedia of American Comics*, p. 187.

33. Les Daniels, *Comix: A History of Comic Books in America*, p. 66.

34. Goulart, *The Encyclopedia of American Comics*, p. 325.

35. Alfred Sundel, letter to author, 17 September 1994.

36. Evans, interview with author, 31 May 1997.

37. Evans, interview with author, 31 May 1997.

38. Jerry DeFuccio, letter to author, 10 November 1993.

39. Goulart, *The Encyclopedia of American Comics*, p. 84; Duin, Richardson, p. 104.

40. George Evans, letter to author, 17 February 1997.

41. *Ibid.*

42. Goulart, *Great History of Comic Books*, p. 300.

43. For a reproduction and analysis of Crandall's "The Squaw," see Les Daniels, *Comix: A History of Comic Books in America*, pp. 102, 107–110.

44. Duin, Richardson, p. 106; George Evans, interview with author, 14 May 1997; Goulart, *The Encyclopedia of American Comics*, p. 84.

XXIII. "The Professional": George R. Evans

1. Alfred Sundel, letter to author, 17 September 1994.

2. George Evans, letter to author, 17 February 1997.

3. Bhob Stewart, "George Evans" in *The Encyclopedia of*

American Comics: From 1897 to the Present, ed. Ron Goulart (New York, Oxford: Facts on File, 1990), p. 122.

4. *Ibid.*
5. Evans, letter to author, 17 February 1997.
6. George Evans, letter to author, 27 May 1997.
7. Stewart, p. 122.
8. Evans, letter to author, 17 February 1997.
9. *Ibid.*
10. George Evans, interview with author, 31 May 1997.
11. Evans, letter to author, 17 February 1997.
12. *Ibid.*
13. *Ibid.*
14. Evans, interview with author, 31 May 1997.
15. Evans, letter to author, 17 February 1997.
16. Stewart, p. 122.
17. Evans, letter to author, 17 February 1997.
18. Evans, letter to author, 27 May 1997.

XXIV. ROBERTA THE CONQUEROR

1. Herb Feuerlicht, interview with author, 25 March 1996.
2. *Ibid.*
3. *Ibid.*
4. Dan Malan, "Roberta Strauss Feuerlicht," *The Classics Collector*, No. 14 (December 1991), p. 19.
5. Hames Ware, interview with author, 7 July 2000.
6. George Evans, letter to author, 17 February 1997.
7. Norman Nodel, interview with author, 20 April 1997.
8. Herb Feuerlicht, interview with author, 29 July 1997.
9. Nos. 1, 2, 3, 4, 5, 6, 7, 8, 9, 10, 12, 18, 19, 23, 24, 35, 38, 39, 42, 45, 50, 52, 54, 56, 60, 63, 68, 71. No. 13 had been assigned before Feuerlicht's association with *Classics Illustrated*.
10. Nos. 1, 2, 3, 4, 5, 6, 7, 8, 9, 10, 12, 15, 16, 18, 19, 21, 22, 23, 24, 25, 26, 27, 28, 29, 30, 31, 32, 34, 35, 36, 38, 39, 41, 42, 45, 46, 47, 48, 49, 50, 51, 52, 54, 55, 56, 57, 58, 59, 60, 61, 62, 63, 64, 65, 67, 68, 69, 70, 71, 72, 75, 76, 77, 78, 79, 80, 90, 93, 103. Nos. 11 and 13 had been commissioned before Feuerlicht's arrival at Gilberton.
11. Malan, p. 19.
12. Herb Feuerlicht, interview with author, 29 July 1997.
13. *Ibid.*
14. *Ibid.*
15. *Ibid.*
16. Feuerlicht, interview with author, 25 March 1996.
17. Malan, p. 19.
18. Feuerlicht, interview with author, 25 March 1996.

XXVI. HIGH TIDE AND GREENBACKS: THE LATE FIFTIES

1. See Les Daniels, *DC Comics: Sixty Years of the World's Favorite Comic Book Heroes* (Boston: A Bulfinch Press Book/Little, Brown and Company, 1995), p. 126; Steve Duin and Mike Richardson, *Comics: Between the Panels* (Milwaukie, Ore.: Dark Horse Comics, 1998), p. 393.
2. Daniels, p. 102.
3. Hames Ware, interview with author, 5 March 2000.
4. Herb Feuerlicht, interview with author, 25 March 1996.
5. Ron Goulart, *The Encyclopedia of American Comics: From 1897 to the Present* (New York, Oxford: Facts on File, 1990), p. 341.
6. *Ibid.*
7. Hames Ware, interview with author, 7 July 2000.
8. Alfred Sundel, letter to author, 17 September 1994.
9. George Evans, interview with author, 31 May 1997.
10. Scotty Moore, "Artist, Author, & Publisher! L.B. Cole," interview in *Comic Book Marketplace* (December 1995), p. 32.
11. Alfred Sundel, letter to author, 21 August 1994.
12. John Benson, "Romance Comics," in *The Encyclopedia of American Comics*, ed. Ron Goulart, p. 313.
13. Moore, p. 32.
14. *Ibid.*
15. Duin and Richardson, p. 90.
16. Feuerlicht, interview with author, 25 March 1996.
17. Moore, p. 32.
18. John Haufe, interview with author, 5 February 2000.
19. Duin and Richardson, "Norm Saunders," in *Comics: Between the Panels*, p. 386.

XXVII. CLASSICAL INTERLUDE: A FAN'S NOTES ON THE 1950s

1. John Haufe, letter to author, 6 June 2000.

XXVIII. "ROBERTA'S REFORMS": THE EARLY SIXTIES

1. Alfred Sundel, letter to author, 17 September 1994.
2. Gray Morrow, letter to author, 22 July 1994.
3. Sundel, letter to author, 17 September 1994.
4. Morrow, letter to author, 22 July 1994.
5. Frank Norris, *The Octopus*, in *Novels and Essays* (New York: The Library of America, 1986), pp. 596, 629.
6. Sundel, letter to author, 17 September 1994.
7. Morrow, letter to author, 22 July 1994.
8. Gerard Jones, "Doom Patrol," in Ron Goulart, ed., *The Encyclopedia of American Comics: From 1897 to the Present* (New York, Oxford: Facts on File, 1990), p. 108.
9. Jerry Bails and Hames Ware, *The Who's Who of American Comic Books*, Vol. IV (Detroit: Jerry Bails, 1976), p. 262.
10. Steve Duin and Mike Richardson, *Comics Between the Panels* (Milwaukie, Ore: Dark Horse Comics, 1998), p. 261.
11. Ron Goulart, "Jack Kirby," in Goulart, ed., *The Encyclopedia of American Comics*, p. 219.
12. *Ibid.*
13. Les Daniels, *DC Comics: Sixty Years of the World's Favorite Comic Book Heroes* (Boston: A Bulfinch Press Book/Little, Brown and Company, 1995), pp. 46, 64, 206.

14. *Ibid.*, p. 106; Mike Benton, *The Comic Book in America: An Illustrated History* (Dallas: Taylor Publishing Company, 1993), p. 43.

15. Daniels, p. 131.

16. The artist's subtle visual representation of Union resolve at Fort Sumter has been analyzed at length in Joseph Witek, *Comics as History: The Narrative Art of Jack Jackson, Art Spiegelman, and Harvey Pekar* (Jackson: University Press of Mississippi, 1989), pp. 20–36.

17. Ron Prager, "My Friend—Jerry Iger," *The Classics Collector*, No. 14 (December 1991), p. 18.

18. Prager, interview with author, 25 May 2000.

19. Les Daniels, *Marvel: Five Decades of the World's Greatest Comics* (New York: Harry N. Abrams, Publishers, 1991), p. 84.

20. Daniels, *DC Comics*, p. 164.

21. Jerry Bails, Hames Ware, *The Who's Who of American Comics*, Vol. III (Detroit: Jerry Bails, 1975), p. 206.

22. Hames Ware, interview with author, 15 April 1997.

23. Alfred Sundel, letter to author, 21 August 1994.

24. Norman Nodel, interview with author, 22 November 1993.

25. Alex Toth, letter to *The Classics Collector*, No. 14 (December 1991), p. 6.

26. Hames Ware, interview with author, 7 July 2000.

27. Jim Vadeboncoeur, Jr., e-mail to author, 21 March 2000.

28. Sundel, letter to author, 21 August 1994.

29. The following are titles and copyright dates for randomly selected contemporary American paperback editions of works that had appeared in *Classics Illustrated*: *The Last of the Mohicans* (Washington Square Press, 1957); *Macbeth* (Dell, 1959); *Gulliver's Travels* (Signet, 1960); *The Red Badge of Courage* (Airmont, 1962).

30. Dan Malan, *The Complete Guide to Classics Collectibles, Volume One: The U.S. Series of Classics Illustrated and Related Collectibles* (St. Louis: Malan Classical Enterprises, 1991), p. 34.

31. *Ibid.*

32. Michael Sawyer, "Albert Lewis Kanter and the Classics: The Man Behind the Gilberton Company," *Journal of Popular Culture*, 20:4 (Spring 1987), p. 14.

33. Sundel, letter to author, 17 September 1994.

XXX. Five Little Series and How They Grew: *Picture Progress; Classics Illustrated Junior; Classics Illustrated Special Issues; The World Around Us; The Best from Boys' Life Comics*

1. William W. Savage, Jr., *Comic Books and America, 1945–1954* (Norman and London: University of Oklahoma Press, 1990), pp. 16–17.

2. Dan Malan, *The Complete Guide to Classics Collectibles, Volume One: The U.S. Series of Classics Illustrated and Related Collectibles*, p. 81.

3. Hubert H. Crawford, *Crawford's Encyclopedia of Comic Books* (Middle Village, N.Y.: Jonathan David Publishers, Inc., 1978), p. 229.

4. Malan, p. 73.

5. Keith Scott, *The Moose That Roared: The Story of Jay Ward, Bill Scott, a Flying Squirrel, and a Talking Moose* (New York: Thomas Dunne Books/St. Martin's Press, 2000), p. 64.

6. Ron Goulart, "M.C. Gaines," in Ron Goulart, ed., *The Encyclopedia of American Comics: From 1897 to the Present* (New York, Oxford: Facts on File, 1990), p. 147.

7. Malan, p. 77.

8. Malan, p. 79.

9. *Ibid.*

10. Alfred Sundel, letter to author, 17 September 1994.

XXXI. "Frawley's Folly" (1967–1971)

1. Robert McG. Thomas, Jr., "Patrick Frawley, Jr., 75, Ex-Owner of Schick," *New York Times* (Monday, 9 November 1998), p. 8B.

2. *Ibid.*

3. Michael Sawyer, "Albert Lewis Kanter and the Classics: The Man Behind the Gilberton Company," *Journal of Popular Culture*, 20:4 (1987), p. 15.

4. Dan Malan, *The Complete Guide to Classics Collectibles, Volume One: The U.S. Series of Classics Illustrated and Related Collectibles* (St. Louis: Malan Classical Enterprises, 1991), p. 36.

5. Frank Walston, *Classics Illustrated Field Manual* (Philadelphia: Curtis Circulation Co., 1968).

6. Sawyer, p. 15; Malan, p. 36.

7. Malan, p. 36.

8. Dan Malan, *The Classics Collector*, No. 17 (January 1996), p. 17.

9. Sawyer, p. 16.

10. Malan, *Complete Guide*, p. 38.

11. Sawyer, p. 16.

12. Malan, *Complete Guide*, p. 93.

13. Sawyer, p. 16.

14. *Ibid.*

15. Albert L. Kanter, quoted in Malan, *Complete Guide*, p. 38.

16. Sawyer, p. 16.

XXXIII. Great Expectations: First Publishing's *Classics* Revival

1. Dan Malan, "Interview: David Batt [Chief Financial Officer, Frawley Group]," *The Classics Collector*, No. 10 (February-March 1990), pp. 27–28.

2. Mike Benton, *The Comic Book in America: An Illustrated History* (Dallas: Taylor Publishing Company, 1993), p. 120.

3. Rick Obadiah, interview with author, May 1990; quoted in Bill Jones, "A Tale of Two Classics," *Spectrum*, No. 126 (June 6–19, 1990), p. 22.

4. Obadiah, in Jones, p. 22.
5. *Ibid.*
6. See Scott McCloud's discussion of the universalizing impulse of sequential art in *Understanding Comics*, pp. 42–54.
7. Dan Malan, *The Complete Guide to Classics Collectibles, Volume One: The U.S. Series of Classics Illustrated and Related Collectibles* (St. Louis: Malan Classical Enterprises, 1991). p. 40.
8. Dan Malan, "CIE Drops NCI," *The Classics Collector*, No. 17 (January 1996), p. 11.
9. *Ibid.*

XXXV. Recalled to Life: Acclaim's *Study Guides*

1. Madeleine Robins, interview with author, 4 April 1997.
2. *Ibid.*
3. Robins, interview with author, 23 July 1997.
4. *Ibid.*

5. Michael Tierney, interview with author, 24 December 1998.

XXXVI. Classical Coda

1. See Bart Beaty, "Featuring Stories by the World's Greatest Authors: *Classics Illustrated* and the 'Middlebrow Problem' in the Postwar Era," *International Journal of Comic Art*, 1:1 (Spring/Summer 1999), 122–139. Notwithstanding a few factual errors (dates, number of issues, and the confusing of the 1950 *Famous Authors* adaptation of *Macbeth* with the 1955 Gilberton edition), Beaty's article is a profoundly perceptive analysis of the cultural context in which *Classics Illustrated* contended and thrived.
2. Jim McLoughlin, interview with author, 31 May 2000.
3. George Eliot, *Middlemarch*, ed. W.J. Harvey (Harmondsworth: Penguin Books, 1965), epigraph, Chapter 70, p. 756.

APPENDICES

Unidentified artist, *The Three Musketeers* (September 1956). Painted cover.

Appendix A

List of *Classic Comics* (Gilberton, 1941–1947) and *Classics Illustrated* (Gilberton, 1947–1967; Frawley, 1967–1971)

Classic Comics Nos. 1–12 (including reprints of first interior art) contained 64 pages; Classic Comics and Classics Illustrated Nos. 13–25 and 27–44 contained 56 pages (most reduced to 48 pages in 1948–1950 reprints); Classic Comics No. 26 contained 48 pages; Classics Illustrated Nos. 45–169 and new editions of earlier titles contained 48 pages.

1. *The Three Musketeers* by Alexandre Dumas. Line-drawing cover and first interior art by Malcolm Kildale; Dumas biography (October 1941; six *CC*, six *CI* printings). Painted cover (September 1956; two printings). Second interior art by George Evans; Dumas biography (May 1959; nine printings).

2. *Ivanhoe* by Sir Walter Scott. Line-drawing cover by Malcolm Kildale, first interior art by Edd Ashe and others; Scott biography (December 1941; six *CC*, seven *CI* printings). Painted cover unattributed, second interior art by Norman Nodel; Scott biography (January 1957; 12 printings; one Twin Circle edition).

3. *The Count of Monte Cristo* by Alexandre Dumas. Line-drawing cover by Ray Ramsey, first interior art by Ray Ramsey, Allen Simon, and Vivian Lipman; "Important Milestones in the Life of Napoleon"; Dumas biography (March 1942; seven *CC*, six *CI* printings). Painted cover unattributed, second interior art by Lou Cameron; Dumas biography (November 1956; ten printings).

4. *The Last of the Mohicans* by James Fenimore Cooper. Line-drawing cover and first interior art by Ray Ramsey; Cooper biography; "SACO [Sino-American Cooperative Organization] is Socko!" by Georgina Campbell [added 1946] (August 1942; six *CC*, six *CI* printings). Painted cover (November 1956; two printings). Second interior art by John P. Severin and Stephen L. Addeo; Cooper biography (May 1959; eight printings; one Twin Circle edition).

5. *Moby Dick* by Herman Melville. Line-drawing cover and first interior art by Louis Zansky; first adaptation by Louis Zansky; Melville biography; "Concord Hymn" by Ralph Waldo Emerson [added 1943] (September 1942; seven *CC*, six *CI* printings). First painted cover unattributed, second interior art by Norman Nodel; Melville biography (March 1956; nine printings). Second painted cover (Winter 1969; two printings).

6. *A Tale of Two Cities* by Charles Dickens. Line-drawing cover and first interior art by Stanley Maxwell (Zuckerberg); first adaptation by Evelyn Goodman, open-book device introduced; Dickens biography (October 1942; seven *CC*, six *CI* printings). First painted cover unattributed, second interior art by Joe Orlando, assisted by George Evans; Dickens biography (May 1956; nine printings). Second painted cover by Norman Nodel (Fall 1968; two printings).

7. *Robin Hood* (uncredited; revised edition based in part on Howard Pyle's *Merry Adventures of Robin Hood*). Line-drawing cover and first interior art by Louis Zansky, inked by Fred Eng, first adaptation by Evelyn Goodman (December 1942; Saks–34th Christmas giveaway with Zansky wraparound cover simultaneously issued; six *CC* printings; six *CI* printings). Painted cover by Victor Prezio (November 1955; one printing). Second interior art by Jack Sparling; second adaptation unattributed (January 1957; ten printings).

8. *Arabian Nights* (anonymous; based on *The Thousand*

and One Nights). Line-drawing cover and first interior art by Lillian Chestney (Zuckerberg), first adaptation by Evelyn Goodman; "The Tyrant of Etreus" by Evelyn Goodman; "Some Wonders of the Ancient World"; "Three Men Named Smith" [added 1944] (February 1943; four *CC*, three *CI* printings). Painted cover unattributed, second interior art by Charles Berger, second adaptation by Alfred Sundel; "Arabian Nights [Antoine Galland]"; "The Splendid East [Friar Odoric]"; "A Japanese Legend [The Boy Who Drew Cats]" (October 1961; one printing).

9. *Les Miserables* by Victor Hugo. Line-drawing cover and first interior art by Rolland Livingstone, first adaptation by Evelyn Goodman, yellow *Classic Comics* rectangle introduced; Hugo biography; "The Bill of Rights: Our Charter of Democracy" [added 1944]; "La Marseillaise"; "The Statue of Liberty: A Gift From France" (March 1943; five *CC*, three *CI* printings). First painted cover by Gerald McCann, second interior art by Norman Nodel, second adaptation by Alfred Sundel; Hugo biography; "Crime and Punishment [18th-century French criminal procedure]"; "The Boy Who Hated Washing [Peter Cooper]" (March 1961; three printings). Second painted cover by Norman Nodel (1968; one printing).

10. *Robinson Crusoe* by Daniel Defoe. Line-drawing cover and first interior art by Stanley Maxwell (Zuckerberg), adaptation by Evelyn Goodman; Defoe biography; Poems of the Sea: "Dover Beach" by Matthew Arnold "Break, Break, Break" by Alfred, Lord Tennyson, "The Three Fishers" by Charles Kingsley; "Joan Fernandez ... Desert Explorer"; "The Bill of Rights: Our Charter of Democracy" [added 1944; replaced 1946 by "With Leg Shot Away—Mans Gun for 8 Hours"] (April 1943; five *CC*, five *CI* printings). Painted cover (January 1956; one printing). Second interior art by Sam Citron and/or Charles Sultan; Defoe biography (September 1957; ten printings; one Twin Circle edition).

11. *Don Quixote* by Miguel de Cervantes. Line-drawing cover and interior art by Louis Zansky, adaptation by Samuel H. Abramson; Cervantes biography; "Captain Arthur Wermuth ... Hero of Bataan" by Evelyn Goodman; Poems from the American Indian: "Ojibwa War Songs," "Lament of a Man for His Son (Paiute)," "Song of the Rain Chant (Navaho)," "The Bear's Song (From the Haida)" (May 1943; four *CC* printings; one Canadian *CI* printing). First painted cover (August 1953; five printings). Second painted cover by Taylor Oughton (1968; one printing).

12. *Rip Van Winkle and The Headless Horseman* by Washington Irving. Line-drawing cover and first interior art by Rolland Livingstone, first adaptation by Dan Levin; Irving biography; "...And One Came Back: The true story of a lone survivor of a bomber crew" by Evelyn Goodman; "The Charge of the Light Brigade" by Alfred, Lord Tennyson (June 1943; five *CC*, five *CI* printings). First painted cover ("*and The Headless Horseman*" dropped from title) (May 1956; one printing). Second interior art by Norman Nodel; Irving biography (May 1959; six printings). Second painted cover by Taylor Oughton (1968; two printings).

13. *Dr. Jekyll and Mr. Hyde* by Robert Louis Stevenson. First line-drawing cover ("horror" cover) and first interior art by Arnold L. Hicks, first adaptation by Evelyn Goodman; Stevenson biography; "Secret Under the Sea" by Dan Kushner (August 1943; four printings). Second line-drawing cover by

Henry C. Kiefer (June 1949; four printings). Painted cover unattributed, second interior art by Lou Cameron; Stevenson biography (October 1953; eight printings; one Twin Circle edition).

14. *Westward Ho!* by Charles Kingsley. Line-drawing cover and interior art by Allen Simon, adaptation by Dan Kushner; Kingsley biography; "The Railway Train [I like to see it lap the miles]" by Emily Dickinson, illustrated by Lillian Chestney; "Victory March" by Evelyn Goodman; "The Cost of Carelessness" by David Butler, Jr.; "Three Men Named Smith" [added 1944, replaced 1946 by "Speaking for America (Truman, Eisenhower, MacArthur, Nimitz)"] (September 1943; four *CC* printings; one *CI* printing).

15. *Uncle Tom's Cabin* by Harriet Beecher Stowe. Line-drawing cover and interior art by Rolland Livingstone; "Flight Over Tokyo" by Michael Sullivan; "The Children's Hour" by Henry Wadsworth Longfellow, illustrated by Vivian Lipman; Stowe biography (November 1943; four *CC*, three *CI* printings). First painted cover; new lettering (March 1954; ten printings). Second painted cover (Winter 1969; two printings).

16. *Gulliver's Travels* by Jonathan Swift. Line-drawing cover and interior art by Lillian Chestney (Zuckerberg), adaptation (from Part I, "A Voyage to Lilliput") by Dan Kushner; "The Purple Heart" by Technical Sergeant Hal Kanter; "I Hear America Singing" by Walt Whitman; Swift biography (December 1943; four *CC*, four *CI* printings). Painted cover unattributed (March 1960; six printings; one Twin Circle edition).

17. *The Deerslayer* by James Fenimore Cooper. Line-drawing cover and interior art by Louis Zansky, adaptation by Evelyn Goodman; Cooper biography; "Annabel Lee" by Edgar Allan Poe; "Bombs ... and ... Sand" by Michael Sullivan; "The Lost Chutists" by Edward Gordon; "Medals for Heroes" (January 1944; four *CC*, six *CI* printings). Painted cover by Stephen L. Addeo (1968; two printings).

18. *The Hunchback of Notre Dame* by Victor Hugo. First line-drawing cover ("horror" cover) and first interior art by Allen Simon, first adaptation by Evelyn Goodman; Hugo biography; "The Story of Staff Sergeant Schiller Cohen and His Fortress 'Stinky'!" by Dan Levin; "The Bells" by Edgar Allan Poe, illustrated by Louis Zansky; (March 1944; four printings). Second line-drawing cover by Henry C. Kiefer (June 1949; five printings). First painted cover (September 1957; two printings). Second painted cover by Gerald McCann, second interior art by Reed Crandall and George Evans, second adaptation by Alfred Sundel; Hugo biography; "The Wanderers [Gypsies]"; "From Osiris to O'Neill" (Fall 1960; seven printings).

19. *Huckleberry Finn* by Mark Twain (Samuel L. Clemens). Line-drawing cover and first interior art by Louis Zansky, first adaptation by Evelyn Goodman; Twain biography; "Air Spies, Their Missions—Their Accomplishments" by June Slater; "Old Ironsides" by Oliver Wendell Holmes; "A Day's Work—Heroes All" by Steve Dale (April 1944; four *CC*, five *CI* printings). Painted cover unattributed; second interior art by Mike Sekowsky (pencils) and Frank Giacoia (inking); Twain biography (March 1956; 12 printings).

20. *The Corsican Brothers* by Alexandre Dumas. Line-drawing cover and interior art by Allen Simon, adaptation by Stephen Burrows; Dumas biography; "Modern Twins in Service" by Hal Kane [Hal Kanter]; "Things For Which We

Fight" by Lieutenant General Brehon Somervell; "The American's Creed" by William Tyler Page; "The Emblem of Invasion" (June 1944; three *CC*, four *CI* printings).

21. *3 Famous Mysteries*. Composite line-drawing cover by Louis Zansky, Allen Simon, and Arnold L. Hicks; three stories: *The Sign of the (sic) Four* by Sir Arthur Conan Doyle; art by Louis Zansky; *The Flayed Hand* by Guy de Maupassant; art by Allen Simon; *The Murders in the Rue Morgue* by Edgar Allan Poe; art by Arnold L. Hicks; Conan Doyle, Maupassant, Poe biographies; "From 'The Kid' to a Fighting Man" by Hal Kane [Hal Kanter] (July 1944; three *CC*, three *CI* printings); Painted cover (December 1953; one printing).

22. *The Pathfinder* by James Fenimore Cooper. Line-drawing cover and first interior art by Louis Zansky, adaptation by Evelyn Goodman; Cooper biography; "Unsung Heroes of the Armed Forces" by Henry Irving; "20-Year-Old Paratrooper Helps Eliminate 500 Germans in Normandy"; "More Ways Than One to Kill Japs" (October 1944; two *CC*, six *CI* printings). Painted cover (November 1963; three printings). Unpublished, unfinished second interior art by Norman Nodel (1962).

23. *Oliver Twist* by Charles Dickens. Line-drawing cover and first interior art by Arnold L. Hicks, first adaptation by Georgina Campbell; Dickens biography; "The Case of the Little Duck" by Georgina Campbell; "Intrepid Medal Winner" (July 1945; two *CC*, six *CI* printings). Painted cover (January 1957; three printings). Second interior art by Reed Crandall and George Evans, second adaptation by Alfred Sundel; Dickens biography; "The Pearl Robbery"; "A Leader of His People [Chaim Weizmann]" (October 1961; six printings).

24. *A Connecticut Yankee in King Arthur's Court* by Mark Twain (Samuel L. Clemens). Line-drawing cover and first interior art by Jack Hearne, first adaptation by Ruth A. Roche and Tom Scott; lettered by Louis L. Goldklang; Twain biography; "Three Pals: 55, 65 and 75" (September 1945; two *CC*, five *CI* printings). Painted cover unattributed, second interior art by Jack Sparling; Twain biography (September 1957; eight printings).

25. *Two Years Before the Mast* by Richard Henry Dana, Jr. Line-drawing cover and interior art by Robert H. Webb and David Heames, adaptation by Ruth A. Roche; Dana biography (page one); "The Yarn of the 'Nancy Bell'" by W.S. Gilbert; "Wild Bill's Cloak and Dagger Outfit" by Georgina Campbell; American Rivers: "The Historic Ohio" (October 1945; two *CC*, five *CI* printings). Painted cover, recolored original art; Dana biography; "Dugout to Diesel"; "Buried Treasure" (May 1960; five printings).

26. *Frankenstein* by Mary W. Shelley. Line-drawing cover and interior art by Robert H. Webb and Ann Brewster, lettered by Louis Goldklang, adaptation by Ruth A. Roche; Shelley biography; "Paul Revere's Ride" by Henry Wadsworth Longfellow; "The 'Ghost of Corregidor'" by Georgina Campbell (December 1945; two *CC*, five *CI* printings). Painted cover by Norman B. Saunders (September 1958; 12 printings).

27. *The Adventures of Marco Polo* (based on *The Travels of Marco Polo*). Line-drawing cover and interior art by Homer Fleming; adaptation by Emanuel Demby; lettered by Louis Goldklang; Biography of John Greenleaf Whittier; "Barbara Frietchie" by J.G. Whittier; "Iroquois: People of the Long House"; "This Is No Joke: A plain-spoken letter from Red

Skelton, one of America's greatest comedy stars" (April 1946; two *CC*, three *CI* printings). Painted cover (January 1960; five printings).

28. *Michael Strogoff* by Jules Verne. Line-drawing cover and interior art by Arnold L. Hicks, adaptation by Pat Adam; Verne biography; "Chaplains Courageous"; "Come On, Balto! Come On, Good Dog!" (June 1946; one *CC*, one *CI* printing). First painted cover (January 1954; four printings). Second painted cover by Norman Nodel (Summer 1969; one printing).

29. *The Prince and the Pauper* by Mark Twain (Samuel L. Clemens). First line-drawing cover ("horror" cover) and interior art by Arnold L. Hicks, adaptation by Scott Feldman and Jack Bass; Twain biography; The American Indian: "The Pequot" (July 1946; one *CC* printing). Second line-drawing cover by Henry C. Kiefer (June 1949; five printings). Painted cover (September 1955; nine printings).

30. *The Moonstone* by William Wilkie Collins. Line-drawing cover and interior art by Don Rico, adaptation by Dan Levin; Collins biography; American Rivers: "The Delaware"; "The Fighting Cheyennes"; Dog Heroes: "Queenie—German Shepherd" (September 1946; one *CC*, two *CI* printings). Painted cover by Leonard B. Cole (March 1960; five printings).

31. *The Black Arrow* by Robert Louis Stevenson. Line-drawing cover and interior art by Arnold L. Hicks, adaptation by Ruth A. Roche and Tom Scott; Stevenson biography; Dog Heroes: "'Blackie': Belgian Shepherd"; Pioneers of Science: "Joseph Priestley, The Father of Soda Water and Discoverer of Oxygen" (October 1946; one *CC*, five *CI* printings). Painted cover (March 1956; eight printings).

32. *Lorna Doone* by Richard Doddridge Blackmore. Line-drawing cover and interior art by Matt Baker, adaptation by Ruth A. Roche; Blackmore biography; Pioneers of Science: "Charles Martin Hall, The Schoolboy Scientist"; American Indians: "The Seminole" by John O'Rourke (December 1946; one *CC*, three *CI* printings). First painted cover, recolored original art with reversed line-drawing cover illustration replacing original first-page splash (May 1957; five printings). Second painted cover (1968; one printing).

33. *The Adventures of Sherlock Holmes* by Sir Arthur Conan Doyle. Line-drawing cover by Henry C. Kiefer (first Kiefer art in series); two stories in first edition: *A Study in Scarlet*; splash, page 1, by Henry C. Kiefer, remainder of interior art by Louis Zansky (deleted after first printing); *The Hound of the Baskervilles*; splash, page 20, by Henry C. Kiefer, remainder of interior art by Louis Zansky; Conan Doyle biography; Pioneers of Science: "William Murdock, Father of Gas-light"; "...Still Echoing ... The Heartbeat of Lincoln"; "Ties Across the Sea" (delayed publication; originally scheduled for March 1943; January 1947; one *CC*, three *CI* printings).

34. *Mysterious Island* by Jules Verne. Line-drawing cover and interior art by Robert H. Webb and David Heames, adaptation by Manning Stokes; Verne biography; American Indians: "The Siouan (Sioux) Family"; Pioneers of Science: "Charles Proteus Steinmetz, The Wizard of Electricity" (February 1947; last *Classic Comics* issue; one *CC*, six *CI* printings). Painted cover (September 1957; six printings).

35. *The Last Days of Pompeii* by Edward Bulwer-Lytton. Line-drawing cover and first interior art by Henry C. Kiefer; Bulwer-Lytton biography; "That Others Might Live"; "Ol' Sea

Dog Sinbad" (March 1947; one printing; first *Classics Illustrated* issue; open-book device reintroduced; one printing). Painted cover unattributed, second interior art by Jack Kirby (pencils) and Dick Ayers (inking); adaptation by Alfred Sundel; Bulwer-Lytton biography; "Pyramus and Thisbe" (from *The Age of Fable* by Thomas Bulfinch); "A Mound of Ruins [Lisbon Earthquake of 1755]" (March 1961; four printings).

36. *Typee* by Herman Melville. Line-drawing cover and interior art by Ezra Whiteman, adaptation by Harry Miller; Melville biography; American Indians: "The Tlingit"; Pioneers of Science: "Marie Sklodowska Curie, Discoverer of Radium" (April 1947; two printings). Painted cover by Gerald McCann (March 1960; four printings). Second interior art by Luis Dominguez (1962, not issued in U.S. series).

37. *The Pioneers* by James Fenimore Cooper. Line-drawing cover and interior art by Rudolph Palais, adaptation by Samuel Willinsky; Cooper biography; "Jungle Promise" by John Ladd; "What's New About the U.N.?"; Pioneers of Science: "Thomas Alva Edison, Wizard of Menlo Park" (May 1947; ten printings). Painted cover by Taylor Oughton (1968; one printing).

38. *Adventures of Cellini* (based on the *Autobiography* of Benvenuto Cellini). Line-drawing cover and first interior art by August M. Froehlich, first adaptation by L. Katz; Pioneers of Science: "Eli Whitney, Inventor of the Cotton Gin"; American Rivers: "The Kennebec"; Dog Heroes: "Shorty the Spaniel" (June 1947; one printing). Painted cover unattributed, second interior art unattributed, second adaptation by Alfred Sundel; Cellini biography; "Waking the Dead [Renaissance]"; "Michelangelo" (Fall 1961; four printings).

39. *Jane Eyre* by Charlotte Brontë. Line-drawing cover and first interior art by Harley M. Griffiths, first adaptation by Harry Miller; Brontë biography; The American Indians: "The Muskohegan Family, The Creek Confederacy"; "Great Heroes of the U.S. Navy" (July 1947; six printings). First painted cover (January 1958; two printings). Second interior art by H.J. Kihl, second adaptation by Alfred Sundel; Brontë biography; "The London Fire"; "Suffering Humanity [Dorothea Dix]" (Spring 1962; four printings). Second painted cover by Norman Nodel (1968; one printing).

40. *Mysteries* by Edgar Allan Poe. Line-drawing cover ("horror" cover) by Henry C. Kiefer; three stories: *The Pit and the Pendulum*; interior art by August M. Froehlich; *The Adventures of Hans Pfall*; interior art by Henry C. Kiefer; *The Fall of the House of Usher*; interior art by Harley M. Griffiths; adaptations by Samuel Willinsky; Poe biography; Pioneers of Science: "Robert Fulton, Inventor of the Steamboat"; Great Lives: "Ludwig Van Beethoven"; American Indians: "The Cherokee Nation" by John H. O'Rourke; "[Excerpt] From a Letter Written by George Washington in 1790" (August 1947; four printings).

41. *Twenty Years After* by Alexandre Dumas. First line-drawing cover ("horror" cover) and interior art by Robert Burns, adaptation by Harry Miller; Dumas biography; Pioneers of Science: "Alexis Carrel" (September 1947; one printing). Second line-drawing cover by Henry C. Kiefer (August 1949; two printings). Painted cover by Doug Roea (May 1960; four printings).

42. *Swiss Family Robinson* by Johann Wyss. Line-drawing cover and first interior art by Henry C. Kiefer, adaptation by Elspeth Campbell; Wyss biography; American Rivers: "The Saint Lawrence"; Pioneers of Science: "Charles Robert Darwin" (October 1947; five printings). Painted cover (March 1956; three printings); Second interior art by Norman Nodel; Wyss biography (September 1959; eight printings).

43. *Great Expectations* by Charles Dickens. Line-drawing cover and interior art by Henry C. Kiefer; Dickens biography; American Indians: "The Navajo"; Pioneers of Science: "Albert Einstein" (November 1947; two printings).

44. *Mysteries of Paris* by Eugene Sue. Line-drawing cover (last "horror" cover) and interior art by Henry C. Kiefer, adaptation by Albert Avitabile; Sue biography; Pioneers of Science: "Michael Faraday"; Dog Heroes: "Just a Bag of Skin and Bones" (December 1947; three printings).

45. *Tom Brown's School Days* by Thomas Hughes. Line-drawing cover and first interior art by Homer Fleming; American Indians: "The Chippewa"; Hughes biography; Great Lives: "Florence Nightingale, 'The Lady of the Lamp'"; Pioneers of Science: "Sir Isaac Newton, Discoverer of 'The Law of Gravitation'" (January 1948; two printings). Painted cover by Gerald McCann, second interior art by John Tartaglione, second adaptation by Alfred Sundel; Hughes biography; "The Learned Monks [Columba and Clement]"; "Children of the Slums [Victorian England]" (March 1961; four printings).

46. *Kidnapped* by Robert Louis Stevenson. Line-drawing cover and interior art by Robert H. Webb, adaptation by John O'Rourke; Stevenson biography; Pioneers of Science: "The Wright Brothers"; Dog Heroes: "Toots, The Collie"; Great Lives: "Joan of Arc" (April 1948; five printings; originally appeared as newspaper *Illustrated Classic*, 30 March–20 April 1947). Painted cover (March 1956; 11 printings).

47. *Twenty Thousand Leagues Under the Sea* by Jules Verne. Line-drawing cover and interior art by Henry C. Kiefer; Verne biography; Dog Heroes: "Hero Rex"; American Indians: "The Hurons"; Pioneers of Science: "Luther Burbank, 'The World's Greatest Naturalist'" (May 1948; five printings; originally appeared as newspaper *Illustrated Classic*, 27 April–18 May 1947). First painted cover (September 1955; ten printings). Second painted cover by Norman Nodel (1968; two printings).

48. *David Copperfield* by Charles Dickens. Line-drawing cover and interior art by Henry C. Kiefer; adaptation by George D. Lipscomb; Dickens biography; Great Lives: "Elizabeth Blackwell, M.D."; American Rivers: "The Hudson"; "Harvard's Marshal Plan" by Nat Shane (June 1948; originally appeared as newspaper *Illustrated Classic*, 25 May–15 June 1947; three printings). Painted cover (July 1954; 12 printings; one Twin Circle edition).

49. *Alice in Wonderland* by Lewis Carroll (Charles Lutwidge Dodgson). Line-drawing cover and interior art by Alex A. Blum (first Blum art in series); Carroll biography; [Dog Heroes:] "Tippy, the Terrier" (different from No. 68); Pioneers of Science: "Galileo Galilei"; Famous Operas: "Carmen" by Georges Bizet (July 1948; three printings; originally appeared as newspaper *Illustrated Classic*, 22 June–13 July 1947). First painted cover (March 1960; four printings). Second painted cover by Taylor Oughton (1968; one printing).

50. *The Adventures of Tom Sawyer* by Mark Twain (Samuel L. Clemens). Line-drawing cover and first interior art by Aldo Rubano; first adaptation by Harry Miller; Twain biography;

[Dog Heroes:] "Bulldog Courage"; Pioneers of Science: "George Westinghouse"; Famous Operas: "Madame Butterfly" by Giacomo Puccini (August 1948; six printings; originally appeared as newspaper *Illustrated Classic*, 17 August–6 September 1947). Painted cover (September 1957; two printings). Second interior art unattributed; Twain biography; "A Lightning Pilot" (adapted from *Life on the Mississippi* by Samuel L. Clemens); "The Seminole Chief [Osceola]" (October 1961; seven printings).

51. *The Spy* by James Fenimore Cooper. Line-drawing cover and interior art by Arnold L. Hicks; Cooper biography; Pioneers of Science: "Wilhelm Konrad Roentgen"; Dog Heroes: "Irma, The Rare Rottweiler Breed"; Famous Operas: "Lohengrin, The Knight of the Swan" by Richard Wagner (September 1948; three printings; originally appeared as newspaper *Illustrated Classic*, 20 July–10 August 1947). Painted cover (July 1957; five printings).

52. *The House of the Seven Gables* by Nathaniel Hawthorne. Line-drawing cover and first interior art by Harley M. Griffiths, adapted by John O'Rourke; Hawthorne biography; Pioneers of Science: "William Crawford Gorgas"; Dog Heroes: "The Spots—One to Four"; Famous Operas: "Rigoletto" by Giuseppe Verdi (October 1948; four printings; originally appeared as newspaper *Illustrated Classic*, 13 September–4 October 1947). Painted cover unattributed, second interior art by George Woodbridge; Hawthorne biography (January 1958; seven printings).

53. *A Christmas Carol* by Charles Dickens. Line-drawing cover and interior art by Henry C. Kiefer; adaptation by George D. Lipscomb/Harry Miller; Dickens biography; Pioneers of Science: "Sir Henry Bessemer"; Dog Heroes: "The Hero of Niagara Falls" (November 1948; one printing; originally appeared as newspaper *Illustrated Classic*, 6–20 December 1947).

54. *The Man in the Iron Mask* by Alexandre Dumas. Line-drawing cover by Henry C. Kiefer, first interior art by August M. Froehlich, adaptation by John O'Rourke; Dumas biography; Pioneers of Science: "Antoine Laurent Lavoisier, The Father of Chemistry"; Famous Operas: "Thais" by Jules Massenet; Dog Heroes: "Brave" (December 1948; three printings; originally appeared as newspaper *Illustrated Classic*, 24 January–14 February 1948). Painted cover unattributed, second interior art by Ken Battefield; Dumas biography (January 1958; six printings).

55. *Silas Marner* by George Eliot (Mary Ann Evans). Line-drawing cover by Henry C. Kiefer, interior art by Arnold L. Hicks; Eliot biography; Dog Heroes: "'Buddy,' The First Seeing-Eye Dog"; [Pioneers of Science:] "Joseph, Lord Lister, The Father of Antiseptic Surgery"; Famous Operas: "The Barber of Seville" by Gioacchino Antonio Rossini (January 1949; three printings; originally appeared as newspaper *Illustrated Classic*, 8–29 November 1947). Painted cover (July 1954; nine printings).

56. *The Toilers of the Sea* by Victor Hugo. Line-drawing cover and first interior art by August M. Froehlich, adaptation by Harry Miller; Hugo biography; Dog Heroes: "No Greater Love"; Pioneers of Science: "William Harvey, Discoverer of Blood Circulation"; Famous Operas: "Tristan und Isolde" by Richard Wagner (February 1949; one printing; originally appeared as newspaper *Illustrated Classic*, 21 February–13 March 1948). Painted cover unattributed, second interior art by An-

gelo Torres, second adaptation by Alfred Sundel; Hugo biography; "The Flood"; "Sea Monsters" (Spring 1962; three printings).

57. *The Song of Hiawatha* by Henry Wadsworth Longfellow. Line-drawing cover and interior art by Alex A. Blum; Longfellow biography; Great Lives: "John Flamsteed, Father of Modern Astronomy"; Famous Operas: "Aida" by Giuseppe Verdi; Dog Heroes: "'Amigo,' Hero of the Andes" (March 1949; four printings). Painted cover (September 1956; seven printings).

58. *The Prairie* by James Fenimore Cooper. Line-drawing cover and interior art by Rudolph Palais; Cooper biography; Pioneer of Science: "Hippocrates, Father of Medicine"; Dog Heroes: "Tunney, the Champ" (April 1949; six printings). Painted cover (September 1958; five printings).

59. *Wuthering Heights* by Emily Brontë. Line-drawing cover and interior art by Henry C. Kiefer, adaptation by Harry Miller; Brontë biography; Pioneers of Science: "Dmitri I. Mendeleyev"; Dog Heroes: "'Pete,' the Peke"; Famous Operas: "The Valkyrie" by Richard Wagner (May 1949; two printings). Painted cover by Geoffrey Biggs (May 1960; four printings).

60. *Black Beauty* by Anna Sewell. Line-drawing cover and first interior art by August M. Froehlich; Sewell biography; Pioneers of Science: "Archimedes, First Teacher of Mathematics"; Famous Operas: "The Girl of the Golden West" by Giacomo Puccini; Dog Heroes: "Jeep—'Just a Plain Dog'" (June 1949; three printings). First painted cover by Leonard B. Cole, second interior art by Leonard B. Cole, Norman Nodel, and Stephen Addeo; second adaptation by Alfred Sundel; Sewell biography; "The Sacred Pet [cats]"; "Child Labor" (Fall 1960; three printings). Second painted cover by Albert Micale (1968; one printing).

61. *The Woman in White* by William Wilkie Collins. Line-drawing cover and interior art by Alex A. Blum, adaptation by John O'Rourke; Collins biography; Pioneers of Science: "Alexander Graham Bell, Inventor of the Telephone"; Famous Operas: "Lucia di Lammermoor" by Gaetano Donizetti; Dog Heroes: "'Duke'—Police Dog"; Great Lives: "Mary Baker Eddy" (July 1949; one printing). Painted cover by Doug Roea (May 1960; three printings).

62. *Western Stories* by Bret Harte; two stories: *The Luck of Roaring Camp* and *The Outcasts of Poker Flat*. Line-drawing cover and interior art by Henry C. Kiefer; Harte biography; Famous Operas: "Pagliacci" by Ruggiero Leoncavallo; Pioneers of Science: "Sir Edgeworth David, Discover[er] of the South Magnetic Pole"; Dog Heroes: "The Breed That Knows No Fear" (August 1949; three printings). First painted cover (author's name misspelled) (March 1957; five printings). Second painted cover by Taylor Oughton (1968; one printing).

63. *The Man Without a Country* by Edward Everett Hale. Line-drawing cover and first interior art by Henry C. Kiefer, adaptation by John O'Rourke; Hale biography; Famous Operas: "Tannhauser" by Richard Wagner; Pioneers of Science: "Simon Lake, Inventor of the First Submarine"; Dog Heroes: "'Spot,' The Crippled Hero" (September 1949; two printings). Painted cover by Gerald McCann (May 1960; one printing). Second interior art by Angelo Torres and Stephen L. Addeo; adaptation by Alfred Sundel; Hale biography; "Burning the *Philadelphia*"; "A Small Case of Forgery" (1962; four printings).

64. *Treasure Island* by Robert Louis Stevenson. Line-

drawing cover and interior art by Alex A. Blum; Stevenson biography; Pioneers of Science: "John A. Roebling, Master of Modern Bridge Building"; Dog Heroes: "'Major,' The Faithful Collie"; Famous Operas: "The Magic Flute" by Wolfgang Amadeus Mozart (October 1949; three printings). Painted cover (March 1956; ten printings). Long John Silver's Seafood Shoppe painted-cover reissue (1989; one printing).

65. *Benjamin Franklin* (based on *The Autobiography of Benjamin Franklin*). Line-drawing cover by Henry C. Kiefer; interior art by Iger shop (Robert Hebberd, Gustav Schrotter, and Alex A. Blum); Pioneers of Science: "Carolus Linnaeus, Father of Botany"; Famous Operas: "Lakme" by Leo Delibes; Dog Heroes: "'Howdy Doody' Saves Family of Four" (November 1949; one printing). Painted cover (March 1956; five printings).

66. *The Cloister and the Hearth* by Charles Reade. Line-drawing cover and interior art by Henry C. Kiefer, adaptation by Leslie Katz; Reade biography; Pioneers of Science: "Marchese Guglielmo Marconi, Inventor of Wireless Telegraphy"; Dog Heroes: "The Mongrel and the Puma"; Famous Operas: "Parsifal" by Richard Wagner (December 1949; one printing).

67. *The Scottish Chiefs* by Jane Porter. Line-drawing cover and interior art by Alex A. Blum, adaptation by John O'Rourke; Porter biography; Pioneers of Science: "Richard Jordan Gatling, Inventor of the Machine Gun"; Dog Heroes: "Skippy, The Funny Looking Dog"; Famous Operas: "Othello" by Giuseppe Verdi (January 1950; three printings). Painted cover (January 1957; four printings).

68. *Julius Caesar* by William Shakespeare. Line-drawing cover and first interior art by Henry C. Kiefer; Shakespeare biography; Pioneers of Science: "Blaise Pascal, The Mathematical Genius"; Dog Heroes: "Tippy, The Terrier" (different from No. 49); Famous Operas: "Manon" by Jules Massenet (February 1950; three printings; originally appeared as newspaper *Illustrated Classic*, 11 October–1 November 1947). Painted cover by Leonard B. Cole (May 1960; one printing). Second interior art by Reed Crandall and George Evans, second adaptation by Alfred Sundel; Shakespeare biography; "The First Roman Emperor [Augustus]"; "Death of a Dictator [Mussolini]" (1962; five printings; one Twin Circle edition).

69. *Around the World in Eighty Days* by Jules Verne. Line-drawing cover and interior art by Henry C. Kiefer; Verne biography; Famous Operas: "Der Meistersinger" by Richard Wagner; Dog Heroes: "Smoky, The Quick Thinking Dog"; Pioneers of Science: "Thomas Wedgwood, Inventor of the Camera" (March 1950; three printings). Painted cover (January 1957; nine printings).

70. *The Pilot* by James Fenimore Cooper. Line-drawing cover and interior art by Alex A. Blum; Cooper biography; Famous Operas: "The Merry Wives of Windsor" by Otto Nicolai; Dog Heroes: "Tatters, The Gentle Protector"; Pioneers of Science: "Phidias, The World's Greatest Sculptor" (April 1950; three printings). Painted cover by Gerald McCann (May 1960; three printings).

71. *The Man Who Laughs* by Victor Hugo. Line-drawing cover and first interior art by Alex A. Blum; Hugo biography; Dog Heroes: "'Pepper,' The 'Heart' Dog"; Famous Operas: "Der Rosenkavalier (The Rose-Bearer)" by Richard Strauss; Pioneers of Science: "Johann Gutenberg, Inventor of Movable Type Printing" (May 1950; one printing). Painted cover unat-

tributed, second interior art by Norman Nodel; Hugo biography; "The Kickapoo Cough Cure"; "Feasts and Fairs" (Spring 1962; two printings).

72. *The Oregon Trail* by Francis Parkman. Line-drawing cover and interior art by Henry C. Kiefer, adaptation by John O'Rourke; Parkman biography; Famous Operas: "La Boheme" by Giacomo Puccini; Pioneers of Science: "Edward Livingstone Trudeau, Isolator of the Tuberculosis Germ"; Dog Heroes: "'Duke,' The Seeing-Eye Cop" (June 1950; three printings). Painted cover (March 1956; eight printings).

73. *The Black Tulip* by Alexandre Dumas. Line-drawing cover and interior art by Alex A. Blum, adaptation by Kenneth W. Fitch; Dumas biography; Pioneers of Science: "Alfred Bernhard Nobel, Inventor of Dynamite"; Dog Heroes: "Tara, The Life Saver"; Famous Operas: "Boris Gudenof" by Modeste Moussorgsky (July 1950; one printing).

74. *Mr. Midshipman Easy* by Frederick Marryat. Line-drawing cover by Alex A. Blum, interior art by Bob Lamme, adaptation by Kenneth W. Fitch; Marryat biography; Pioneers of Science: "Baron Gottfried Leibnitz, Inventor of the Calculating Machine"; Dog Heroes: "Trixie, the Tough Shepherd"; Famous Operas: "Faust" by Charles Gounod (August 1950; one printing).

75. *The Lady of the Lake* by Sir Walter Scott. Line-drawing cover and interior art by Henry C. Kiefer, adaptation by George D. Lipscomb; Scott biography; Famous Operas: "The Flying Dutchman" by Richard Wagner; Pioneers of Science: "Pythagoras, Discoverer of the Solar System"; Dog Heroes: "'Chubby,' A Mongrel" (September 1950; three printings; originally appeared as newspaper *Illustrated Classic*, 27 December 1947–17 January 1948). Painted cover (July 1957; six printings).

76. *The Prisoner of Zenda* by Anthony Hope (Hawkins). Line-drawing cover and interior art by Henry C. Kiefer, adaptation by Kenneth W. Fitch; Hope biography; Famous Operas: "Pelleas and Melisande" by Claude Debussy; Pioneers of Science: "Roald Amundsen, Discoverer of the South Pole"; "Dog Heroes: "'Lady,' A Beagle Hound" (October 1950; three printings). Painted cover (September 1955; six printings).

77. *The Iliad* of Homer. Line-drawing cover and interior art by Alex A. Blum; Homer biography; Pioneers of Science: "Samuel Pierpont Langley, American Astronomer and Physicist"; Famous Operas: "La Gioconda" by Amilcare Ponchielli; Dog Heroes: "'Deacon,' A St. Bernard" (November 1950; three printings). Painted cover (July 1957; seven printings).

78. *Joan of Arc* (biography). Line-drawing cover and interior art by Henry C. Kiefer, adaptation by Samuel Willinsky; Dog Heroes: "Skeeter—A Sleeper"; Pioneers of Science: Friedrich, Baron von Humboldt, Discovery of the Science of Geography"; Famous Operas: "The King's Henchman" by Deems Taylor (December 1950; three printings). First painted cover (September 1955; eight printings). Second painted cover by Taylor Oughton (1969; one printing).

79. *Cyrano de Bergerac* by Edmond Rostand. Line-drawing cover and interior art by Alex A. Blum; adaptation by Kenneth W. Fitch; Rostand biography; Famous Operas: "Don Carlos" by Giuseppe Verdi; Dog Heroes: "'Foxy,' Hero of the Underground"; Pioneers of Science: "Friedrich Froebel, Father of the Modern Kindergarten" (January 1951; three printings). Painted cover (1957; three printings). (*Note*: Although the first painted-cover edition's HRN is 133, which would suggest a

1956 publication date, the column arrangement, in which the first three vertical rows end with Nos. 32, 76, and 122, corresponds to lists ending in HRNs 138 to 143, published between May 1957 and March 1958; the cover's paper stock resembles the grade used by Gilberton for reprints in 1957 and early 1958.)

80. *White Fang* by Jack London. Line-drawing cover and interior art by Alex A. Blum; adaptation by Kenneth W. Fitch; London biography; "History of U.S. Coins: How the phrase 'In God We Trust' came to be on the coins of the United States"; Famous Operas: "Die Fledermaus (The Bat)" by Johann Strauss; Pioneers of Science: "Johannes Kepler, Discoverer of the Laws of the Motions of Planets" (February 1951; three printings; last line-drawing cover; last 10-cent issue). Painted cover (May 1956; eight printings).

81. *The Odyssey* of Homer. First painted cover by Alex A. Blum; interior art by Harley M. Griffiths; Homer biography; Justinian, Creator of the Roman Code of Laws"; Dog Heroes: "Bosco, A 'Disobedient' Dog"; Famous Operas: "Il Trovatore (The Troubaour)" (March 1951; three printings; art completed in 1947; first painted-cover issue; first 15-cent issue). Second painted cover by Tony Tallarico (Spring 1969; one printing).

82. *The Master of Ballantrae* by Robert Louis Stevenson. First painted cover by Alex A. Blum, interior art by Lawrence Dresser, adaptation by Kenneth W. Fitch; Stevenson biography; Pioneers of Science: "Gottlieb Daimler, Father of the Modern Automobile"; Dog Heroes: "Windy"; Famous Operas: "Das Rheingold (The Gold of the Rhine) by Richard Wagner (April 1951; two printings). Second painted cover by Siryk (1968; one printing).

83. *The Jungle Book* by Rudyard Kipling; three stories: *Mowgli's Brothers*; *The King's Ankus*; *Red Dog*. First painted cover by Alex A. Blum (vertical tablet with issue number and price replaces open-book device); first interior art by Alex A. Blum and William Bossert; Kipling biography; Pioneers of Science: "Charles Goodyear, The Luckless Inventor of Vulcanized Rubber"; Dog Heroes: "'Chief': A Fire Dog"; Famous Operas: "Siegfried" by Richard Wagner (May 1951; 11 printings). Second painted cover and second interior art by Norman Nodel, same script as original edition (1968; one printing).

84. *The Gold Bug and Other Stories* by Edgar Allan Poe. Painted cover by Alex A. Blum; three stories, adaptations by John O'Rourke: *The Gold Bug*, art by Alex A. Blum; *The Tell-Tale Heart*, art by Jim Wilcox; *The Cask of Amontillado*, art by Rudolph Palais; Poe biography (June 1951; two printings).

85. *The Sea Wolf* by Jack London. Painted cover and interior art by Alex A. Blum, adaptation by John O'Rourke; London biography; Pioneers of Science: Nicholas Copernicus, Key Man in the Study of the Solar System"; Famous Operas: "The Tales of Hoffman" by Jacques Offenbach; Dog Heroes: "Pistol Head" (July 1951; eight printings).

86. *Under Two Flags* by Ouida (Marie Louise de la Ramee). Painted cover by Alex A. Blum (open-book device restored); interior art by Maurice del Bourgo; adaptation by Kenneth W. Fitch; Ouida biography; Pioneers of Science: "Edward Jenner, Discoverer of Small Pox Vaccination"; Dog Heroes: "'Brownie': Just a Faithful Dog"; Famous Operas: "Iolanthe" by W.S. Gilbert and Arthur Sullivan (August 1951; seven printings).

87. *A Midsummer Night's Dream* by William Shakespeare. Painted cover and interior art by Alex A. Blum, adaptation by Samuel Willinsky; Shakespeare biography; Pioneers of Sci-

ence: "Robert Wilhelm Bunsen, Inventor of the Bunsen Burner"; Dog Heroes: "The 'M' Dogs of the U.S. Army"; "The World of Books," quotation from *The Story of the Yale University Press Told by a Friend* by Clarence Day (September 1951; five printings).

88. *Men of Iron* by Howard Pyle. Painted cover by Alex A. Blum, interior art by Lawrence Dresser, Gustav Schrotter, and Harry Daugherty; adaptation by John O'Rourke; Pyle biography; "Courtship in Miniature"; Dog Heroes: "Just a Wandering Dog"; Pioneers of Science: "Euclid, Father of Geometry" (October 1951; four printings).

89. *Crime and Punishment* by Fyodor Dostoevsky. Interior art by Rudolph Palais; Dostoevsky biography; "So Proudly We Hailed…," art by Maurice del Bourgo; Famous Operas: "Mignon" by Ambroise Thomas (November 1951; five printings).

90. *Green Mansions* by William Henry Hudson. First painted cover and interior art by Alex A. Blum, adaptation by George D. Lipscomb; Hudson biography; Pioneers of Science: "Sir Richard Arkwright, Father of the Modern Factory"; "Barnum's Buffalo Hunt"; Famous Operas: "Don Giovanni" by Wolfgang Amadeus Mozart (December 1951; on printing). Second painted cover by Leonard B. Cole (January 1959; five printings).

91. *The Call of the Wild* by Jack London. Painted cover by Alex A. Blum; interior art by Maurice del Bourgo; adaptation by Kenneth W. Fitch; London biography; "The Universal Declaration of Human Rights"; Stories of Early America: "Clippers to the West" (January 1952; 11 printings).

92. *The Courtship of Miles Standish* and *Evangeline* by Henry Wadsworth Longfellow. Painted cover and interior art by Alex A. Blum; Longfellow biography; "The Jersey Tea Party" by Wendell Smith; American Indians: "The Apache"; Pioneers of Science: "Cyrus McCormick, Inventor of the Reaper" (February 1952; five printings; *The Courtship of Miles Standish* originally appeared as newspaper *Illustrated Classic*, 21 March 1948).

93. *Pudd'nhead Wilson* by Mark Twain (Samuel L. Clemens). First painted cover and interior art by Henry C. Kiefer; Twain biography; Stories from the World of Sports: "With an Assist from Mother Nature"; Stories of Early America: "The Capture of Fort Ticonderoga"; American Presidents: "An Incident in the Life of George Washington" (March 1952; one printing). Second painted cover by Gerald McCann (Spring 1962; three printings).

94. *David Balfour* by Robert Louis Stevenson. Painted cover unattributed; interior art by Rudolph Palais, adaptation of *Catriona*, a sequel to *Kidnapped*; Stevenson biography; "Stories from the World of Sports: 'Babe' Ruth's Great Moment"; "Bonnie Prince Charlie: The Rebellion of '45"; Stories of Early America: "John Sutter and the Gold Rush" (April 1952; three printings).

95. *All Quiet on the Western Front* by Erich Maria Remarque. Painted cover unattributed, interior art by Maurice del Bourgo, adaptation by Kenneth W. Fitch; Remarque biography; Stories of Early America: "Give Me Liberty or Give Me Death"; Stories from the World of Sports: "The Dean Brothers" (May 1952; three printings).

96. *Daniel Boone: Master of the Wilderness* by John Bakeless. First painted cover unattributed, interior art by Alex A.

Blum, adaptation by Kenneth W. Fitch; Bakeless biography; Stories from the World of Sports: "Old Pete's Greatest Moment"; American Presidents: "How Abraham Lincoln Gained National Prominence" (June 1952; nine printings). Second painted cover by Tony Tallarico (Winter 1969; one printing).

97. *King Solomon's Mines* by H. Rider Haggard. Painted cover and interior art by Henry C. Kiefer, adaptation by Kenneth W. Fitch; Rider Haggard biography; Great Lives: "Samuel Gompers"; Stories of Early America: "Wings of Salvation"; Stories from the World of Sports: "The 'Iron Horse' of Baseball" (July 1952; eight printings).

98. *The Red Badge of Courage* by Stephen Crane. First painted cover unattributed, art by Gustav Schrotter (originally scheduled for publication in *Famous Authors Illustrated*); Crane biography; 15-page illustrated filler story: *An Outline History of the Civil War*; art by Maurice del Bourgo; Stories of Early America: "Seward's Folly"; Stories from the World of Sports: "The Wild Horse of the Osage"; Great Lives: "George Jones, The Crusading Publisher" (August 1952; nine printings). Second painted cover by Taylor Oughton (1968; one printing).

99. *Hamlet* by William Shakespeare. First painted cover and art by Alex A. Blum, adaptation by Samuel Willinsky; Shakespeare biography; Stories of Early America: "Remember the Alamo!"; Great Lives: "Damon and Pythias"; Stories from the World of Sports: "Christy Mathewson's Great Series" (September 1952; seven printings). Second painted cover by Edward Moritz (Spring 1969; one printing).

100. *Mutiny on the Bounty* by Charles Nordhoff and James Norman Hall. Painted cover by Henry C. Kiefer, interior art by Morris Waldinger, adaptation by Kenneth W. Fitch; Nordhoff and Hall biographies; American Presidents: "An Incident in the Life of Franklin D. Roosevelt"; Stories of Early America: "Duel of Honor"; Stories from the World of Sports: "Knute Rockne" (October 1952; nine printings).

101. *William Tell* by Frederick Schiller (Johann Christoph Friedrich von Schiller). Painted cover by Henry C. Kiefer, interior art by Maurice del Bourgo, adaptation by Kenneth W. Fitch; Schiller biography; "Jean LaFitte and the Battle of New Orleans," art by Henry C. Kiefer; Great Lives: "Henry Bergh, Founder of the A.S.P.C.A." (November 1952; eight printings).

102. *The White Company* by Sir Arthur Conan Doyle. Painted cover unattributed, interior art by Alex A. Blum, adaptation by Kenneth W. Fitch; Conan Doyle biography; "How Much Land Does a Man Need?" (Russian folk tale); Great Lives: "Nathan Hale" (December 1952; three printings).

103. *Men Against the Sea* by Charles Nordhoff and James Norman Hall. First painted cover by H.C. Kiefer, interior art by Rudolph Palais, adaptation by Kenneth W. Fitch; Nordhoff and Hall biographies; Stories of Early America: "The Panama Canal"; Great Lives: "The Great Houdini" (January 1953; two printings). Second painted cover (March 1956; four printings).

104. *Bring 'Em Back Alive* by Frank Buck with Edward Anthony. Painted cover and interior art by Henry C. Kiefer, adaptation by Kenneth W. Fitch; Buck biography; Great Lives: "Mathew Brady, Photographer of the Civil War"; American Presidents: "An Incident in the Life of Ulysses S. Grant"; Stories of Early America: "A Volcano Changes the Course of History" (February 1953; eight printings).

105. *From the Earth to the Moon* by Jules Verne. Painted cover and interior art by Alex A. Blum; Verne biography; American Presidents: "An Incident in the Life of Andrew Johnson"; Great Lives: "Ponce de Leon and the Fountain of Youth"; Stories of Early America: "The Oklahoma Land Run" (March 1953; 12 printings).

106. *Buffalo Bill* (possibly based on *An Autobiography of Buffalo Bill* by Colonel William F. Cody). Painted cover unattributed, interior art by Maurice del Bourgo; Bad Men of the West: "William Quantrill"; Great Lives: "Henry Clay, The Great Compromiser"; Stories of Early America: "Wreck Ashore!" (April 1953; eight printings).

107. *King—of the Khyber Rifles* by Talbot Mundy. Painted cover unattributed, interior art by Seymour Moskowitz, adaptation by Kenneth W. Fitch; Mundy biography; Great Lives: "Balboa, Discoverer of the Pacific Ocean"; Stories from the World of Sports: "The Miracle of 1951" (May 1953; seven printings).

108. *Knights of the Round Table* (possibly based on Arthurian books by Sidney Lanier or Howard Pyle). Painted cover unattributed (Alex A. Blum?), interior art by Alex A. Blum, adaptation by John Cooney; Stories of Early America: "The Lost Colony"; Our American Heritage: "The Liberty Bell"; Stories from the World of Sports: "Baseball Comes Back" (June 1953; six printings).

109. *Pitcairn's Island* by Charles Nordhoff and James Norman Hall. Painted cover unattributed, interior art by Rudolph Palais, adaptation by Kenneth W. Fitch; Nordhoff and Hall biographies; American Presidents: "The Humor of Abraham Lincoln"; Great Lives: "Johnny Appleseed" (July 1953; four printings).

110. *A Study in Scarlet* by Sir Arthur Conan Doyle. Painted cover unattributed; two stories: *A Study in Scarlet* and *The Adventure of the Speckled Band*, art by Seymour Moskowitz, adaptations by Kenneth W. Fitch; Conan Doyle biography; Our American Heritage: "The Story of 'Yankee Doodle'"; Stories from the World of Sports: "Short and Rough: The Dempsey-Firpo Fight" (August 1953; two printings).

111. *The Talisman* by Sir Walter Scott. Painted cover and interior art by Henry C. Kiefer (last Kiefer art in series), adaptation by Kenneth W. Fitch; Scott biography; Stories of Early America: "Discovery of the Yellowstone"; Great Lives: "Theodore Roosevelt and the Rough Riders" (September 1953; four printings).

112. *The Adventures of Kit Carson* (biography). First painted cover unattributed, interior art by Rudolph Palais, adaptation by Kenneth W. Fitch; Stories of Early America: "The Cardiff Giant"; Stories from the World of Sports: "Harold 'Red' Grange, The Galloping Ghost" (October 1953; eight printings). Second painted cover by Edward Moritz (Winter 1969; one printing).

113. *The Forty-Five Guardsmen* by Alexandre Dumas. Painted cover unattributed, interior art by Maurice del Bourgo; Dumas biography; Great Lives: "Jeb Stuart"; Stories of Early America: "The Seminole War" (November 1953; two printings).

114. *The Red Rover* by James Fenimore Cooper. Painted cover by Jo Polseno, interior art by Peter Costanza; Cooper biography; Great Lives: "Frederick Remington, Illustrator of the Old West"; Stories of Early America: "The Prospector's Decision: The Settlement of Alaska" (December 1953; two printings).

115. *How I Found Livingstone* by Henry Morton Stanley.

Painted cover unattributed, interior art by Sal Trapani and Sal Finocchiaro; Stanley biography; Great Lives: "Clara Barton, Schools For All"; Stories of Early America: "Reindeer to the Rescue" (January 1954; two printings).

116. *The Bottle Imp* by Robert Louis Stevenson; two stories from *Island Nights' Entertainments*: *The Bottle Imp*, adaptation by Richard E. Davis; *The Beach of Falesa*, adaptation by Harry Miller. Painted cover unattributed, interior art by Lou Cameron; Stevenson biography; Great Lives: "Sam Houston, 'The Raven'"; Stories of Early America: "The Conquest of the Colorado" (February 1954; two printings).

117. *Captains Courageous* by Rudyard Kipling. Painted cover unattributed, interior art by Peter Costanza, adaptation by Ira Zweifach; Kipling biography; "Ghosts of the Sea"; Stories of Early America: "Return With Valor" (March 1954; three printings).

118. *Rob Roy* by Sir Walter Scott. Painted cover unattributed, interior art by Rudolph Palais and Walter Palais, adaptation by Harry Miller; Scott biography; "Hero of the Highlands [Rob Roy]"; Stories of Early America: "Winning the Northwest Territory" (April 1954; two printings).

119. *Soldiers of Fortune* by Richard Harding Davis. Painted cover unattributed, interior art by Kurt Schaffenberger, adaptation by Harry Miller; Davis biography; Great Lives: "Lawrence of Arabia"; Stories of Early America: "The Sinking of the *Maine*" (May 1954; three printings).

120. *The Hurricane* by Charles Nordhoff and James Norman Hall. Painted cover and interior art by Lou Cameron, adaptation by Harry Miller; Nordhoff and Hall biographies; "The Dreyfus Case"; Stories of Early America: "The Great Fire" (June 1954; two printings).

121. *Wild Bill Hickok* (biography). Painted cover unattributed, interior art by Sal Trapani and Medio Iorio, adaptation by Ira Zweifach; Stories of Early America: "Gallant Retreat [Nez Perces]"; Bad Men of the West: "Jesse James" (July 1954; last monthly issue; eight printings).

122. *The Mutineers* by Charles Boardman Hawes. Painted cover unattributed, interior art by Peter Costanza, adaptation by Harry Miller; Hawes biography; Great Lives: "John Paul Jones"; "The Barbary Pirates" (September 1954; first bimonthly issue; seven printings).

123. *Fang and Claw* by Frank Buck. Painted cover unattributed, interior art by Lin Streeter; Buck biography; Great Lives: "Aesop, Teller of Animal Tales"; "The Animal That Never Was: The Unicorn" (November 1954; six printings).

124. *The War of the Worlds* by H.G. (Herbert George) Wells. Painted cover and interior art by Lou Cameron, adaptation by Harry Miller; Wells biography; "Nostradamus: Prophet or Impostor?"; "The War That Never Was [Orson Welles]" (January 1955; 11 printings).

125. *The Ox-Bow Incident* by Walter Van Tilburg Clark. Painted cover unattributed, interior art by Norman Nodel (first Nodel art in series), adaptation by Lorenz Graham; Clark biography; "The Colorado Gold Rush: 'Pike's Peak of Bust'"; "Trial by Terror [William Lynch]" (March 1955; eight printings).

126. *The Downfall* by Emile Zola. Painted cover and interior art by Lou Cameron; Zola biography; "Napoleon's Return"; "The Last Lesson" by Alphonse Daudet (May 1955; three printings).

127. *The King of the Mountains* by Edmond About.

Painted cover unattributed, interior art by Norman Nodel; About biography; "The Story of Great Britain, Part 1: The Celtic Invasion" (Lou Cameron); "The Death of Socrates" (July 1955; three printings).

128. *Macbeth* by William Shakespeare. Painted cover unattributed, interior art by Alex A. Blum (last Blum art in series), adaptation by Lorenz Graham; Shakespeare biography; "The Story of Great Britain, Part 2: The Roman Conquest" (Lou Cameron); "Banquo's Descendant [James I]" (September 1955; eight printings; one Twin Circle edition).

129. *Davy Crockett* (based on *A Narrative of the Life of David Crockett of the State of Tennessee* by David Crockett). Painted cover unattributed, interior art by Lou Cameron; "The Story of Great Britain, Part 3: Saxon England" (Lou Cameron); "James Bowie" (November 1955; two printings).

130. *Caesar's Conquests* by Julius Caesar (based on Caesar's *Gallic War*). Painted cover unattributed, interior art by Joe Orlando and others, adaptation by Annete Rubinstein; Caesar biography; "The Story of Great Britain, Part 4: The Norman Conquest" (Lou Cameron); "The Roman Army" (January 1956; seven printings).

131. *The Covered Wagon* by Emerson Hough. Painted cover unattributed, interior art by Norman Nodel, adaptation by Annete Rubinstein; Hough biography; "The Story of Great Britain, Part 5: The Middle Ages" (Lou Cameron); "Jim Bridger" (March 1956; eight printings).

132. *The Dark Frigate* by Charles Boardman Hawes. Painted cover unattributed, interior art by Robert H. Webb and Ed Waldman, adaptation by Annete Rubinstein; Hawes biography; "The Story of Great Britain, Part 6: The Tudor Kings" (Lou Cameron); "The Battle of Trafalgar" (May 1956; four printings).

133. *The Time Machine* by H.G. (Herbert George) Wells. Painted cover unattributed, interior art by Lou Cameron, adaptation by Lorenz Graham; Wells biography; "The Story of Great Britain, Part 7: The Elizabethan Age" (Lou Cameron); "Charles Darwin" (July 1956; nine printings).

134. *Romeo and Juliet* by William Shakespeare. First painted cover unattributed, interior art by George Evans; Shakespeare biography; "The Story of Great Britain, Part 8: The Puritan Revolution" (Lou Cameron); "A Penny a Play" (September 1956; five printings). Second painted cover by Edward Moritz (Winter 1969; one printing).

135. *Waterloo* by Erckmann-Chatrain (Emile Erckmann and Louis-Alexandre Chatrain). Painted cover by Alex A. Blum, interior art by Graham Ingels; Erckmann-Chatrain biographies; "The Story of Great Britain, Part 9: The Restoration" (Lou Cameron); "Retreat From Moscow" (November 1956; five printings).

136. *Lord Jim* by Joseph Conrad. Painted cover unattributed, interior art by George Evans; Conrad biography; "The Story of Great Britain, Part 10: The Age of Revolution" (Lou Cameron); Great Lives: "Albert Schweitzer" (January 1957; five printings).

137. *The Little Savage* by Frederick Marryat. Painted cover unattributed, interior art by George Evans; Marryat biography; "The Story of Great Britain, Part 11: The Victorian Era" (Lou Cameron); "High Diving Birds" (March 1957; seven printings).

138. *A Journey to the Center of the Earth* by Jules Verne.

Painted cover unattributed, interior art by Norman Nodel; Verne biography; "The Story of Great Britain, Part 12: Great Britain Today" (Lou Cameron); "Cave Exploring [spelunking]" (May 1957; eight printings).

139. *In the Reign of Terror* by G.A. (George Alfred) Henty. Painted cover unattributed, interior art by George Evans, adapted by Ferrin Fraser; Henty biography; "The Revolutionist [Maximilien Robespierre]"; "Fight for Freedom [Greek War of Independence]" (July 1957; five printings).

140. *On Jungle Trails* by Frank Buck. Painted cover unattributed, interior art by Norman Nodel; Buck biography; "The Wreck of the *Essex*" (September 1957; five printings).

141. *Castle Dangerous* by Sir Walter Scott. Painted cover unattributed, interior art by Stan Campbell; Scott biography; "The Rebellious Scots [William Wallace, Robert Bruce, and Lord James Douglas]"; "Elves and Urisks" (November 1957; four printings).

142. *Abraham Lincoln* (biography). Painted cover by Gerald McCann, interior art by Norman Nodel; "Soldier, Lawyer and Justice [Oliver Wendell Holmes, Jr.]"; "Conspiracy [Lewis Paine and David Herold]" (January 1958; seven printings).

143. *Kim* by Rudyard Kipling. Painted cover unattributed, interior art by Joe Orlando; Kipling biography; "Buddha"; "The Abominable Snowman" (March 1958; five printings).

144. *The First Men in the Moon* by H.G. (Herbert George) Wells. First painted cover by Gerald McCann; interior art by George Woodbridge, Al Williamson, Angelo Torres, and Roy Krenkel; Wells biography; "The Mysterious Moon [lunar folklore]"; "Celestial Streaks [comets]" (May 1958; six printings). Second painted cover (Fall 1968; two printings).

145. *The Crisis* by Winston Churchill. Painted cover unattributed, interior art by George Evans; "Attack at Harpers Ferry"; Churchill biography (July 1958; five printings).

146. *With Fire and Sword* by Henryk Sienkiewicz. Painted cover unattributed, interior art by George Woodbridge, adaptation by Betty Jacobson; Sienkiewicz biography; "Two Polish Masters [Chopin and Paderewski]"; "The Cossack Revolution" (September 1958; four printings).

147. *Ben-Hur* by Lew Wallace. First painted cover by Gerald McCann, interior art by Joe Orlando, adaptation by Betty Jacobson; Wallace biography; "Fame or Death [Roman gladiators]"; "Emperor of Rome [Nero]" (November 1958; seven printings); Second painted cover by Taylor Oughton (Fall 1968; one printing).

148. *The Buccaneer* (movie tie-in, based on Paramount screenplay by Jessie L. Lasky, Jr. and Berenice Mosk). Painted cover by Norman B. Saunders, interior art by George Evans and Robert L. Jenney, adaptation by Jeanie Macpherson; "Blood and Plunder [Henry Morgan and William Kidd]"; "Sunken Treasure" (January 1959; originally scheduled for release as No. 145; five printings).

149. *Off On a Comet* by Jules Verne. First painted cover unattributed, interior art by Gerald McCann; Verne biography; "The Dwarf and the Giant [Mercury and Jupiter]"; "Heavenly Heroes [Callisto, Orion, Pleiades, Ariadne]" (March 1959; six printings). Second painted cover by Edward Moritz (Fall 1968; one printing).

150. *The Virginian* by Owen Wister. Painted cover by Doug Roea, interior art by Norman Nodel; Wister biography;

"T.R. and the Thieves"; "The Capture of Geronimo" (May 1959; four printings).

151. *Won By the Sword* by G.A. (George Alfred) Henty. Painted cover unattributed, interior art by John Tartaglione; Henty biography; "Wallenstein"; "The Thirty Years' War" (July 1959; four printings).

152. *Wild Animals I Have Known* by Ernest Thompson Seton. Painted cover and interior art by Leonard B. Cole; Seton biography; "Noah and His Ark"; "Bold Adventurers [Francisco Pizarro]" (September 1959; five printings).

153. *The Invisible Man* by H.G. (Herbert George) Wells. Painted cover by Geoffrey Biggs, interior art by Norman Nodel, adaptation by Alfred Sundel; Wells biography; "The Vanished Race [Etruscans]"; "The Strange Visitor [Lincoln and the supernatural]" (November 1959; seven printings).

154. *The Conspiracy of Pontiac* by Francis Parkman. Painted cover and interior art by Gerald McCann, adaptation by Alfred Sundel; Parkman biography; "Driven River [1836 battle between Cheyennes and Pawnees]"; "Sutter's Dream [John Augustus Sutter]" (January 1960; four printings).

155. *The Lion of the North* by G.A. (George Alfred) Henty. Painted cover by Gerald McCann, interior art by Norman Nodel; adaptation by Alfred Sundel; Henty biography; "Sweden on the Delaware [Peter Minuit]"; "A Storm of Stones [development of cannon]" (March 1960; three printings).

156. *The Conquest of Mexico* by Bernal Diaz del Castillo. Painted cover and interior art by Bruno Premiani, adaptation by Alfred Sundel; Diaz biography; "Prophecy of Doom [return of Quetzalcoatl]"; "The Old World [16th-century Europe]" (May 1960; four printings).

157. *Lives of the Hunted* by Ernest Thompson Seton. Painted cover by Leonard B. Cole, interior art by Norman Nodel, adaptation by Alfred Sundel; Seton biography; "The Secret of the Cave [prehistoric paintings]"; "Escape to Freedom [slave narrative]" (July 1960; three printings).

158. *The Conspirators* by Alexandre Dumas. Painted cover and interior art by Gerald McCann, adaptation by Alfred Sundel; Dumas biography; "The Grand Monarch [Louis XIV]"; "The Fortress at Eagle's Nest [The Old Man of the Mountains and the Assassins]" (September 1960; three printings).

159. *The Octopus* by Frank Norris. Painted cover by Leonard B. Cole, interior art by Gray Morrow, adaptation by Alfred Sundel; Norris biography; "An Earthly Paradise [early history of California]"; "Food for the Hungry [United Nations Relief and Rehabilitation Administration]" (November 1960; three printings).

160. *The Food of the Gods* by H.G. (Herbert George) Wells. Painted cover by Gerald McCann, interior art by Tony Tallarico, adaptation by Alfred Sundel; Wells biography; "Garden of Miracles [Brookhaven National Laboratories]"; "The War Against Machines [early Industrial Revolution mob violence]" (January 1960; three printings).

161. *Cleopatra* by H. Rider Haggard. Painted cover by Poch, interior art by Norman Nodel, adaptation by Alfred Sundel; Rider Haggard biography; "The Roman Power Struggle [Octavius and Antony]"; "The Realm of the Dead [Egyptian tombs]" (March 1961; three printings).

162. *Robur the Conqueror* by Jules Verne. Painted cover by Casey Jones (final issue with number and price in open-book device); interior art by Don Perlin, adaptation by Alfred Sundel;

Verne biography; "Who Knows?" (Part I) by Guy de Maupassant; "The Bride Comes to Yellow Sky" (Part I) by Stephen Crane; Men of Action: "Joshua," art by Sidney Miller (?) (May 1961; three printings).

163. *Master of the World* by Jules Verne. Painted cover unattributed (first issue with number and price in yellow rectangle); interior art by Gray Morrow; adaptation by Alfred Sundel; Verne biography; "Who Knows?" (Part II) by Guy de Maupassant; "The Bride Comes to Yellow Sky" (Part II) by Stephen Crane; Men of Action: "Socrates," art by Sidney Miller (?) (July 1961; three printings).

164. *The Cossack Chief (Taras Bulba)* by Nikolai Gogol. Painted cover unattributed, interior art by Sidney Miller, adaptation by Alfred Sundel; Gogol biography; "Who Knows?" (Part III) by Guy de Maupassant; "The Bride Comes to Yellow Sky" (Part III) by Stephen Crane; Men of Action: "Thutmosis III" (October 1961; three printings).

165. *The Queen's Necklace* by Alexandre Dumas. Painted cover unattributed, interior art by Gray Morrow, adaptation by Alfred Sundel; Dumas biography; "Who Knows?" (Part IV) by Guy de Maupassant; "The Bride Comes to Yellow Sky" (Part IV) by Stephen Crane; Men of Action: "Caupolican," art by Bruno Premiani (January 1965; three printings).

166. *Tigers and Traitors* (from *The Steam House*) by Jules Verne. Painted cover unattributed, interior art by Norman Nodel, adaptation by Alfred Sundel; Verne biography; "Who Knows? (Part V) by Guy de Maupassant; "The Sepoy Revolt"; Men of Action: "Frederick Barbarossa," art by Norman Nodel (May 1962; three printings).

167. *Faust* by Johann Wolfgang von Goethe. Cover penciled by Norman Nodel, colored by Sidney Miller; interior art by Norman Nodel, adaptation by Alfred Sundel; Goethe biography (August 1962; three printings).

168. *In Freedom's Cause* by G.A. (George Alfred) Henty. Painted cover unattributed, interior art by Reed Crandall and George Evans, adaptation by Alfred Sundel; Henty biography (scheduled for release in 1962; issued in British series as No. 160 in 1963; issued in U.S. series in Winter 1969; one printing).

169. *Negro Americans—The Early Years* (biographical profiles and sketches of Crispus Attucks, Peter Salem, Prince Hall, Prince Whipple, Oliver Cromwell, Spy James, Deborah Gannett, Benjamin Banneker, Phillis Wheatley, James Beckwourth, Harriet Tubman, Frederick Douglass, Robert Smalls, William Carney, Martin R. Delaney, Charles H. Davis, Henry Flipper, Isaiah Dorman, Nat Love, Daniel Hale Williams, Elijah McCoy, Garrett A. Morgan, Granville T. Woods, Booker T. Washington, George Washington Carver, and Matthew Henson). Painted cover and interior art by Norman Nodel, script by Deena Weintraub (Spring 1969; last issue in U.S. series; two printings).

Appendix B

List of *Classics Illustrated* Giant Editions (Gilberton, 1949)

An Illustrated Library of Great Adventure Stories: reprints of *A Tale of Two Cities*, *Robin Hood*, *Arabian Nights*, and *Robinson Crusoe* (Stanley Maxwell Zuckerberg, Louis Zansky, Lillian Chestney versions) (1949).

An Illustrated Library of Great Indian Stories: reprints of *The Last of the Mohicans* (Ray Ramsey version), *The Deerslayer*, *The Pathfinder*, and *The Pioneers* (1949).

An Illustrated Library of Great Mystery Stories: reprints of *Dr. Jekyll and Mr. Hyde* (Arnold L. Hicks version), *3 Famous Mysteries*, *The Moonstone*, and *Mysteries* by Edgar Allan Poe (1949).

Appendix C

List of *Classics Illustrated Educational Series* (Gilberton 1951–1953)

Both Educational Series *issues were 16 pages in length.*

1. *Shelter Through the Ages*. Painted cover and interior art by Henry C. Kiefer (1951).

[No number] *The Westinghouse Story: The Dreams of a Man*. Painted cover and interior art by Henry C. Kiefer (1953).

Appendix D

List of *Picture Parade/ Picture Progress* (Gilberton, 1953–1955)

Picture Parade and Picture Progress *issues were 24 to 32 pages in length.*

Vol. 1, No. 1. *Andy's Atomic Adventures*. Art by Peter Costanza (September 1953); reprinted in *Special Issue* No. 138A.

Vol. 1, No. 2. *Around the World With the United Nations* (October 1953).

Vol. 1, No. 3. *The American Indian* (November 1953).

Vol. 1, No. 4. *A Christmas Adventure*. Art by Lin Streeter (December 1953; last issue as *Picture Parade*); reissued as giveaway, with painted cover by Norman Nodel (1969).

Vol. 1, No. 5. *News in Review—1953* (January 1954; first issue as *Picture Progress*).

Vol. 1, No. 6. *The Birth of America*. Art by Lin Streeter (February 1954); reprinted in *Special Issue* No. 132A.

Vol. 1, No. 7. *The Four Seasons* (March 1954).

Vol. 1, No. 8. *Paul Revere's Ride*. Art by Peter Costanza (April 1954); reprinted in *Special Issue* No. 132A.

Vol. 1, No. 9. *The Hawaiian Islands* (May 1954).

Vol. 2, No. 1. *The Story of Flight*. Art by Peter Costanza (September 1954); reprinted in *Special Issue* No. 138A.

Vol. 2, No. 2. *A Vote for Crazy River (The Meaning of Elections)* (October 1954).

Vol. 2, No. 3. *The Discoveries of Louis Pasteur*. Art by Peter Costanza (November 1954); reprinted in *Special Issue* No. 138A.

Vol. 2, No. 4. *The Star-Spangled Banner*. Art by Tom Hickey (December 1954); reprinted in *Special Issue* No. 132A.

Vol. 2, No. 5. *1954—News in Review* (January 1955).

Vol. 2, No. 6. *Alaska: "The Great Land"* (February 1955).

Vol. 2, No. 7. *Life in the Circus* (March 1955).

Vol. 2, No. 8. *The Time of the Cave Man* (April 1955).

Vol. 2, No. 9. *Summer Fun* (May 1955).

Vol. 3, No. 1. *The Man Who Discovered America*. Art by Lou Cameron (September 1955); reprinted in *Special Issue* No. 132A.

Vol. 3, No. 2. *The Lewis and Clark Expedition*. Art by Norman Nodel (October 1955).

Appendix E

List of *Classics Illustrated Junior* (1953–1971)

All Classics Illustrated Junior *issues were 32 pages in length. Additional features are listed. The author owes a special debt of gratitude to Hames Ware for assistance in identifying unsigned art.*

501. *Snow White and the Seven Dwarfs* by the Brothers Grimm. Cover unattributed; interior art by Alex A. Blum; *Fillers*: "The Farmer in the Dell" (Alex A. Blum); "Lion" (William A. Walsh) (October 1953; nine printings).

502. *The Ugly Duckling* by Hans Christian Andersen. Cover and interior art by William A. Walsh; *Fillers*: "The Cat and the Fiddle" (Alex A. Blum); "Polar Bear" (William A. Walsh) (November 1953; nine printings).

503. *Cinderella* by Charles Perrault. Cover by Dik Browne; interior art by Peter Costanza; *Fillers*: "Jack and Jill" (Alex A. Blum); "Giant Panda" (William A. Walsh) (December 1953; 11 printings).

504. *The Pied Piper* by Robert Browning. Cover and interior art by Dik Browne; *Fillers*: "Sing a Song of Sixpence" (Alex A. Blum); "Elephants" (William A. Walsh) (January 1954; nine printings).

505. *The Sleeping Beauty* by Charles Perrault/Brothers Grimm. Cover by Dik Browne; interior art by Peter Costanza; *Fillers*: "Simple Simon" (Alex A. Blum); "Camel" (William A. Walsh) (February 1954; nine printings).

506. *The 3 Little Pigs* by Joseph Jacobs. Cover and interior art by William A. Walsh; *Fillers*: "I Saw a Ship a-Sailing" (Alex A. Blum); "Cheeta" (William A. Walsh) (March 1954; eight printings).

507. *Jack and the Beanstalk* by William Godwin. Cover by Dik Browne; interior art by Alex A. Blum; "My Shadow" by Robert Louis Stevenson (Alex A. Blum); "Gorilla" (William A. Walsh) (April 1954; eight printings).

508. *Goldilocks and the Three Bears* by Robert Southey. Cover by Dik Browne; interior art by William A. Walsh; *Fillers*: "Foreign Lands" by Robert Louis Stevenson (Alex A. Blum); "Bison" (William A. Walsh) (May 1954; seven printings).

509. *Beauty and the Beast* by Gianfrancesco Straparola/Charles Perrault. Cover and interior art by Dik Browne;

Fillers: Aesop's Fables: "The Dog and the Shadow" (William A. Walsh); "Ride a Cock-Horse" (Alex A. Blum); "Hippopotamus" (William A. Walsh) (June 1954; eight printings).

510. *Little Red Riding Hood* by Charles Perrault/Brothers Grimm. Cover by Dik Browne; interior art by William A. Walsh; *Fillers*: Aesop's Fables: "The Fox and the Grapes" (William A. Walsh); "Little BoPeep" (Alex A. Blum); "Rhinoceros" (William A. Walsh) (July 1954; seven printings).

511. *Puss-in-Boots* by Gianfrancesco Straparola/Charles Perrault. Cover by Dik Browne; interior art by William A. Walsh; *Fillers*: Aesop's Fables: "The Fox and the Stork" (William A. Walsh); "There Was a Crooked Man," "Peter Piper" (Alex A. Blum); "Platypus" (William A. Walsh) (August 1954; seven printings).

512. *Rumpelstiltskin* by the Brothers Grimm. Cover by Dik Browne; interior art by William A. Walsh; *Fillers*: Aesop's Fables: "The Miller, His Son, and Their Donkey" (William A. Walsh); "To Market, To Market," "Three Wise Men of Gotham" (Alex A. Blum); "Giraffe" (William A. Walsh) (September 1954; seven printings).

513. *Pinocchio* by Carlo Collodi. Cover and interior art by William A. Walsh; *Fillers*: Aesop's Fables: "The Ant and the Grasshopper" (William A. Walsh); "Pirate Story" by Robert Louis Stevenson (Alex A. Blum); "Grizzly Bear" (William A. Walsh) (November 1954; nine printings).

514. *The Steadfast Tin Soldier* by Hans Christian Andersen. Cover and interior art by Dik Browne; *Fillers*: Aesop's Fables: "The Actor and the Farmer" (Alex A. Blum); "Young Night Thought" by Robert Louis Stevenson (Alex A. Blum); "Dingo" (William A. Walsh) (January 1955; five printings).

515. *Johnny Appleseed*. Cover and interior art by William A. Walsh; *Fillers*: "Pecos Bill" (William A. Walsh); "If All the Seas Were One Sea" (Alex A. Blum); "Kangaroo" (William A. Walsh) (March 1955; seven printings).

516. *Aladdin and His Lamp*. Cover and interior art unattributed; *Fillers*: Aesop's Fables: "The Boy and the Wolf" (unattributed); "The Fat Man of Bombay," "Wee Willie Winkie" (Alex A. Blum); "Sperm Whale" (William A. Walsh) (May 1955; seven printings).

517. *The Emperor's New Clothes* by Hans Christian Andersen. Cover by Dik Browne; interior art by William A. Walsh; *Fillers*: Aesop's Fables: "The City Mouse and the Country Mouse" (William A. Walsh); "Peter, Peter," "Baa, Baa, Black Sheep" (Alex A. Blum); "The Swing" by Robert Louis Stevenson (Alex A. Blum) (July 1955; six printings).

518. *The Golden Goose* by the Brothers Grimm. Cover by Dik Browne; interior art by Mike Sekowsky and Frank Giacoia; *Fillers*: Aesop's Fables: "The Lion and the Mouse" (Mike Sekowsky); "Hark! Hark!", "Humpty Dumpty" (Alex A. Blum); "Rain" and "At the Seaside" by Robert Louis Stevenson (Alex A. Blum) (September 1955; five printings).

519. *Paul Bunyan* by W.B. Laughead. Cover by Dik Browne; interior art by Mike Sekowsky and Frank Giacoia; *Fillers*: Aesop's Fables: "The Donkey and the Little Dog" (Mike Sekowsky); "Little Boy Blue" (Alex A. Blum); "Where Go the Boats" by Robert Louis Stevenson (Alex A. Blum) (October 1955; eleven printings).

520. *Thumbelina* by Hans Christian Andersen. Cover by Dik Browne; interior art by Lin Streeter and William A. Walsh (background); *Fillers*: Aesop's Fables: "The Crow and the Pitcher" (Mike Sekowsky); "Bed in Summer" by Robert Louis Stevenson (Alex A. Blum); "Cock Robin and Jenny Wren" (Alex A. Blum) (November 1955; seven printings).

521. *The King of the Golden River* by John Ruskin. Cover by Mike Sekowsky; interior art by Mike Sekowsky and Frank Giacoia; Aesop's Fables: "The Unhappy Crow" (Mike Sekowsky); "The Land of Nod" by Robert Louis Stevenson (Alex A. Blum); "This Is the Way" (Alex A. Blum) (December 1955; six printings).

522. *The Nightingale* by Hans Christian Andersen. Cover and interior art by Dik Browne; *Fillers*: Aesop's Fables: "The Hare and the Tortoise" (Dik Browne); "The Moon" by Robert Louis Stevenson (Alex A. Blum); "Mary Had a Little Lamb" (Alex A. Blum) (January 1956; five printings).

523. *The Gallant Tailor* by the Brothers Grimm. Cover by Mike Sekowsky; interior art by Mike Sekowsky and Frank Giacoia; *Fillers*: Aesop's Fables: "The Fox and the Crow" (Mike Sekowsky); "Windy Nights" by Robert Louis Stevenson (Alex A. Blum); "Wouldn't It Be Funny?", "Jack Be Nimble" (Alex A. Blum) (February 1956; six printings).

524. *The Wild Swans* by Hans Christian Andersen. Cover and interior art by William A. Walsh; *Fillers*: Aesop's Fables: "The Raven and the Swan" (William A. Walsh); "I Saw Three Ships Come Sailing By" (Alex A. Blum); "The Wind" by Robert Louis Stevenson (Alex A. Blum) (March 1956; six printings).

525. *The Little Mermaid* (based on "The Mermaid") by Hans Christian Andersen. Cover and interior art by William A. Walsh; *Fillers*: Aesop's Fables: "The Milkmaid and Her Pail" (William A. Walsh); "Ding, Dong, Bell!", "A Cat Came Fiddling" (Alex A. Blum); The Animal World: The Raccoon" (William A. Walsh) (April 1956; six printings).

526. *The Frog Prince* by the Brothers Grimm. Cover and interior art by Lin Streeter; *Fillers*: Aesop's Fables: "The Hares and the Frogs" (William A. Walsh); "Pussy Cat, Pussy Cat," "What Are Little Boys Made Of?" (Alex A. Blum); The Animal World: "The Condor" (William A. Walsh) (May 1956; six printings).

527. *The Golden-Haired Giant* by the Brothers Grimm. Cover and interior art by William Walsh; *Fillers*: Aesop's Fables: "The Fox and the Goat" (William A. Walsh); "There Was a Maid" (Alex A. Blum); The Animal World: "The Moose" (William A. Walsh) (June 1956), six printings).

528. *The Penny Prince* (based on "The Swineherd") by Hans Christian Andersen. Cover by Dik Browne; interior art by Tom Hickey; *Fillers*: Aesop's Fables: "The Two Goats" (William A. Walsh); "Three Little Kittens" (Alex A. Blum); The Animal World: "The Rabbit" (William A. Walsh) (July 1956; six printings).

529. *The Magic Servants* by the Brothers Grimm. Cover and interior art by William A. Walsh; *Fillers*: Aesop's Fables: "The Wolf in Sheep's Clothing" (William A. Walsh); "Froggie Went a'Courtin'" (Alex A. Blum); The Animal World: "The Tiger" (William A. Walsh) (August 1956; four printings).

530. *The Golden Bird* by the Brothers Grimm. Cover by Dik Browne; interior art by Lin Streeter; *Fillers*: Aesop's Fables: "The Wind and the Sun" (Lin Streeter); "London Bridge" (Alex A. Blum); The Animal World: "The Seal" (William A. Walsh) (September 1956; five printings).

531. *Rapunzel* by the Brothers Grimm. Cover and interior art by Lin Streeter; *Fillers*: Aesop's Fables: "The Mice in Council [Belling the Cat]" (Lin Streeter); "Little Miss Muffet" (Alex A. Blum); The Animal World: "The Reindeer" (William A. Walsh) (October 1956; six printings).

532. *The Dancing Princesses* by the Brothers Grimm. Cover by Dik Browne; interior art by William A. Walsh; *Fillers*: Aesop's Fables: "The Lark and Her Young Ones" (William A. Walsh); "Little Jack Horner" (Alex A. Blum); The Animal World: "The Porcupine" (William A. Walsh) (November 1956; seven printings).

533. *The Magic Fountain*. Cover by Mike Sekowsky; interior art by Mike Sekowsky and Frank Giacoia; *Fillers*: "The Straw, the Coal and the Bean" (Mike Sekowsky); "Where, O Where" (Alex A. Blum); The Animal World: "The Squirrel" (William A. Walsh) (December 1956; five printings).

534. *The Golden Touch* by Nathaniel Hawthorne. Cover by Dik Browne; interior art by William A. Walsh; *Fillers*: Aesop's Fables: "Stone Soup" (William A. Walsh); "Mistress Mary" (Alex A. Blum); The Animal World: "The Turtle" (William A. Walsh) (January 1957; five printings).

535. *The Wizard of Oz* by L. Frank Baum. Cover by Dik Browne; interior art by Mike Sekowsky; *Fillers*: Aesop's Fables: "The Fox and the Lion" (Mike Sekowsky); "Old Mother Hubbard" (Alex A. Blum); The Animal World: "The Koala" (William A. Walsh) (February 1957; seven printings; one Twin Circle edition).

536. *The Chimney Sweep* by Hans Christian Andersen. Cover and interior art by William A. Walsh; *Fillers*: Aesop's Fables: "The Fisherman and the Little Fish" (William A. Walsh); "Pat-a-Cake" (Alex A. Blum); The Animal World: "The Beaver" (William A. Walsh) (March 1957; six printings).

537. *The Three Fairies*. Cover and interior art by Lin Streeter; Aesop's Fables: "The Ant and the Dove" (Lin Streeter); "Rub-a-Dub-Dub" (Alex A. Blum); The Animal World: "The Flamingo" (April 1957; five printings).

538. *Silly Hans* by the Brothers Grimm. Cover and interior art by William A. Walsh; *Fillers*: Aesop's Fables: "The Lion and the Dolphin" (William A. Walsh); "The North Wind" (Alex A. Blum); The Animal World: "The Penguin" (William A. Walsh) (May 1957; five printings).

539. *The Enchanted Fish* by the Brothers Grimm. Cover and interior art by Lin Streeter; *Fillers*: Aesop's Fables: The Four Oxen and the Lion" (William A. Walsh); "The Queen of Hearts" (Alex A. Blum); The Animal World: "The Armadillo" (William A. Walsh) (June 1957; six printings).

540. *The Tinder-Box* by Hans Christian Andersen. Cover and interior art by William A. Walsh; *Fillers*: Aesop's Fables: "The Lioness and Her Family"(William A. Walsh); "Hickety, Pickety" (Alex A. Blum); The Animal World: "The Kinkajou" (William A. Walsh) (July 1957; six printings).

541. *Snow White and Rose Red* by the Brothers Grimm. Cover and interior art by William A. Walsh; *Fillers*: Aesop's Fables: "The Rich Man's Guest" (William A. Walsh); "The Duck and the Kangaroo" by Edward Lear (William A. Walsh); The Animal World: "The Cougar" (William A. Walsh) (August 1957; five printings).

542. *The Donkey's Tale*. Cover and interior art by Stan Campbell; *Fillers*: Aesop's Fables: "The Oak and the Reed" (Stan Campbell); "The Owl and the Pussycat" by Edward Lear (Stan Campbell); The Animal World: "The Flying Squirrel" (William A. Walsh) (September 1957; five printings).

543. *The House in the Woods* by the Brothers Grimm. Cover and interior art by Lin Streeter; *Fillers*: Aesop's Fables: "The Treasure in the Vineyard" (Lin Streeter); "The Broom, the Shovel, the Poker, and the Tongs" by Edward Lear (unattributed); The Animal World: "The Skunk" (William A. Walsh) (October 1957; five printings).

544. *The Golden Fleece* by Nathaniel Hawthorne. Cover by Alex A. Blum; interior art by William A. Walsh; *Fillers*: Aesop's Fables: "The Donkey and the Cricket" (William A. Walsh); "The Daddy Long-Legs and the Fly" by Edward Lear (William A. Walsh); The Animal World: "The Jaguar" (William A. Walsh) (November 1957; six printings).

545. *The Glass Mountain*. Cover and interior art unattributed; *Fillers*: Aesop's Fables: "The Donkey and the Salt" (unattributed); "There Was an Old Man With a Beard" by Edward Lear (unattributed); The Animal World: "The Otter" (William A. Walsh) (December 1957; five printings).

546. *The Elves and the Shoemaker* by the Brothers Grimm. Cover and interior art by William A. Walsh; *Fillers*: Aesop's Fables: "The Greedy Lion" (William A. Walsh); "There Was an Old Lady of France" by Edward Lear (William A. Walsh); The Animal World: "The Heron" (William A. Walsh) (January 1958; five printings).

547. *The Wishing Table* by the Brothers Grimm. Cover and interior art by Lin Streeter; *Fillers*: Aesop's Fables: "The Two Frogs" (Lin Streeter); "There Was an Old Person of Brigg" by Edward Lear (unattributed); The Animal World: "The Aardvark" (William A. Walsh) (February 1958; five printings).

548. *The Magic Pitcher* (*The Miraculous Pitcher*) by Nathaniel Hawthorne. Cover and interior art by William A. Walsh; *Fillers*: Aesop's Fables: "The Arab and His Camel" (William A. Walsh); "There Was an Old Man Who Said, `Hush!'" by Edward Lear (William A. Walsh); The Animal World: "The Albatross" (March 1958; six printings).

549. *Simple Kate* by the Brothers Grimm. Cover and interior art unattributed (Jerry Fasano?); *Fillers*: Aesop's Fables: "The Spendthrift and the Swallow" (unattributed); "There Was a Young Lady of Welling" by Edward Lear (unattributed); The Animal World: "The Alligator" (William A. Walsh) (April 1958; six printings).

550. *The Singing Donkey* (*The Bremen Town Musicians*) by the Brothers Grimm. Cover and interior art by Stan Campbell; *Fillers*: Aesop's Fables: "The Fortune Teller" (Stan Campbell); "There Was an Old Man Who Said, `Well!'" by Edward Lear (unattributed); The Animal World: "The Caribou" (William A. Walsh) (May 1958; five printings).

551. *The Queen Bee* by the Brothers Grimm. Cover and interior art by William A. Walsh; *Fillers*: Aesop's Fables: "The Plane Tree" (William A. Walsh); "There Was an Old Man of Kilkenny" by Edward Lear (William A. Walsh); The Animal World: "The Puma" (William A. Walsh) (June 1958; five printings).

552. *The Three Little Dwarfs* by the Brothers Grimm, Cover and interior art by William A. Walsh; *Fillers*: Aesop's Fables: "The Woodcutters and the Ax" (William A. Walsh); "There Was an Old Man of the West" by Edward Lear (William A. Walsh); The Animal World: "The Salamander" (William A. Walsh) (July 1958; five printings).

553. *King Thrushbeard* by the Brothers Grimm. Cover and interior art by William A. Walsh; *Fillers*: Aesop's Fables: "The Man and the Satyr" (William A. Walsh); "There Was an Old Man in a Boat" by Edward Lear (William A. Walsh); The Animal World: "The Hamster" (William A. Walsh) (August 1958; six printings).

554. *The Enchanted Deer* by the Brothers Grimm. Cover and interior art by Joe Sinnott; *Fillers*: Aesop's Fables: "The Deer and the Hunters" (Joe Sinnott); "There Was a Young Lady Whose Bonnet" by Edward Lear (Joe Sinnott); The Animal World: "The Ostrich" (William A. Walsh) (September 1958, six printings).

555. *The Three Golden Apples* by Nathaniel Hawthorne. Cover and interior art by Mike Sekowsky; *Fillers*: Aesop's Fables: "The Boy and the Filberts" (Mike Sekowsky); "There Was an Old Man With a Nose" by Edward Lear (Mike Sekowsky); The Animal World: "The Swan" (William A. Walsh) (October 1958; four printings).

556. *The Elf Mound* by Hans Christian Andersen. Cover and interior art by William A. Walsh; *Fillers*: "The Shepherd Goes to Sea" (William A. Walsh); "There Was an Old Man in a Tree" by Edward Lear (William A. Walsh); The Animal World: "The Lobster" (William A. Walsh) (November 1958; five printings).

557. *Silly Willy* by the Brothers Grimm. Cover and interior art by Mike Sekowsky; *Fillers*: Aesop's Fables: "The Donkey's Shadow" (Mike Sekowsky); "There Was an Old Man on a Hill" by Edward Lear (Mike Sekowsky); The Animal World: "The Ground Hog" (William A. Walsh) (December 1958; five printings).

558. *The Magic Dish*. Cover by L.B. Cole; interior art by George Peltz; *Fillers*: Aesop's Fables: "The Wolf and the Kid" (George Peltz); "There Was an Old Person of Dover" by Edward Lear (George Peltz); The Animal World: "The Chinchilla" (William A. Walsh) (February 1959; four printings).

559. *The Japanese Lantern* by Lafcadio Hearn. Cover by L.B. Cole; interior art by George Peltz; *Fillers*: Aesop's Fables:

"Hercules and the Wagon Driver" (George Peltz); "There Was a Young Lady Whose Chin" by Edward Lear (George Peltz); The Animal World: "The Badger" (William A. Walsh) (April 1959; four printings).

560. *The Doll Princess.* Cover by L.B. Cole; interior art by William A. Walsh; *Fillers:* Aesop's Fables: "The Man and His Two Wives" (William A. Walsh); "There Was an Old Lady of Chertsey" by Edward Lear (William A. Walsh); The Animal World: "The Bat" (William A. Walsh) (June 1959; four printings).

561. *Hans Humdrum.* Cover by L.B. Cole; interior art by George Peltz; *Fillers:* "The Camel and the Pig" (George Peltz); "There Was an Old Man Who Said `How'" by Edward Lear (George Peltz); The Animal World: "The Walrus" (William A. Walsh) (August 1959; four printings).

562. *The Enchanted Pony*, a Russian fairy tale. Cover by L.B. Cole; interior art by William A. Walsh; *Fillers:* Aesop's Fables: "The Two Maids and the Cock" (William A. Walsh); "There Was a Young Lady Whose Eyes" by Edward Lear (William A. Walsh); The Animal World: "The Katydid" (William A. Walsh) (October 1959; four printings).

563. *The Wishing Well.* Cover by L.B. Cole; interior art by William A. Walsh; *Fillers:* Aesop's Fables: "The Boy Bathing" (William A. Walsh); "There Was a Young Lady Whose Nose" by Edward Lear (William A. Walsh); The Animal World: "The Alpaca" (L.B. Cole) (December 1959; four printings).

564. *The Salt Mountain*, a Russian fairy tale. Cover by L.B. Cole; interior art by George Peltz; *Fillers:* Aesop's Fables: "The Father and His Two Daughters" (George Peltz); "There Was a Young Lady of Norway" by Edward Lear (George Peltz); The Animal World: "The Pelican" (L.B. Cole) (February 1960; four printings).

565. *The Silly Princess.* Cover by L.B. Cole, interior art by William A. Walsh; *Fillers:* "Fortune and the Beggar" (William A. Walsh); "There Was a Young Lady of Bute" by Edward Lear (William A. Walsh); The Animal World: "The Chameleon" (L.B. Cole) (April 1960; four printings).

566. *Clumsy Hans* by Hans Christian Andersen. Cover by L.B. Cole; interior art by William A. Walsh; *Fillers:* Aesop's Fables: "The Mouse, the Cat and the Rooster" (William A. Walsh); "The Table and the Chair" by Edward Lear (William A. Walsh); The Animal World: "The Prairie Dog" (L.B. Cole) (June 1960; four printings).

567. *The Bearskin Soldier* by the Brothers Grimm. Cover by L.B. Cole; interior art by George Peltz; *Fillers:* "The Red-Bud Tree" (George Peltz); "There Was a Young Lady of Russia" by Edward Lear (George Peltz); The Animal World: "The Swordfish" (L.B. Cole) (August 1960; five printings).

568. *The Happy Hedgehog* by the Brothers Grimm. Cover by L.B. Cole; interior art by George Peltz; *Fillers:* Aesop's Fa-bles: "The Mouse, the Frog, and the Hawk" (L.B. Cole); "There Was an Old Man of the Dee" by Edward Lear (George Peltz); The Animal World: "The Buffalo" (Jay Disbrow) (October 1960; four printings).

569. *The Three Giants.* Cover unattributed; interior art by George Peltz; *Fillers:* "The String of Carts" (George Peltz); "Spots of Greece" by Edward Lear (George Peltz); The Animal World: "The Ibex" (Norman Nodel) (December 1960; four printings).

570. *The Pearl Princess.* Cover unattributed; interior art unattributed; *Fillers:* "The Three Fish" (unattributed); "There Was an Old Person of Troy" by Edward Lear (unattributed); The Animal World: "The Grebe" (unattributed) (February 1961; four printings).

571. *How Fire Came to the Indians*, a Native American tale. Cover unattributed; interior art by Tony Tallarico; *Fillers:* "The Good King" (Tony Tallarico); "There Was a Young Person in Pink" by Edward Lear (unattributed); The Animal World: "The Tarsier" (unattributed) (April 1961; four printings).

572. *The Drummer Boy* by the Brothers Grimm. Cover unattributed; interior art by Sidney Miller (?); *Fillers:* Aesop's Fables: "The Hare and the Hound" (Charles Berger); "There Was an Old Man in a Garden" by Edward Lear (unattributed); The Animal World: "The Road Runner" (June 1961; three printings).

573. *The Crystal Ball* by the Brothers Grimm. Cover unattributed; interior art by Sidney Miller (?); *Fillers:* "The Fish and the Cat" (unattributed); "There Was an Old Person of Wilts" by Edward Lear (unattributed); The Animal World: "The Mastodon" (H.J. Kihl) (August 1961; three printings).

574. *Brightboots.* Cover unattributed; interior art by Tony Tallarico; *Fillers:* "The Shepherd's Bride" (Tony Tallarico); "There Was an Old Man of Dee-side" by Edward Lear (Erhard); The Animal World: "The Sloth" (unattributed) (October 1961; three printings).

575. *The Fearless Prince* by the Brothers Grimm. Cover unattributed; interior art by "Boris"; *Fillers:* "The Nail" (Erhard); "There Was an Old Person of Dean" by Edward Lear (Erhard); The Animal World: "The Panglion" (unattributed) (February 1962; three printings).

576. *The Princess Who Saw Everything* by the Brothers Grimm. Cover and interior art by Pat Pritchard; *Fillers:* "The Unhappy Cow" (Erhard); "There Was an Old Man in a Tree" by Edward Lear (unattributed); The Animal World: "The Hummingbird" (unattributed) (June 1962; three printings).

577. *The Runaway Dumpling* based on a Japanese folktale, told by Lafcadio Hearn. Cover and interior art by Pat Pritchard (Winter 1969; one printing).

Appendix F

List of *Classics Illustrated Special Issues* (1955–1962)

The Special Issues *were 96 pages in length; the cover price was 35 cents.*

129A. *The Story of Jesus.* "Jesus on the Mountain" cover by Victor Prezio, interior art by William A. Walsh and Alex A. Blum, adaptation by Lorenz Graham; "Birth and Boyhood of Jesus"; "Preparation for Life's Work"; "The Galilean Ministry"; "Jesus at Jerusalem"; "Betrayal, Trial and Crucifixion"; "Resurrection" (December 1955; three printings, not consecutive); "Three Camels" cover unattributed (December 1958; one printing).

132A. *The Story of America.* Cover unattributed; "The Man Who Discovered America" (Lou Cameron); "The Birth of America" (Lin Streeter); "Paul Revere's Ride" (Peter Costanza); "The Star-Spangled Banner" (Tom Hickey); all sections originally appeared in *Picture Parade/Picture Progress* series (June 1956, one printing).

135A. *The Ten Commandments.* Cover and interior art by Norman Nodel, adaptation by Lorenz Graham; "Oppression in Egypt"; "Early Life of Moses"; "God Calls Moses"; "The Plagues"; "Exodus"; "The Commandments"; "The Tabernacle" (December 1956; one printing).

138A. *Adventures in Science.* Cover unattributed; "The Story of Flight" (Peter Costanza); "Andy's Atomic Adventures" (Peter Costanza); "The Discoveries of Louis Pasteur" (Peter Costanza); "From Tom-Tom to TV" (Lin Streeter); *Fillers*: Great Lives: "Amelia Earhart"; Pioneers of Science: "Joseph Priestley" (June 1957; three printings).

141A. *The Rough Rider,* Cover unattributed; interior art by George Evans (pencils); *Fillers*: "This He Believed…"; "Theodore Roosevelt" by Hermann Hagedorn (December 1957; one printing).

144A. *Blazing the Trails West.* Cover unattributed; page-one splash by George Evans; "Daniel Boone" (George Evans); "The Lewis and Clark Expedition" (George Evans); "The Santa Fe Trail" (George Evans); "Fur and Mountains" (George Evans); "Kit Carson" (George Evans); "Texas and the Alamo" (John P. Severin); "The Mexican War" (John P. Severin);

Fillers: "End of an Empire"; "Frontier Fun" (June 1958; one printing).

147A. *Crossing the Rockies.* Cover by Gerald McCann; page-one splash by Norman Nodel; "The Oregon Trail" (Norman Nodel); "Death and the Donners" (Norman Nodel); "'This Is the Place'" (Norman Nodel); "The Gold Rush" (George Evans); "The Apache Wars" (Joe Orlando); "The Overland Mail" (Joe Orlando): "Pony Express" (Joe Orlando); "Bound By Rails" (Joe Orlando); *Fillers*: "Meanwhile, Back in the East…"; "The Magic Wire" (December 1958; one printing).

150A. *Royal Canadian Mounted Police.* Cover by Gerald McCann; page-one splash by L.B. Cole; "March to Fort Whoop-Up" (Sam Glanzman); "Pony Soldiers" (Graham Ingels); "Indians and Outlaws" (Sid Check); "Unrest and Rebellion" (Kirner); "Patrolling the Prairies" (Sam Becker); "The Gold Rush" (unattributed); "Into the Far North" (Norman Nodel); "The Modern Mountie" (Stan Campbell); Manhunt!" (Ray Ramsey); "Molding a Mountie (Norman Nodel); *Fillers*: "Mountie Museum"; "Heroic Rescues" (June 1959; one printing).

153A. *Men, Guns and Cattle.* Cover by Gerald McCann; page-one splash by L.B. Cole; "Horns and Hoofs" (George Evans); "Iron Fisted Marshal" (George Evans); "The Chisholm Trail" (George Evans); "The Lincoln County War" (Gerald McCann); "Dodge City Lawman" (Gerald McCann); "The Last War" (Everett Raymond Kinstler); "The West's Wildest Town" (Norman Nodel); "The Death of Tombstone" (Everett Raymond Kinstler); "Koohoppers and Cactus Cats" (George Peltz); "The Closing Frontier" (Gerald McCann); *Fillers*: "Guns and Gunfighters"; "Git Along Little Dogies" (December 1959; one printing).

156A. *The Atomic Age.* Cover by Gaylord Welker; page-one splash by Norman Nodel; "Adventure North" (Norman Nodel); "The Smallest Particle" (Bruno Premiani); "Inside the Atom" (Edd Ashe); "The Atomic Furnace" (Gerald McCann);

"The Magic Mineral" (Sam Glanzman); "How to Build a Radiation Detector" (George Evans); "Alpha, Beta and Gamma" (Everett Raymond Kinstler); "Atoms for Power" (George Evans); "The Radioscope" (Sam Glanzman); "Atoms and Industry" (John Tartaglione); "Atoms and Agriculture" (Gerald McCann); "Atoms and Medicine" (Angelo Torres); "The Healing Rays" (Gerald McCann); "The Atom Tomorrow" (Bruno Premiani); *Fillers*: "The Ages of Energy"; "The Search for Uranium" (June 1960; one printing).

159A. *Rockets, Jets and Missiles*. Cover by Simon; page-one splash by Gerald McCann; "Flight of the X–1" (George Evans); "Space Talk" I (Sam Glanzman); "The Moon" (Gerald McCann); "The Jet is Born" (Gerald McCann); "Space Talk" II (Sam Glanzman); "Mercury" (John Tartaglione); "Jet Engines" (John Tartaglione); "Jets Around the World" (John Tartaglione); "Space Talk" III (Sam Glanzman); "Venus" (John Tartaglione); "Rockets Through Time" (H.J. Kihl); "Space Talk" IV (Sam Glanzman); "Mars" (Gerald McCann); "The Wizard of Worcester" (Gerald McCann); "Space Talk" V (Sam Glanzman); "Jupiter" (Gerald McCann); "Rocket Engines" (John Tartaglione); "Don't Do It Yourself" (Jack Abel); "Space Talk" VI (Sam Glanzman); "Saturn" (Gerald McCann); "Rockets and Missiles Around the World" (Gerald McCann); "Artifical Moons" (Sam Glanzman); "Space Talk" VII (Sam Glanzman); "Uranus" (John Tartaglione); "Seven For Space" (Gray Morrow); "Space Talk" VIII (Sam Glanzman); "Neptune" (John Tartaglione); "Off Into Orbit" (Gray Morrow); "Space Talk" IX (Sam Glanzman); "Pluto" (Gerald McCann); "Doorway to Tomorrow" (Sam Glanzman); *Fillers*: "Stones From Space"; "Other Worlds" (December 1960; one printing).

162A. *The War Between the States*. Cover by Geoffrey Biggs; page-one splash by Jack Kirby; "April, 1861: Fort Sumter" (Jack Kirby); "The Causes" (Sam Glanzman); "July, 1861: Bull Run" (Till Goodan); "Battle Report" I (George Peltz); "April, 1862: Shiloh" (George Evans); "April, 1862: New Orleans" (Edd Ashe); "April–July, 1862: The Peninsula" (Jack Kirby); "July, 1862: Kentucky" (John Tartaglione); "Battle Report" II (Till Goodan); "June, 1863: Brandy Station" (George Peltz); "June–July, 1863: Gettysburg" (Sam Glanzman); "April–July, 1863: Vicksburg" (Jack Kirby); "September–November, 1863: Chattanooga" (Edd Ashe); "Battle Report" III (George Peltz); "May–September, 1864: Georgia" (Till Goodan); "October, 1864: The Atlantic" (Stan Campbell); "November, 1864: New York City" (Jack Kirby); "April, 1865: Appomattox Court House" (Till Goodan); "Final Report" (Till Goodan); "Reconstruction" (George Evans); *Fillers*: The Exile's Dream"; "The Peasants' Revolt" (June 1961; one printing).

165A. *To the Stars!* Page-one splash by Angelo Torres; "Man in the Skies" (Angelo Torres); "Earth in Space" (George Evans): "The Magic Eye" (George Evans); "The Giant of Palomar" (George Evans); "A Simple Telescope (Jack Kirby); "Lines and Signals" (Jack Kirby); "Viewing the Spectrum" (Jack Kirby); "Our Neighbor—The Moon" (Sam Glanzman); "The Copper Moon" (Sam Glanzman); "The Inner Planets" (Jo Albistur); "The Giants" (Jo Albistur); "The Georgian Planet"

(George Evans); "Uranus" (Jo Albistur); "Neptune" (Jo Albistur); "Planet X"(Jo Albistur); "Pluto" (Jo Albistur"); "Are There Other Planets?" (Jo Albistur); "Fiery Streaks and Tails" (Sam Glanzman); "Figures in the Sky" (Sam Glanzman); "Star Facts" (Sam Glanzman); "Our Nearest Star" (Sam Glanzman); "The Disappearing Sun" (Norman Nodel); "Light Years" (Norman Nodel); "The Universe" (Norman Nodel); "The Universe and Life" (Norman Nodel); *Fillers*: "The Swiss Patent Clerk"; "Days and Years" (December 1961; one printing).

166A. *World War II*. Page-one splash by Angelo Torres; "Blitzkrieg" (Angelo Torres); "The Fuehrer" (Angelo Torres); "War on the High Seas" (Angelo Torres); "Il Duce" (Angelo Torres); "The Conquest of Western Europe" (George Evans); "The Battle of Britain" (Norman Nodel); "Warships and Wolf Packs" (Norman Nodel); "The Resistance" (George Evans); "The Eastern Front" (Norman Nodel); "The Big Three" (Angelo Torres); "War in the Pacific" (Norman Nodel); "The Doolittle Raid" (George Evans); "Guadalcanal" (George Evans); "Tarawa" (George Evans); "War Leaders" I (Angelo Torres); "Stalingrad" (Angelo Torres); "War Leaders" II (Angelo Torres); "Lidice and Warsaw" (Norman Nodel); "The Death Camps" (Norman Nodel); "North Africa" (Norman Nodel); "War Leaders" III (Angelo Torres); "The Italian Campaign" (Norman Nodel); "Blockbusters and Buzz Bombs" (George Evans); "The Normandy Invasion" (George Evans); "The Battle of the Bulge" (Norman Nodel); "Victory in Europe" (Norman Nodel); "War Leaders" IV (Angelo Torres); "Leyte Gulf" (Angelo Torres); "The Mainland War" (Angelo Torres); War Leaders" V (Angelo Torres); "Iwo Jima and Okinawa" (Angelo Torres); "Victory in the Pacific" (Angelo Torres); "Crimes Against Humanity" (Angelo Torres) (1962; one printing).

167A. *Prehistoric World*. Page-one splash by Angelo Torres; "In Search of the Past" (Angelo Torres); "Survival of the Fittest" (Angelo Torres); "The Wonderful Earth Movie" (Angelo Torres); "The First Fishes" (Angelo Torres); "Living on Land" (Angelo Torres); "The Dinosaurs" (Angelo Torres); "A Missing Link" (Angelo Torres); "Mammals, Bones and Stones" (Angelo Torres); "The Treasure of Flaming Cliffs" (Angelo Torres); "End of an Era" (Angelo Torres); "The Age of the Mammals" (Angelo Torres); "Prehistoric Man" (Angelo Torres); "The Bulls of Altamira" (Angelo Torres); "The Dawn Men" (George Evans); "Neanderthal Man" (George Evans); "Homo Sapiens" (Norman Nodel); "Cro-Magnon Man" (George Evans); "The Reindeer Age" (Jo Albistur); "The Races of Man" (Jo Albistur); "The Early Farmers" (Jo Albistur); "The Long Journeys: Into America, Into Africa" (Gerald McCann); "The Long Journeys: The Mixing of Peoples, Across the Pacific" (Norman Nodel); "The Stone Builders" (Norman Nodel); "The Fuegian Experiment" (Norman Nodel); "Primitives Today" (Norman Nodel) (July 1962; two printings).

[No number] *The United Nations*. Interior artwork by George Evans, Angelo Torres, Bruno Premiani, and unknown artists; not part of U.S. series; printed in Norway for sale at United Nations headquarters (1964; one printing).

Appendix G

List of *The Best from Boys' Life Comics* (1957–1958)

The Best from Boys' Life Comics, Number 1 (tornado cover); reprinted material (October 1957).

The Best from Boys' Life Comics, Number 2 (rescue cover); reprinted material (January 1958).

The Best from Boys' Life Comics, Number 3 (space cover); reprinted material (April 1958).

The Best from Boys' Life Comics, Number 4 (canoeing cover); reprinted material (July 1958).

The Best from Boys' Life Comics, Number 5 (hiking cover); reprinted material (October 1958).

Appendix H

List of *The World Around Us* (1958–1961)

The first 14 issues contained 80 pages; the length decreased to 72 pages in W15, and there was a final reduction to 64 pages in W21. No World Around Us *issue was reprinted. The cover price was 25 cents.*

W1. *The Illustrated Story of Dogs.* Cover and page-one splash by Ernest H. Hart; Heroic Dogs: "Moustache," "Balto," "Bob of Carmel" (George Evans); "How the Dog Began" (Ernest H. Hart); Dogs of War: "Chips," "Andy," "Peefka," "Sandy," "Bruce" (Ernest H. Hart); "Canine Clippings" (George Peltz); "Breeds" (unattributed); "Dog Diagram" (Ernest H. Hart); Dogs of Peace: "The Far Frontiers," "Dog Paratroopers" (Lin Streeter); "Guide to the Blind"(Ernest H. Hart); "Their Human Friends" (George Peltz); "Their Animal Friends" (George Peltz); "You and Your Dog" (William A. Walsh); "How Would Your Dog Rate You?" (Ernest H. Hart) (September 1958).

W2. *The Illustrated Story of Indians.* Cover by Gerald McCann; page-one splash by Sam Glanzman; "Buffalo Hunt" (Sam Glanzman); "The White Buffalo" (John Forte); "Play the Chunkey Game," "First in America" (George Tukell); "Chief Joseph" (Till Goodan); "Test of Friendship" (Alfonso Green); "Make an Indian Bonnet" (H.J. Kihl); "Sequoya" (John Tartaglione); "Sign Talk" (Ann Brewster); "First Among the Indians" (Sid Check) (October 1958).

W3. *The Illustrated Story of Horses.* Cover by Leonard B. Cole; page-one splash by John Forte; "The Indian and His Horse" (Gerald McCann); "Mustang!" (Sam Glanzman); "The Cowboy and His Horse" (Gerald McCann); "Know Your Oats," "Horse Diagram" (E.H. Hart); "Horses in War" (John Forte); "Horses in Sport" (Ernest H. Hart); "Harness Racing," "Heroic Horsemen" (Gerald McCann); "Stories and Legends" (Leonard B. Cole); "You and Your Horse" (John Forte); "Riding Through the Looking Glass" (H.J. Kihl); "Yesterday and Today" (Ann Brewster); "Parades" etc. (Gerald McCann) (November 1958).

W4. *The Illustrated Story of Railroads.* Page-one splash by Leonard B. Cole; "A Weapon of War" (Marvin Stein); "Birth of the Locomotive" (Kirner); "A Very Merry Ride" (unattributed); "A Steel Driving Man" (Norman Nodel); "Stopped by

Wind" (Leonard B. Cole and others); "The Way West" (Sam Becker); "Highball!" (Leonard B. Cole); "Casey's Last Ride" (George Klein); "Today and Tomorrow" (John Tartaglione) (December 1958).

W5. *The Illustrated Story of Space.* Cover by Gay Welker; page-one splash by Marvin Stein; "Training for Space" (Marvin Stein); "Rocket Around the Moon" (John Tartaglione); "What is Space?" (Sam Glanzman); "Birth of the Rocket" (Gerald McCann); "Man-Made Moons" (Ernest H. Hart); "Countdown!" (Graham Ingels); "Assignment Space Station" (Sam Glanzman); "Planet Patter," "Life On Other Planets?" (H.J. Kihl) (January 1959).

W6. *The Illustrated Story of the FBI.* Page-one splash by Gerald McCann; "The FBI in War: Spies on the Beach" (George Evans); "The FBI in War: Double Agents" (Graham Ingels); "The FBI in War: The Doll Woman" (Ann Brewster); "The FBI in War: The Spy Scientists" (Jim Infantino); "How It Began" (Gerald McCann); "G-Men" (H.J. Kihl); "The FBI in Peace: Planes Over Paradise" (Ann Brewster); "The FBI in Peace: Wanted" (Ray Ramsey); "The FBI in Peace: Playing Many Parts" (John Tartaglione); "Solved by Science" (George Klein); "Telltale Fingerprints" (Jay Disbrow); "If You Join" (Ray Ramsey); "Make-Believe Cases" (Ray Ramsey); "To Catch a Thief" (Stan Campbell); "You're an Agent" (Jay Disbrow) (February 1959).

W7. *The Illustrated Story of Pirates.* Page-one splash by Gerald McCann; "The Buccaneer Chief [Henry Morgan]" (Gerald McCann); "The World's Greatest Treasure [William Phips]" (Jay Disbrow); "The First Buccaneers [Pierre Le Grand]" (Ann Brewster); "The Pirate Who Couldn't Swim [Batholomew Portuguese]" (John Forte); "Robin Hood of the Sea [Red Legs Greaves]" (Ernest H. Hart); "The Amateur Pirate [Francis Drake]" (unattributed); "Pirate Patter" (H.J. Kihl); "Marooned [Alexander Selkirk]" (Sam Glanzman); "The

World's Greatest Pirate [Madame Ching]" (Stan Campbell); "A-Robbing Upon the Salt Sea" (Norman Nodel); "Caesar's Revenge" (Ann Brewster); "Bloody Blackbeard" (Graham Ingels); "Captain Kidd" (H.J. Kihl); "Pirate and Patriot [Jean Lafitte]" (John Tartaglione); "The Last Pirates" (H.J. Kihl); "Are You in Ship Shape?" (Gerald McCann); "Buried Treasure" (Gerald McCann) (March 1959).

W8. *The Illustrated Story of Flight.* Cover by Stan Campbell; page-one splash by Gerald McCann; "Blizzard Rescue" (John Tartaglione); "Wings of Myth," "Wings of Man," "Leonardo's Dream of Flight" (H.J. Kihl); "First in the Sky" (Graham Ingels); "From Gliders to Gasoline" (Ann Brewster); "The Great Almost" (Gerald McCann); "The First to Fly" (Stan Campbell); "What Makes an Airplane Fly?" (H.J. Kihl); "Pioneer Pilots" (Ann Brewster); "A New Weapon" (Sam Becker); "The Red Knight of Germany" (George Evans); "Between the Wars" (Stan Campbell); "A Deadly Weapon" (Sam Glanzman); "Brick Wall in the Sky" (John Tartaglione); "Flight of the Future" (Stan Campbell) (April 1959).

W9. *The Illustrated Story of the Army.* Cover by Doug Roea; page-one splash by Gerald McCann; "Follow Old Minick" (John Tartaglione); "Here Comes Yankee Doodle" (Ann Brewster); "Frontier Forts" (Graham Ingels); "The Corps of Cadets" (George Klein); "Two Too Many" (Edd Ashe); "Rifles and Arrows" (Sam Glanzman); "Custer's Last Stand" (Gerald McCann); "Northern Raiders" (Edward Moritz); "The Army in War: The War of 1812" (Ann Brewster); "The Army in War: The Mexican War" (Ray Ramsey); "The Army in War: The Civil War" (Joe Orlando); "The Army in War: The Spanish-American War" (Stephen L. Addeo); "The Army in War: World War I" (Jay Disbrow); "The Army in War: World War II" (Norman Nodel); "The Army in War: The Korean War" (Norman Nodel); "The Army in Peace" (Gerald McCann); "Scooter Burke's Peak" (Sam Glanzman) (May 1959).

W10. *The Illustrated Story of the Navy.* Cover by Gay Welker; page-one splash by Gerald McCann; "The First Hero" (Gerald McCann); "The First Fleet" (H.J. Kihl); "They Shall Fight Today" (Gerald McCann); "A Bet is Paid" (Everett Raymond Kinstler); "Learning to Lead" (Jay Disbrow); "Fighting Words" (Gerald McCann); "The Navy in War: An Impossible Task" (Everett Raymond Kinstler); "The Navy in War: Battle After Breakfast" (Ann Brewster); "The Navy in War: The Unseen Enemy" (Everett Raymond Kinstler); "The Navy in War: Full Speed Ahead!", "The Navy in War: The Wonderful Blunder" (Sam Glanzman); "Cheese-Box on a Barrelhead" (H.J. Kihl); "The Navy in Peace" (George Klein); "The Fleet Below" (Gerald McCann); "The Good Old Days" (George Peltz); "Mission to Mindanao" (Sam Glanzman) (June 1959).

W11. *The Illustrated Story of the Marines.* Cover by Alex A. Blum; page-one splash by Gerald McCann; "The Shores of Tripoli" (Gerald McCann); "Fighting Leathernecks," "The Halls of Montezuma" (Everett Raymond Kinstler); "The Marines Have Landed" (Joe Orlando); "Six Outposts to Charlemagne" (Graham Ingels); "Devil Dogs" (George Woodbridge); "Becoming a Marine" (John Tartaglione); "Peacetime Firemen" (Stan Campbell); "Circle of Death" (Sidney Check); "Rocks, Sand and Bullets" (Sam Glanzman); *Fillers*: "The Terrible Tiger"; "A Gentle Hand [Florence Nightingale]"; "The Piltdown Hoax"; "The Floating Laboratory" (July 1959).

W12. *The Illustrated Story of the Coast Guard.* Page-one splash by Gerald McCann; "Four Last Words," "Revenues and Rescues" (Edd Ashe); "Send For Black Maria" (George Peltz); "Cutters at War" (Stan Campbell); "The Matchbox Fleet" (Kirner); "Training for Duty" (Ann Brewster); "Sea Patrol" (Graham Ingels); "Mayday!" (John Tartaglione); "Six Subs in Twelve Hours" (Edd Ashe); "The Long March" (Sam Glanzman); *Fillers*: "The Gallant Mare [Dick Turpin and Black Bess]"; "The Mystery of Stonehenge"; "The Fatal Fever"; "First Around the World [Magellan]" (August 1959).

W13. *The Illustrated Story of the Air Force.* Page-one splash by Gerald McCann; "We Need the Ship!" (Sam Glanzman); "The Air Force is Born" (Gerald McCann); "Seek Out the Enemy" (Edd Ashe); "Brave Men Must Die" (H.J. Kihl); "Between Two Wars" (Norman Nodel); "Victory in the Air" (Gerald McCann); "A Separate Service" (Ann Brewster); "Fourteen to One" (George Klein); "SAC, TAC and ADC" (H.J. Kihl); "End of an Ace" (Sam Glanzman); *Fillers*: "The White Whale"; "Henry's Six Wives"; "The Blizzard of '88"; "Frontier Heroines [Molly Pitcher, Betty Zane]" (September 1959).

W14. *The Illustrated Story of the French Revolution.* Page-one splash by Gerald McCann; "To the Bastille!", "Seeds of the Revolution," "Fanning the Flames" (Gerald McCann); "The Tennis Court Oath" (Everett Raymond Kinstler); "The End of Feudalism" (Everett Raymond Kinstler); "The Rights of Man" (George Klein); "Escape to Varennes" (George Klein); "To Arms, To Arms, Ye Brave!", "Death of a King" (Norman Nodel); "The Enemy at the Gate," "The Committee of Public Safety," "The Reign of Terror," "Death of a Queen" (George Evans, inked by Graham Ingels); "The End of Terror" (H.J. Kihl); "The Mystery of the Dauphin" (Norman Nodel); "The Rise of Napoleon" (Ann Brewster); "Liberty! Equality! Fraternity!" (Norman Nodel); *Fillers*: "The Death of Byron"; "Inca Gold"; "He Followed the River [La Salle]"; "The First Hypnotist [Mesmer]" (October 1959).

W15. *The Illustrated Story of Prehistoric Animals.* Cover by Geoffrey Biggs; page-one splash by Gerald McCann; "The Fish That Never Died" (Gerald McCann); "Birth of a Planet," "Life Begins" (Stephen L. Addeo); "Backbones, Lungs and Shells" (Gray Morrow); "Giants in the Earth" (Sam Glanzman); "Tracks, Teeth and Bones" (Gray Morrow); "Fixing Fossils" (Stephen L. Addeo); "Death of the Dinosaur," "Mammals, Men and Ice" (Al Williamson); "Icebox in Siberia" (George Peltz); "Science, Strata and Species" (Gerald McCann); "Living Fossils" (Till Goodan); *Fillers*: "Forbidden Land"; "The Smallest Continent"; "For the Honor of Our Country"; "The Schoolboy and the Scientists" (November 1959).

W16. *The Illustrated Story of the Crusades.* Cover by Gerald McCann; page-one splash by Gerald McCann; "The Cross Bearers" (Gerald McCann); "The Road to War" (Gerald McCann); "The Red Lion" (Everett Raymond Kinstler); "The Walled City" (Bruno Premiani); "The Holy Lance" (Edd Ashe); "Defeat" (Gerald McCann); "Richard the Lion-Hearted" (H.J. Kihl); "Jerusalem, Jerusalem" (Bruno Premiani); *Fillers*: "Dante's Lesson"; "Faithful Unto Death [Mary Dyer]"; "Search for a Home"; "Art and Inspiration" (December 1959).

W17. *The Illustrated Story of Festivals.* Page-one splash by George Evans; "A Visit from St. Nicholas" (George Evans); "A Child Is Born: The Presepe" (Bruno Premiani); "A Child Is Born: The Posadas" (William A. Walsh); "Christmas Long

Ago: Myrtle and Mistletoe" (H.J. Kihl); "Christmas Long Ago: Christmas in America" (Alex A. Blum); "Christmas Long Ago: Feasting and Firing" (George Peltz); "The New Year" (John Tartaglione); "The Earth Unlocks: The Death of Winter," "The Earth Unlocks: Easter" (Bruno Premiani); "The Earth Unlocks: "Preparing Papaquis, Watch Me Tap This Easter Egg" (H.J. Kihl); "The Earth Unlocks: Merry May Day" (George Peltz); "Summer Is a-Comin' In" (Edd Ashe); "Harvest Home" (Norman Nodel); "Festivals of Freedom: July 4, 1776, 'To the Bastille!'" (H.J. Kihl); "Festivals of Freedom: Buzkashi Races" (George Peltz); "Festivals of Freedom: A Great Miracle" (Norman Nodel); "A Grab-Bag of Festivals" (John Tartaglione); *Fillers*: "The Ancient Games"; "Washington's Vision"; "A Leprechaun I Spied"; "The Wrath of Juno" (January 1960).

W18. *The Illustrated Story of Great Scientists.* Cover by Norman Nodel; page-one splash by George Evans; "The Earth Is Round" (George Evans); "Famous Geographers [Unknown Chinese inventor of compass, Marco Polo, Mercator, Byrd]" (George Evans); "Fun With Geography" (Stephen L. Addeo); "The Body is Charted" (Edd Ashe); "Famous Physiologists [Herophilus, Harvey, Virchow, Pavlov]" (Edd Ashe); "The Earth Moves" (Al Williamson); "Famous Astronomers [Thales, Copernicus, Kepler, Tombaugh]" (Al Williamson); "Fun With Astronomy" (Stephen L. Addeo); "Nature Has Laws" (John Tartaglione); "Famous Mathematicians [Euclid, Al-Khwarizimi, LaPlace, Mach]" (John Tartaglione); "Fun With Mathematics" (Stephen L. Addeo); "The Earth's Secrets" (Bruno Premiani); "Famous Geologists [Buffon, Smith, Murchison, Ewing]" (Bruno Premiani); "Fun With Geology" (Stephen L. Addeo); "Germs Cause Disease" (Gray Morrow); "Famous Biologists [Leeuwenhoek, Darwin, Mendel, Fleming]" (Gray Morrow); "Fun With Biology" (Stephen L. Addeo); "The Ways of Mankind" (Sam Glanzman); "Famous Anthropologists [Blumenbach, Galton, Boas, Mead] (Sam Glanzman); "Fun With Anthropology" (Stephen L. Addeo); "The Magic Element" (Norman Nodel); "Famous Chemists [Paracelsus, Priestley, Lavoisier]" (Norman Nodel); "Fun With Chemistry" (Stephen L. Addeo); "The Inner Man" (Angelo Torres); "Famous Psychologists [Locke, James, Munsterberg, Adler]" (Angelo Torres); "Fun With Psychology" (Stephen L. Addeo); "The Atom Splits" (H.J. Kihl); "Famous Physicists [Gilbert, Marconi, Goddard, Yukawa]" (Stephen L. Addeo); "Fun With Physics" (Stephen L. Addeo); *Fillers*: "House of Hope"; "Water For Springfield"; "Ten Thousand Muskets"; "Classroom to an Age" (February 1960).

W19. *The Illustrated Story of the Jungle.* Cover, page-one splash, and page two by Gerald McCann; "The Explorer" (Sid Check); "A Spear for Buth Mwon" (John Tartaglione); "The Lion and the Fox" (George Peltz); "Jungle Riddles" (George Peltz); "African Wildlife" (Sam Glanzman); "The Hunter" (Gray Morrow); "The Missionary" (Gray Morrow); "Asian and North Australian Wildlife" (Sam Glanzman); "The Scientist" (Gerald McCann); "Central and South American Wildlife" (Gerald McCann); "Today and Tomorrow" (Gerald McCann); *Fillers*: "Island of Mystery"; "Age of Iron"; "Insect Giants"; "The Impossible Canal" (March 1960).

W20. *Through Time and Space: The Illustrated Story of Communications.* Page-one splash by Gerald McCann; "The First Words" (Gerald McCann); "Signs and Sounds" (Gerald McCann); "Signals and Speed" (Bruno Premiani); "Mounted Messengers" (George Peltz); "The Art of Printing" (John Tartaglione); "A Moving Stream" (H.J. Kihl); "Words Over Wires" (Gerald McCann); "Linking Two Worlds" (Angelo Torres); "Talking by Telegraph" (George Evans); "Words Without Wires" (Ann Brewster); "The Electronic Ear" (Sam Glanzman); "The Electronic Eye" (H.J. Kihl); "Today and Tomorrow" (Edd Ashe); *Fillers*: "The Liberty to Know"; "Death of an Age"; "The Artist Who Did Not Starve [El Greco]"; "The Clue to Life" (April 1960).

W21. *The Illustrated Story of American Presidents.* Cover by Harry Myers; page-one splash by George Evans; "The Founding Fathers" (George Evans); "First in Peace" (George Evans); "Mansion in the Mud" (Norman Nodel); "Is This the Fourth?" (Edd Ashe); "Madison and Monroe" (H.J. Kihl); "Old Man Eloquent" (Gerald McCann); "Old Hickory" (Gray Morrow); "Before the Great War" (H.J. Kihl); "The Nation's Wounds" (Norman Nodel); "From Johnson to McKinley" (H.J. Kihl); "The Rough Rider" (Gerald McCann); "From Boom to Bust" (H.J. Kihl); "The Nation Asks For Action" (Norman Nodel); "The Atomic Age" (Gerald McCann); "Electing the President" (George Peltz); *Fillers*: "The Asphalt Trap"; "March Across the Alps [Hannibal]"; "Buried City [Mycenae]"; "The Unlucky Submarine" (May 1960).

W22. *The Illustrated Story of Boating.* Cover by Gerald McCann; page-one splash by Norman Nodel; "Race Against Time" (Norman Nodel); "Boat Talk" (H.J. Kihl); "Boats For Sport" (Gerald McCann); "From Trunk to Outboard" (Edd Ashe); "From Kayak to KuDru" (John Tartaglione); "Racing Sails" (Gerald McCann); "Ski Tips" (George Peltz); "Course Contest" (H.J. Kihl); "Wrecks and Rescues" (Gray Morrow); "The Open Boat" by Stephen Crane (Norman Nodel); "A Safe Voyage" (Sam Glanzman); "Till Next Season" (H.J. Kihl); *Fillers*: "The Flying Windmill"; "Revolution in Electricity"; "The Enchanted Isles"; "When the Earth Was Flat" (June 1960).

W23. *The Illustrated Story of Great Explorers.* Cover by Gerald McCann; page-one splash by George Evans; "Passage to the Indies" (George Evans); "The Land of El Dorado" (Gray Morrow); "Famous Explorers [Eric the Red, Columbus, Magellan]" (H.J. Kihl); "The Mysterious Continent" (Gerald McCann); "Famous Explorers [Scott, Amundsen, Byrd]" (H.J. Kihl); "The Great Wilderness" (John Tartaglione); "The Pathmarker [Fremont]" (George Evans); "Famous Explorers [Cartier, Bering, Parry] (H.J. Kihl); "To the North Pole" (Gray Morrow); "Famous Explorers [Fuchs, Heyerdahl, Herzog]" (H.J. Kihl); "The Roof of the World" (Gerald McCann); *Fillers*: "A Storm of Peace"; "Emmeline [Pankhurst] Went Marching"; "The Mine of Death"; "The Duel [Hamilton and Burr]" (July 1960).

W24. *The Illustrated Story of Ghosts.* Page-one splash by George Evans; "The Hitch-Hiker" (George Evans); "Room For the Night" (Gray Morrow); "The Ghost of Gold Gulch" (Jack Abel); "Ghosts That Make a Racket" (Gray Morrow); "The House of Flying Objects" (William A. Walsh); "The Talking Mongoose" (H.J. Kihl); "The Mummy's Foot" by Théophile Gautier (George Peltz); "The Sixth Sense" (John Tartaglione); "The Scientific Search" (Norman Nodel); "A Question of Ghosts" (Gray Morrow); *Fillers*: "The Chinese Sage [Confucius]"; "Olga's Revenge"; "The Mysterious Lake"; "The Yellow Star" (August 1960).

W25. *The Illustrated Story of Magic.* Cover by Gray Morrow; page-one splash by George Evans; "The Wizard of France [Robert-Houdin]" (George Evans); "The First Magicians" (George Peltz); "The Cursed Trick" (Ann Brewster); "The Great Houdini" (Norman Nodel); "The Most Marvelous Trick in the World" (George Peltz); "Witches, Magic and Medicine" (John Tartaglione); "The Truth Will Out" (Gray Morrow); "What's Magic About It?" (George Evans); *Fillers*: "Secrets of the Pharaohs"; "The Beheading Game [Cuchulainn]"; "The Mysterious Traveler [Paracelsus]"; "A Man of Sense [Omar Khayyam]" (September 1960).

W26. *The Illustrated Story of the Civil War.* Cover by Norman Nodel; page-one splash by Gray Morrow; "Before the Storm" (Gray Morrow); "The Storm Breaks," "War Leaders [Lincoln, Davis]" (H.J. Kihl); "The General Who Fought" (Angelo Torres); "The Great Train Chase" (George Peltz); "Flames on the Sea" (Sam Glanzman); "The Iron Ships" (George Peltz); "War Leaders [Grant, Lee, Farragut]"; "War Drums" (Gray Morrow); "These Brave Fields" (Sam Glanzman); "The Men in Uniform" (George Peltz); "War Leaders [Pickett, Meade, Jackson]" (H.J. Kihl); "The Gray Ghost" (Sam Glanzman); "The People at Home" (George Peltz); "War Leaders [Kearny, Stuart, Sherman]" (H.J. Kihl); "The Final Days" (Gerald McCann); "An April Day" (George Peltz); "The Aftermath" (Norman Nodel); *Fillers*: "Restless Conspirator [Mazzini]"; "Trial of the Century [Nuremberg]"; "The Ghost Dance"; "The Prophet From Hoboken [John Stevens]" (October 1960).

W27. *High Adventure: The Illustrated Story of Men Against Mountains.* Page-one splash by George Evans; "The Highest Mountain" (George Evans); "How Mountains Are Made" (Tony Tallarico); "Men of the Mountains" (Tony Tallarico); "Conquering the Barriers" (Gerald McCann); "In Seas and Space" (Sam Glanzman); "The Home of the Gods" (Gray Morrow); "The Fiery Mound" (Gray Morrow); "The Father of Mountaineering [Saussure]" (George Peltz); "Fun and Danger" (Gerald McCann); "The Mysterious Footprints" (Sam Glanzman); *Fillers*: The World of Story: "The Notorious Jumping Frog of Calaveras County" by Samuel L. Clemens (George Peltz); Serials: "D-Day, Part 1: The Key to Victory" (George Evans); "The Red Planet, Part 1: The True Orbit" (Gray Morrow); The World of Science: "How Grass Holds Water" (Stephen L. Addeo) (November 1960).

W28. *The Illustrated Story of Whaling.* Page-one splash by Gray Morrow; "The Long Voyage" (Gray Morrow); "Whale Facts: Sperm Whale" (Sam Glanzman); "Whale Lore [whale as a mammal]" (Norman Nodel); "The Great Hunt" (Gerald McCann); "Whale Facts: Arctic Right Whale" (Sam Glanzman); "Yankee Whaling" (Angelo Torres); "Whale Lore: Gamming, Scrimshaw, Natucket Sleigh Ride" (Norman Nodel); "Stove By a Whale" (Bruno Premiani); "Whale Facts: Northern Bottle-Nosed Dolphin, Killer Whale, Blackfish" (Sam Glanzman); "Whale Lore: Spouting, Sounding" (Norman Nodel); "Whale Facts: Blue Whale" (Sam Glanzman); "Captain Larsen's Ship" (Bruno Premiani); "Whale Facts: Finback Whale, Sei Whale, Common Porpoise" (Sam Glanzman); "Whale Lore [accounts of men swallowed by whales]" (Norman Nodel); "Whaling Today" (Gray Morrow); *Fillers*: The World of Story: "An Episode of War" by Stephen Crane (H.J. Kihl); Serials: "D-Day, Part 2: Target Normandy" (George

Evans); "The Red Planet, Part 2: Mars Is a World" (Angelo Torres); The World of Science: "Jets in the Bathtub" (Gray Morrow) (December 1960).

W29. *The Vikings.* Cover by Gerald McCann; page-one splash by George Evans; "The Dragon Ships" (George Evans); "The Home Shores" (Norman Nodel); "The Longship" (Gerald McCann); "Rivers of Blood" (Gray Morrow); "The Viking Gods" (Norman Nodel); "The Uneasy Throne" (Angelo Torres); "The Colonists" (Sam Glanzman); "The Strongest of Vikings" (Tony Tallarico); "The Far Shores" (Bruno Premiani); "End of an Age" (George Evans); *Fillers*: The World of Story: "The Convicts and the Eagle" (from *The House of the Dead*) by Fyodor Dostoevsky (Norman Nodel); Serials: "D-Day, Part 3: The Decision" George Evans); "The Red Planet, Part 3: The Martian Canals" (Angelo Torres); The World of Science: "What the Weather Will Be" (Sam Glanzman) (January 1961).

W30. *Undersea Adventures.* Cover by Jay Scott Pike; page-one splash by Jack Kirby; "The Frogmen" (Angelo Torres); "Mines Below" (Angelo Torres); "Underwater Conquest" (Sam Glanzman); "Sea Monsters—False and True" (unattributed); "Sunken Treasure" (Lou Morales); "Skin Diving" (Tony Tallarico); "In Magellan's Wake" (Sam Glanzman); "Seven Miles Down" (Stan Campbell); *Fillers*: The World of Story: "The Duel" by Guy de Maupassant (unattributed); Serials: "D-Day, Part 4: Night Drop" (George Evans); "The Red Planet, Part 4: A Trip to Mars" (Angelo Torres); The World of Science: "Blue Skies" (Jack Kirby) (February 1961).

W31. *Hunting.* Page-one splash by Jack Kirby; "The Rogue Elephant" (Till Goodan); "Early Hunters" (Jack Kirby); "Mythical Monsters" (Pete Morisi); "Mythical Monsters [continued]" (George Peltz); "From Falcon to Fox" (Stan Campbell); "Wanton Killing" (Sam Glanzman); "An End to Slaughter" (Jack Kirby); "The Trapped Trapper" (Sam Glanzman); "Bringing Them Back Alive" (Till Goodan); "Malay Tiger" (Luis Dominguez); "Hunting Today" (unattributed); "Dogs and Guns" (H.J. Kihl); "A New Way to Hunt" (Sam Glanzman); *Fillers*: The World of Story: "Two Tales of Baron Munchausen" by Rudolf Erich Raspe (unattributed); Serials: "D-Day, Part 5: The Landing" (George Evans); "Desert Treasure, Part 1: The Dead Sea Scrolls" (Norman Nodel); The World of Science: "A Puff of Steam" (Pete Morisi) (March 1961).

W32. *For Gold and Glory.* Cover photo by Alfred Sundel; page-one splash by Gray Morrow; "The Golden Shore" (Gray Morrow); "The Aztecs" (George Tukell); "The Great City" by Bernal Diaz del Castillo (Aztec pictographs); "The Mayas" (Jack Kirby); "Omens of Evil" (Jack Kirby); "The Incas" (Jack Kirby); "Peru! Peru!" (George Evans); "The Long Journey" (Sam Glanzman); "The Seven Cities of Gold" (Maxwell Elkan); "The Golden Man" (Gray Morrow); "The Glory" (Gray Morrow); *Fillers*: "Two Merry Pranks of Till Eulenspiegel" (Charles Berger); Serials: "D-Day, Part 6: Beachhead" (George Evans); "Desert Treasure, Part 2: Unraveling the Mystery" (Norman Nodel); The World of Science: "A Balancing Act" (Jack Kirby) (April 1961).

W33. *Famous Teens.* Cover by Geggan; page-one splash by Angelo Torres; "Victory at Orleans" (Till Goodan); "Teens as Rulers [Charles XII, Prince Edward, Victoria]" (Norman Nodel); "Mr. Farragut, Sir!" (Angelo Torres); "Teens in War [Anne Frank, Marquis de Montcalm, Horatio Nelson] (Angelo Torres); "The Young Engineer [John Ericsson]" (Stan Campbell);

"Teens in Science [Perry Klein, Raphael Soifer, Tycho Brahe, Blaise Pascal, Eli Whitney, Karl Friedrich Gauss, William Henry Perkin]" (Angelo Torres); "The Boy Mozart" (Gray Morrow); "Teens in the Arts [Pliny the Younger, John Singleton Copley, Franz Schubert, Sarah Bernhardt, Ernestine Schumann-Heink, Gian-Carlo Menotti, Yehudi Menuhin, Margot Fonteyn]" (Tony Tallarico); "Olympic Champion [Bob Mathias]" (Maxwell Elkan); "Teens in Sports [Babe Didrikson, Murray Rose]" (Angelo Torres); *Fillers*: "The Knight of the Couchant Leopard" (from *The Talisman*) by Sir Walter Scott (Charles Berger); Serials: "The Battle of Tours, Part 1: The Threat From the East" (George Evans); "Desert Treasure, Part 3: Fortress of Faith" (Norman Nodel); The World of Science: "Getting a Lift" (unattributed) (May 1961).

W34. *Fishing.* Page-one splash by Jo Albistur; "The Salmon of Miramichi" (Jo Albistur); "Hook, Line and Sinker" (Sam Glanzman); "Gills and Grunts" (Sam Glanzman); "Lungs and Lures" (Sam Glanzman); "Angler's Angles" (Sam Glanzman); "Salt-Water Game Fish" (Sam Glanzman); "The Compleat Angler" by Sir Izaak Walton (first page by Angelo Torres, remainder by Pat Pritchard?); "FreshWater Game Fish" (Sam Glanzman); "A Share for Awang" (Sidney Miller?); "From Drags to Kites" (Sam Glanzman); "Fish for Food" (Sam Glanzman); "The Secret Fleet" (Sidney Miller); "Know the Law" (Jo Albistur); "A Home Aquarium" (Jo Albistur); *Fillers*: The World of Story: "The Champion of Rum Alley" (from *Maggie*) by Stephen Crane (unattributed); Serials: "The Battle of Tours, Part 2: The Franks Fight Back" (George Evans); "Desert Treasure, Part 4: The Fate of Qumran" (Norman Nodel); The World of Science: "Upside Down and Inside Out" (Sidney Miller) (June 1961).

W35. *Spies.* Page-one splash by Norman Nodel; "Most Conspicuous Courage [Noor Khan]" (George Evans); "From Moses to Madrid" (Norman Nodel); "The Conspirators" (Edd Ashe); "The Spy Who Was a Traitor [Alfred Redl]" (Jo Albistur); "The Master Saboteur [Franz von Rintelen]" (George Evans); "Sky Spies" (Jack Kirby); "The Business of Spying" (Jack Kirby); "Famous Spies [Chevalier d'Eon de Beaumont, Nathan Hale, John André, Sir Robert Baden-Powell, Eugene Azeff, Mata Hari, Thomas E. Lawrence, Cicero] (Jo Albistur); "Tricks of the Trade" (Jack Kirby); "Codes and Ciphers" (unattributed); *Fillers*: The World of Story: "The Death of Captain Cook" by Captain King (unattributed); Serials: "The Battle of Tours, Part 3: The Moslems Retreat" (George Evans); "Witches in Salem, Part 1: The First Accusations" (unattributed); The World of Science: "Floating in the Air" (Sidney Miller) (August 1961).

W36. *Fight for Life.* Page-one splash by Jo Albistur; "The Field Surgeon [Ambroise Pare]" (Jo Albistur); "The Ancient Heritage" (Jo Albistur); "The Middle Ages" (Jo Albistur); "The Great Awakening" (Tony Tallarico); "The Black Death" (from *A Journal of the Plague Year*) by Daniel Defoe (unattributed); "Ending Epidemics" (Jo Albistur); "The Germ Fighters [Pasteur, Koch, Semmelweiss, Lister]" (Tony Tallarico); "Triumph Over Pain" (unattributed); "The Native Cure" (unattributed); "Quacks and Quackery" (Jack Kirby); "The Branches of Medicine" (Jack Kirby); "The Pure Substance" (Jack Kirby); "The War on Insects" (Jack Kirby); "Machines of Modern Medicine" (Tony Tallarico); "Aid From the Atom" (Tony Tallarico); "The Challenge of Space" (Jack Kirby); *Fillers*: "The Gift of the Plow" (from *The Age of Fable*) by Thomas Bulfinch (Sidney Miller?); Serials: "The Armada, Part 1: The Sea Powers" (Norman Nodel); "Witches in Salem, Part 2: The Suspicion Spreads" (unattributed); The World of Science: "The Weight of Air" (Sidney Miller) (October 1961).

Appendix I

List of *Classics Illustrated*: Second Series (First Publishing/ Berkley Publishing Group, 1990–1991)

All editions were 48 pages in length; author biographies were included. Issues 1 through 17 were priced at $3.75 U.S./$4.75 Canada; issues 18 through 27 were increased to $3.95 U.S./$4.95 Canada.

1. *The Raven and Other Poems* by Edgar Allan Poe; illustrated by Gahan Wilson (February 1990).

2. *Great Expectations* by Charles Dickens; adapted and illustrated by Rick Geary (February 1990).

3. *Through the Looking-Glass* by Lewis Carroll; adapted and illustrated by Kyle Baker (February 1990).

4. *Moby Dick* by Herman Melville; adapted and illustrated by Bill Sienkiewicz (February 1990).

5. *Hamlet* by William Shakespeare; adapted by Steven Grant; illustrated by Tom Mandrake; lettered by Gary Fields (March 1990).

6. *The Scarlet Letter* by Nathaniel Hawthorne; adapted by P. Craig Russell; illustrated by Jill Thompson; lettered by Bill Pearson (March 1990).

7. *The Count of Monte Cristo* by Alexandre Dumas; cover by Pat Boyette; adapted by Steven Grant; illustrated by Dan Spiegle; colored by Les Dorscheid; lettered by Carrie Spiegle (April 1990).

8. *Dr. Jekyll and Mr. Hyde* by Robert Louis Stevenson; adapted and illustrated by John K. Snyder III; lettered by Paul Fricke (April 1990).

9. *The Adventures of Tom Sawyer* by Mark Twain; adapted and illustrated by Michael Ploog; lettered by Willie Schubert (May 1990).

10. *The Call of the Wild* by Jack London; adapted by Charles Dixon; illustrated by Ricardo Villagran; lettered by Gary Fields (June 1990).

11. *Rip Van Winkle* by Washington Irving; adapted and illustrated by Jeffrey Busch; lettered by Willie Schubert (July 1990).

12. *The Island of Dr. Moreau* by H.G. Wells; cover by Jeffrey K. Potter; adapted by Steven Grant; illustrated by Eric Vincent; lettered by Ken Bruzenak; colored by Steve Oliff and Olyoptics (August 1990).

13. *Wuthering Heights* by Emily Brontë; adapted and illustrated by Rick Geary (October [*sic*] 1990).

14. *The Fall of the House of Usher* by Edgar Allan Poe; adapted by P. Craig Russell; illustrated by Jay Geldhof; lettered by Willie Schubert; colored by Steve Oliff and Olyoptics (September [*sic*] 1990).

15. *The Gift of the Magi and Other Stories* by O. Henry; Contents: "The Gift of the Magi," "The Pimienta Pancakes," "A Retrieved Reformation," "The Cop and the Anthem," "The Voice of the City," and "The Last Leaf"; adapted and illustrated by Gary Gianni (November 1990).

16. *A Christmas Carol* by Charles Dickens; cover by Gary Gianni; adapted and illustrated by Joe Staton; lettered by Willie Schubert; colored by Les Dorscheid (December 1990).

17. *Treasure Island* by Robert Louis Stevenson; adapted and illustrated by Pat Boyette (January 1991).

18. *The Devil's Dictionary and Other Works* by Ambrose Bierce; Contents: "The Devil's Dictionary," "The Boarded Window," "Dead," and "An Imperfect Conflagration"; adapted and illustrated by Gahan Wilson (February 1991).

19. *The Secret Agent* by Joseph Conrad; adapted and illustrated by John K. Snyder III; lettered by Paul Fricke (February 1991).

20. *The Invisible Man* by H.G. Wells; adapted and illustrated by Rick Geary (March 1991).

21. *Cyrano de Bergerac* by Edmond Rostand; adapted by

Peter David; illustrated and lettered by Kyle Baker (March 1991).

22. *Robinson Crusoe* by Daniel Defoe; cover by Bill Wray; adapted by Sam Wray; illustrated by Pat Boyette; lettered by Gary Fields (April 1991).

23. *The Jungle Books* by Rudyard Kipling; adapted and illustrated by Jeffrey Busch; lettered by Willie Schubert (April 1991).

24. *The Rime of the Ancient Mariner* by Samuel Taylor Coleridge; adapted and illustrated by Dean Motter; lettered by Willie Schubert (May 1991).

25. *Ivanhoe* by Sir Walter Scott; adapted by Mark Wayne Harris; illustrated by Ray Lago; lettered by Willie Schubert (May 1991).

26. *Aesop's Fables*; adapted and illustrated by Eric Vincent; lettered by Patrick Owsley (June 1991).

27. *The Jungle* by Upton Sinclair; adapted by Peter Kuper and Emily Russell; illustrated by Peter Kuper; lettered by Willie Schubert (June 1991).

Appendix J

List of *Classics Illustrated Study Guides* (Acclaim Books, 1997–1998)

[SG1.] *The Adventures of Tom Sawyer* by Mark Twain; digest reissue of 1948 edition; essay by Andrew Jay Hoffman (February 1997).

[SG2.] *Romeo and Juliet* by William Shakespeare; cover by Rebecca Guay; digest reissue of 1956 edition; essay by Susan Shwartz (February 1997).

[SG3.] *A Tale of Two Cities* by Charles Dickens; cover by Enrique Alcatena; digest reissue of 1956 edition; essay by Stuart Christie (February 1997).

[SG4.] *Jane Eyre* by Charlotte Brontë; cover by Rebecca Guay; digest reissue of 1947 edition; essay by David Hoover (February 1997).

[SG5.] *Hamlet* by William Shakespeare; digest reissue of 1952 edition; essay by Debra Doyle (March 1997).

[SG6.] *The Odyssey* by Homer; cover by Enrique Alcatena; digest reissue of 1951 edition; essay by Maurice A. Randall (March 1997).

[SG7.] *Huckleberry Finn* by Mark Twain; digest reissue of 1956 edition; essay by Andrew Jay Hoffman (March 1997).

[SG8.] *Crime and Punishment* by Fyodor Dostoevsky; cover by Dennis Calero; digest reissue of 1951 edition; essay by Andrew Jay Hoffman (March 1997).

[SG9.] *A Midsummer Night's Dream* by William Shakespeare; cover by Richard Case; digest reissue of 1951 edition; essay by Bruce Glassco (April 1997).

[SG10.] *Great Expectations* by Charles Dickens; cover by Chuck Wotjkiewicz; digest reissue of 1947 edition; essay by Michael Doylen (April 1997).

[SG11.] *The Prince and the Pauper* by Mark Twain; cover by Bo Hampton; digest reissue of 1946 edition; essay by Andrew Jay Hoffman (April 1997).

[SG12.] *Moby Dick* by Herman Melville; cover by Chuck Wotjkiewicz; digest reissue of 1942 edition; essay by Debra Doyle (April 1997).

[SG13.] *Macbeth* by William Shakespeare; cover by Richard Case; digest reissue of 1955 edition; essay by Karen Karbiener (May 1997).

[SG14.] *Oliver Twist* by Charles Dickens; digest reissue of 1945 edition; essay by Deborah Condon (May 1997).

[SG15.] *A Connecticut Yankee in King Arthur's Court* by Mark Twain; cover by Bo Hampton; digest reissue of 1957 edition; essay by Andrew Jay Hoffman (May 1997).

[SG16.] *Les Miserables* by Victor Hugo; cover by Alexander Maleev; digest reissue of 1961 edition; essay by Sherwood Smith (May 1997).

[SG17.] *Stories by Poe* ("The Adventure of Hans Pfall"; "The Tell-Tale Heart"; "The Cask of Amontillado") by Edgar Allan Poe; cover by Jen Marrus; digest reissue of excerpts from 1947 and 1951 editions; essay by Gregory Feeley (June 1997).

[SG18.] *The Three Musketeers* by Alexandre Dumas; cover by John Paul Leon; digest reissue of 1959 edition; essay by Sherwood Smith (June 1997).

[SG19.] *Cyrano de Bergerac* by Edmond Rostand; cover by Richard Case; digest reissue of 1951 edition; essay by Sherwood Smith (June 1997).

[SG20.] *Uncle Tom's Cabin* by Harriet Beecher Stowe; cover by Rebecca Guay; digest reissue of 1943 edition; essay by Karen Karbiener (June 1997).

[SG21.] *Treasure Island* by Robert Louis Stevenson; cover by Tommy Lee Edwards; digest reissue of 1949 edition; essay by Trevor Pickering (June 1997).

[SG22.] *Typee* by Herman Melville; cover by Clem Robins; digest reissue of 1947 edition; essay by Debra Doyle (June 1997).

[SG23.] *20,000 Leagues Under the Sea* by Jules Verne; cover by John Paul Leon; digest reissue of 1948 edition; essay by Beth Nachison (July 1997).

[SG24.] *The Mysterious Island* by Jules Verne; cover by Richard Case; digest reissue of 1947 edition; essay by Beth Nachison (July 1997).

[SG25.] *A Journey to the Center of the Earth* by Jules Verne; cover by Lou Harrison; digest reissue of 1957 edition; essay by Howard Hendrix (July 1997).

[SG26.] *From the Earth to the Moon* by Jules Verne; cover by Jim Calafiore; digest reissue of 1953 edition; essay by Gregory Freeley (July 1997).

[SG27.] *Gulliver's Travels* by Jonathan Swift; cover by Bo Hampton; digest reissue of 1943 edition; essay by Gregory Feeley (July 1997).

[SG28.] *Ivanhoe* by Sir Walter Scott; cover by Bo Hampton; digest reissue of 1957 edition; essay by Susan Schwartz (July 1997).

[SG29.] *More Stories by Poe* ("The Pit and the Pendulum"; "The Murders in the Rue Morgue"; "The Fall of the House of Usher"; "The Raven") by Edgar Allan Poe; cover by Jen Marrus; digest reissue of excerpts from 1944, 1947, and 1990 editions; essay by Gregory Feeley (August 1997).

[SG30.] *The Man in the Iron Mask* by Alexandre Dumas; cover by Jay Geldof; digest reissue of 1958 edition; essay by Beth Nachison (August 1997).

[SG31.] *Julius Caesar* by William Shakespeare; cover by Lou Harrison; digest reissue of 1950 edition; essay by Julie Bleha (August 1997).

[SG32.] *David Copperfield* by Charles Dickens; cover by Gene Ha; digest reissue of 1948 edition; essay by Emily Woudenberg (August 1997).

[SG33.] *Pudd'nhead Wilson* by Mark Twain; cover by Clem Robins; digest reissue of 1952 edition; essay by Andrew Jay Hoffman (August 1997).

[SG34.] *The Jungle Book* by Rudyard Kipling; cover by Alex Maleev; digest reissue of 1951 edition; essay by Gregory Feeley (August 1997).

[SG35.] *Lord Jim* by Joseph Conrad; cover by Dennis Calero; digest reissue of 1957 edition; essay by John Barnes (September 1997).

[SG36.] *The Hunchback of Notre Dame* by Victor Hugo; cover by Alexander Maleev; digest reissue of 1960 edition; essay by Howard Hendrix (September 1997).

[SG37.] *The Red Badge of Courage* by Stephen Crane; cover by John Paul Leon; digest reissue of 1952 edition; essay by Julie Bleha (September 1997).

[SG38.] *The House of the Seven Gables* by Nathaniel Hawthorne; cover by Chuck Wotjkiewicz; digest reissue of 1958 edition; essay by Joshua Miller (September 1997).

[SG39.] *Robinson Crusoe* by Daniel Defoe; cover by Scott Hampton; digest reissue of 1957 edition; essay by June Foley (September 1997).

[SG40.] *The Call of the Wild* by Jack London; cover by Leonardo Manco; digest reissue of 1952 edition; essay by Joshua Miller (September 1997).

[SG41.] *Frankenstein* by Mary Shelley; cover by Jordan Raskin; digest reissue of 1945 edition; essay by Debra Doyle (October 1997).

[SG42.] *The Invisible Man* by H.G. Wells; cover by Tony Harris; digest reissue of 1959 edition; essay by Beth Nachison (October 1997).

[SG43.] *The Legend of Sleepy Hollow* by Washington Irving; cover by Bo Hampton; digest reissue of 1943 edition; essay by Debra Doyle (October 1997).

[SG44.] *Dr. Jekyll and Mr. Hyde* by Robert Louis Stevenson; cover by Tony Harris; digest reissue of 1953 edition; essay by Andrew Jay Hoffman (October 1997).

[SG45.] *Captains Courageous* by Rudyard Kipling; cover by Chuck Wotjkiewicz; digest reissue of 1954 edition; essay by Debra Doyle (November 1997).

[SG46.] *The Master of Ballantrae* by Robert Louis Stevenson; cover by Enrique Alcatena; digest reissue of 1951 edition; essay by Debra Doyle (November 1997).

[SG47.] *Silas Marner* by George Eliot; cover by Scott Hampton; digest reissue of 1949 edition; essay by Andrew Jay Hoffman (November 1997).

[SG48.] *Wuthering Heights* by Emily Brontë; cover by Rebecca Guay; digest reissue of 1949 edition; essay by Abigail Burnham Bloom (November 1997).

[SG49.] *Don Quixote* by Miguel de Cervantes; cover by Tommy Lee Edwards; digest reissue of 1943 edition; essay by Gregory Feeley (December 1997).

[SG50.] *A Christmas Carol* by Charles Dickens; cover by Doug Tropea-Wheatley; digest reissue of 1948 edition; essay by Debra Doyle (December 1997).

[SG51.] *The Iliad* by Homer; cover by Enrique Alcatena; digest reissue of 1950 edition; essay by Maurice A. Randall (December 1997).

[SG52.] *The Last of the Mohicans* by James Fenimore Cooper; cover by Alexander Maleev; digest reissue of 1959 edition; essay by June Foley (December 1997).

[SG53.] *Kidnapped* by Robert Louis Stevenson; cover by Scott Hampton; digest reissue of 1948 edition; essay by Andrew Jay Hoffman (January 1998).

[SG54.] *The Count of Monte Cristo* by Alexandre Dumas; cover by Alexander Maleev; digest reissue of 1956 edition; essay by Susan Shwartz (January 1998).

[SG55.] *Around the World in 80 Days* by Jules Verne; cover by Lou Harrison; digest reissue of 1950 edition; essay by Beth Nachison (January 1998).

[SG56.] *All Quiet on the Western Front* by Erich Maria Remarque; cover by Tommy Lee Edwards; digest reissue of 1952 edition; essay by A.J. Scopino, Jr. (January 1998).

[SG57.] *Kim* by Rudyard Kipling; cover by Vince Evans; digest reissue of 1958 edition; essay by Debra Doyle (February 1998).

[SG58.] *Faust* by Johann Wolfgang von Goethe; cover by Ray Lago; digest reissue of 1962 edition; essay by Debra Doyle (February 1998).

[SG59.] *Henry IV—Part 1* by William Shakespeare; original Acclaim edition; cover by George Pratt; interior art by Patrick Broderick; adaptation by Gregory Feeley; essay by Susan Shwartz (February 1998).

[SG60.] *The War of the Worlds* by H.G. Wells; cover by Clem Robins; digest reissue of 1955 edition; essay by Joshua Miller (February 1998).

[SG61.] *Narrative of the Life of Frederick Douglass* by Frederick Douglass; original Acclaim edition; cover by Steven Musgrave; interior art by Jamal Igle, Ravil Lopez, and Mike DeCarlo; lettering by Jade Moede; adaptation by Len Wein and Christine Vallada; essay by Joshua Miller (March 1998).

[SG62.] *The Scarlet Pimpernel* by Baroness Emmuska Orczy; original Acclaim edition; cover by Linda Fennimore; interior art by Patrick Broderick and Ralph Reese; coloring by Colorpillar; lettering by Jade Moede; adaptation by Madeleine Robins; essay by Beth Nachison (April 1998).

The Deerslayer by James Fenimore Cooper; scheduled (March 1998) but not issued.

Alice in Wonderland by Lewis Carroll; scheduled (March 1998) but not issued.

Twenty Years After by Alexandre Dumas; scheduled (March 1998) but not issued.

Henry IV—Part 2 by William Shakespeare; scheduled (April 1998) but not issued.

Pride and Prejudice by Jane Austen; scheduled (May 1998) but not issued.

The First Men in the Moon by H.G. Wells; scheduled (May 1998) but not issued.

Henry V by William Shakespeare; scheduled (June 1998) but not issued.

White Fang by Jack London; scheduled (June 1998) but not issued.

Beowulf; scheduled (July 1998) but not issued.

The Ox-Bow Incident by Walter Van Tilburg Clark; scheduled (July 1998) but not issued.

Appendix K

List of British *Classics Illustrated* Titles Not Included in U.S. Series

143. *Sail With the Devil* by Daniel Defoe (1962).

146. *Adventures of Baron Munchausen* by Rudolph E. Raspe (1962).

147. *Through the Looking Glass* by Lewis Carroll (1962).

148. *Nights of Terror* by William Wilkie Collins and Charles Dickens (1962).

149. *The Gorilla Hunters* by Robert M. Ballantyne (1962).

150. *The Canterville Ghost* by Oscar Wilde (1962).

156. *The Dog Crusoe* by Robert M. Ballantyne (1962).

157. *The Queen of Spades* by Alexander Pushkin (1962).

158A. *Doctor No* by Ian Fleming (1963).

159. *Master and Man* by Leo Tolstoy (1963).

161. *The Aeneid* by Virgil (1963).

162. *Saga of the North* by Pierre Loti (1963).

163. *The Argonauts* by Appolonius of Rhodes (1963).

Appendix L

List of *Fast Fiction/Stories by Famous Authors Illustrated* (1949–1951)

Seaboard Publishers, Inc., changed the name of this competing line of literary adaptations from Fast Fiction *to* Stories by Famous Authors Illustrated *with No. 6. Issue length varied between 32 and 48 pages. The series was purchased and put out of business by Gilberton Co., Inc., in 1951.* The Red Badge of Courage, *scheduled to appear as* Famous Authors *No. 14, was issued as* Classics Illustrated *No. 98. The* Famous Authors *trademark was preserved by Gilberton as the nominal publisher of the* Classics Illustrated Junior *series.*

FAST FICTION

1. *The Scarlet Pimpernel* by Baroness Orczy; cover and interior art by Jim Lavery; adaptation by Dick Davis (October 1949); *Famous Authors* reprint with cover by Henry C. Kiefer (1950).

2. *Captain Blood* by Rafael Sabatini; cover and interior art by Henry C. Kiefer (November 1949); *Famous Authors* reprint with new cover by Henry C. Kiefer (1950).

3. *She* by H. Rider Haggard; cover by Henry C. Kiefer; interior art by Vincent Napoli; adaptation by Dick Davis (December 1949); *Famous Authors* reprint (1950).

4. *The 39 Steps* by John Buchan, cover and interior art by Jim Lavery (January 1950); *Famous Authors* reprint (1950).

5. *Beau Geste* by P.C. Wren; cover and interior art by Henry C. Kiefer (March 1950); *Famous Authors* reprint (1950).

STORIES BY FAMOUS AUTHORS ILLUSTRATED

6. *Macbeth* by William Shakespeare; cover and interior art by Henry C. Kiefer; lettered by H.G. Ferguson; adapted by Dana E. Dutch (August 1950).

7. *The Window* by Cornell Woolrich; cover and interior art by Henry C. Kiefer; lettered by H.G. Ferguson; adapted by Dana E. Dutch (September 1950).

8. *Hamlet* by William Shakespeare; cover and interior art by Henry C. Kiefer; adapted by Dana E. Dutch (October 1950).

9. *Nicholas Nickleby* by Charles Dickens; cover and interior art by Gustav Schrotter; adapted by Dick Davis (November 1950).

10. *Romeo and Juliet* by William Shakespeare; cover and interior art by Henry C. Kiefer (December 1950).

11. *Ben-Hur* by Lew Wallace; cover and interior art by Gustav Schrotter (January 1951).

12. *La Svengali (Trilby)* by George du Maurier; cover and interior art by Gustav Schrotter (February 1951).

13. *Scaramouche: The Days Before the Terror* by Rafael Sabatini; cover and interior art by Henry C. Kiefer (March 1951).

Bibliography

BOOKS, JOURNALS, MAGAZINES, AND OTHER PRINTED MATTER

Bails, Jerry, and Hames Ware. *The Who's Who of American Comic Books, Volume One*. Detroit: Jerry Bails, 1973.

_____. *The Who's Who of American Comic Books, Volume Two*. Detroit: Jerry Bails, 1974.

_____. *The Who's Who of American Comic Books, Volume Three*. Detroit: Jerry Bails, 1975.

_____. *The Who's Who of American Comic Books, Volume Four*. Detroit: Jerry Bails, 1976.

Beaty, Bart. "Featuring Stories by the World's Greatest Authors," *International Journal of Comic Art*, 1:1 (Spring/Summer 1999), 122–139

Beerbohm, Robert L., and Richard D. Olson, Ph.D. "In the Beginning: New Discoveries Beyond the Platinum Age," in Robert M. Overstreet, *The Overstreet Comic Book Price Guide*, 30th Edition. New York: Gemstone Publishing, Inc./HarperCollins Publishers, Inc., 2000.

Benton, Mike. *The Comic Book in America: An Illustrated History*. Dallas: Taylor Publishing Company, 1993.

_____. *Crime Comics: The Illustrated History*. Dallas: Taylor Publishing Company, 1993.

_____. *Horror Comics: The Illustrated History*. Dallas: Taylor Publishing Company, 1991.

Carter, Henry A. "Chemistry in the Comics: Part 2. Classic Chemistry," *Journal of Chemical Education*, 66:2 (February 1989).

Collins, William Wilkie. *The Woman in White*. New York: Alfred A. Knopf, Inc./Everyman's Library, 1991.

Crawford, Hubert H. *Crawford's Encyclopedia of Comic Books*. Middle Village, N.Y.: Jonathan David Publishers, Inc., 1978.

Daniels, Les. *Comix: A History of Comic Books in America*. New York: Outerbridge & Dienstfrey, 1971.

_____. *DC Comics: Sixty Years of the World's Favorite Comic Book Heroes*. Boston: A Bulfinch Press Book/Little, Brown and Company, 1995.

_____. *Marvel: Five Decades of the World's Greatest Comics*. New York: Harry N. Abrams, Publishers, 1991.

Duin, Steve, and Mike Richardson. *Comics: Between the Panels*. Milwaukie, Ore.: Dark Horse Comics, Inc., 1998.

Eisner, Will. *Comics and Sequential Art*. Tamarac, Fla.: Poorhouse Press, 1985.

Evory, Ann, ed. *Contemporary Authors, New Revision Series*, Vol. 4. Detroit: Gale Research Company, 1981.

Glut, Donald F., "Frankenstein Meets the Comics," in *The Comic-Book Book*, eds. Don Thompson and Dick Lupoff. New Rochelle, N.Y.: Arlington House, 1973.

Goulart, Ron. *Ron Goulart's Great History of Comic Books*. Chicago: Contemporary Books, 1986.

Goulart, Ron, ed. *The Encyclopedia of American Comics: From 1897 to the Present*. New York, Oxford: Facts on File, 1990.

Hagenauer, George. "Cameron and the Count," *The Classics Reader*, No. 10 (February 1978), 30.

Hamill, Pete. *A Drinking Life: A Memoir*. Boston: Little, Brown and Company, 1994.

Harvey, Robert C. *The Art of the Comic Book: An Aesthetic History*. Jackson: University Press of Mississippi, 1996.

Iger, Jerry. "Jerry Iger Talks About Matt Baker," in *Jerry Iger's Famous Features*, Vol. I, No. 1. San Diego: Pacific Comics, July 1984, p. 9.

Inge, M. Thomas. "Edgar Allan Poe and the Comics Connection," *Comic Book Marketplace* (March 2000).

Irving, Washington. "Rip Van Winkle," *The Sketch Book of Geoffrey Crayon, Gent.*, in *Tales and Sketches*. New York: The Library of America, 1983.

_____. *The Headless Horseman of Sleepy Hollow*, retold by Cherney Berg; illustrated by Norman Nodel. Mahwah, N.J.: Educational Reading Service, 1970.

Jones, Bill. "A Tale of Two Classics," *Spectrum*, No. 126 (6–19 June 1990), pp. 1, 22.

Kanter, Hal. *So Far, So Funny: My Life in Show Business*. Jefferson, N.C.: McFarland & Company, Inc., Publishers, 1999.

Malan, Dan. "CI#124, *The War of the Worlds* Model, *The Classics Collector*, No. 17 (January 1996), 13.

_____. "CIE Drops NCI," *The Classics Collector*, No. 17 (January 1996), 11.

_____. *The Complete Guide to Classics Collectibles, Volume One: The U.S. Series of Classics Illustrated and Related Collectibles*. St. Louis: Malan Classical Enterprises, 1991.

_____. *The Complete Guide to Classics Illustrated, Volume Two: Foreign Series and Related Collectibles*. St. Louis: Malan Classical Enterprises, 1993, rev. 1996.

_____. "Interview: David Batt [Chief Financial Officer, Frawley Group]," _The Classics Collector_, No. 10 (February-March 1990), 27–28.

_____. "Roberta Strauss Feuerlicht," _The Classics Collector_, No. 14 (December 1991), 19.

_____. [Untitled item], _The Classics Collector_, No. 17 (January 1996), 17.

McCloud, Scott. _Understanding Comics: The Invisible Art_. Northampton, Mass.: Kitchen Sink Press, 1993.

Moore, Scotty. "Artist, Author, & Publisher! L.B. Cole," interview in _Comic Book Marketplace_ (December 1995).

Nollen, Scott Allen. _Robert Louis Stevenson: Life, Literature and the Silver Screen_. Jefferson, N.C.: McFarland & Company, Inc., Publishers, 1994.

Norris, Frank. _The Octopus_, in _Novels and Essays_. New York: The Library of America, 1986.

Nyberg, Amy Kiste. _Seal of Approval: The History of the Comics Code_. Jackson: University Press of Mississippi, 1998.

Prager, Ron. "My Friend—Jerry Iger," _The Classics Collector_, No. 14 (December 1991).

Rice, Anne. "Giving 100%" (interview), _Comic Buyers Guide #_ 1340 (23 July 1999).

Richardson, Donna. "Classics Illustrated," _American Heritage_ (June 1993).

Robbins, Trina, and Catherine Yronwode. _Women and the Comics_. [No publication site given]: Eclipse Books, 1985.

Sabin, Roger. _Comics, Comix & Graphic Novels: A History of Comic Art_. London: Phaidon Press Limited, 1996.

Sands, Jim. "Maurice del Bourgo [Interview with Maurice del Bourgo]," _The Classics Reader_, No. 4 (August 1975).

_____. "M.D.B. [Interview with Maurice del Bourgo]," _The Classics Reader_, No. 5 (October 1975).

Savage, William W., Jr. _Comic Books and America, 1945–1954_. Norman and London: University of Oklahoma Press, 1990.

Sawyer, Michael. "Albert Lewis Kanter and the Classics: The Man Behind the Gilberton Company," _The Journal of Popular Culture_, 20:4 (Spring 1987).

Scott, Keith. _The Moose That Roared: The Story of Jay Ward, Bill Scott, a Flying Squirrel, and a Talking Moose_. New York: Thomas Dunne Books/St. Martin's Press, 2000.

Shakespeare, William. _Julius Caesar_, in _The Complete Works_, ed. Stanley Wells and Gary Taylor. New York: Oxford University Press, 1986.

"Shakespeare Bows to 'Comics' Public: Play Texts Will Be Produced in Picture Form to Interest World's Popular Audience," _New York Times_ (9 March 1950), p. 24.

Stevenson, Robert Louis. _Dr Jekyll and Mr Hyde_, in _Dr Jekyll and Mr Hyde and Other Stories_, ed. Jenni Calder. Harmondsworth: Penguin Books, 1979.

_____. _Treasure Island_. New York: Charles Scribner's Sons, 1911.

Thomas, Robert McG., Jr. "Patrick Frawley Jr., 75, Ex-Owner of Schick," _New York Times_ (Monday, 9 November 1998), p. 8B.

Toth, Alex. Letter, _The Classics Collector_, No. 14 (December 1991).

Walston, Frank. _Classics Illustrated Field Manual_. Philadelphia: Curtis Circulation Co., 1968.

Warshow, Robert. "Paul, the Horror Comics, and Dr. Wertham," _Commentary_, 17: 596–604 (June 1954).

Wertham, Fredric. _Seduction of the Innocent_. New York: Rinehart & Company, Inc., 1954.

Who's Who in American Art: 1999–2000. New Providence, N.J.: Marquis/Reed Elsevier Inc., 1999.

Wiater, Stanley, and Stephen R. Bissette. _Comic Book Rebels_. New York: Donald I. Fine, Inc., 1993.

Witek, Joseph. _Comics as History: The Narrative Art of Jack Jackson, Art Spiegelman, and Harvey Pekar_. Jackson: University Press of Mississippi, 1989.

Zansky, Louis. Resume for art show, 1976.

CORRESPONDENCE

Ashe, Edd. Letter to Raymond S. True, 17 February 1972.

Briggs, Bill. Letter to author, 30 June 2000.

Cameron, Lou. Letter to author, 4 November 1993.

_____. Letter to author, 20 November 1993.

De Fuccio, Jerry. Letter to author, 10 November 1993.

Evans, George. Letter to author, 17 February 1997.

_____. Letter to author, 27 May 1997.

Griffiths, Harley M., Jr. Letter to author, 30 May 1995.

Haufe, John. Letter to author, 6 June 2000.

Lamme, Bob. Letter to Charles Heffelfinger, 11 October 1977.

Morrow, Gray. Letter to author, 22 July 1994.

Nodel, Norman. Letter to author, 25 July 1997.

Palais, Rudolph. Letter to author, 30 December 1993.

Sundel, Alfred. Letter to author, 21 August 1994.

_____. Letter to author, 17 September 1994.

Vadeboncoeur, Jim, Jr. E-mail to author, 21 March 2000.

Ware, Hames. Letter to Mike Nicastre, March 1997.

Zansky, Jeanette. Letter to author, 16 June 1997.

INTERVIEWS

Evans, George. Interview with author, 31 May 1997.

_____. Interview with author, 28 January 2000.

_____. Interview with author, 30 January 2000.

Feuerlicht, Herb. Interview with author, 25 March 1996.

_____. Interview with author, June 1997.

_____. Interview with author, 29 July 1997.

Haufe, John. Interview with author, 5 February 2000.

Mahler, Nancy. Interview with author, 15 June 2000.

Nodel, Norman. Interview with author, 22 November 1993.

_____. Interview with author, 20 April 1997.

_____. Interview with author, 12 May 1997.

Obadiah, Rick. Interview with author, May 1990.

Palais, Rudolph. Interview with author, 1 November 1993.

Prager, Ron. Interview with author, 25 May 2000.

_____. Interview with author, 31 May 2000.

Robins, Madeleine. Interview with author, 4 April 1997.

_____. Interview with author, 23 July 1997.

Swayze, Marc. Interview with author, 1 June 2000.

Tierney, Michael. Interview with author, 24 December 1998.

True, Raymond. Interview with author, 16 January 2000.

Ware, Hames. Interview with author, 21 July 1994.

_____. Interview with author, 22 July 1994.

_____. Interview with author, 20 February 1996.
_____. Interview with author, 27 January 1997.
_____. Interview with author, 23 February 1997.
_____. Interview with author, 12 March 1997.
_____. Interview with author, 20 March 1997.

_____. Interview with author, 31 March 1997.
_____. Interview with author, 15 April 1997.
_____. Interview with author, 5 March 2000.
_____. Interview with author, 7 July 2000.
Zansky, Jeanette. Interview with author, 25 July 1994.

Index

Key to parenthetical identification: Acclaim = Acclaim Books; Cassette = Cassette Book Company; CC = Classic Comics; CI = Classics Illustrated; CI Jr. = Classics Illustrated Junior; CI Special = Classics Illustrated Special Issue; FA = Stories by Famous Authors Illustrated; First = First Publishing/First Classics, Inc.; FO = Famous Operas; King = King Classics; PP = Picture Parade *or* Picture Progress; WAU = World Around Us. *Most* World Around Us *titles have been shortened* (e.g., The Illustrated Story of Horses *is listed as* Horses). **Bold** *numbers refer to illustrations.*